The Admirable Heart of Mary

The Admirable Heart of Mary

By
Saint John Eudes

Translated from the French by
Charles di Targiani and Ruth Hauser

Immaculate Heart Publications
Buffalo, New York USA

Imprimi Potest:

> A. D'AMOUR, C.J.M.
>> *Praepositus Provincialis*

Laval-des-Rapides, P.Q.,
die 15ᵃ septembris, 1947

Nihil Obstat:

> JOHN M. A. FEARNS, S.T.D.
>> *Censor Librorum*

Imprimatur:

> ✠ FRANCIS CARDINAL SPELLMAN
>> *Archbishop of New York*

December 5, 1947

Published by :

IMMACULATE HEART PUBLICATIONS
In USA - Box 1028, Buffalo, New York 14205
In Canada - 452 Kraft Road, Fort Erie, Ontario L2A 4M7
Call toll free - 1-800-263-8160
Telephone - 1-905-871-8041
www.fatima.org <http://www.fatima.org>

Under license from:
Loreto Publications
P. O. Box 603, Fitzwilliam, New Hampshire 03447 USA

ISBN - 1-896384-05-6
Library of Congress - 2007930946

Printed and bound in Canada.

General Preface

Saint John Eudes has been called "the wonder of his age." Missionary, founder, reformer of the clergy, he crowded into a life of seventy-nine years so many and such varied accomplishments that one marvels how a single man could achieve so much. In addition to the activities of an incessant and many-sided apostolate, he wrote a number of valuable books, which rank him among the most prolific ascetic writers of the seventeenth century.

For many years the devotional works of Saint John Eudes were practically unknown.[1] Occasionally a volume was discovered in the library of some seminary or religious house. Many others preserved in manuscript form were lost in the chaos of the French Revolution.[2] At the beginning of the present century the sons of Saint John Eudes united in a tribute of filial piety to bring out a complete edition of the works of their spiritual father, seeking them in public and private libraries throughout the world.[3] About twenty volumes were found and edited in 1905 by the late Fathers Charles Lebrun, C.J.M., and Joseph Dauphin, C.J.M. The first edition in French, *Oeuvres Complètes du Vénérable Jean Eudes*, ran into twelve octavo volumes with introductions, explanatory notes, analytic and alphabetic indexes of great value.

1 Before the French Revolution the works of Saint John Eudes were popular in France. In 1792, the houses of the Congregation of Jesus and Mary were confiscated by the Government and its members were massacred or dispersed throughout Europe. With the suppression of the Eudists, their rich literary heritage was widely scattered and partially destroyed. It was not until the reestablishment of the Congregation of Jesus and Mary in 1826 that effort was made to recover the printed and manuscript works of Saint John Eudes. The research was carried on until the latter part of the nineteenth century. In the "Preface Générale" to the *Oeuvres Complètes* (Vannes, 1905), Father Charles Lebrun points out that one of the purposes of the edition was to unearth these works buried too long in oblivion, *exhumer ces ouvrages ensevelis depuis trop longtemps dans l'oubli* . . .

2 The following manuscripts were not found: *The Christian Man, All Jesus, The Divine Office, The Admirable Sacrifice of the Mass, Meditations* (2 vols.), *Sermons of Saint John Eudes* (3 vols.), *Favors Obtained by the Diocese of Coutances through the Blessed Virgin, The Divine Childhood of Jesus. The Devotion to the Sacred Heart of Jesus, The Admirable Life of Mary des Vallées* (incomplete copy found at Laval University Library, Quebec) and *Correspondence of Saint John Eudes*.

3 Cf. *Oeuvres Complètes*, p. xiv.

These writings constitute a complete summa of ascetic and pastoral theology. The list is as follows:

Volume I. The Life and Kingdom of Jesus in Christian Souls. In this work the Saint develops his spiritual teaching on the Christian life, namely, that the Christian life is simply the life of Jesus extended and continued in each one of us.

Volume II. This volume contains six short treatises on subjects relating to the Christian life:

1. *A Treatise on the Respect Due to Holy Places*, which is an echo of the fiery denunciations he pronounced during his missions against profaners of the temple of God.

2. *Meditations on Humility*, a series of meditations on the profession of humility as used daily in his order of priests, the Congregation of Jesus and Mary.

3. *Interior Colloquies of the Soul with God*, meditations on creation, the end of man and the grace of Baptism.

4. *Man's Contract with God in Holy Baptism*, a summary of the teachings of Sacred Scripture and Tradition on the Sacrament of Baptism.

5. *The Practice of Piety*, a brief explanation of what is necessary in order to live a Christian life.

6. *Catechism of the Mission*, an outline of the catechetical instructions given during a mission.

Volume III. Contains two important works on sacerdotal perfection:

1. *The Memorial of the Ecclesiastical Life*, an explanation of the dignity and duties of the priesthood.

2. *A Manual of Piety for Use in an Ecclesiastical Community*, in which the author explains how the means of sanctification he recommended to his priests should be practically applied in their daily lives.

Volume IV. Comprises significant works on the priestly ministry.

1. *The Apostolic Preacher* is one of the first treatises written on the ministry of the Word of God and is even yet one of the most practical.

2. *The Good Confessor* explains the qualities and obligations of the minister of the Sacrament of Penance.

3. *Counsels for Mission Confessors* suggests practical means of assisting penitents to make their examination of conscience and excite themselves to contrition.

4. *The Manner of Serving Mass* explains the dignity and holiness of this act and what one must do to perform it devoutly and worthily.

Volume V. The Admirable Childhood of the most Holy Mother of God. This book treats of the holy childhood of Mary and the practical means of honoring the mysteries and virtues of her early life.

Volumes VI, VII, VIII contain the entire writings of the Saint on the Sacred Hearts of Jesus and Mary. The work is entitled: *The Admirable Heart of the most Holy Mother of God.* It comprises twelve books covering the complete theology of the devotion to the Sacred Hearts. Eleven books discuss the theory, history, and practice of the devotion to the Immaculate Heart of Mary. The last book deals with the devotion to the Sacred Heart of Jesus. It is this work, together with the Offices of the Sacred Hearts, that merit for him the title of Father, Doctor and Apostle of the Devotion to the Sacred Hearts.

Volume IX. The Rules and Constitutions of the Congregation of Jesus and Mary.

Volume X. Contains *The Rules and Constitutions of the Order of Our Lady of Charity,* the *Directory* of the Order, and a collection of two hundred and forty letters.

Volumes XI and XII embrace the Saint's *Liturgical Works,* comprising twenty-five Offices and Masses for feasts to which he urged special devotion, the *Memorial of God's Blessings* and several other minor works.

The second French edition appeared in 1935, *Oeuvres Choisies de Saint Jean Eudes,* prepared under the direction of Father Lebrun, the leading authority on Eudistic research. It comprises nine volumes: *The Life and Kingdom of Jesus in Christian Souls, Meditations of Various Subjects, Regulae Vitae Christianae et Sacerdotalis, Man's Contract with God in Holy Baptism, Letters and Minor Works, Writings on the Priesthood, The Sacred Heart of Jesus, The Admirable Heart of Mary* and *The Admirable Childhood of the Mother of God.* The format of these volumes is compact and more convenient than the 1905 edition, which is now out of print.

The publication of the works of Saint John Eudes revealed the extent and depth of their spiritual doctrine. Cardinal Pitra, who was associated with the cause of Beatification, discovered in the writings of Saint John Eudes a remarkable depth of thought and purity of doctrine. Cardinal Vivès has more recently expressed his admiration:

> I was acquainted with the Doctors of the Order of Saint Francis; I was acquainted with Saint Teresa and

Saint John of the Cross, the mystical writers of my own country, Spain; but I was completely ignorant of the writings of Father Eudes. As a member of the Sacred Congregation of Rites it was my duty to study his life and his works, and I am in admiration. Blessed John Eudes must be ranked with the great lights of the Church. His spiritual doctrine is profound and of wonderful exactitude. He is one of the writers who has best propounded the doctrine of the Gospel.[4]

The late Father Ange Le Doré, for fifty years Superior General of the Congregation of Jesus and Mary, wrote:

> The works of Blessed John Eudes, although they do not bear the scientific touch of the professional theologian, are nevertheless proofs of his remarkable theological, ascetic and scriptural knowledge. . . . He is not a Doctor after the fashion of the scholastics of the thirteenth century or of the great theologians of the sixteenth and seventeenth centuries. As they, he might have built up theses and composed books didactic in form; but he was before all a saver of souls. For him the science of theology found its chief field of usefulness in the practice of virtue and in the acquisition of sanctity of which it is the principle. . . . He was a Doctor after the manner of the Apostles, the Fathers of the Church, Saint Francis de Sales and Saint Alphonsus de Liguori. The science which shines in his works not only emits light; it engenders piety and sanctity.[5]

The spiritual doctrine expounded by Saint John Eudes follows the teaching of Cardinal Pierre de Bérulle and Father Charles de Condren, two prominent members of the seventeenth century French School of Spirituality. Saint John Eudes applies this doctrine to the devotion to the Sacred Hearts of Jesus and Mary, developing and rendering it more precise and practical. He has the rare gift of expressing the most sublime truths in simple, familiar language. He also excels in condensing into a few pages a complete scheme of Christian life and perfection.

The wish was repeatedly expressed that these inspirational writings could be made available to English speaking readers. Excellent abridged editions of certain books were published in England and in Canada, but

4 Quoted by P. A. Bray, C.J.M., *Saint John Eudes* (Halifax, 1925), p. 116.
5 Quoted by Bray, *op. cit.*, p. 117.

they did not do justice to the literary value of the Saint. Consequently, the Eudist Fathers commemorating their tercentenary in 1943 resolved to publish a complete translation of the principal works of their founder. Competent translators were secured and much time and effort were expended to produce readable volumes in modern English, faithful to the spirit and style of the original.

The first English edition, *Selected Works of Saint John Eudes*, is the result. In presenting it to the public the Eudist Fathers and the Religious of Our Lady of Charity of the Refuge, and of the Good Shepherd, wish to thank all those who contributed to the success of this comprehensive undertaking. They are especially grateful to the distinguished churchmen who have so graciously accepted to introduce these volumes to Catholic readers, because they consider that the works of Saint John Eudes should be more widely known. The Saint in his apostolic work and in his writings ranks with the eminent figures who belong not to one country and to one religious order but to the universal Church. Three centuries have passed since he wrote the works now being printed in the new world, a striking illustration that he wrote for all time. He still speaks in accents that penetrate the mind and heart of the reader to enlighten, purify and sanctify so that Jesus Christ may live and reign in the Christian soul.

WILFRID E. MYATT, C.J.M.
PATRICK J. SKINNER, C.J.M.
Editors

Holy Heart Seminary
Halifax, N. S.
Feast of Saint John Eudes, 1945

Table of Contents

Part Six
Third Foundation of the Devotion: The Heart of God the Holy Ghost
Inspired Texts Referring to the Admirable Heart of Mary

Part Seven
Inspired Catholic Tradition Concerning the Admirable Heart of Mary

Part Eight
Fourth Foundation of the Devotion:
Sanctity of the Admirable Heart of Mary Exposition of Its Excellence

Part Nine
Practice of the Devotion to the Admirable Heart of Mary

Part Ten
The Canticle of the Admirable Heart of Mary
Exposition of the Magnificat, Treating Its Significance Verse by Verse

Appendix One

Appendix Two

Part One

OBJECT OF THE DEVOTION TO THE
ADMIRABLE HEART OF MARY

Chapter One

Reasons for the Name "Admirable"

Jesus Christ, the only begotten Son of God, chose the incomparable Virgin Mary from among all creatures to be His Mother and deigned to be nourished and governed by her. In His infinite goodness He also gave her to us to be our Queen, our Mother and our sure Refuge in all our needs. He therefore wishes us to honor her as He honors her and to love her as He loves her.

According to the Apostle Saint Paul, Christ is the Head of His Mystical Body, the Church, and we are the members.[1] We must therefore be animated by His Spirit; we must follow His inspirations, walk the path He has traced, and continue, as it were, His life on earth by practicing the virtues which were His own. It follows that our devotion to His Holy Mother must be a continuation of His devotion to her. We must be filled with the sentiments of respect, submission and affection which He entertained for her on earth and still entertains in Heaven. Mary always held and will hold forever the first place in the Sacred Heart of her divine son; she always was and will never cease to be the first object of His love after the eternal Father; and so He wishes that, next to God, she should be the principal object of our devotion. For this reason, after the veneration we owe to the divine majesty of God, we cannot render a greater service to Jesus Christ or do anything more pleasing to Him than to serve and honor His most worthy Mother.

The human will is not, however, moved to love a fellow creature unless the intellect first knows what renders it worthy of respect and esteem. The infinite zeal with which the Son of God is inflamed for all that concerns His dear Mother, has urged Him to reveal to us through the inspired words of Sacred Scripture and through the writings of the Fathers some small measure of the perfections with which He has enriched her. The reality far surpassing our knowledge of her in this vale of darkness will be revealed only in Heaven, the land of unclouded light.

1 1 Cor. 12, 27; Eph. 5, 30.

3

Among the divinely inspired passages of Sacred Scripture I select one from the twelfth chapter of the Apocalypse, which is a compendium of all the great things that can be said or thought of our marvelous Queen. "A great sign appeared in Heaven: A woman clothed with the sun, and the moon under her feet, and on her head a crown of twelve stars."[2]

What is this great sign? Who is this miraculous woman? Saint Epiphanius,[3] Saint Augustine,[4] Saint Bernard[5] and many other holy doctors agree that the woman is Mary, the Queen among women, the Sovereign of angels and men, the Virgin of virgins. She is the woman who bore in her chaste womb the perfect man, the God-Man. "A woman shall compass a man."[6]

Mary appears in Heaven because she comes from Heaven, because she is Heaven's masterpiece, the Empress of Heaven, its joy and its glory, in whom everything is heavenly. Even when her body dwelt on earth, her thoughts and affections were all rapt in Heaven.

She is clothed with the eternal sun of the Godhead and with all the perfections of the divine essence, which surround, fill and penetrate her to such an extent that she has become transformed, as it were, into the power, goodness and holiness of God.

She has the moon under her feet to show that the entire world is beneath her. None is above her, save only God, and she holds absolute sway over all created things.

She is crowned with twelve stars that represent the virtues which shine so brightly in her soul. The mysteries of her life are as many stars more luminous by far than the brightest lights of the sky. The privileges and prerogatives God has granted to her, the least of which is greater than anything shining in the firmament of Heaven, as well as the glory of the saints of Paradise and of earth, are her crown and her glory in a much fuller sense than the Philippians could be said to be the crown and joy of Saint Paul.[7]

But why does the Holy Ghost call Mary "a great sign"? It is simply to tell us that everything in her is wonderful, and that the marvels that fill her being should be proclaimed to the entire world, so that she may become an object of the admiration for the inhabitants of Heaven as well as for mankind on earth, and so that she may be the sweet delight of angels and men.

2 Apoc. 12, I.
3 Hares., 78.
4 De Symbolo. lib. 4.
5 Sermo in Signum Magnum.
6 Jer. 31. 22.
7 Phil. 4, I.

This is likewise the reason why the Holy Ghost inspires the faithful throughout the world to sing in her praise: *Mater admirabilis*. "O Mother Most Admirable." Moreover, according to the testimony of several trustworthy authors,[8] a holy Jesuit who once asked the Mother of God to reveal to him which of the many titles in her Litany was most pleasing to her received this same answer: *Mater admirabilis*.

Mary is truly admirable in all her perfections and in all her virtues.[9] But what is most admirable in her is her virginal heart. The heart of the Mother of God is a world of marvels, an abyss of wonders, the source and principle of all the virtues which we admire in our glorious Queen: "All the glory of the king's daughter is within." It was through the humility, purity and love of her most holy heart that she merited to become the Mother of God and to receive the graces and privileges with which God enriched her on earth. These same sublime virtues of her Immaculate Heart have rendered her worthy of the glory and happiness that surround her in Heaven, and of the great marvels that God has wrought in and through her.

Do not be surprised if I say that the virginal heart of this Mother of Fair Love is an admirable heart indeed. Mary is admirable in her divine maternity because as Saint Bernardine of Siena says, "to be Mother of God is the miracle of miracles," *miraculum miraculorum*. But the august heart of Mary is also truly admirable, for it is the principle of her divine maternity and of the wonderful mysteries this privilege implies.

Of Mary's admirable heart I shall attempt to speak in this book although to speak and write worthily of the holy heart of God's own Mother one would need a heart of fire. To know and proclaim the perfections of the noble heart of the Queen of Angels one should have the intellect of a cherub and the flaming love of a seraph. Nay more, it would be necessary to possess the mind, the heart, the tongue and the hand of Jesus Christ, the King of all hearts, to understand, honor, proclaim or commit to writing the treasures of sanctity contained in the holy heart of Mary, the worthiest, most royal and most marvelous of all hearts after the most adorable heart of our Saviour Himself.

I am not so presumptuous as to believe that I can enclose within the pages of this book the immense treasure and the innumerable wonders contained in the incomparable heart of Mary which is and will forever be the object of the ecstatic contemplation of the happy citizens of Heaven.

---

8 Cf. *Triple Couronne de la Mère de Dieu* by Reverend Francis Poiré S.J., Treatise 4, ch. 9, pg. 89. The book was published in Paris in 1630. In 1858 the Benedictine Fathers of Solesmes brought out a new edition.
9 The Saint enumerates here many of Mary's admirable perfections. Since most of these passages are found elsewhere, we have omitted them in this edition.

When the angels beheld their Queen and ours at the moment of her Immaculate Conception they were filled with admiration at such fullness of grace and in their wonderment exclaimed, "Who is she that cometh forth as the morning rising, fair as the moon, bright as the sun, terrible as any army set in array?"[10] What then must their rejoicing be, now that they behold in Heaven all the marvelous perfections of her heart from the first moment of her life on earth until the last?

The God of angels finds even the footsteps of this glorious Queen so holy and so pleasing to His divine majesty that He exclaims, "How beautiful are thy steps in shoes, O prince's daughter!"[11] Under His divine inspiration Holy Church, both Militant and Triumphant, celebrates on earth and in Heaven Our Lady's visitation to her cousin Elizabeth. From this we see how great is Our Lord's desire that we should admire and honor as He does the many holy and admirable actions which were inspired in the most amiable heart of His peerless Mother.

If the smallest virtuous act of this heavenly Virgin represented in Sacred Scripture by one of her hairs, is so pleasing to God as to make Him proclaim that she has wounded and ravished His heart with a hair of her neck,[12] what must we think of the manifold acts of love which, like sacred flames, were constantly darting from the burning furnace of her virginal heart ablaze with divine love? These flames were incessantly rising to Heaven to the heart of the most Holy Trinity.

Holy Church, whom the Divine Spirit guides in all things, celebrates on earth and will forever celebrate in Heaven several feasts to honor the various events in the earthly life of the Mother of God, such as her Presentation, in which she offered herself to God in the temple of Jerusalem; her Purification, to honor her obedience to a law that did not apply to her; the feast of Our Lady of Snows, in memory of the dedication of the first church consecrated to her. What praises and homage her holy heart then deserves, that heart which for at least sixty-three years offered up so many acts of faith, hope, love of God and charity towards men, humility, obedience and every other virtue? What mind can understand and what tongue express the richness of this incomparable heart, the Sovereign of all hearts consecrated to Jesus?

Her heart is a vast sea of grace, a measureless ocean of perfections, an immense furnace of love. Would that I might lose myself as a drop of water in this ocean or be consumed like a straw in this furnace, so

10 Cant. 6, 9.
11 Cant. 7, 1.
12 Cant. 4, 9. "Thou hast wounded my heart, my sister, my spouse: thou hast wounded my heart . . . with one hair of thy neck."

that nothing of what I write could be considered as coming from me, but only from Jesus Christ who is the unique source of all good!

O most holy Mary, Thy divine son, Jesus, hath created thy heart, and He alone knows the great treasures he has hidden therein. He it was who lit the fire burning in this furnace, and none but He can measure the heights reached by the flames which leap from its abyss. He alone can measure the vast perfections with which He has enriched the masterpiece of His all-powerful goodness, or count the innumerable graces He has poured into this ocean of grace: "He created her in the Holy Ghost, and saw her, and numbered her, and measured her."[13]

And now I beseech thee, O most Blessed Virgin Mary, through thy heart and for the honor of that very heart to offer me to thy beloved son and to pray that He may annihilate my personality and set Himself in the place of my nothingness, so that not my voice but His may be heard. May Jesus Christ be the author of this book, and I but the instrument of His surpassing love for thee and of the zeal with which He watches over the honor of thy most worthy heart. May He inspire the thoughts He wishes to see expressed in this book and the very words He desires I should use. May His blessing rest in fullest measure on the readers of this book, and may He transform all its words into bright and ardent coals, so that their hearts may be purified, enlightened and inflamed with the sacred fire of His love. In a word, may they become worthy to live according to God's heart and to be numbered among the children of the maternal heart of God's own Mother.[14]

13 Ecclus. 1, 9.
14 It is usual in the devotional works of the seventeenth century to find prayers scattered throughout the doctrinal parts. Saint John Eudes follows this custom in the present volume. The last two paragraphs of this chapter make up a beautiful prayer to the Immaculate Heart of Mary.

Chapter Two

THE HEART OF MARY IN GENERAL

Before expounding the prodigious virtues and the incomparable marvels of the Admirable Heart of Mary, according to the lights which He Who is the Source of all light will be pleased to give me, I shall point out the various meanings of the word "heart" in Sacred Scripture.

1. The word "heart," first of all, signifies the *material and corporeal heart* which beats within our breast, the noblest part of the human body. It is the principle of life, the first organ to begin to live and the last to be stilled in death; it is the seat of love, hatred, joy, sadness, fear and every passion of the soul. Of this heart does the Holy Ghost speak when He says, "With all watchfullness keep thy *heart*, because life issueth out from it."[1]

2. "Heart" is also employed in Scripture to signify the *memory*. This is, no doubt, its meaning in these words of Our Lord: "Lay it up therefore in your *hearts*, not to meditate before how you shall answer. For I will give you a mouth and wisdom which all your adversaries shall not be able to resist and gainsay."[2] That is, *remember* when you are brought before kings and judges for my name's sake, not to prepare an answer for your enemies because I will give you wisdom, which your enemies will not be able to gainsay.

3. It likewise denotes *the intellect*, with which we meditate. Meditation is, in fact, discursive reasoning on the things of God, tending to persuade and to convince us of the truth of Christian doctrine. This is the heart alluded to in the words: "The meditation of my *heart* (is) always in thy sight."[3] In other words, "my heart, that is, my intellect, is always occupied in meditating and contemplating Thy glory, mysteries and works."

4. The word "heart" expresses the *free will* of the superior and rational part of the soul, the queen of the other faculties, the root of

1 Prov. 4, 23.
2 Luke 21, 14-15.
3 Ps. 18, 15.

good and evil, and the mother of virtue and of vice. Our Lord refers to this heart when He says, "A good man out of the good treasure of his *heart* bringeth forth that which is good: and an evil man out of the evil treasure bringeth forth that which is evil."[4] Here, "a good heart" means the righteous will of the just man, from which all kinds of good can come; and "an evil heart" means the bad will of the wicked, which is a source of all kinds of evil.

5. We must also understand by the word "heart" that highest part of the soul which theologians call the *point of the spirit*. It is the seat of contemplation, which consists in turning the mind directly toward God and viewing Him in all simplicity, without discursive reasoning or multiplicity of thoughts. The Fathers of the Church apply to this power of the soul those words which the Holy Ghost puts in the mouth of the Blessed Virgin Mary: "I sleep, and my *heart* watcheth."[5] According to Saint Bernardine of Siena and several other writers, sleep and rest of the body did not prevent Mary's holy heart, that is, the highest part of her mind, from being always united to God in sublime contemplation.[6]

6. At times "heart" stands for the *whole interior life of man*; I mean, of course, the spiritual life, as indicated by these words spoken by the Son of God to the faithful soul, "Put me as a seal upon thy *heart*, as a seal upon thy arm,"[7] that is, stamp the image of my interior and exterior life in your interior and exterior life, in your soul and in your body, by a perfect imitation of Me.

7. The word "heart" can also signify the *Holy Spirit*, the veritable heart of the Father and the Son, Whom They desire to give us for our own mind and heart. "And I will give you a new *heart*, and put a new spirit within you."[8]

8. The *Son of God* is called the heart of the eternal Father in Sacred Scripture, and it is of this heart that the Father speaks to His spouse, the Blessed Virgin, when He says to her, "Thou hast wounded my *heart*, my sister, my spouse,"[9] or according to the Septuagint, "Thou hast ravished my heart." And the Son of God Himself is called in Scripture "The breath of our mouth,"[10] that is, the soul of our soul and our heart's very heart.

---

4 Luke 6, 45.
5 Cant 5, 2.
6 *Somnus qui abyssat ei sepelit nobis rationis et liberi arbitrii actus, non credo quod talia in Virgine fuerit operatus, sed anima ejus libere ac meritorio actu tunc tendebat in Deum. Unde illo tempore erat perfectior contemplatrix, quam unquam fuerit aliquis dius dum vigilavit.* Serm. 51, art. i, c. 2.
7 Cant. 8, 6.
8 Ezech. 36, 26.
9 Cant. 4, 9.
10 Lam. 4, 20.

All these hearts are to be found in Mary, the Mother of Fair Love, and they form in her one single heart, because all the faculties of the superior and the inferior part of her soul were always harmoniously united. Moreover, Jesus, who is the heart of His Father, and the Holy Ghost, who is the heart of the Father and the Son, were given to Mary to be the soul of her soul and the heart of her heart.

To understand more clearly what is meant by the heart of the Blessed Virgin Mary, we must recall that, just as we adore in the most Holy Trinity and in the Incarnate Word three hearts which form but one heart, so also do we honor in the Mother of God three hearts united in one.

The first heart to be found in the Blessed Trinity is *the Son of God,* who is the heart of the eternal Father, as we have seen above.[11] The second is *the Holy Ghost,* who is the heart of the Father and the Son. The third is *divine love itself,* an adorable attribute of the divine essence, which can be considered as the heart of the Father, of the Son and of the Holy Ghost. These three hearts are in reality only one single heart, and with it the three eternal Persons love one another as They deserve to be loved. They also love mankind with an incomparable charity.

The first heart to be found in our Loving Saviour, Jesus Christ, the God-Man, is His *heart of flesh,* deified like all the other parts of His sacred body by its hypostatic union with the Divine Word. The second is His *spiritual heart,* that is, the superior faculties of His holy soul, including His memory, His understanding and His will, all most specially deified by the hypostatic union. The third is His *divine heart,* that is, *the Holy Ghost,* by whom His adorable humanity has always been animated in a higher degree than by its own soul and heart.

Thus we have in Jesus Christ, the God-Man, three hearts forming but one, because His divine heart constituted the soul, the heart and the life of His spiritual and bodily hearts. Moreover God has established such perfect unity between them that these three hearts form only a single heart, filled with infinite love towards the Blessed Trinity and with surpassing charity towards men.

The first heart of Mary, the Mother of God, is *the heart of flesh* enclosed in her virginal breast. Although this heart is corporeal, it is nevertheless completely spiritualized by the spirit of grace and the spirit of God which fill it.

The second heart is her *spiritual heart,* made God-like, not indeed by the hypostatic union as in the Incarnate Word, but by a superlative participation in the divine perfections, as we shall see in the following pages. This heart is referred to by the words of the Holy Ghost, "All the

11   See no. 8, p. 9.

glory of the king's daughter is within,"[12] that is, has its origin in her heart and her inmost soul.

The third heart of Mary is *Divine* and is truly *God Himself,* for it is none other than the *love of God.* This is the heart of which she says, "I sleep, and my heart watcheth,"[13] which means according to the interpretation of several holy Doctors, "While I grant necessary rest to my body, my son Jesus, who is my heart and whom I love like my own heart, is always watching over me and for me."

These three hearts of the Mother of God constitute a single heart, through the holiest and most intimate union that ever was and will be, next to the hypostatic union. Of these three hearts, or rather, of this single heart, the Holy Ghost has said twice, "Mary kept all these words, pondering them in her heart."[14]

Our Lady cherished the mysteries and marvels of her son's life, first of all, in her material and corporeal heart, the principle of life, the seat of love and of the other physical emotions. All the movements, every beat of this virginal heart, the material functions that it accomplished and the emotions that swayed it, existed solely for Jesus and for the things that concerned Him. Her love was spent in loving Him, her hatred in hating all that is contrary to Him, her joy in rejoicing in His glory and His grandeurs, her sorrow and compassion in bewailing His trials and sufferings. The same may be said of every emotion of her bodily heart.

Secondly, Mary kept all these things in her spiritual heart, that is, in the noblest part of her soul, in the inmost recesses of her mind. All the faculties of her soul were constantly applied to contemplating and adoring everything that took place in the life of her beloved son, down to the very smallest details.

Thirdly, Our Lady kept all these things in her divine heart, that is, in her son Jesus, who was the mind of her mind and the heart of her heart. He in turn kept them for her and recalled them to her mind when necessary, that she might feed herself in contemplation upon the mysteries of His life, rendering them due honor and adoration, and repeating them to the holy apostles and disciples, who were to preach them to the faithful.

This, then, is what is meant by the Admirable Heart of the beloved Mother of God. This is the worthy subject of which I shall have to speak in this book. The next three chapters will treat in greater detail of the corporeal, spiritual and divine heart of Mary. In the rest of the

12   Ps. 44, 14.
13   Cant. 5, 2.
14   Luke 2, 19 and 51.

book, you will find comments proper to her corporeal heart, others concerning her spiritual heart, others pertaining only to her divine heart, while additional characteristics will be common to all three. Every word that I write, every point that I make, will further the spiritual progress of my readers, if they will but lift up their hearts to God as they read, in praise and thanksgiving for the innumerable graces and treasures of the heart of Mary.

O Jesus, Son of God and son of Mary, my task is great and beyond my power, but I trust in Thy goodness and in the love of Thy Holy Mother. I seek nothing, as I, a sinner, strive to show forth the wonders of the heart of Mary; nothing, except to make some small return for the countless graces received from Thy paternal heart through the loving heart of Thy Mother. To Thee, O Jesus, I surrender myself, my mind, my heart and my pen for one purpose only: that my readers may understand and cultivate a lively devotion to the most Admirable Heart of Thy Blessed Mother.

Chapter Three

The Corporeal Heart of Mary

Just as everything in Our Lord Jesus Christ is great and admirable, so also everything that concerns Mary, His holy Mother, is replete with grandeur and marvels. Every part of the sacred humanity of the Son of God is deified and raised to an infinite dignity through its union with the Divinity; so likewise everything in the Blessed Virgin Mary is ennobled and sanctified by her divine maternity. There is no part of the sacred body of the God-Man that is not worthy of the eternal admiration of angels and men, and there is nothing in the virginal body of the Mother of God that is unworthy of the eternal praise of all creatures.[1]

The Holy Ghost, the Son of God and His saints have given high praise to the sacred members of Mary's immaculate body. We may therefore conclude that her blessed heart, the first and worthiest part, is deserving of especial veneration. Shall we not share the sentiments of Jesus Christ, our Head, and follow the example He gives us? Mary's divine son, who has willed to be our Head and our Brother, manifests great zeal in honoring even the smallest exterior detail of the person of His Most Blessed Mother. Who therefore can dare to criticize[2] the other children of this Mother of Fair Love, if, following the spirit and example of their divine head and elder brother, they render special homage to her maternal heart and celebrate a feast in its honor with the permission of Holy Church?

There are five marvelous prerogatives of the corporeal heart of Mary which render it forever worthy to receive the veneration of men and angels.

---

1 In the original edition, the Saint here proceeds to exalt the body of the Blessed Virgin Mary, supporting his exposition with texts from Sacred Scripture, the Fathers of the Church and the writings of various Saints. Cf. *Oeuvres Completes* V. 6, p. 41, ff.
2 When Saint John Eudes wrote this work, the devotion to the Heart of Mary was new. It was attacked and criticized by the Jansenists. This opposition explains why the Saint in this book never misses an opportunity to silence those "who dare to criticize," by setting forth the proofs for the devotion to the Immaculate Heart of Mary.

The *first* prerogative consists in the fact that the heart is the principle of the life of our holy Mother. It is the principle of all the functions of her bodily, material life, ever holy in itself and in its every function and employment. It is the source of the life of the Mother of God, the life of her who gave birth to the only Son of God, the life of the woman through whom God gave life to all the children of Adam, sunk as they were in the abyss of eternal death. Finally, her heart is the source of a life so holy, so noble, so sublime that it is more precious in the sight of God than the lives of all the angels and men.

The *second* prerogative of the corporeal heart of Mary is that it produced[3] the virginal blood with which the sacred body of the God-Man was formed in the chaste womb of His Blessed Mother.

The *third* prerogative of Mary's heart of flesh is that it was the source of the human, material life of the Infant Jesus during the nine months that He dwelt in Mary's sacred womb. While the infant is in its mother's bosom, the mother's heart is to such an extent the source of the infant's life that both mother and infant can be said to depend upon it for their existence. Mary's Admirable Heart was therefore the source of the two most noble and precious lives, at once the source of the holy life of the Mother of God and of her only son, the humanly divine as well as the divinely human life of the God-Man.

The *fourth* prerogative of the amiable heart is noted in the words of the holy Bride to the divine Bridegroom, that is, of Mary to Jesus, who is her son and her Father, her Brother and her Spouse, "Our bed is flourishing,"[4] that is, our bed is covered and perfumed with flowers. What is this bed? It is the pure heart of the Blessed Virgin where the divine Infant so gently rested.

It was a great privilege for Saint John, the beloved disciple, to have rested once on the Saviour's adorable breast, from which he drew such great light and derived the knowledge of so many marvelous secrets.

But not only once but many times did our divine Saviour rest on the virginal heart of His dearest Mother. What abundance of lights, of grace and of blessings the eternal sun, the very source of light and grace,

---

3   Saint John Eudes thought that the blood, which carries life through the organism, is produced in the heart, or at least receives its final perfection there, so that before having passed through the heart it is unfit either to nourish the body or to assist in the performance of its vital functions. He was mistaken in that notion, as were all his contemporaries. But it still remains true that the heart influences the entire organism in sending the blood through it. "All vital movement springs from the heart," says Claude Bernard, "and thus it is the heart which gives indication of life. . . . It is still at work when the other organs surrounding it lie dormant. . . . It never rests; while everything else sleeps, the heart is beating. As long as it remains in motion, life can reassert itself, but when it ceases to pulsate, life is irrevocably lost. Just as its first movement was the unmistakable indication of life, its last beat is the sure sign of death." Quoted by Reverend Ange Ledoré in *Les SS. Coeurs ei le V. Jean Eudes*, V. 2, p. 25. Father Charles Lebrun's work, *La Dévotion au Coeur de Marie* (Paris, 1917), p. 289.

4   Cant. 1, 15.

must have poured into that maternal heart, on which He rested so often! Her heart never interposed the slightest obstacle to divine grace. On the contrary, she was always disposed to welcome every celestial favor. Our Lord loved her heart more than all other hearts put together, and was in turn loved by it more perfectly than by the hearts of all the Seraphim. What union, what intimacy, what understanding, what correspondence between these two hearts! What fire in these two furnaces of love constantly inflamed by the breath of the Holy Spirit!

And now we come to the *fifth* prerogative of this holy heart. It is the altar upon which a great and perpetual sacrifice, most agreeable to God, is constantly offered. On it are immolated all the natural passions which reside in the human heart.[5] There are found at once the concupiscible and the irascible appetites of the soul, given by God to man that they may be led to hate, fear, avoid, combat and destroy the things that hurt them, and to love, desire, hope for and seek that which will benefit them. These two principal passions comprise eleven others, which are like soldiers fighting under two captains, or like weapons and instruments used to attain the two ends mentioned above.

The irascible appetite possesses five passions, namely hope, despair, daring, fear and anger. The concupiscible appetite includes six: love, hatred, desire, abhorrence, delight and sadness.

Man's revolt against the commandments of God caused all these passions to revolt against self and to fall into such disorder that instead of being completely subject to the will, which is the queen of all the soul's faculties, they often make it their slave. Instead of being the guardians of the heart in which they reside, preserving it in peace and tranquillity, the passions usually become as many executioners who torment the heart and fill it with conflict and war.

5   Saint John Eudes stresses the connection between the heart and the passions in order to bring out a final prerogative of the corporeal heart of Mary. There is, indeed, a close relationship between the heart and the perceptible feelings. "We feel our hearts affected by our emotional states, and even our moral dispositions," says Father Bainvel. "We feel that our emotional states and our moral dispositions are connected with certain states and movements of the heart. We are not simply using a metaphor when we say: 'My heart is panting; my heart is full; my heart is oppressed; my heart is gladdened.' These expressions translate for us a physiological reality as well as a psychical." Cf. Bainvel, *La Dévotion an Sacré-Coeur de Jésus*, p. 183.

Following the physiology of his day, Saint John Eudes looked upon the heart as the *seat of the passions* and *the organ of love*. This was the prevailing opinion in the eighteenth century. Even in recent years this theory found adherents. The late Cardinal Billot, an outstanding theologian, boldly made the following statement in his treatise, *De Verbo Incarnato* (Rome, 1904) 4th edition, p. 348: *Cor non solum symbolum amoris est, sed etiam organum; imo symbolum quia organum; inquam, amoris sensitivi ei compassivi qui subjectatur in conjuncto.* "The heart is not merely the symbol of love (of the senses); it is also its organ. It is its symbol, in fact, only because it is its organ." This is also the opinion of Bainvel in *La Dévotion an Sacré-Coeur*, p. 122, and Vermeersch, *Pratique et Doctrine de la Dévotion au Sacré-Coeur*, p. 392. It must be noted, however, that most modern physiologists teach that the heart can do no more than experience the repercussions of the emotions, the organ of which is the brain together with the nervous system. Cf. Lebrun, *Oeuvres Complétes du Vénérable Jean Eudes* (Vannes, 1907), v. 6, p. xxv.

Such was not the case with the passions that reside in the corporeal heart of the Queen of Angels, for they were always entirely subject to her reason and to the divine will that held sovereign sway over every part of her soul and body.

Just as these passions were rendered divine in the adorable heart of Our Lord Jesus Christ, so were they sanctified most excellently in the holy heart of His Blessed Mother. The fire of divine love, burning day and night in the ardent furnace of this virginal heart, so purified, consumed and transformed her passions into its own substance, that, as this heavenly fire had no other object save God alone, towards whom it constantly tended with incomparable ardor and impetuosity, so these passions were always turned towards God and exercised in His service. They were moved and led exclusively by the love of God, which possessed, animated and inflamed them in so marvelous a manner that they became a perpetual and admirable sacrifice in honor of the Blessed Trinity.

We may consider the most pure body of Mary as a sacred temple, indeed as the most august temple that ever was or will be, next to the temple of the sacred humanity of Jesus Christ, her divine son. We see her virginal heart as the sacred altar of this temple. We behold Divine Love as the high priest offering to God uninterrupted sacrifices in this temple and on this altar. We contemplate the divine will bringing many victims to be sacrificed on this altar of Mary's heart. Among the victims we distinguish the eleven natural passions slaughtered by the flaming sword which the high priest holds in his hand, that is, by the efficacy of divine love. They are consumed and transformed into the heavenly fire which burns upon the altar of her heart; they are immolated to the most Holy Trinity in a sacrifice of praise, of glory and of love.

Thus did the great high priest, Divine Love, sacrifice on the holy altar of Mary's heart, all her passions, inclinations and sentiments of love, hatred, desire, aversion, joy, sadness, hope, distrust, daring, fear and anger.

And this sacrifice commenced the first instant the holy heart of Mary began to beat in her virginal breast, that is, the very first instant of this Immaculate Virgin's life. It continued uninterruptedly until her last breath, gaining in sanctity and in love with every passing moment.

O great and truly admirable sacrifice, so wonderfully agreeable to the God of hearts! O blessed heart of the Mother of Fair Love, consecrated altar whereon so divine a sacrifice was offered! Blessed art thou, O most holy heart, for having loved and desired nothing but Him who alone is amiable and desirable! Blessed art thou for having established thy joy and thy contentment in loving and honoring Him, who alone is capable of satisfying the heart of man, and for having known no other grief than that caused by the offenses committed against His divine majesty!

O blessed heart, thou hast hated nothing, fled from nothing, feared nothing, except what could injure the interests of thy beloved son, and hast never known anger except towards that which was opposed to His glory!

O blessed heart, so completely closed to the vanities of the earth and of self interest that not one trace of them ever found place in thee! Thy confidence in God was equalled by thy firm trust in divine bounty, and, fired with holy generosity, never didst thou give way before the obstacles raised by hell and the world to prevent thee from advancing along the path of sacred love, but thou didst always surmount them with unremitting constancy and invincible strength.

These are some of the marvelous prerogatives of the Admirable Heart which beats in the virginal breast of the Mother of God. Is it not true that, even if we considered only the material and corporeal heart of the Queen of Heaven, it would still be worthy of the greatest honor and veneration?

Blessed indeed are the hearts of the true children of Mary, who strive to live in conformity with the most holy heart of their Mother most admirable!

Think, think of the honour that is due to her heart, most noble part of the virginal body that gave human flesh to the eternal Word, forever the center of adoration of the angels and saints in Heaven! What honour is due to her heart, life principle of the Mother of God and of God made man!

Above all, what great veneration is merited by the heart that God Himself loved and glorified most highly, the heart that adored and loved God more perfectly than all the hearts in Heaven and upon earth! May every heart praise and magnify thee forever and ever!

Chapter Four

THE SPIRITUAL HEART OF MARY

The Holy Ghost is wont to describe many things with few words. Wishing to praise the principal faculties of the body and soul of His spouse, the Blessed Virgin Mary, and to exalt the merits of her heart, He uses very few words, which nevertheless contain many meanings. What does He say? How does He praise Mary, the sovereign of hearts? He utters only three words: *Quod intrinsecus latet*.[1] But these three words encompass all the great and admirable utterances that can be said or thought of her royal heart; they reveal to us that it is a treasure hidden from the most enlightened eyes of Heaven and earth, a treasure so filled with celestial riches that God alone can have a perfect knowledge of its wonders.

Notice that the Holy Spirit pronounces these words not only once, but twice in the same chapter. He does this in order to impress them more strongly on our minds and to oblige us to consider them with greater attention, as well as to manifest to us both the corporeal heart of the Queen of Heaven, which was the subject of the preceding chapter, and her spiritual heart, of which I shall speak now.

What is the spiritual heart? In order to understand it, we must remember that, although the soul is essentially one, it can nevertheless be considered as having a threefold life.

The first and lowest life is that of the vegetative soul, which is similar in nature to that of plants, for the soul in this state has no other function than to nourish and sustain the body. The second is the sensitive life, which we have in common with animals. The third is the intellectual life, like that of angels, comprising the intellectual memory, the intellect proper and the will, together with the highest part of the mind, which theologians call the point, the summit or the eminence of the spirit. This last power is led not by the light of complex reasoning, but by a clear intuition of the intellect and a simple movement of the will whereby the soul submits to the truth and the will of God.

1 Cant, 4, 1 and 3 "what is hid within."

It is this third life called *spirit,* the mental, superior part of the soul, which renders us like the angels and carries with it in its natural state the image of God and in the state of grace, a participation of the divine nature.

This intellectual part is the heart and the noblest portion of the soul, for, first, it is the principle of the natural life of the rational soul, which consists in the knowledge it can obtain of supreme truth with the aid of the natural light of its intelligence, and in its natural love for sovereign goodness. Animated by the spirit of faith and grace, it becomes the principle of the supernatural life of the soul, which knows God by celestial light and loves Him with supernatural love. "This is eternal life: That they may know thee, the only true God."[2]

Secondly, this intellectual part is the heart of the soul, because in it is centered the will, the faculty and capacity of loving, but in a manner much more spiritual and noble and exalted and with a love incomparably more excellent, more lively, more active, more solid and durable than the love which proceeds from the sensitive and corporeal heart.

The will, enlightened by the light of the intellect and the torch of faith, is the principle of this love. When it is led only by the light of human reason and acts only in virtue of its natural capacities, the will produces only a human and natural love incapable of uniting the soul to God. But when it follows the torch of faith, and is moved by the impulses of the spirit of grace, it becomes the source of a supernatural and divine love, which makes the soul worthy of God.

Thirdly, sacred theology teaches us that, even though grace, faith, hope and charity spread their heavenly influence and divine movements to the other faculties of the inferior part of the soul, they nevertheless reside and have their true natural dwelling in the superior part. Hence it follows that this same part is the real heart of the Christian soul, because divine charity can have no other abode than the heart which possesses it, according to the words of Saint Paul, "The charity of God is poured forth in our hearts."[3]

Fourthly, Saint Paul proclaims to all Christians, "Because you are sons, God hath sent the Spirit of his Son into your hearts,"[4] and assured them that he bends his knees to the Father of Our Lord Jesus Christ to obtain the privilege that His Divine Son may dwell in their hearts.[5] Now, what is this heart, if not the superior part of our soul, since the God of grace and love cannot dwell in a Christian soul elsewhere than in the part where grace and charity reside?

2 John 17, 3.
3 Rom. 5, 5.
4 Gal. 4, 6.
5 Ephes. 3, 14-17.

All this clearly demonstrates that the true and proper heart of the rational soul is the intellectual part, called spirit, the mental, superior part.

This being so, the spiritual heart of the Blessed Virgin Mary is the intellectual element of her soul, comprising her memory, intelligence, will and the supreme point of her spirit. This is the heart which expresses itself in the first words of her admirable Canticle, the *Magnificat*, "My soul doth magnify the Lord: and my spirit hath rejoiced in God my Saviour."[6] It is the spirit, the soul's first and noblest part, which must, in a very special manner, glorify God and rejoice in Him.

Of this marvelous heart I have great things to say. But to use the language of Saint Paul, even all human and angelic tongues together pronouncing everything that could be said would still fall far short of its perfections. "Of whom we have much to say, and hard to be intelligibly uttered."[7]

If the virginal heart beating in the consecrated breast of the Virgin of virgins, the most excellent organ of her holy body, is so admirable, as we have already seen, what must be the marvels of her spiritual heart, the noblest portion of her soul? Is it not true that, as the condition of the soul surpasses that of the body, so also does the spiritual heart excel the corporeal? We have already considered the rare prerogatives of her heart of flesh, and we shall now endeavor to express the incomparable gifts and inestimable treasures with which her spiritual heart is filled.

I shall place before you only a short summary to encourage you to bless the source of so many marvels, to praise her who made herself worthy of so many graces, and to honor her most holy heart, which so faithfully preserved her graces and privileges and used them so perfectly.

First of all, divine bounty miraculously preserved the heart of the Mother of Our Saviour from the stain of sin, which never touched it because God filled it with grace from the moment of its creation, and clothed it with purity so radiant that, next to God's, it is impossible to conceive of greater purity. His divine majesty possessed her heart so completely from its first instant that it never ceased for a moment to belong entirely to Him and to love Him more ardently than all the holiest hearts of Heaven and earth united. Such is the opinion of many great theologians.

In the second place, the Father of light has filled this beautiful sun with the most brilliant lights of nature and of grace. If we consider the natural illumination shining within Mary, we see that God gave to the chosen spouse of the Holy Ghost a natural intellect more clear, lively, profound, vaster and more perfect in every way than any

6 Luke 1, 46-47.
7 Heb. 5, 11.

other intellect, an intellect worthy of the Mother of God, worthy of the woman destined to guide and rule divine Wisdom, worthy of the Mistress of the Church and Queen Regent of the universe, worthy of her who was to converse familiarly on earth with the angels of Heaven, and what is more, with the King of Angels, for thirty-four years, an intellect worthy of the lofty functions and sublime contemplation to which she was consecrated.

As regards supernatural light, the luminous heart of Mary, Seat of Wisdom, was so filled with its radiance that the learned Albert the Great, nurtured in the school of the Mother of God, plainly teaches, together with many other holy Doctors, that there was nothing Our Lady did not know.[8] They assert that she possessed infused knowledge of every science, and in a much more eminent degree than the most learned minds that ever existed.[9]

The vast knowledge of the Blessed Virgin Mary was dedicated to a most holy use, employed only to urge her to love God with greater ardor, to procure the salvation of souls with greater fervor, to hate sin more vigorously, to humble herself more profoundly, to despise still further everything that the world esteems and to prize and embrace with greater affection the things it detests, namely poverty, abjections and suffering.

Moreover, Our Lady never experienced undue pleasure in the lights that God imparted to her, never became attached to these favors, never preferred herself to other beings on account of them, but always returned them to God as pure as they sprang from their source.

Such was the knowledge of the Admirable Heart of Mary. What shall we now say of the twofold love that inflamed her heart, her love for God and incomparable charity for men?

It was by the force of love and humility that Mary attracted the well-beloved Son of God, the heart of the eternal Father, to be the heart of her heart.

The love of Mary's most blessed heart makes it an inexhaustible source of gifts, favors and blessings for all those who truly love their Mother most amiable, and honor with affection her most lovable heart, according to the words the Holy Ghost puts on her lips, "I love them that love me."[10]

Finally, it is this heart which has loved and glorified God above all the hearts of angels and men, and therefore, can never be revered adequately.

---

8 *Tract. super Missus est*, cap. 149—After enumerating the various aspects of Mary's knowledge, Saint Albert the Great summarizes thus: . . . *est conclusio ex praedictis omnibus, quod nullius rei proprie habuit ignorantiam.*
9 Here Saint John Eudes describes in detail the different types of knowledge possessed by the Blessed Virgin Mary. Cf. *Oeuvres Complètes*, v. 6, p. 97 ff.
10 Prov. 8, 17.

What honor is due to such great and admirable wonders! What veneration should be shown to the heart of Mary, the noblest part of the holy soul of the Mother of God! What praises must be rendered to all the faculties of the spiritual heart of the Virgin Mother, namely her memory, her intellect, her will, and the most intimate part of her spirit, which were never exercised except for God and by motivation of the Holy Ghost.

What respect her holy memory commands, which only remembered the unutterable favors she had received from the divine munificence, and the graces God constantly showers on every creature, in order to thank Him incessantly!

What veneration is due to her intellect, always engaged in considering and meditating on God's mysteries and His divine perfections in order to honor and imitate them! What veneration is also due to her will, perpetually absorbed by the love of God!

What honor the supreme part of her spirit commands, which was day and night absorbed in contemplating and glorifying His divine majesty most excellently!

Is there any praise not merited by the marvelous heart of the Mother of the Saviour, a heart which never encompassed anything that could in the least displease Him, a heart so filled with light and grace, a heart possessing the perfection of all virtues, all the gifts, all the fruits of the Holy Ghost, with all the evangelical beatitudes?

Will you not admit, dear reader, that, if Heaven and earth were to exalt the Admirable Heart of Mary eternally with all possible strength and if the entire universe were to thank God for having filled her heart with such a wealth of marvels, this honor and thanksgiving could never fittingly be made.

Chapter Five

THE DIVINE HEART OF MARY

Jesus Christ, the heart of the eternal Father, is the heart of His Holy Mother.[1] Is not the heart the principle of life? And what is the Son of God to His dear Mother? He always was and will be forever the heart of her heart, the soul of her soul, the spirit of her spirit, and the sole principle of all the movements, uses and functions of her most holy life. Saint Paul tells us that it is not himself who lives but Jesus Christ who lives in him.[2] Our Lord is the life of all Christians:[3] so who could doubt that He abides in His holy Mother, and that He is the life of her life, the heart of her heart, in a union incomparably more excellent even than with Saint Paul and the other faithful saints?

Let us listen to what Our Lady revealed to Saint Brigid, "My son was truly my heart to me. When He left my bosom to be born, it seemed as though half of my heart were going forth from me. When He suf-

---

1 Between the Sacred Heart of Jesus and the holy heart of Mary there exists a union so perfect that there never has been and never will be "a closer one aside from the hypostatic union." Saint John Eudes calls both Jesus and the Holy Ghost the divine Heart of Mary. We must remember, however, that no matter how close is the union between Jesus and Mary it does not destroy the distinction of persons. *Jesus Christ, the divine Heart of Mary,* so closely united to her corporeal and spiritual hearts, *is nevertheless extrinsic to her person.* It therefore cannot belong to the immediate object of the devotion to the holy heart of Mary because the devotion concerns Mary herself and cannot have any object other than whatever belongs properly to her person. Thus it is that *the particular object of the devotion to the holy heart of Mary must be limited to her corporeal and spiritual hearts.*

Nevertheless, it must be noted that the devotion to the Blessed Virgin Mary and to the saints, when it is well understood, never confines itself to their persons; it ascends to God Who is the author of their holiness and Who is no less adorable in what He effects in His saints than in what He is in Himself. Without this consideration, devotion to Mary and to the saints would not be an act of religion, for religion relates to God and if now and then the acts which it inspires are addressed to creatures, it is because of their special union to the Divinity. "The devotion we have for the saints," says Saint Thomas, "never ends with them; it passes to God, for it is God Himself whom we honor in the saints." *Sum. Theol.* 2a 2ae, q. 82, art. 2, ad 3.

Saint John Eudes was convinced and rightly so that all honor rendered to the Blessed Virgin Mary and to the saints in the Catholic Church implies homage to the person of Jesus Christ, who is the *final object,* together with the Father and the Holy Ghost. Cf. Lebrun, *La Dévotion au Coeur de Marie* (Paris, 1917), p. 312 ff.

2 Gal. 2, 20.

3 Col. 3, 4.

fered, I felt His pain as though my heart endured the identical sorrows and torments that He endured. When my son was being scourged and torn with whips, my heart was scourged and whipped with Him. When He looked at me from the Cross, and I at Him, two streams of tears gushed from my eyes; and when He saw me oppressed with sorrow, He experienced such violent anguish at my desolation that the pain caused by His sorrow was my sorrow as His heart was my heart. Because Adam and Eve together betrayed the world for one, single forbidden fruit, so did my beloved son wish that I should cooperate with Him in redeeming it with one heart, *quasi cum uno Corde*.[4]

You see, therefore, how the Son of God is the heart and life of His holy Mother, in the most perfect union conceivable. The Holy Ghost, speaking by Saint Paul, proclaims that our adorable Saviour must so live in all His servants that His life be manifested in their bodies. "That the life also of Jesus may be made manifest in our mortal flesh."[5] Who could consequently understand with what abundance and perfection Our Lord communicates His divine life to her from whom He received a divinely human and a humanly divine life because she conceived and begot the God-Man?

Jesus lives in her soul and in her body, and in each faculty of her body and soul. He lives in her entirely, which means that whatever is in Jesus is also in Mary. His heart abides in her heart, His soul in her soul, His spirit in her spirit. The memory, intellect and will of Jesus are alive in the memory, intellect and will of Mary; His interior and exterior senses in her interior and exterior senses. His passions in her passions; His virtues, mysteries and divine attributes are living in her heart. Nay, more than living, they hold sovereign sway, producing inconceivably marvelous effects and impressing a living image of themselves as her heart mirrors His Sacred Heart.

So it is that Jesus is the principle of life in His most holy Mother. So it is that He is the heart of her heart and the life of her life. Saint Brigid once heard her say, "Every homage rendered to my son is likewise rendered to me, and who dishonors Him dishonors me. We have always had such perfect mutual love that we seemed to have as it were but one heart for both. *Quasi cor unum ambo fuimus*."[6]

This Admirable Heart it is, which receives our respect and praise, which must be esteemed an object of veneration for all Christians, for to honor Mary's marvelous heart means to honor countless holy and divine mysteries deserving of the eternal veneration of angels and men.

4 *Revel.* Lib. 1, cap. 35.
5 2 Cor. 4, 11.
6 *Revel.* Lib. 1, cap. 8.

It also means to honor all the functions of the corporeal and material life of the Queen of Heaven, of which the heart is the principle, that life superlatively holy in itself and in every use she made of it. It means honoring the perfect functions of her memory, her will, her intellect, and the highest part of her spirit. It means honoring innumerable great and ineffable mysteries which were perfected in the superior part of her soul.

It means above all to honor the great love and ardent charity of this Mother of Fair Love toward God and men, together with the effects which that love and charity produced in her thoughts, words, prayers, actions, sufferings, and in the exercise of every virtue.

This veneration of Mary means honoring the corporeal heart, the spiritual heart and the divine heart of Jesus, which are also the hearts, or rather, the one and only heart of Mary. It means giving glory to Our Lord, Jesus Christ, who is the heart of the eternal Father, and has willed to become the heart of His Holy Mother.

It means honoring and glorifying all the effects of light, grace, and sanctity which this divine heart of Mary, who is Jesus Christ Himself, has effected, and all the movements of the heavenly life of which He was the principle in her soul, and also the great fidelity with which she cooperated, on her part, with all that His grace accomplished in her heart during so many years. What tongue could proclaim, what mind could conceive, what heart could worthily honor so many great and admirable wonders of grace!

If Holy Church celebrates an annual feast in honor of the chains of Saint Peter, the prince of the Apostles, how great a solemnity does not the august heart of the Queen of Apostles deserve! If the holy name of Mary is so greatly venerated by all the faithful, if the oracles of the Holy Spirit, the Fathers and Doctors of the Church, like Saint Germanus, Patriarch of Constantinople, Saint Anselm, Saint Bernard and many others, have said such wonderful things concerning the name of Mary, if one of them[7] assures us that "after the adorable name of Jesus, Mary's name is above every name, so all creatures in Heaven, on earth, and in Hell must bend their knees to honor it, and that every tongue must proclaim the holiness, glory and virtue of this holy name"; if the Church celebrates its feast annually in many places what must we say, what must we think of the marvelous heart of our holy Mother, that heart far more precious than her name? What should we do to honor it? Indeed every heart, every pen and every tongue should be employed in loving, in writing and in speaking of the incomparable heart of Mary. The entire universe should therefore celebrate the Feast of Mary's Immaculate Heart.

7 Raym. Jordan. *Contempl. B. V.*~ Part 4 Contempl. 1.

You all know that in various great churches throughout the Christian world there are venerated constantly, with special feasts, treasured relics of the most holy Mother of God, for example her veil. If Holy Church has proclaimed feasts in veneration of the least and smallest objects traditionally belonging to Our Lady, how much more should we not celebrate the praises of her most exalted and most sublimely honorable heart?

To conclude the first part of my treatise, I would have you realize, dear reader, that Our Lord Jesus Christ, who is the heart of the eternal Father, willed to become the heart or life principle of His Most Blessed Mother, and He likewise wills to become the heart of your own life.

Having granted you the grace to become one of the members of His mystical body, He seeks to share your life so that you may say with Saint Paul, "Christ liveth in me!"[8] Such is the infinite plan of God, such His burning desire. Our Lord seeks to establish His life, not only in your soul, but in your body, that His spirit may become your spirit and His heart your heart, united in all its love, thoughts and actions, by self surrender, even as His heart was completely and perfectly the heart of His admirable Mother.

If the will of God is to become your will, and if the spiritual and corporeal faculties of the sacred humanity of Our Lord are to animate the faculties of your soul and body, what must you do? You must cooperate.

First, you must seek the death of every activity of your soul and body that is displeasing to God, bearing in your body the mortification of Christ.[9] Then, having mortified your faculties, their powers and exercise must be turned towards virtue.

Above all, offer yourself frequently to the Son of God. Beg Him to deign to exercise the almighty power of His arm to destroy within you everything that is contrary to His holy will, and to establish over you the reign of His divine soul and His crucified body.

Especially useful is the most devout prayer of Saint Augustine, the *Anima Christi, Sanctifica Me.* "Soul of Christ, sanctify me.[10] It will help you to attain your purpose at all times, but particularly after you have received Our Saviour within your heart, either during the Holy Sacrifice of the Mass, or in Holy Communion. When you are speaking to the divine heart of Jesus, if you realize His actual and veritable pres-

8 Gal. 2, 20.
9 2 Cor. 4, 10.
10 Saint John Eudes attributes this prayer to Saint Augustine, but does not give any reasons for doing so. Although Saint Ignatius places it at the beginning of the *Spiritual Exercises,* he is not looked upon as the author of the prayer. The *Anima Christi* was first indulgenced in 1330 by Pope John XXII, who is thought to have written it. Cf. Dreves, *Laacher stimmen,* 1898. To this well-known prayer Saint John Eudes adds the invocation: *Cor Jesu, purifica me, accende me.* "Heart of Jesus, purify me, enlighten me, inflame me."

ence within you, you will pronounce this prayer with greater fervor and receive greater blessing for its recitation.

But I must return to thee, O Mother Most Admirable, to exclaim that in thee are accomplished all things most perfectly, most gloriously, in union with thy divine son. Whether it be corporeal, spiritual or divine, His heart is thine, He is the life of thy life and the heart of thy heart. May He be blessed, praised and glorified forever by all creatures, because of the graces imparted to thee, O Mary, and all the greatness of His humanity and His divinity!

Part Two

FIRST FOUNDATION OF THE DEVOTION:
THE HEART OF GOD THE FATHER

SIX SYMBOLIC PICTURES

Chapter One

GOD THE FATHER, DELINEATOR OF THE ADMIRABLE HEART OF MARY

The exposition I have made in Part One ought to suffice to show that, next to the sacred humanity of Christ, there exists in the universe no creature more deserving of honor and veneration than the Admirable Heart of His most pure Mother, and that this devotion is specially pleasing to the divine majesty of God and most beneficial for all Christians.

But in order to foster and strengthen this devotion more and more deeply in the hearts of the faithful where it already exists, and to spread and establish it among those who so far have no place for it, I wish to show fully that devotion to the heart of Our Lady, instead of being without basis and reason, is a cult established on foundations so firm, with roots so strong, that all the powers of earth and Hell cannot possibly shake or weaken it.

The first foundation and the primary source of the devotion to the most holy heart of Mary is the adorable heart of the eternal Father and His unfathomable love for the Blessed Mother of His only begotten Son. This infinite love induced our heavenly Father to give us many beautiful images and figures of the most worthy heart of His holy Mother.

God the Father, to whom we assign by appropriation the creation of the world, together with the establishment and fulfillment of the Old Law, was pleased to foreshadow, in every part of the universe and in all the mysteries, sacrifices and ceremonies of the Old Testament, His only Son through whom He created and willed to renew all things. Likewise, the eternal Father lovingly prefigured, both in the visible world and in the rites of the Mosaic Law, Mary, the woman chosen from all eternity to be the Mother of the adorable Redeemer. "It was she whom the Prophets foretold long before her birth," says Saint Jerome. "It was she whom the Patriarchs described in many figures; it was she who was announced by the Evangelists."[1] "Toward her converge all the predictions of the Prophets, all the mysteries of

1 Serm. de Assumpt.

Scripture," says Saint Ildephonsus.[2] Elsewhere he writes, "The Holy Ghost foretold her through the Prophets, announced her by the divine oracles, manifested her in figures, promised her by means of the things which preceded her birth, and fulfilled in her the things which followed it."[3]

Saint John Damascene[4] says that the earthly paradise, Noe's ark, the burning bush, the Tables of the Law, the Ark of the Covenant, the golden vessel containing the manna, the golden candlesticks in the Tabernacle, the table with the loaves of proposition, Aaron's rod, the furnace of Babylon, were all figures of the incomparable Virgin Mary.

The eternal Father did not content Himself with prefiguring the person of His Son Jesus in His prototypes, Abel, Noe, Melchisedech, Isaac, Jacob, Moses, Aaron, Josue, Samson, Job, David and many other holy persons who lived under the Old Law, which preceded His Son's appearance on earth. God also wished to give us several beautiful representations of His mysteries in detail, such as His divine espousal of human nature in the Incarnation, His Passion, Death, Resurrection and Ascension.

In like manner, God the Father was not satisfied to foreshadow and represent the person of the Mother of His beloved Son merely in the person of Mary, sister of Moses, in the prophetess Debbora, wise Abigail, chaste and generous Judith, beautiful and compassionate Esther, and many other valiant women. Beyond this, the eternal Father deigned to entrust to us special pictures and images of the mysteries and qualities of His incomparable Mother, her virtues and even the more noble faculties of her virginal body. Several passages of Sacred Scripture reveal these pictures, especially the twenty-fourth chapter of Ecclesiasticus, and the Canticle of Canticles, where her Immaculate Conception is represented by the lily growing among thorns without being wounded by them, "As the lily among thorns;"[5] her Nativity, by the rising dawn;[6] her Assumption, by the Ark of the Covenant which Saint John saw in Heaven;[7] the sublime eminence of her dignity, her power and her holiness, by the height of the cedar of Lebanon;[8] her charity, by the rose;[9] her humility, by the spikenard;[10] her mercy, by the olive;[11] her virginity, by the

---

2 Serm. 1.
3 *Lib. de Virginitate Mariae.*
4 *Orat. 1 de Dormit. Mariae.*
5 Cant. 2, 2.
6 *Ibid.*, 6, 9.
7 Apoc. 11, 19.
8 Ecclus. 24, 17.
9 *Ibid.*, 39, 17.
10 Cant. 1, 11.
11 Ecclus. 24,19.

closed gate of the Temple which God showed to Ezechiel the prophet.[12]

But above all else, Our Heavenly Father has willed to place before our eyes a wealth of beautiful figures and marvelous representations of Mary's most holy heart. He has done this to show us how much He values and cherishes this lovable heart and because the rare and wondrous perfections that fill it are well-nigh innumerable and can be represented and described only through a great number of figures and symbolic pictures.

Among the many images and representations of the Admirable Heart of Mary, I can distinguish twelve of surpassing beauty. Six of them are found in the principal divisions of the universe; namely, the heavens, the sun, the center of the earth, the inexhaustible fountain of Genesis, the sea and the Garden of Eden. The six others appear in six of the most important manifestations witnessed by the world from the time of Moses to the death of Our Lord. They are the burning bush of Mount Horeb, the mysterious harp of David, the magnificent throne of Solomon, the marvelous Temple of Jerusalem, the miraculous furnace of Babylon, and the holy mount of Calvary.

In this part we shall consider one by one the first six manifestations of the august heart of the Queen of Heaven. We shall dwell at length upon them so that we may be inspired to bless and praise the hand of the divine artist who drew them, to reverence and admire the rare perfections of the prototype whose too inadequate reflection they are, and to evoke a higher esteem for the devotion to the holy heart of Mary. It is a well-founded devotion, resting on a solid basis, because its first origin and firm foundation is the adorable heart of the eternal Father, Who drew these symbolic pictures for us.

12 Ezech. 44, 2.

Chapter Two

MARY'S HEART, THE HEAVENS

The first symbolic picture of the Admirable Heart of Mary which the eternal Father has given to us is the heavens. Mary's pure heart is truly a heaven of which the sky over our heads is a mere shadow and image. It is a heaven exalted above all others, of which the Holy Ghost speaks when He says that the Saviour of the world went out from a heaven surpassing all others in excellence, when He came on earth to redeem mankind: *A summo, caelo egressio ejus*.[1] As Our admirable Mother had formed her divine son in her heart before conceiving Him in her womb,[2] we can truly say that, having remained hidden in her heart for a little while even as He had been in the heart of His Heavenly Father from all eternity, Our Blessed Saviour emerged from it to manifest Himself to men. But just as He went forth from Heaven and His Father's bosom, without however relinquishing them: *Excessit, non recessit*,[3] so also is His Mother's heart a heaven whence He came forth in such a manner that He nevertheless remained and will remain forever in it, "For ever, O Lord, thy word standeth firm in Heaven."[4]

The heavens are called the special work of God's hands, "The heavens are the works of thy hands,"[5] but the heart of the Mother of God is the unequalled masterpiece of His omnipotence, His unfathomable wisdom and His infinite goodness.

---

1 Ps. 18, 7.
2 Saint John Eudes repeats very often that Mary conceived her divine son in her heart through faith and love before conceiving Him in her womb. In this connection he likes to quote the words of Saint Augustine (*Lib. de S. Virginitate*, c. 3), "Mary's maternal relationship would have availed nothing, if she had not borne Christ in her heart more happily than in her body"; and also the saying of Saint Leo the Great, "She conceived (Christ) in her soul before conceiving Him in her body." (*Serm. 1 de Nativitate Domini*).
3 Tertull.
4 Ps. 118, 89.
5 Ps. 101, 26.

God made Heaven to be the particular abode of His divine majesty, "The Lord hath prepared his throne in Heaven."[6] It is true that He fills both Heaven and earth with His divinity, "I fill Heaven and earth,"[7] but Heaven to a far greater degree than earth, for He has established there the fullness of His grandeur, power and divine magnificence, "Thy magnificence is elevated above the heavens."[8] In like manner, we can truly say of the heart of the Blessed Mother of God that it is a real heaven of the Divinity, of the divine attributes and of the most Blessed Trinity.

The Admirable Heart of Mary is an empyrean heaven, that is, a heaven all fire and flames, ever burning with the fire and flames of celestial love, holier and more ardent than the love of the Seraphim and of the greatest saints who dwell in the empyrean heaven.

Mary's pure heart is the heaven of heavens, created for God alone, because it is the priceless inheritance and rich portion of the Lord, who always possessed it most entirely, "The heaven of heaven is the Lord's."[9] Yes, the most holy heart of the Queen of Angels is the heaven of heavens for three significant reasons.

First of all, Jesus Christ is truly the Heaven of the Blessed Trinity. The Holy Ghost assures us that the fullness of the Divinity abides in Him, "For in him dwelleth all the fullness of the Godhead,"[10] and this same Jesus has forever fixed His dwelling in the blessed heart of His most worthy Mother. This must not surprise us, for Sacred Scripture reveals that even in this present life, He maintains His dwelling in the hearts of all who believe in Him with a firm and perfect faith. We can therefore conclude that, as our most lovable Saviour is Himself a Heaven, possessing no abode more glorious and delightful, next to the adorable bosom of His eternal Father, than the heart of His holy Mother, which is itself a heaven, He is truly Heaven dwelling within a Heaven. In this way, the heart of the Mother of Jesus can be said to be the Heaven of Heaven.

Secondly, Mary's Immaculate Heart is the Heaven of Heaven because the spotless Virgin is really a Heaven considered in her own person. This is the quality ascribed to her by the Holy Ghost, according to a learned and holy writer, "From Heaven the Lord hath looked upon the earth."[11] As this commentator explains it, "the Lord, dwelling in the Blessed Virgin Mary, as in a Heaven, has turned the eyes of His

6 Ps. 102, 19.
7 Jer. 23, 24.
8 Ps. 8, 2.
9 Ps. 113, 16.
10 Col. 2, 9.
11 Ps. 101, 20.

mercy towards the earth, that is, towards sinners."[12] Then the same author goes on to say that this marvelous Virgin is a Heaven because, as all living things in the order of nature receive their life from the influence of Heaven, so does Holy Church teach us that the life of grace is given to us through the Blessed Virgin Mary: *Vitam datam per Virginem*."[13] Now if this incomparable Virgin is a Heaven, our own Heaven in this world of grace, because next to God the source of our spiritual life, we can well say that her heart is the Heaven of Heaven, having been the principle of her corporeal and spiritual life on earth and of the eternal life that she now enjoys in Heaven.

Thirdly, the Admirable Heart of Mary is the Heaven of Heaven, because, as Saint Bernard says, it contains the entire Church, which is called in Sacred Scripture the Kingdom of Heaven, and because all the children of the Church receive through Mary the life of grace.[14] If Saint Paul assured the Christians of his time that they were in his heart,[15] who would dare to contradict Saint Bernardine of Siena,[16] who tells us that the most Blessed Virgin Mary, like a good mother, carries all her children in her heart? Who will contradict me if I add that Our Lady will forever carry all the inhabitants of Heaven in her inmost heart, which becomes the Heaven of Heaven, and a true paradise of the elect, in which they find the fullness of delight and joy, due to the inconceivable love for each soul which consumes her maternal heart? Thus the blessed will forever sing: *Sicut laetantium omnium nostrum habitatio est in corde tuo, sancta Dei Genetrix.* O holy Mother of God, thy boundless charity has so vastly extended thy maternal heart that it has become like a great city, or rather an immense Heaven, full of ineffable consolations and unspeakable joys for thy beloved children, whose happy dwelling it shall be for all eternity.

The heart of our Holy Mother is thus truly a Heaven, an empyrean Heaven, the Heaven of Heaven. O Heaven, more exalted, more extensive and more vast than all the Heavens! O Heaven, enclosing Him whom the Heaven of Heavens cannot contain! O Heaven, filled with more praise, glory and love of God than the Heaven where eternal bliss resides! O Heaven, wherein the King of Heaven reigns more completely than in all other Heavens! O Heaven, where the most Holy Trinity dwells more worthily and accomplishes wonders far greater than in the empyrean Heaven! O Heaven, in which divine mercy has established its throne and deposited its treasures, where it hearkens to the

12 *Ignotus* in Ps. 101.
13 *Ignotus* in Ps. 101.
14 *Serm. 3 Super Salve.*
15 2 Cor. 7, 3.
16 *Serm.* 6, art. 22, cap. 2.

cry of the unfortunate and helps them in all their necessities! "O Lord, thy mercy is in Heaven."[17]

Let us draw nigh to this throne of grace and with great confidence present our requests to the Mother of grace and mercy. Through the intercession of her heart, most exalted, yet most tender, we shall obtain the graces that we need to become pleasing in the sight of the celestial majesty of God.

Rejoice, O readers, rejoice, you whose great happiness it is to be numbered among the true children of the Mother of pure love, for your names are written in her maternal heart! Lift up your eyes and your hearts to that beautiful Heaven! It is there that your hearts will find light, strength, powerful aid in the battle of life, guidance and succor, and above all inspiration to love your Creator and Redeemer, the Lord of Heaven, strongly, purely and above all things.

17 Ps. 35, 6.

Chapter Three

Mary's Heart, the Sun

The sun is the second symbolic picture which God, the Creator of Heaven and earth, has deigned to give us of the Immaculate Heart of the Queen of Heaven and earth. God did not create the natural sun, our wonderful luminary, merely to enlighten our material world; He made it also to be a representation of the excellent perfections which shine in the luminous heart of the world's Sovereign Lady.

We should remember that the infinite power of God has divided this great universe into three different states or orders; namely the state of nature, the state of grace and the state of glory. His divine wisdom has nevertheless established such a perfect bond, relationship and resemblance among these three states and among the beings existing in these orders that whatever is in the order of nature is an image of the things belonging to the order of grace, and whatever belongs to the order of nature and grace is a figure of what is to be seen in the state of glory. Hence, the sun, which is truly the heart of the visible world, and the most beautiful and glowing gem of nature, gives us, in spite of its dazzling light, only a very faint shadow of our heavenly sun, the heart of the Mother of God.

Sacred Scripture calls the sun an admirable vessel, the work of the Sovereign Lord. "An admirable instrument, the work of the Most High. Great is the Lord that made him."[1] But we can say of the most excellent heart of the Mother of God that it is an incomparable masterpiece of God's almighty hand. It is a compendium of all the marvels He has worked in pure creatures, and will be the eternal object of the admiration and delight of angels and men. Great indeed is He who made it, because His divine magnificence appears in her Admirable Heart more clearly than in all the other wonderful things of nature, grace and glory.

The sun, which gives light to our visible world and which is, so to speak, its heart, is entirely luminous, is light itself and the source from

1 Ecclus. 43, 2 and 5.

which the other heavenly bodies receive their light. Mary's heart is surrounded, filled, penetrated by light, and her light is incomparably more brilliant and radiant than all the lights of the celestial spaces. It is all light, and after God, it is the first source of the lights which shine in the firmament of the Church. "I made that in the Heavens there should rise light that never faileth."[2]

The sun is, moreover, the principle of the vegetative, sensitive and animal life in the visible world. The heart of the Blessed Virgin Mary is the source of life of three great worlds. We have already seen[3] that it is the source of life of the Mother of God, who is a world unto herself, filled with marvels far greater and more wonderful than the world we contemplate with our bodily eyes.

But I shall add that the pure heart of Mary is the source of three different lives to be found in this holy Mother; namely the natural and human life that animated her body on earth; the spiritual and supernatural life which her soul then possessed; and the glorious, eternal life which both her body and soul enjoy in Heaven. Everyone agrees that the heart, in the sense in which we have defined it, is the source of the corporeal life; we must likewise admit that it is the source of love and charity, the virtues which constitute the true life of a Christian soul in time and in eternity, and hence can be said very truly to be the very element which fosters the life of the soul for earth as well as for Heaven.

Secondly, the Immaculate Heart of Mary is the principle of the life of a second world, infinitely more admirable than the preceding one. What is this world? It is the God-Man, filled with countless rare marvels. Now, this God-Man is the son of Mary, and Mary's heart is consequently the source of His life, since the mother's heart is the principle of the child's life as well as her own.

Thirdly, the heart of the Mother of Our Saviour is the origin of life for a third world, composed of true children of God, who are vivified by grace on earth and glory in Heaven, because under God they derive both the life of grace and the life of glory from the Mother of Him who is their Head and whose members they themselves are. They are indebted for this benefit to her holy heart, whose original purity, profound humility and ardent love, made her worthy to become the Mother of God and of all the children of God. Saint John Chrysostom is surely right when he says that the heart of Saint Paul was "the heart of the whole world. For it is through that apostolic heart that the Spirit of Life was poured forth on all things and given to the members of Jesus Christ."[4] But how much more true is

2 Ecclus. 24, 6.
3 Part One, Ch. 3.
4 *In cap. 16, Epist. ad Rom. homil,* 23.

this of the incomparably loving heart of the Queen of Apostles? Yes, hers is indeed the heart of the entire world, the heart of Heaven and earth, the heart of the Church Militant, Suffering and Triumphant, since the Holy Spirit bids us sing: *Vitam datam per Virginem, genies redemptae plaudite.* "All ye nations, redeemed by the Precious Blood of Jesus Christ, rejoice, sing the praises of your Redeemer and His glorious Mother! You were condemned to eternal death, and the son of Mary has made you free; the Mother of Jesus has restored life to you, even eternal life, by giving you her son, who is Life essential and the source of all life."

The solar sun has been in perpetual motion since its creation in space, and it travels so rapidly that mathematicians calculate its speed to be over one million leagues an hour. Similarly, the holy heart of Mary, from the moment of her Immaculate Conception, has been completely kept in motion by love for God and charity towards mankind. As long as Mary, the admirable sun of light and purity, was on earth, she sped or rather flew with such celerity on the path of sanctity that the speed of our material sun is simply a shadow and a figure by comparison. For this holy sun, Mary's Immaculate Heart, progressed incomparably farther in the mystical and supernatural way of the world of grace than the material sun which revolves around our visible world.

Sacred Scripture teaches us that the sun is the tabernacle of God. "He has set his tabernacle in the sun."[5] This is infinitely more true of the heart of the Blessed Virgin Mary. Saint Ambrose applies these words to her, and we should refer them especially to her heart, in which God resides more gloriously and works far greater wonders than in the sun of any universe. I hear the eternal Father pronounce that the throne of His only begotten Son is like to a sun before His face, "His throne (is) as the sun before me. . . ."[6] What is this throne of Christ, if not the heart of His dearest Mother, which is therefore the ever brilliant sun shining before the Father of lights?

If the material sun radiates its light, heat and influence over all living things on earth, still more does this mystical sun, the heart of Mary, make its holy light, divine warmth and celestial influence felt everywhere in Heaven and earth, over men and angels, "There is no one who can hide himself from his heat."[7] The earthly sun gladdens with its rays the inhabitants of the lowly world; the heavenly sun enriches the whole universe with its great and boundless charity towards all God's creatures. *Gaudium annuntiat universo mundo.* It is the consolation of the suffering souls in Purgatory, the joy of the faithful on earth, the

5 Ps. 18, 6.
6 Ps. 88, 38.
7 Ps. 18, 7.

exultation of the angels and saints in Heaven, and the delight of the most Blessed Trinity. Saint Germanus of Constantinople calls the heart of Mary the happiness of the entire world. *Commune mundi gaudium.*[8] And Saint John Damascene says that it is an ocean of inexhaustible delight: *Gaudii pelagus inexhaustum.*[9]

"Take away the sun that enlightens our material world," says Saint Bernard, "what will become of day or light? Take away Mary, the Star of the Sea, or take away the heart of Mary, the true sun of the Christian world, and what would be left? Without Mary's radiance, nothing is left but enveloping darkness, the shadow of death and the frightful night of the grave."[10]

O excellent heart of my Queen, my most amiable sun, blessed are the hearts that love thee! Happy the minds that meditate on thy greatness, and the tongues that preach and praise thee! Blessed are the eyes that contemplate thee, O radiant Mary! The more they gaze on thee, the greater their desire, the stronger the light and strength they receive to enable them to gaze yet more upon thy dazzling light!

O beautiful sun, enlighten our darkness, melt our frigidity, dispel the clouds and fogs of our minds, inflame our hearts with thy sacred fire! Make us ever receptive to thy sweet influence, that every Christian virtue may flourish in our souls, so that they may be rendered fertile in all kinds of good works. By thy intercession, obtain that we may lead a heavenly life on earth, and never seek any joy here below except the joy of the children of God, which consists in pleasing their Heavenly Father and obeying His adorable will in all things.

O radiant sun, let our hearts become like clear and polished mirrors, and be pleased to impress thy likeness on them, that they may bear a perfect image of thy humility, purity and submission to the divine will as well as of thy charity, love, sanctity and all the other virtues and perfection of thine Admirable Heart. This we ask for the glory of God who made our hearts for Himself alone.

8 *Homil. de Nativit. Mariae.*
9 *Orat. 2 de dorm. Deip.*
10 *In Serm. de Aquaeductu in Nativit. B. Mariae.*

Chapter Four

Mary's Heart, the Center of the Earth

The third symbolic picture of the most noble heart of Mary is described in the inspired words, "God hath wrought salvation in *the midst of the earth.*"[1]

What is this earth and what is its center? I find several meanings of the word "earth" as mentioned in Sacred Scripture, among which two seem to be most important. The first is the earth created by God at the beginning of the world, which He gave to Adam and his descendants. "But the earth he has given to the children of men."[2] The second is the earth made for the new man, Jesus Christ, Our Lord, to whom the following words were spoken, "Lord, thou hast blessed thy land."[3]

The first earth incurred the wrath of God because the first man sinned. Cursed is the earth in thy work.[4] The fallen earth is a land of misery and darkness, of disorder and death, a land of never-ending woe. In the words of Job, it is "a land of misery and darkness, where the shadow of death, and no order, but everlasting horror dwelleth."[5]

The second earth is a land of blessings, grace and light, a land of eternal life, a land that has become nobler, more august, more luminous and holier than all the Heavens. What is this priceless renewed earth? It is the most Blessed Virgin Mary, of whom the first earth, considered as it left the hands of God and existed before being cursed by God, is only an imperfect image and sketch. Of this earth did the Holy Ghost speak in Scripture: when He said through the Prophet, Isaias, "Let the earth be opened, and bud forth a saviour."[6]

It was in Mary, the center of this blessed earth, that God worked out the salvation of mankind. "He hath wrought salvation in the midst

1 Ps. 73, 12.
2 Ps. 113, 16.
3 Ps. 84, 2.
4 Gen. 3, 17.
5 Job 10, 22.
6 Isa. 45, 8.

41

of the earth."[7] Both Saint Jerome and Saint Bernard[8] apply these words to the Blessed Virgin Mary. Notice, however, that the Holy Ghost who uttered these words through the lips of the royal prophet David, does not proclaim merely that God worked the salvation of the world in this earth, but *in the midst of the earth, in medio terrae,* or according to another version, *in intimo terrae, in the center* or *in the heart of the earth.* By that is meant the heart and bosom of the spotless Virgin Mary. Yes, it was in the midst of this "good earth," or better, in the good and excellent heart of Mary, Mother of Jesus Christ, "in a good and perfect heart,"[9] that the eternal Word, coming forth from the Father's bosom to save mankind, was received and zealously nourished, producing fruit a hundredfold and one hundred thousand times a hundredfold.

All this was declared in that divine prophecy of the Holy Spirit which reveals so many great and admirable mysteries, "There shall be a firmament on the earth on the tops of mountains, above Libanus shall the fruit thereof be exalted: and they of the city shall flourish like the grass of the earth;"[10] or according to another version, "A full measure of wheat scattered over the lofty mountains, shall grow so tall that, stirred by the breath of the wind, its undulations shall imitate the verdant woods of Lebanon."

What is this overflowing measure of wheat, if not the only Son of God, the true wheat of the elect, the bread of God, Who is the life and strength of man's heart? "Bread may strengthen man's heart."[11] The eternal Father scattered this sanctifying wheat when He gave us His divine Son with such great love in the mystery of the Incarnation and He still scatters it every day in full measure when He continues to give us Our Lord daily with consummate goodness in the Blessed Eucharist. What are the lofty mountain-tops, if not His most worthy Mother, whom the Holy Spirit sets before our eyes under the name and figure not of a single mountain but of many mountains? Mary possesses in the highest degree all that is most excellent in the sacred mountains, that is in all the saints, who are called in Sacred Scripture "the holy mountains,"[12] and "the everlasting hills."[13] What are the mighty summits of these mountains, if not the exalted prerogatives and sublime perfections of the Sovereign Lady of the Universe?

7 Ps. 73, 12.
8 *Serm. 2 in die Pentec.*
9 Luke 8, 15.
10 Ps. 71, 16.
11 Ps. 103, 15.
12 Ps. 86, 1.
13 Ps. 75, 5.

Now then it was up on these holy mountains with lofty summits in the midst of this sacred soil, in the excellent heart of the best of Mothers, that the adorable wheat of redemption was first sown and planted, since she received Our Saviour in her heart before conceiving Him in her womb. It was later scattered throughout the world by the preaching of the Apostles, animated by the Holy Ghost as by an impetuous wind and became infinitely multiplied in the hearts of all Christians.

We can, therefore, say in truth that Jesus is the fruit of Mary's heart as well as of her womb, and that the faithful are the fruits of the same heart, because the very virtues of faith, humility, purity, love and charity, which rendered her worthy to become the Mother of God, made her also the Mother of all God's children. As the eternal Father gave her the power to conceive His Son in her heart and in her virginal womb, by clothing her with the divine virtue whereby He generates His divine Son from all eternity in His own adorable bosom, so also did God grant her the power to form Christ and give birth to Him in the hearts of the children of Adam, who thus became members of Jesus Christ and sons of God.

Even as Mary conceived and will eternally bear her son Jesus Christ in her heart, she also conceives and holds forever in the same heart all the holy members of our divine head. They are her beloved children, the fruits of her maternal heart, and she offers them to the divine majesty as a perpetual sacrifice.

Thus did Our Lady, "the good earth," fructify the grain of wheat which she received from God. Her son had to die even as the seed must die and, as it were, become annihilated that He might not remain alone, but might produce numberless other grains. In this sense did the King of Kings work out our salvation in the center of the earth.

I could quote many holy Fathers and illustrious Doctors to show how almighty God saved mankind "in the midst of the earth," that is, in the holy heart of Mary, Mother of Jesus. Her heart cooperated with His divine mercy, having received such a plenitude of grace, according to the Angelic Doctor, Saint Thomas, that she became enabled to cooperate with her son in the salvation of all men.[14] This inspires Saint Bonaventure to say that her heart is the source of universal salvation. "All salvation springs from Mary's heart."[15]

All this being conceded, what must be our obligations towards the most charitable heart of our Blessed Mother! What gratitude can we

14 *Magnum est in quolibet Sancto, quando habet tantum de gratia, quod sufficit ad salutem multorum; sed quando haberet tantum, quod sufficeret ad salutem omnium hominum de mundo, hoc esset maximum, et hoc est in Christo, et in beata Virgine. Opusc. 8.*
15 *In Psalt. B. Virg. ps. 79.*

show, what praises can we sing, what feast can we celebrate in honor of her heart, that will be worthy of her excessive charity towards us, and of the favors granted to us by divine mercy through her intercession?

Mary is the center of the earth in which our salvation was wrought. She is also the center of the renewed world, the Christian world, the world of the new man, the world of divine love and holy charity. Here are three reasons to show that Mary's heart is the center of the Christian world.

First, all beings consider their center the seat of their repose, their conservation, and, as it were, their salvation. The salvation of man having taken place in the heart of Mary, all Christians must consider her as the source of their life after God and as the cause and the center of their happiness.

The words of the Fathers of the Church will bear us out in this. Here is what Saint Bernard has to say. His words refer to the person of the Blessed Virgin, but can be applied especially to her heart. "With good reason is Mary called the center of the earth, for all the inhabitants of Heaven, and those of Hell, those who come before us, and those who will come after us, their children's children and their entire posterity look to her as to the midst and the center of the earth. She is, in fact, next to her divine son, the mediator between God and Man, between the Head and the members of the Mystical Body, the Church, between the Old and New Testament, between Heaven and earth, between justice and mercy. They look to her as to the Ark of God, Ark of the Covenant and of peace between God and His people, as the cause of all that is good and the masterpiece of all ages, past and to come. The inhabitants of Heaven, that is, the angels, look to her as to the one through whom the losses inflicted on them by sin will be repaired; those who are in the fiery torment, which here means Purgatory, look to her as to the one through whose mediation they will be delivered, those who came before us see in her the fulfillment of the ancient prophecies, those who shall follow us consider her as the means whereby they will one day be crowned with immortal glory."[16]

These words of Saint Bernard not only may be applied to the heart of the Mother of God, but are actually more applicable to her heart than to her person. The cause being nobler than its effects, her heart so full of humility is, as we shall see, the cause and the source of all virtues which adorn Our Lady and render her worthy to be the object, the refuge, and as it were, the center of every creature past, present and to come. Hence I conclude that her marvelous heart is indeed the midst and center of the world of the new man.

16 Serm. 2 in die Pentec.

Secondly, I say that the heart of Mary is the center of this new world, meaning the world of divine love and holy charity, a world of tenderness and dilection, having charity as its only law, because all holy love and divine charity contained in the hearts of angels and men, who love God for Himself and their neighbor for the love of God, are found united in the heart of the Mother of Fair Love as in their center. Mary's heart is like a beautiful mirror, large enough to reflect all the sun's rays focussed on its polished surface.

Thirdly, you will remember that the most humble and pure Virgin ravished and attracted to herself the adorable heart of the eternal Father, His beloved Son, and that He became the heart of her heart. Jesus is, therefore, the true heart of Mary. Is not this amiable Jesus the love, the delight, the center and the joy of Heaven and earth? Is it not certain, therefore, that the true heart of Mary, namely Jesus, is the center of all the hearts of angels and men? They must ever be turned towards it, gaze upon it unceasingly and make it the object of their aspirations and desires. It is the seat of their perfect repose and of their supreme felicity. Out of it there is only trouble, fear, anxiety, death and hell.

O Jesus, true heart of Mary, take possession of our hearts, and draw them nigh to Thee. Inspire them to love, desire, seek and relish only Thee. May they ever long for Thee, may they always seek their rest and happiness in Thee, may they remain in Thee forever and be consumed in the ardent furnace of Thy divine heart so as to be transformed eternally in Thee!

Chapter Five

MARY'S HEART, THE INEXHAUSTIBLE FOUNTAIN

The fourth symbolic picture of Our Lady's most blessed heart is the wonderful fountain that God caused to spring from the ground at the beginning of the world, as described in the second chapter of Genesis. "A spring rose out of the earth, watering all the surface of the earth."[1] Bonaventure tells us that this fountain was a figure of the Blessed Virgin Mary. "She was prefigured in the fountain that sprang from the earth."[2] But we have equal reason to say that this represented her heart, which is truly a living fountain whose heavenly waters irrigate not only the whole earth, but every created thing in Heaven as well as on earth.

Mary is the sealed fountain of the holy spouse, which her divine bridegroom calls "a fountain sealed up,"[3] for it remained sealed not only against the world, the devil and every kind of sin, but it was closed even to the Cherubim and Seraphim, who could not penetrate the marvelous secrets or comprehend the inestimable treasures hidden by God in Our Lady's pure heart.

Sacred Scripture states that the heart of man is evil and inscrutable.[4] But the heart of the Queen of Heaven inspires these words, "God created her in the Holy Ghost, and saw her, and numbered her, and measured her."[5] In other words, so holy and impenetrable is the heart of Mary that only God Who enclosed within His treasures of grace and put His seal upon it, can know the quality, quantity and price of the graces hidden in this sealed fountain. All we can say is that Mary's Immaculate Heart is a fountain of light, a fountain of holy and blessed water, a fountain of living and life-giving water, a fountain of milk and honey and a fountain of wine. It is the source of

1 Gen. 2, 6.
2 *Figurata fuit per fontem quae ascendebat de terra. In opusc. inscripto Laus Virg.*
3 Cant. 4, 12.
4 Jer. 17, 9.
5 Ecclus. 1, 9.

a great river, nay, of four miraculous streams, and finally, it is the source of an infinity of blessings and goodness.

Mary's peerless heart is a *fountain of light*, that foreshadowed in the person of Queen Esther, who is represented in Sacred Scripture as a small fountain that becomes a great light and is turned into the sun. "The little fountain which grew into a river, and was turned into a light, and into the sun . . ."[6] It is the fountain of the sun, *fons solis*, mentioned in chapters fifteen and seventeen of the Book of Josue.

The heart of Mary, as well as her name, which means "enlightened" or "the one who enlightens," and also "star of the sea," is indeed a true fountain of light. Holy Church considers and honors her as the resplendent door of pure light; *Tu porta lucis fulgida*, and salutes her as the portal through which divine Light entered the world: *Salve porta, ex qua mundo lux est orta*. Truly the heart of Mary is the fountain of the sun, because Mary is the Mother of the sun of justice, and this divine sun is the fruit of Mary's heart.

O incredible wonder! O inconceivable miracle! Who could ever have thought that the sun could be born of a star, or that a fountain could be the source of the sun, *fons solis*. Thus, then, the virginal heart of Mary is a true fountain of light.

Mary's heart is a *fountain of water*, but one of blessed, holy and precious water. I here speak of the innumerable tears that poured from this sacred fountain and, united with those of the Redeemer Himself, cooperated in our redemption. O Mary, how many streams of tears have flowed from thine eyes, with their source in thy loving, charitable, devoted and merciful heart! Tears of love, tears of charity, tears of joy, of sorrow and of compassion! How often did not the ardent love of the maternal heart for thy infinitely lovable son cause thee to shed bitter tears, beholding Him so little loved, so much hated, offended and dishonored by the majority of men, although it was the duty of man to serve Him? How often thy burning charity for souls caused thee to weep because through their own malice, millions of precious souls would be lost, notwithstanding all that He did and suffered in order to save them? How many times have the holy angels witnessed tears of sublime devotion coursing down thy beautiful face, as thou wast absorbed in holy communion with the divine majesty? All the saints were granted the gift of tears, which could not possibly have been wanting in the Mother of Sorrows who has assured us that she possesses the fullness of gifts bestowed on all the saints. *In plenitudine sanctorum detentio mea.*[7]

6 Esther 10, 6.
7 Ecclus. 24, 16.

O Mother of Jesus, the joy which filled thy peerless heart on so many occasions while thou wast on earth with thy beloved son caused sweetest tears to flow from thine eyes. Those were tears of joy and consolation, for example, when He assumed our human nature in thy sacred womb, when thou didst visit thy saintly cousin Elizabeth, when thy dear son was born in Bethlehem, when the three Holy Kings came to adore Him, when, after having lost Him for three days, thou didst find Him in the temple among the Doctors, when He visited thee after the resurrection and when thou didst watch His triumphant ascension into Heaven.

Alas, thy consolations in this life were negligible compared to the sufferings thou didst have to endure. If the joys of thy heart caused tears of rapture to flow from thine eyes, the poignant sorrows that were so often thine, especially at the time of the passion and death of thy beloved son, made thee shed floods of bitter tears. Then were the sacred words fulfilled in thee, "Let tears run down like a torrent day and night: give thyself no rest, and let not the apple of thy eye cease."[8]

Now then are not all these tears of joy, love, charity, devotion, sorrow and compassion like so many waters streaming from the holy fountain of Mary's Immaculate Heart? Oh, with what good reason, therefore, do we call her Admirable Heart a fountain of blessed, holy and precious water!

The most pure heart of Mary is also a *fountain of living water*, which means a fountain of grace. This ought not to astonish us, for the Archangel Gabriel declared long ago that the Mother of the Saviour was full of grace, *gratia plena*, and the Church calls her *Mater gratiae*, Mother of Grace, and *Mater divinae gratiae*, Mother of Divine Grace. The Angelic Doctor, Saint Thomas, affirms that Our Lady is so full of grace that out of her abundance she can dispense graces to all men.[9]

Her most generous heart is indeed a fountain of living waters whose salutary streams flow on all sides, over the land of the wicked as well as of the just, in imitation of the all-good and all-merciful heart of our heavenly Father who causes His providential rain to fall on the good and the bad alike. This is the reason why the Holy Ghost calls the charitable heart of the Mother of Mercy "the fountain of gardens," *fons hortorum*.[10] In another passage He names it the fountain that "shall water the torrent of thorns."[11]

What are these gardens, what is this torrent of thorns, watered by this beautiful fountain?

8 Lam. 2, 18.
9 Opusc. 8.
10 Cant. 4, 15.
11 Joel 3, 18.

The gardens are all the Orders of the Church that lead a truly Christian and holy life. They are delicious gardens for the Son of God, blooming with flowers and fruit that the spouse longs for when she exclaims, "Stay me up with flowers, compass me about with apples: because I languish with love."[12] These mystical gardens likewise represent all holy souls, no matter what their state or condition, in whom the heavenly bridegroom finds His delight among the flowers of holy thoughts, desires and affections, and among the refreshing fruits of virtues and good works.

These gardens of delight are constantly watered by the fountain which is called by the Holy Ghost "the fountain of gardens," according to many holy Doctors who apply these words to the Blessed Virgin Mary.[13]

But Mary's heart is not only the fountain of gardens whose waters impart refreshment to just and holy souls. Saint Jerome also refers to the Holy Mother of God these words of the prophet Joel, ". . . a fountain shall come forth of the house of the Lord, and shall water the torrent of thorns."[14] What are these thorns and this torrent? The thorns represent the wicked, whose lives are infested with the thorns of their sins. This torrent is the world, which resembles an impetuous torrent, full of refuse and evil odors, making much noise, but flowing swiftly past, dragging the majority of men into the abyss of perdition. "The world passeth away, and the concupiscence thereof."[15]

But the heart of the Mother of Mercy is so full of goodness that its effects are felt even by the torrent of thorns, or rather, by the poor thorns which are swept in this torrent to be thrown into the eternal whirlpool of Hell. The wonderful waters of her holy fountain, coming in contact with these barren and dead thorns, fit only for eternal fire, cause many of them to awaken to new life, and some are even transformed into beautiful trees that bear quantities of good fruit, worthy to be placed on the table of the eternal King. The reason is that this fountain's divine waters are not only living, but lifegiving. Mary's heart is, therefore, not only a fountain of living waters but a fountain of life, and of life eternal.

But it is not enough to love life without furnishing the substance to nourish and sustain it. For this reason, Mary's maternal heart is not only a fountain of living and life-giving waters; it is, moreover, *a fountain of milk, of honey, of oil and of wine.*

It is a fountain of milk and honey, for we hear the divine spouse

12 Cant. 2, 5.
13 Cf. Rupert. *in Cantio.*
14 Joel 3, 18.
15 1 John 2, 17.

saying to Mary, "Thy lips, my spouse, are as a dropping honeycomb, honey and milk are under thy tongue,"[16] which means, Thy words are full of sweetness and tenderness, and thy heart must consequently be filled with them. Mary's heart and tongue always agree, and there is perfect conformity between her words and her sentiments. If therefore she has milk and honey in her mouth, she must also have them in her heart; and they are under her tongue and upon her lips only because her heart is filled with incomparable sweetness.

Hence, the inspired words, "My spirit is sweet above honey, and my inheritance above the honey and the honeycomb."[17] We must, therefore, conclude that her heart is a real fountain of milk and honey, whose streams flow incessantly into the hearts of her children, thus verifying the saying of the Holy Ghost, ". . . you shall be carried at the breasts, and upon the knee, (she) shall caress you, as one whom the mother caresseth."[18] Happy are they who raise no obstacles to the fulfillment of these consoling words! Happy are those who do not close their ears to the voice of the sweetest Mother constantly crying, "As newborn babes, desire the rational milk without guile, that thereby you may grow unto salvation."[19] Come, my well-beloved, come, eat of my honey and drink of my milk, that you may taste and see how sweet and delightful it is to serve and love Him Who has made me so amiable and tender towards His children, and how my heart is full of love and affection for those who love me in return. "I love them that love me."[20]

We see therefore that the heart of the Mother of Fair Love is a fountain of milk and honey for all her children, especially for those who are still weak, tender and delicate, not yet capable of taking more solid food.

Her heart is also a fountain of oil, that is, of mercy for all sinners. It is, moreover, a fountain of wine to give strength and vigor to the weak and comfort to the sorrowful and afflicted, according to the divine words, "Give strong drink to them that are sad: and wine to them that are grieved in mind."[21]

All those who comfort other men for the sake of charity, and, above all, who work for the salvation of their neighbor, should be inebriated with the wine of divine love! To such as these our charitable Mother, ever burning with zeal for the salvation of souls, cries in a loud voice, "Come, children, come beloved of my heart, come, draw from the fountain of your Mother's heart the heavenly wine of divine love;

16 Cant. 4, 11.
17 Ecclus. 24, 27.
18 Isa. 66, 12–13.
19 1 Peter 2, 2.
20 Prov. 8, 17.
21 Prov. 31, 6.

drink long and deep; filled with the rapture of the spirit, you need fear
no excess. 'Drink, and be inebriated, my dearly beloved.'[22] Drink of this
pure wine, father of virginity and of all holy virgins. 'Wine springing
forth virgins.'[23] This heavenly wine fills the Seraphim with delight; it
inebriated the Apostles of my divine Son; it filled the Redeemer
Himself with holy rapture when, in the excess of His love for you, He
renounced the grandeurs of His divinity and humbled Himself in the
lowly crib and on the ignominious Cross. Drink with Him of this delicious wine, that you may forget and despise what the world loves and
esteems, that you may love and value God alone, and exert yourself
with all your might to establish the reign of His love and His glory in
the souls of men. Thus will you become the beloved children of His
heart and of my own."

Who will give me a voice strong enough to be heard in all the
world, crying to all men, "All you that thirst, come to the waters: and
you that have no money make haste, buy, and eat: Come ye, buy wine
and milk without money, and without any price."[24]

You who thirst vainly after the false honors of the world, come
instead to the most honorable heart of the Queen of Heaven, and you
will learn by the example of this heart's thirst for the glory of God
alone, that true honor consists in following His divine majesty, "It is
great glory to follow the Lord."[25] Every other honor is only smoke, vanity and illusion. You who thirst after the riches of earth, come hither,
and you will find incomparable treasures.

You who thirst after worldly pleasures, come and you will find the
contentment of the angels, the delights of God, the peace and joy of the
children of God and of God's Mother, according to the divine promise
addressed to each faithful soul, "Behold I will bring upon her as it were a
river of peace, and as an overflowing torrent the glory of the Gentiles."[26]

Emerge from the filth of the world's horrible torrent, of the torrent
of thorns that is whirling you into the abyss of perdition! Emerge and
enter the sweet waters of the river of peace. Give yourself up in holy
ecstasy to this torrent of delights. *Properate*, hasten, why do you wait?

Do you fear to slight the incomparable goodness of the heart of
Jesus, your God and Redeemer, if you invoke the charity of His
Mother's heart? Do you not know that Mary is nothing, possesses nothing, and can do nothing except in, through and by Jesus? Do you not
know that Jesus is everything and that He can and does accomplish

22 Cant. 5, 1.
23 Zach. 9, 17.
24 Isa. 55, 1.
25 Ecclus. 23, 38.
26 Isa. 66, 12.

everything through her? Do you not know Jesus made Mary's heart as it is, and that He willed it to be the fountain of light, of consolation and of every possible grace for those who will have recourse to it in their necessities? Do you forget that not only does Jesus reside and dwell perpetually in Mary's heart, but that He is in truth the heart of her heart and the soul of her soul; and that therefore coming to the heart of Mary means to honor Jesus and to invoke her heart is to invoke Jesus?

Our Lady asks of you only one thing, which is, that if you seek to taste the sweetness of the milk and honey flowing from the fountain of her heart, and experience the potency of its wine, you must renounce all evil feasting and give up all tasting of the wine of the demons. It is impossible to drink of the chalice of Our Saviour and of the goblet of the devil, to partake of the heavenly banquet of God and at the same time to eat at the table of the devil.[27] You must choose between them. It should be so very easy to make your choice!

Consider how strange it is! The world offers nothing but crumbs and dregs of feasting, empty fame, wealth and fleeting pleasure, but it sells you these stale crumbs and dregs at the costly price of worry, pain, bitterness, restlessness, anguish, often even at the price of your very life. As Sacred Scripture exclaims, "Why do you spend money for that which is not bread, and your labour for that which doth not satisfy you?"[28] Furthermore, the libations that the world sells so dearly are not only stagnant and bitter, completely unable to satisfy you in this life, but their venom is poison bringing eternal death. What satisfaction can you possibly expect to derive from waters as bitter as those of Egypt?[29]

On the other hand, the divine Son of God and of Mary offers you the refreshment and rapture of the fountain of the fullness of the House of God, of which you are free to drink forever. O what blind, blind folly it is to choose the goblet of sin instead of the chalice of Our Saviour! God Himself has exclaimed in amazement at this, through the prophet Jeremias, saying:

"Be astonished, O ye Heavens at this, and ye gates thereof, be very desolate. . . . For my people have done two evils. They have forsaken me, the fountain of living water, and have digged to themselves cisterns, broken cisterns, that can hold no water."[30]

O dearest Lord, have pity on such wretchedness, and by the pure heart of Thy most Blessed Mother, grant unto us the living water that flows from Thee through the miraculous fountain of her heart. Stifle in

27 1 Cor. 10, 21.
28 Isa. 55, 2.
29 Jer. 2, 18.
30 Jer. 2, 12–13.

our hearts the dangerous thirst for worldly things and grant us instead the thirst that burns only to please Thee, to love Thee, to seek our delight and refreshment in following Thy holy will, in imitation of the Admirable Heart of Mary, fountain of sweetness and grace, who knew no joy or paradise except to accomplish Thy divine will most perfectly.

Chapter Six

MARY'S HEART, THE SEA

The Admirable Heart of the Blessed Virgin Mary is not only a fountain, as we have seen, it is also a *sea*, of which the ocean created by God on the third day is a beautiful figure. This is the fifth symbolic picture or representation of Our Lady's Immaculate Heart.

Saint John Chrysostom says that the heart of Saint Paul is a sea: *Cor Pauli Mare Est*,[1] but the Holy Ghost Himself gives this name to the most holy Mother of God, and therefore to her heart, to which the title is even more applicable than to her person, for we shall show that her heart is the principle of all the holy qualities that adorn her.

The Holy Spirit declares that Mary, His most worthy bride, is a sea. A humble and learned writer who, while revealing his brilliant gifts in his excellent commentary on the psalms, has chosen that his name and person remain unknown,[2] teaches us that the name of sea is given in Sacred Scripture to the glorious Virgin because she is indeed a sea of purity, vast in extent and in usefulness. We shall consider shortly that Mary is an ocean in purity and in extent. As for usefulness, this holy Doctor tells us that just as the sea does not permit the adjoining land to remain sterile, so the souls who approach the Mother of God with true devotion bring forth abundant fruits of benediction, thanks to the graces she lavishly bestows on them. Let us say of her heart that it is a sea full of great and wondrous riches.

In the order of nature, the sea is one of the greatest marvels of God's omnipotence. "Wonderful are the surges of the sea."[3] God, Who is great everywhere, is especially admirable in the sea. "Wonderful is the Lord in the depths."[4] The holy heart of Mary is an ocean of wonders and an abyss of miracles. It is the extraordinary mas-

---

1 In cap. 28 *Act. Apost.* homil. 55.
2 Incognitus, in *Ps. 71*.
3 *Ps.* 92, 4.
4 *Ibid.*

terpiece of essential and uncreated Love, in which the effects of infinite power, wisdom and goodness shine more brilliantly than in all the hearts of angels and men.

What is the sea? It is the gathering of the waters, says Sacred Scripture, or if you prefer, it is the place where all the waters are gathered. "Let the waters that are under the Heaven, be gathered together into one place."[5] And the sacred text adds, "The gathering together of the waters, he called seas."[6] Now what is the august heart of Mary? It is the place where are gathered and united the living waters of all graces springing from the heart of God, as from their first source. Saint Jerome says, "Grace is divided among other saints, but Mary possesses the plenitude of sanctity."[7] For the same reason Saint Peter Chrysologus calls Mary *collegium sanctitatis*,[8] that is the place where all grace and holiness are assembled and gathered together; and Saint Bernard, *mare admirabile gratiarum*,[9] a prodigious sea of graces.

"All the rivers run into the sea, yet the sea doth not overflow," says the Holy Ghost.[10] Thus also all the streams, all the torrents and all the rivers of heavenly grace run into the heart of the Mother of Grace, and are readily contained there. All the graces of Heaven and earth merge their waters in the great sea of the holy heart of the Mother of the Saint of Saints. "In me is all grace of the way and the truth."[11] In Mary's heart are all the graces of the angels and of men, all the graces of the Seraphim, Cherubim, Thrones, Dominations, Virtues, Powers, Principalities, Archangels and Angels, all the graces of the holy Patriarchs, Prophets, Apostles, Evangelists, disciples of Jesus, martyrs, priests and levites, confessors, hermits, virgins and widows, of the Holy Innocents and of all the blessed in Heaven. There is no overflow of grace in Mary, she is not overwhelmed, for her heart is worthy of all the gifts and all the liberalities of God's infinite goodness, and is capable of receiving and using them all for the glory of His divine majesty.

Saint Bernardine of Siena tells us that all the gifts and graces of the Holy Ghost descended into the soul and heart of this heavenly Virgin in such fullness, especially when she conceived the Son of God within her chaste womb, that her heart forms an abyss of grace which no human or angelic intellect can comprehend. The mind of God, that

5 Gen. 1, 9.
6 *Ibid.* 10.
7 *Caeteris per partes: Mariae vero simul se tota infundit plenitudo gratiae, Serm. de Assumpt. B. Mariae.*
8 *Serm.* 1, 46.
9 *Serm. de B. Virg.*
10 Eccles. 1, 7.
11 Ecclus. 24, 25.

of her son, Jesus Christ, and her own, are alone capable of understanding the abundance and perfection of this ocean of grace.[12]

The sea does not hoard its waters, but freely dispenses them to the earth through the rivers, which flow into the ocean only to come out of it again, that they may water the whole earth and make it bear all kinds of fruit. "Unto the place from whence the rivers come, they return, to flow again." The heart of our munificent Queen does not withhold any of the graces she receives from the generous hand of God. She returns them all to the first source, and waters the barren earth of our hearts to the extent needed to make them fruitful for God and for eternity. "That we may bring forth fruit to God."[13]

Saint Bernard's words on this subject are most beautiful. He tells us that Mary desires to become everything to everyone. In her abundant charity, she denies no man a claim upon her heart. She opens the door of her mercy and the portals of her generous heart to all, that all may receive of her fullness. To the captive, she brings redemption; to the sick, healing; to the afflicted, comfort; to the sinner, forgiveness; to the just, increase of grace. She augments the joy of the angels; to the Son of God she gives the substance of human flesh, and to the most Blessed Trinity glory and everlasting praise. The love and charity of her heart make themselves felt by the Creator Himself and by all His creatures.[14]

Yes, Mary's Admirable Heart is indeed a sea, being, after Our Lord Himself, the basis and sustenance of the Christian world, a sea of charity and love, a sea more solid and firm than that which sustained the feet of Saint Peter as he walked upon its surface. Her heart is an ocean more strong than the firmament itself, that sea of which Saint John speaks in the *Apocalypse*, "And in the sight of the throne was, as it were, a sea of glass like to crystal; a sea of glass mingled with fire, and them that had overcome the beast . . . standing on the sea of glass, having the harps of God."[15]

Let us study the symbolism of the vision of the Evangelist. Glass is a product which owes its clarity, shape and perfection to moulding in the heat of intense fire. Similarly, the heart of Mary was fashioned in the all-consuming fire of the Blessed Trinity, the furnace of the Holy Spirit, of which it is the most perfect work. Also, during her life on earth, the heart of Mary was tempered, like glass, in the furnace of suffering.

Saint John speaks of glass like to crystal, meaning glass that is both transparent and shining, absorbing and radiating clear light, the most

12 *Serm. 5 de Nativ. B. Virg.* cap. 12.
13 Rom. 7, 4.
14 *Serm. de verb. Apoc.* Signum magnum.
15 Apoc. 4, 6 and 15, 2.

vivid symbol of purity. The sea like unto crystal is the ocean of Mary's heart shining in its flawless purity. Glass made by man is dark in darkness, needing light to be luminous, shining most brilliantly in the direct brightness of the sun, reflecting the measure of light it receives. Similarly, the Admirable Heart of Mary absorbs and reflects most marvelously the full celestial radiance of the eternal sun.

She is the sea of crystal "in the sight of the Throne" that is, directly before the face of the divine majesty, her entire existence being to receive and to reflect the image of God, not only as a sea but as a shining mirror.

Saint John also speaks of the vision of a miracle, a sea mingled with fire, and thus he explains the inspired words of the Canticle of Canticles, "Many waters cannot quench charity, neither can the floods drown it."[16] These floods represent the torrent of sorrow that engulfed the heart of Mary, the beloved spouse, particularly during the passion of her divine son. ". . . O Virgin daughter of Sion, for great as the sea is thy destruction."[17] Yet even the ocean of sorrow did not overwhelm the fire of love in the heart of Mary, but rather caused its flames to glow more brightly.

The Evangelist envisions the saints standing upon the sea of crystal, because their salvation has been founded upon Mary and they have chosen to dwell with her beloved son. Because of her, they have won the grace to chant forever the canticle of the Lamb, the hymn of praise, of joy, of victory over evil; therefore they stand upon the sea of her heart, bearing harps.

O adorable Jesus, grant unto us that we may sing with thee, with Thy Mother most admirable, and with the entire company of the saints, this miraculous canticle in praise of the adorable heart of the Blessed Trinity, which is the source of the countless wonders and perfections enriching the heart of Mary, the ocean of grace and charity.

O Mary, thou sea of love unquenched by sorrow, behold my heart, the least and smallest of all hearts, a mere drop of water seeking to unite itself with thy vast ocean, to become lost in thy depths forever! O Mary, Queen of all hearts consecrated to Jesus, look down upon the tiny drop, my unworthy heart, offered to thee, to become merged forever in the sea of thy glowing love! Mother of Mercy, thou seest us here below, tossed upon a stormy sea of raging trial and temptation. In thy great mercy, deign to be our strength, our guiding star, our sustenance, that, standing firm upon that crystal sea before the Throne, thy Admirable Heart, which tempests cannot assail, we may sing without fear:

Thy royal heart is our pure light, our refuge safe. Why should I fear? Her goodness is firm support of our lives. Nothing can trouble our hearts.

16 Cant. 8, 7.
17 Lam. 2, 13.

Chapter Seven

MARY'S HEART, THE GARDEN OF EDEN

The Garden of Eden described in the second and third chapters of Genesis is one of the most expressive figures drawn by the omnipotent and all-wise hand of God to represent the heart of His beloved daughter, the Blessed Virgin Mary. His infinite goodness has given us an excellent picture of her Immaculate Heart. The earthly paradise of Scripture is the perfect representation of another paradise; it is the paradise of the first man, Adam, excellently portraying the paradise of the second man, Jesus Christ, our Redeemer.

To view this picture in its true light, we must consider many aspects of it.

Let us begin with the name. If we consult Sacred Scripture, we shall learn that the first paradise was called "a paradise of pleasure,"[1] "a place of pleasure."[2] The name of the garden of delights can very properly be applied to the Admirable Heart of the Mother of God, true paradise of the new man, Jesus Christ. It is a garden of the beloved, a garden sealed and doubly barred, a garden of delights. The divine Spirit gives three names to the heart of His holy Bride, and they contain many profound meanings.

In the first place, Mary's heart is the *Garden of the Beloved*. Do we not hear the Holy Ghost inspiring her to say, "Let my beloved come into his garden."[3] Who is the beloved of whom she speaks? Is it not her son Jesus, the single and only object of her love? Into what garden does she invite Him to come, if it be not her virginal heart, into which He was attracted, as we have said, by her humility and her love? Such is the explanation of the learned Balingham.[4] The Garden of the Beloved, therefore, is the heart of the beloved bride; the heart of Mary is the Garden of Jesus.

1 Gen. 2, 8.
2 *Ibid.* 2, 10.
3 Cant 5, 1.
4 *In locis commun. Sacr. Script. verbo Cor.* § 4.

In the second place, the Admirable Heart of the Mother of God is a *sealed garden*. Her heavenly spouse says of her, "My sister, My spouse, is a garden enclosed, a garden enclosed, a fountain sealed up."[5] But why does He twice repeat that it is an enclosed garden? He thereby means to teach us that the heart of His beloved bride is absolutely shut against two things: it is shut against sin, which together with the serpent, the author of sin, never entered there: and it is shut against the world and all things of the world, against everything that is not God. He alone has always occupied this garden entirely, and there never existed place in it for anything else.

The third name given by the Holy Ghost has reference to the prophetic figure, the first paradise, and He calls it a garden of delights, *locus voluptatis,*[6] *paradisus voluptatis.*[7] Mary's spotless heart is indeed a garden of rapture for the Son of God; a garden where He experienced joys which were His greatest delights after those enjoyed from all eternity in the heart and bosom of His eternal Father.

If Thou dost assure us, O Jesus, that Thy delight is to be with the children of men,[8] even though they are full of sin, ingratitude and infidelities, what must not have been Thy delight in the most amiable heart of Thy Blessed Mother, where Thou didst never meet anything displeasing to Thee, but found Thyself always praised, glorified and loved more perfectly than in the Paradise of the Cherubim and Seraphim? One can easily say that, after the adorable bosom of the eternal Father, no place ever was or will be so holy, so worthy of Thy majesty, so filled with glory and contentment for Thy delectation as the virginal heart of Thy most amiable Mother.

Hence it is, O Saviour, that after hearing the invitation to come into her garden, that is, her heart, expressed in the words, "Let my beloved come into his garden,"[9] thou dost answer her, "I am come into my garden, O my sister, my spouse, I have gathered my myrrh, with my aromatical spices: I have eaten the honeycomb with my honey, I have drunk my wine with my milk."[10] The myrrh represents the mortifications and anguish of thy loving heart which I have gathered as well as all acts of virtue thou hast practiced for love of Me, and I shall keep them in my heart forever to be eternal joy and glory. I have also eaten honey, and drunk my wine and milk, that is, I find so many delights in

5 Cant. 4, 12.
6 Gen. 2, 8 and 10.
7 *Ibid.* 3, 23 and 24.
8 Prov. 8, 31.
9 Cant. 5, 1
10 *Ibid.*

this paradise given to me by my heavenly Father, that I seem to be constantly feasting therein on honey.

These inspired words certainly define for us the name of "paradise."

Do you wish to know the Creator of this earthly paradise? Listen to the Word of God; "The Lord God had planted a paradise of pleasure from the beginning."[11] It was His infinite goodness towards the first Adam, that impelled God to plant this first paradise for men and posterity. If men had been obedient to God, they would have passed from an earthly, temporal paradise to an eternal and celestial Heaven.

The unfathomable love of the eternal Father for the second Adam, namely His divine Son, Jesus Christ, led Him also to create a second paradise for Christ and all His true children, who will abide therein forever with their all-good Father. He causes them to participate even now as well as for all eternity in the holy and divine delights He there enjoys. For this reason, having told His most worthy Mother that He has come into her garden to eat His honey and to drink His wine and milk, He turns to His children and says to them, "Eat, O friends, and drink, and be inebriated, my dearly beloved."[12]

I see three principal objects in the garden of the first Adam. I see the tree of life and the tree of knowledge of good and evil, planted in the center of paradise. I see also many other trees bearing all kinds of fruit, agreeable to look upon and delightful to taste.

In the second Garden, I behold incomparably better trees, of which the first are but shadows. I see the real *Tree of Life*, Jesus Christ, the only Son of God, Whom the Father planted in the midst of this divine paradise of the virginal heart of His most Holy Mother, when the Angel said to her, "The Lord is with thee." Saint Augustine thus explains this passage, "The Lord is with thee, to abide first in thy heart and then in thy virginal womb, to fill thy soul before descending into thy chaste bosom."[13]

Was it not the fruit of this Tree of Life that restored to us the eternal life which we had lost by eating another fruit given to us by a woman whose name was Eve? Was not the fruit of everlasting life given to us by the hands of a celestial woman whose name was Mary? "What didst thou say, O Adam?" exclaims Saint Bernard. "'The woman whom Thou didst give to me gave me of the fruit, and I did eat.' These words tend to increase thy guilt, rather than diminish it. Change this unjust excuse into words of gratitude, and say: 'Lord, the woman thou gavest me, gave me of the fruit of the Tree of Life, and I did eat, and my mouth found it sweeter

11 Gen. 2, 8.
12 Cant. 5, 1.
13 *De sanctis*, serm. 18.

than honey, because by this precious fruit Thou hast restored me to life.'"
Then the Saint adds, "O marvelous Virgin, worthy of every honor! O
woman to whom the highest veneration is due, who are admirable above
all others, who hast repaired thy parents' fault and hast imparted life to
those who will come after thee!"[14]

Such is the first tree I behold in the second paradise, the virginal
heart of Mary, which is more of Heaven than of earth. But I also see
there the Tree of Knowledge of Good and Evil, because the luminous
and most enlightened heart of the Mother of God has been filled with
the science of the saints, with the wisdom and science of Jesus Christ,
the Saint of Saints. Her heart is the dwelling place of the sun, ever
united to Him in Whom all the treasures of God's wisdom and knowledge are hidden. Mary's heart has therefore perfectly known the sovereign good, which is God, and the supreme evil, which is sin. She did
not know sin, however, as Adam and Eve knew it, by transgressing the
commands of God; she knows sin in the light of God and as God
knows it, hating it as God hates it. The fruit of this tree did not harm
her as the fruit of the Tree of Knowledge in the first paradise harmed
the first man and woman. Adam and Eve lost themselves and their
posterity by eating of its fruit, because they ate of it against God's will.
But our true Eve, the real Mother of the Living, sanctified herself and
contributed to the sanctification of her children by eating of the fruit
of the Tree of Knowledge which God had planted in her heart. She ate
of it as God does, and as God wished that she should eat, that is, in
using her knowledge as God employs His divine omniscience, availing
herself of knowledge only to love God as God loves Himself, and to
hate sin as God hates it.

God said of Adam, after his sin, in a sense implying his confusion and condemnation, "Behold Adam is become as one of us,
knowing good and evil."[15] So also can He say of our incomparable
Virgin, but in a sense that contributes to her praise and glory,
"Behold Mary is become like one of us, knowing good and evil in the
same light as we know them, and thus becoming a clear image of our
holiness and perfection."

I see many other trees in our new Garden, that is, in the heart of
Mary, laden with excellent fruits most agreeable to the sight and delightful to the taste of Him who planted them. Does she not have these fruits
in mind when she says to her beloved, "Let my beloved come into his
garden, and eat the fruit of his apple trees?"[16] Her faith, her hope, her

14 *Homil.* 2 sup. Missus est.
15 Gen. 3, 22.
16 Cant. 5, 1.

charity, her submission to the divine will, are as many holy trees planted in her heart and bearing an infinite variety of fair fruits.

Her virginal purity is another heavenly tree which bore the fruit of
fruits, Christ, the King of Virgins, and later the thousands of virgins
who will ever be found in the Church of God. Mary's ardent zeal for the
glory of God and the salvation of souls is a divine tree upholding as
many fruits as there are souls in whose salvation she has cooperated.
Our Lady speaks of these fruits, which she also calls flowers, when, in
the excess of her love for souls, she exclaims, "Stay me up with flowers,
compass me about with apples: because I languish with love."[17] With
the flowers she indicates newly converted souls who have just begun to
serve God; with the fruits, those souls who have made progress and are
more steadfast in virtue.

Such then are the trees to be found in the first and the second gardens
of Eden. Are any flowers to be found there? Sacred Scripture does not mention the presence of any blossoms in the first garden; yet who can doubt
that a garden of delight must have contained flowers in great abundance?
It is certain, however, that the garden of Jesus is filled with heavenly flowers, the most beautiful and sweet scented imaginable. The heart of Christ's
Mother is a celestial flower bed dotted with the holy blossoms of all
Christian virtues, immortal flowers, which never fade, whose ravishing
beauty and delightful fragrance remain in every season. They fill the universe with their sweet perfume and give joy to the angels, yea, even, to God
Himself. They are at once flowers and fruits, for the Holy Ghost inspires
the words, "My flowers are the fruit of honour and riches."[18]

The eternal King adorns His garden with these flowers, and by
means of their divine fragrance attracts innumerable hearts to Himself.
He eats of these fruits, which are among the choicest viands of His heavenly table, and gives them as nourishment to His children. He assures
us, moreover, that He takes His rest and refreshment in the works of
mercy which are among the first flowers of His garden, "This is my rest,
refresh the weary, and this is my refreshing."[19] So also does He feast with
delight on the other acts of virtue which proceed from devoted hearts,
and especially from the perfect heart of His glorious Mother. With them
He nourishes and strengthens the souls of His children.

This is what God meant when He said that He came into His garden, ate His honey and drank His wine with milk, and then invited His
friends and children to eat, drink and be inebriated with Him.[20]

17 Cant. 2, 5.
18 Ecclus. 24, 23.
19 Isa. 28, 12.
20 Cant. 5, 1.

Among the flowers in Mary's garden for her divine spouse, Saint Bernard admires especially the perfume of violets, the whiteness of lilies and brilliant color of the roses. Here are his words, "Thou art an enclosed garden, O Mother of God, wherein we cull all kinds of flowers. Among them, we gaze with particular admiration on thy violets, thy lilies and thy roses, which fill the House of God with their sweet fragrance. Thou art, O Mary, a violet of humility, a lily of chastity, and a rose of charity."[21] We may add, Thou art, O Mary, a carnation of mercy, a double carnation, because thy wondrous heart is filled with mercy and compassion, not only for our corporal infirmities, but still more for our spiritual misery, which is infinitely more painful and complex than our bodily ills can ever be. O Mother of Mercy, have pity on all who are miserable, and especially on those who remain unaware of their own misery.

And now I go on to another object to be envisioned in the earthly paradise. In the second chapter of Genesis, we read that God brought to the first man the animals and the birds He had created that Adam might give them suitable names, as a sign of his dominion over them and of their dependence on him. Several learned Doctors are of the opinion that Adam offered some of the animals to God in sacrifice at that time.

We may now ask if any qualities of the heart of the Queen of Heaven can have been symbolized by such humble things as animals and birds? Yes, and this should not surprise you, since her son, Who is God Himself, willed to be represented by oxen, sheep, lambs, and several other beasts which, under the Old Law, were sacrificed to God.

What, then, is represented by the animals and birds subjected by God to the dominion of Adam in paradise? They represent the natural passions that have their seat in the corporeal and physical heart of man. These passions are of two kinds, that is, the more earthly and animal instincts, such as anger, hatred, fear, sadness, aversion, distrust, which are represented by the animals, and the more spiritual emotions, such as love, desire, hope, courage and joy typified by the birds.

All these passions existed as we have seen,[22] in the heart of the Blessed Virgin Mary, just as they are found in the hearts of all children of Adam, but she enjoyed the greatest privilege that in her heart they were completely subject to reason, just as the savage beasts were under the complete control of Adam in the earthly paradise. The spirit of Christ, the new man, reigned so perfectly in Mary's heart and so absolutely ruled her passions, that they never experienced any motivation contrary to the will of God. She never employed them except

21 *In deprecat. et laude ad B. Virg.*
22 See Part 1, Chapter 3.

63

under the guidance of God's Holy Spirit and for the glory of His divine majesty. She never loved anything besides God; she never desired anything except to please Him; she feared nothing save to displease Him. All the difficult tasks she undertook were accomplished in His service and for His glory, the sole cause of her joy, even as the offense and dishonor afforded Him by sin were the only motives of her hatred, her aversion, and her anger. So truly were her natural passions uplifted and almost annihilated towards the world and all worldly objects and concerns, even with regard to herself and her own interests, that her emotions existed and vibrated only for what was pleasing to Him who possessed, animated and directed them in all thoughts.

From this we learn that the heart of the Blessed Virgin Mary was truly the earthly paradise, in which there was no war, trouble or disorder of any kind, but peace, tranquility and marvelous order, combined with ceaseless praise and adoration of the God who had established His throne in this paradise. All her passions, being entirely subject to reason and the Spirit of God, and perfectly blended together, blessed and praised Him with admirable harmony in the variety of their distinct motions, uses and functions. They were all guided by the same Spirit and all directed towards the same end, to glorify the divine majesty.

Now let us study the gardeners. In the first terrestrial paradise, Adam was appointed "to dress it, and to keep it,"[23] but instead of cherishing his beautiful garden, he sold it to his arch-enemy the serpent, for a mere taste of the forbidden fruit. Instead of cultivating the Garden of Eden, Adam brought sin into it, filling it with thorns and thistles. What an unfaithful guardian! What a wicked gardener!

But in the second paradise, the enclosed garden of the heart of Mary, the gardener is wisdom, eternal, watchful and faithful, and the three assistant gardeners are love, which digs and prepares the soil to receive the seed of heavenly inspiration, grace which sows the seed, and patience, that cultivates it to fruition by perseverance. Thus the flowers of Mary's heart grow ever more beautiful, more admirable to us and more delightful to God, while the fruits of her garden multiply a hundred thousandfold.

As for the significance of the events that transpired, I consider that the marriage of our first parents in the Garden of Eden, a holy union designated directly by God, was symbolic of the hypostatic union between the divinity and humanity of the eternal Word, and the mystical alliance of Our Saviour and His Church. Yet where was the contract for these divine alliances drawn up, if not in the Garden of the heart of Mary, the handmaid of God Almighty and the beloved

23 Gen. 2, 15.

spouse of the Holy Spirit? There took place the secret and ineffable negotiations between the eternal Father and the Blessed Virgin concerning the mystery of the Incarnation. There she made the offering and surrender of herself to the divine will, and gave her consent to have a part in the divine Espousals, not only between the august Trinity and herself, but between divine and human nature, between the Son of God and Holy Church.

In the original garden of paradise, God sought for man, saying "Where art thou?"[24] because sin made Adam seek to hide and blot himself out in fear. In the second paradise, God sought to hide Himself and His great glory for love, concealing His royal splendour so that the three Kings, who came from afar to adore Him, had to ask. "Where is he?" It was sin that caused the annihilation of Adam, but love achieved the annihilation of the new Adam, the Son of God, who descended into the garden of Mary to draw us from the nothingness of sin.

In the first garden, God pronounced sentence upon the serpent, "The woman shall crush thy head and thou shalt lie in wait for her heel."[25] In the garden of Mary's heart, this pronouncement was fulfilled. Her Immaculate Conception crushed original sin, her sanctity routed the powers of evil, and her love obtained the commutation of our death sentence, bringing us the Saviour of the world.[26]

Man, having rebelled against God in the first paradise, was driven from that garden and banished forever with all his posterity, and at the gate was placed an angel with a flaming sword in his hand to prevent the children of Adam from reentering the Garden of Eden. From this we learn that to enter and share the second paradise, namely the pure heart of the Mother of the new Adam, we must cease to be sons of Adam and become children of Jesus Christ, that is, our old life must die.

This death seems fearful; the sword of the cherubim is terrifying; yet actually it is a sword of love, which wounds, or even slays the blessed, in order to heal their souls and make them live the life of God. "Precious in the sight of the Lord is the death of his saints"[27] says Sacred Scripture, meaning the death that is not death but the beginning of eternal life.

Now that I have shown you, dear reader, the Admirable Heart of Mary as the garden of delectation of the God-Man, I would warn you that your own heart must be one of two things, either a hell of torment for yourself, or a paradise of delights for you and for Jesus Christ. If you

---

24 Gen. 3, 9.
25 Gen. 3, 15.
26 Cf. Saint John Damascene: *Orat 2 de dormit. B. Mariae.*
27 Ps. 115, 15.

banish sin and self love from the garden of your heart, opening wide the door to grace and to the King of Virtue, He will enter in and find repose in that place.[28] If you drive away grace and mortification, letting sin grow in your garden, then the demons will enter and make it their abode, a veritable hell instead of paradise. But if you strive to imitate Mary, your Queen, tending your heart with wisdom, love, grace and patience, God will not refuse you the full measure of His gifts so that you may cultivate your garden fruitfully, and make it, like Mary's, a paradise of delight for your Lord and Saviour, as well as a place of refreshment, deep sweetness and peace for yourself.

28 Prov. 15, 15.

Part Three

SIX ADDITIONAL SYMBOLIC PICTURES

Chapter One

MARY'S HEART, THE BURNING BUSH OF MOSES

John Gerson, very learned and devout chancellor of the famous University of Paris, when commenting on the *Magnificat*, says that Mary's incomparable heart was prefigured by the burning bush seen by Moses on Mount Horeb.[1] Gerson does not speak thus without good reason. The extraordinary spectacle of a bush burning in the midst of a blazing fire without being consumed is a beautiful representation of the heart of Mary, which it excellently portrays in several ways.

First, we should consider that the mountain on whose slopes the bush grew is called in Sacred Scripture "the mountain of God," *mons Dei*.[2] It is also spoken of as "a holy mountain," for Moses heard a voice saying to him, "The place whereon thou standest is holy ground."[3] We shall easily be convinced, therefore, that it represents the most Blessed Virgin Mary, who is the true mountain of God, a mountain of holiness of whom we can well say with Saint Gregory the Great[4] that she is the mountain foretold by the prophet Isaias as the peak towering above all other heights, "A mountain . . . on the top of mountains,"[5] because God has raised her in dignity, in sanctity and power above the chief Seraphim and the greatest saints.

Secondly, we ought not to despise this insignificant bush, a lowly shrub, the least of all plants. On the contrary, we should regard it with respect, since God so honored this bush as to choose it in preference to the tallest cedars of Lebanon for this manifestation of His glory, amid the fire and flames of its miraculous blaze. Would you know the reason of this? Listen to the Holy Ghost, "The Lord is high and looketh on the low: and the high he knoweth afar off."[6] Though God is most high and

---

1 *Altare Cordis (Mariae) in quo semper ignis ardebat holocausti. Fuit enim rubus ardens incombustus.* Tract. 9 super *Magnificat*, part. 1.
2 Exod. 3, 1.
3 *Ibid.* 3, 5.
4 *In Reg.* 1.
5 Isa. 2, 2.
6 Ps. 137, 6.

infinitely above His creatures, nevertheless it delights His divine providence to look with a kind and loving eye at that which is small and lowly. While He draws near to the humble, He surveys the great and mighty from afar, as though He disregarded and despised them.

Thus was He attracted by the humility of Mary, His handmaid. *Respexit humilitatem ancillae suae.*[7] Saint Bernard speaks as follows of the profound humility of Mary's heart, "She who in her own mind and heart was the least of all creatures, has rightly been made the first, because, even though she was in fact the first, she considered herself as being the last."[8] This humility of the heart of Heaven's Queen is represented by the lowliness of the mysterious bush of Mount Horeb.

Thirdly, we must not be frightened or horrified by the sharp thorns which guard this bush on all sides, both outside and inside. This should, on the contrary, make us love it more, because God Himself loves it for this reason. It is obvious that God loves all His creatures and hates none of the works of His hands, for it is written, "Thou lovest all things that are, and hatest none of the things which thou hast made."[9] It is also obvious that God cherished a specially tender love for this little bush, that His heart was there and that He took pleasure in it. He chose it to be His throne, the place where He would manifest His glory to His servant Moses, where He would speak to His prophet, disclose divine secrets and reveal His providential designs to deliver the chosen people from Egyptian bondage.

God loved the burning bush because the fire that encompassed without consuming it represented the fire of divine love which filled the heart of Mary, a love far greater than that of all the hearts of men and angels. The thorns symbolized the bitter sorrow and unspeakable anguish which pierced the heart of the Mother of God, suffering that she accepted for the love of God and the salvation of mankind.

Moreover, God descended from Heaven into the bush on Mount Horeb and manifested Himself to Moses, "in the flame of fire," to show His love and charity towards his people, and spoke "from the midst of the bush," or according to another version "from the heart of the bush," to declare His intention of delivering the children of Israel from the captivity of Pharao through the instrumentality of Moses. In like manner the Son of God, in the excess of His love, descended from the bosom of the eternal Father into His Mother's heart, ablaze as it was with love for God and charity towards men, in order to bring about our redemption and to associate her with Himself as the instrument of this great work.

7 Luke 1, 48.
8 *In Assumpt.* Serm. 5, De Verbo Apoc. *Signum Magnum.*
9 Wisd. 11, 25.

God remained in the burning bush only a short time, but He has always been and will forever abide in the heart of our glorious Mother. *Deus in medio ejus, non commovebitur.*[10] "God is in the midst thereof, it shall not be moved." According to another rendering, *Deus in intimo ejus non amovebitur,* "God is in the inmost heart and shall never depart therefrom."

The principal characteristic we should consider about the burning bush, however, is marked by the words of Moses, "I will go and see this great sight, why the bush is not burnt."[11] The sacred text says that Moses saw the bush in the midst of a glowing fire, which nevertheless did not destroy it. "He saw that the bush was on fire and was not burnt."[12]

This is truly a great miracle. Yet it is only a figure of the much greater wonder that took place in the heart of our admirable Mother. Mary's heart was a galaxy of marvels, and one of the most stupendous was that, while the Mother of Fair Love remained in this world, her heart became inflamed with love for God to such intensity that this sacred flame would have consumed her corporeal life if she had not been miraculously preserved in the midst of such heavenly fervor. It was, therefore, a greater wonder to behold Our Lady living surrounded by heavenly fire, without being annihilated, than to watch the burning bush of Moses in the midst of fire without being consumed.

From the foregoing we may therefore conclude that the burning bush of Mount Horeb was indeed a significant representation of the most holy heart of the Mother of God.

Likewise, dear reader, do not forget that your heart must burn with the loving fire that enkindled the virginal heart of Mary, the fire that the Son of God came to spread upon earth, or else it must burn forever in the dreadful conflagration prepared for the devil and his cohorts. Oh, what a difference between these two kinds of fire! The devouring flames that torment eternally without consuming, and the delightful, joyous flames that constantly ravish the hearts of the ardent seraphim!

Rejoice, each one of you who reads or listens to these words! Give thanks to God that you are still alive, that yours is still the power to choose which of these fires shall enkindle your heart. Strive earnestly to extinguish the flame of self love, of worldliness, the burning of anger, lust, envy and ambition. Give your heart entirely to Jesus Christ, asking Him to set it on fire with His love. For this purpose there is no better prayer than the words of Saint Augustine:

10 Ps. 45, 6.
11 Exod. 3, 3.
12 *Ibid.* 3, 2.

"O divine fire that burneth always and is never extinguished; O love always ardent and never growing cold, enkindle my being! Set me on fire completely, so that I may become nothing but a glowing flame of love for Thee."

Chapter Two

MARY'S HEART, THE HARP OF KING DAVID

The mysterious harp of King David, mentioned in several passages of Sacred Scripture, is another symbolic picture of the holy heart of Mary. It is an excellent representation because her pure heart was indeed the harp of the true David, namely Our Lord Jesus Christ. He fashioned it with His own hands; He alone always possessed it. No other fingers but His ever evoked its melodies, because her virginal heart never vibrated with sentiments, affections or impulses other than those inspired by the Holy Ghost.

The strings of this royal harp are the virtues of Mary's heart, especially her faith, hope, love of God, charity towards her neighbor, religion, humility, purity, obedience, patience, mercy, hatred of sin, love of the cross. On these twelve strings the divine Spirit played with wondrous harmony melodious canticles of love which so greatly charmed the ears of the eternal Father that He forgot His anger against sinners, He laid aside the thunderbolts wherewith He vowed to destroy mankind and gave His own Son to be the Saviour of humanity.

Sacred Scripture tells us that King David employed his harp specially on four great occasions and we see Jesus, the son of David, using His mystical harp to accomplish four infinitely greater achievements.

In the first instance, David, the man of God, by the mere sound of his harp, put to flight the evil spirit which possessed Saul. Similarly, the new David used the heart of His loving Mother as a sublime harp and consequently freed by its divine music the human race that grovelled under the evil dominion of Satan.

The prophet David also employed His harp to sing many psalms and canticles to the honor and glory of God. Our true David, likewise, sang with His instrument five types of canticles in praise of the most Blessed Trinity. The *first* were *canticles of love*, the strongest, purest, most perfect love that ever was or shall be. The *second* were *canticles of praise and thanksgiving* for the benefits of divine goodness on behalf of all creatures, for the Blessed Virgin Mary did not limit herself to thanking God for the infinite favors she received from His hand, but she praised Him unceasingly for the graces He pours on all created beings. The *third* were *canticles of sorrow, of anguish and bereavement* at the time of the sufferings and death of her beloved son. The *fourth* were *canticles of triumph* for all the victories won by herself as general of the great King's armies over His enemies and, we may truly say, over Himself, having so often disarmed divine vengeance when it stood ready to destroy the world and punish its innumerable crimes. The *fifth* were *canticles of prophecy* to announce the great designs of God for the future, many of which were foretold by the Queen of Prophets in the wonderful canticle she composed when greeting her cousin Saint Elizabeth.

The third purpose for which King David used his harp was to praise God and especially to praise Him *with joy*. In like manner, Christ the second David, not only attuned His holy Mother's heart to praise and bless His divine majesty in every way, but He also induced Mary to seek her joy and bliss exclusively in His praises, and in all the acts she performed for His glory and in His service.

King David chose as the fourth function of his harp to excite and attract other men to the praise of God, with hearts full of joy and gladness like his own. So too Christ the King attracts innumerable souls to the love and praise of His heavenly Father by the sweet sound of His precious harp, that is, by means of the blessed heart of His glorious Mother. The extraordinary virtues of her vibrant heart resound so loudly and harmoniously throughout the entire Christian Church that numberless persons of all ranks and conditions find themselves urged to imitate the perfections which adorn it, thus beginning to carry out on earth what the angels and saints achieve in Heaven. In other words, they place their entire contentment and felicity in all that concerns the sovereign Monarch in Heaven and earth.

Another point worthy of special mention is that Christ, our adorable David, possesses many other harps given to Him by the eternal Father to satisfy His boundless desire to hear the praise of God unceasingly in every place, at every time, in all things and in every way.

His first and sovereign harp is His own Sacred Heart. It is this harp that He speaks of when He says, "I will sing to thee with the harp, thou holy one of Israel."[1] On this harp, in fact, He sang continually during His mortal life on earth, and will forever sing in the glory of Heaven a thousand canticles of love, praise and thanksgiving to His heavenly Father, in His own home as well as in the name of all His members and of all creatures God has made. But the love that inspires these canticles

1 Ps. 70, 22.

is infinitely higher, their song is immeasurably holier than those of the canticles He sings on His second harp, which we have just described, namely the heart of His peerless Mother.

These two hearts and these two harps are nevertheless so closely attuned that in a certain sense they constitute one single harp, vibrating in unison, giving forth but one sound and one song, singing the same canticle of love. If the first sounds a canticle of praise, the second echoes it with its own chords. If the heart of Jesus loves God the Father, Mary's heart unites in that love; if the heart of Jesus pours itself out in thanksgiving before the most Holy Trinity, Mary's heart sings an identical hymn of gratitude. The heart of Mary loves and hates all that the heart of Jesus loves and hates. What rejoices the son's heart rejoices the heart of the Mother as well; what crucifies the heart of the son likewise nails the Mother's heart to the Cross. "Jesus and Mary," says Saint Augustine, "were two mystical harps. What sounded on the one, also sounded on the other, even though no one touched it. When Jesus was in sorrow, Mary was in sorrow; when Jesus was crucified, Mary was crucified."[2]

The eternal Father gave His divine Son innumerable other harps, namely, the hearts of all the angels and saints, on which to praise and glorify His almighty Father while they were pilgrims on earth, and forever to praise and glorify Him in blissful eternity. All the glory, honor and praise that ever was or will be rendered to God the Father by the angels and saints was and will be rendered through His divine Son, Jesus Christ. "By Him, and with Him, and in Him, is to thee, God the Father almighty, all honor and glory."

These are the harps mentioned in several passages of the Apocalypse,[3] where Saint John tells us that God permitted him to behold the saints all holding harps on which they sang many canticles in honor of the Lamb of God. But a learned author,[4] in his commentaries on the Apocalypse, notices a striking difference between these harps and the harp of the Mother of God. The former, while on earth, were often discordant, and because of human weakness and frailty, they sometimes wearied of praising God; hence it was necessary to tune them from time to time and urge them to do their duty. The harp of the Queen of all Saints, on the other hand, never suffered any weakening or interruption in its song, having praised and glorified the most Blessed Trinity with a changeless love and the most perfect harmony. Hence Viegas says that Our Lady did not exclaim, as

2 *Serm. de Pass. Dom.*
3 Apoc. 5, 8; 14, 2; 15, 2.
4 Viegas, *in Apoc.*

though exhorting herself: *Magnifica, anima mea, Dominum, but Magnificat anima mea Dominum;*[5] not "O my soul, magnify the Lord," but "My soul doth magnify the Lord."

The eternal Father has given His beloved Son yet another harp, which like the hearts of all Christians is meant to chant the praises of His Holy Name, and this harp is your own heart. Beware lest you follow the miserable example of those who take away from Christ the hearts given to Him by the heavenly Father and purchased by His Precious Blood. Unlike an ordinary instrument, the harp of your heart cannot remain silent. It must be played either by the hand of God or by the hand of the devil. Either it will sing the divine canticles of Our Lady and of the saints, or it will echo the cursed and unhappy songs of the worldlings here below in dishonour to God its Maker, and vibrate eternally with the blasphemies and horrid dirges of the damned in Hell.

To make your heart a harp of Our Saviour, the true David, you must pluck out the strings of vice and replace them with the strings of virtue, which must be set in tune with the peace and charity of the hearts of your fellow men. Sound your harp in unison with the inspired paeans of true Christians, of the angelic host and of the saints, above all with the sublime harp of the heart of Mary, Queen of all saints, joining in the chorus of praise and love of Almighty God, led by the royal harpist, Our Lord, "singing with one voice: Holy, Holy, Holy, Lord God of Hosts."

5 Luke 1, 46.

Chapter Three

MARY'S HEART, THE THRONE OF KING SOLOMON

Among the many beautiful qualities attributed by the Holy Ghost to the Blessed Virgin Mary, one stands out preeminently. It is contained in these words of the eighty-sixth psalm, which Holy Church and her Doctors apply to the Mother of God, "Glorious things are said of thee, O city of God."[1]

Mary is indeed the great and glorious city of God, the holy city, the city of Jerusalem, the city of peace, the royal city, "the city of the great King."[2] The King of Kings built this city with His own hands; He exempted her entirely from the infamous tribute of sin; He honored her with countless great and extraordinary privileges; He enriched her with inestimable gifts and treasures and He established His first and most glorious abode within her heart. In her He chose to reveal the rarest marvels of His power and royal magnificence.

O Holy City of God, what high and admirable things must be said and thought of thee! Thou are not only the city of the great King, O incomparable Virgin, thou art also His royal and eternal palace. "Yes," says Saint Bonaventure, "this heavenly maiden is the sacred palace of the great God: *Sacratum Dei palatium*.[3] Now, if Mary is the palace of the King of Kings, her heart must be the King's imperial throne.

This magnificent throne is perfectly represented by the throne of King Solomon, as described in the Book of Kings.[4] We read there that this great king erected a throne of ivory in his house on Libanus and covered it with brilliant gold. Six steps led up to this throne; the top of it was rounded at the back, and there were two hands on either side to hold the seat, with two large lions standing near, while small lions stood upon either side of the six steps. Never was any similar throne made in any kingdom of the world.

1 Ps. 86, 3.
2 Ps. 47, 3.
3 *In Carminibus* super Salve Regina.
4 3 Kings 10, 18–20.

There is another throne of King Solomon which also represents Our Lady's heart most perfectly. The third chapter of the Canticle of Canticles describes it as follows, "King Solomon hath made him a litter of the wood of Libanus. The pillars thereof he made of silver, the seat of gold, the going up of purple: the midst he covered with charity for the daughters of Jerusalem."[5]

In the same chapter, immediately before the description of this throne, mention is made of Solomon's bed with the following words, "Behold threescore valiant ones of the most valiant of Israel surrounded the bed of Solomon. All holding swords, and most expert in war; every man's sword upon his thigh, because of fears in the night."[6]

What does all this mean? Here is the answer.

The throne and the couch of Solomon symbolize the same representation, namely the holy heart of the Queen of the world, the couch representing the heart in contemplation, the litter describing in it action. Mary's heart is at once the throne and the bed of the true Solomon, Jesus Christ, Our Lord. It is the bed on which He rests in the sweetness and calm of contemplation. It is the litter in which love and charity that set Him on this throne, carry Him from place to place, that He may reign everywhere for the glory of God and the salvation of souls. An illustrious commentator expresses a similar thought when he says, "The bed of Solomon represents the heart resting in the sweetness of contemplation. His litter is the heart going about in the exercise of good works."[7]

Who are the valiant ones surrounding Solomon's bed well armed and expert in war? According to Saint Bernard and several other learned Doctors, they are the angels and the mightiest among the angels, namely the Seraphim, who armed with God's strength and expert in combat against His enemies, always kept watch around the seraphic heart of their Empress, in the world's dark night. They kept guard against the fears in the night, that is, they prevented the powers of darkness to approach and in any way trouble the divine Solomon as He rested on this holy couch.[8]

But let us return to Solomon's litter. He designed it with his own hands like the throne of the palace on Libanus: *Fecit sibi*.[9] In like manner, our adorable Solomon is himself the author of the incomparable masterpiece of Mary's heart. He prepared for Himself a throne worthy of His infinite grandeur and eternal majesty in the august heart of His glorious Mother.

---

5 Cant. 3, 9–10.
6 Cant. 3, 7–8.
7 Hugh of Saint Victor, *Erudit, Theolog.*, lib. 1, tit. 61.
8 S. Bern. *in Deprecat. ad Virgin*; Honorius Augustodum. Presbyter.
9 Cant. 3, 9.

We have good reason to call Solomon's litter a figure of the throne of the King of Kings, namely of the heart of the most holy Mother of this great King. Saint Gregory of Nyssa tells us that this throne of Solomon is "a figure of the heart of every faithful Christian,"[10] and a famous Doctor says that "the heart of the true Christian is the litter of the Son of God, because it goes where the one it bears wills that it should go, and never elsewhere."[11] This was fulfilled more perfectly in the heart of the holy Virgin than in the hearts of even the holiest of creatures. Her virginal heart never experienced inclinations or affections other than those it derived from the Master who held absolute sway over it.

Solomon's throne was made of incorruptible wood of the cedar of Libanus, to show that the Immaculate Heart of the Mother of God was not only preserved from the corruption of sin, but also that its superabundance of heavenly graces rendered it incapable of sin by grace, as God is incapable of sin by nature.

The four columns of Solomon's throne are the four cardinal virtues, which sustain the throne of the true Solomon, namely justice, prudence, fortitude and temperance. The pillars made of silver denote the candor of innocence preserved in the heart that possesses them. This symbol was eminently verified in the most pure and innocent heart of the Queen of all virtues.

The gold seat represents free will transformed by love into the adorable love of God. It can be truly said with David, the royal prophet, "Whatever befall me, my soul shall trust the Lord in all things, with humility and submission to His will. From Him is my salvation. He is my God, my stronghold, my living rock, nothing can shake me."[12] Every human will attaining this state of submission becomes the seat of the throne of Jesus, and in the will of His Blessed Mother this was accomplished in a most perfect manner. Therefore Saint Peter Damian calls her "the golden seat on which, after the tumult and disorder occasioned by the sins of angels and men, He sought and found His rest."[13]

The "going up" or back of purple represents ardent desire for the glory of God, for the sanctification of His name and the accomplishment of His will on earth as it is accomplished in Heaven. It symbolizes the divine love that constantly urged the zealous heart of the Mother of Love upward and onward to do and suffer great things towards the fulfillment of the designs of the Creator.

Finally, our beloved Christ prefigured by Solomon, filled His throne with charity for the daughters of Jerusalem, that is, for all souls, especially

10 Homil. 7.
11 Richard of Saint Victor.
12 Ps. 61, Philip des Portes' version.
13 *Serm. de Annunt.*

for each Christian soul, and more particularly still for the beloved children of His Blessed Mother's heart. These are the humble, pure and charitable souls who entertain a singular devotion towards her maternal heart. Yes, our lovable Solomon filled the virginal heart with charity towards us, for He did everything for us, as the Apostle Saint Paul says, "All things are for your sakes."[14] If He created the world, it was for us; if He became Man, it was for us; if He was born in a stable, it was for our sake. For us He remained thirty-four years in this world, accomplished and suffered so many great and extraordinary things and shed the last drop of His Precious Blood. For our sake, He died on the Cross, ascended into Heaven, established Holy Church, confided the sacraments to her care, and especially the most Holy Sacrament of the Altar where He resides in person. All this was for us: *Omnia propter vos.* In like manner, if He willed to have a true Mother on earth, it was for our sake. If He made her so good, so wise, so powerful, so full of incomparable privileges and extraordinary powers, it was that she might possess the knowledge, power and desire to protect and assist us in all our necessities. He gave her a heart filled with charity, benignity, zeal, care and vigilance towards us, that we might profit thereby, if we but invoke it in our needs with utmost confidence. He set His throne in her heart for two purposes, both equally useful and profitable to us: Our Saviour made Mary's heart a throne of honor and glory and established it as a throne of grace and mercy.

Her heart is a *throne of honor and glory*, where Our Lord wills to be honored and glorified more than in the hearts of all angels and saints, even though they also are thrones of glory given to Him by His omnipotent Father. "The soul of the just is the seat of wisdom." It is a throne on which all the citizens of Heaven adore and glorify Him without end. It is the throne of which Holy Church speaks when she says, "Upon a high throne I saw a man sitting, whom a multitude of angels adore singing together: Behold Him the name of whose empire is to eternity."[15] Notice that it is during the Octave of the Epiphany that Holy Church, guided by the divine Spirit, utters and sings these heavenly words, for the three Kings found and adored the Messias in the arms close to the heart of His most worthy Mother as up on His royal throne. "They found the child with Mary his mother."[16] If they had had the eyes of angels, they would have beheld and adored Him enthroned within her heart, as well as reposing against it. On this throne, Christ wills to receive our homage and humble respects, and the children of the Church Militant must join those of the Church Triumphant in adoring and glorifying Him.

14 2 Cor. 4, 15.
15 Introit for First Sunday after Epiphany.
16 Matt. 2, 11.

Our Lady's heart is also a *throne of grace and mercy*, where Christ absolves all sinners who approach Him in a spirit of humility and penance, where He abundantly dispenses His gifts and graces to those who ask Him. Our Lord grants with extraordinary goodness the requests presented by those who render to Him, in the heart of His most honored Mother, the homage He desires to receive there. He wishes to be praised and glorified in the hearts and even in the bodies of His saints and "Glorify and bear God in your body."[17] How much more, then, should we not honor and magnify Our Saviour in the heart of His Blessed Mother?

Let us approach with humility, respect and confidence this throne of grace and mercy, and the Son of God will grant us every blessing we ask through the heart of His glorious Mother. "Let us go therefore with confidence to the throne of grace: that we may obtain mercy, and find grace."[18]

17 1 Cor. 6, 20.
18 Heb. 4, 16.

Chapter Four

MARY'S HEART, THE TEMPLE OF JERUSALEM

In the time of the Mosaic Law one of the greatest wonders of the world was the temple of Jerusalem. Yet this stupendous temple was merely a figure and an image of the multitude of temples to be found in the Christian world. It prefigured particularly the sacred humanity of the Son of God, for Christ referring to His own body said to the Jews, "Destroy this temple, and in three days I will raise it up."[1]

The temple of Jerusalem was a figure of Holy Church and a figure of each Christian. It prefigured our churches and cathedrals, but was also a representation of a temple far more holy and august than any material structure. What then is the true temple? It is the holy heart of the most Blessed Virgin Mary. The Church says of her person that Mary is "the temple of the Lord, the sanctuary of the Holy Ghost," and we can apply these words with still better reason to her Admirable Heart, having seen that it is the source of all the qualities and excellences with which she is adorned. If, according to the divine Word, the body of each Christian is the temple of God,[2] who will dare to deny this characterization to the most worthy heart of the Mother of all Christians? I affirm, therefore, that the holy heart of Mary is the true temple of the Divinity, the sanctuary of the Holy Ghost, the Holy of Holies of the Blessed Trinity.

This temple was not like Solomon's built by a host of workmen, but by the almighty Hand of God, Who can achieve greater wonders in a single instant than all the powers of Heaven and earth can accomplish during the whole of eternity.

The temple of Mary's heart was consecrated by the Sovereign Pontiff, Our Lord Jesus Christ Himself. It was never profaned by the slightest sin and stood adorned with a tremendous wealth of ordinary and extraordinary graces, and by all Christian virtues practiced in the highest degree.

1 John 2, 19.
2 1 Cor. 6, 19.

Not only is her heart entirely covered with King Solomon's gold, but it is itself wrought of the finest and purest gold, of a metal infinitely more precious than all the material gold to be found in the universe. The heart of our amiable Mother is filled with love of God and charity towards us. It is entirely transformed into love and charity, and completely identified with the purest love and the most perfect charity. Its love is more ardent, more pure and divine, its charity more fervent, holier and more excellent than the love and charity of all the Seraphim. The temple of Mary contains all the riches of God together with all the treasures of Heaven and earth because it keeps within its cloister all the mysteries of the life of the Son of God. "His Mother kept all these words in her heart." [3] Her heart possesses the very Son of God Himself, the treasure of the eternal Father, Who encompasses all the wealth and beauty of the most Holy Trinity.

In this temple Christ, the Sovereign Priest, offered His first sacrifice at the time of the Incarnation. Christ, the Doctor of doctors and the Preacher of preachers, Who taught and preached so often in the temple of Jerusalem, imparts to us from the temple of His Mother's heart as many instructions and lessons as there are virtues exemplified in this virginal heart.

In this temple God is adored more profoundly and worthily, praised and glorified more perfectly than in all other material or spiritual temples that ever were and shall be in Heaven and on earth, the sacred humanity of Jesus alone excepted. The smallest acts of virtue and even the prayerful thoughts of Mary's holy heart are more agreeable to the divine majesty and render God greater honor and glory than the greatest actions of the foremost among the saints.

The heart of the heavenly Mary is indeed a temple; and a temple filled with rarest marvels. God entrusted to King David a description of the temple of Jerusalem written by His own hand, as recorded in the words, "All these things came to me written by the hand of the Lord."[4] The eternal Father willed to place several remarkable objects in this temple to foreshadow and represent many great and wondrous mysteries that were to be found in the Admirable Heart of His holy Mother. Among them I notice seven principal objects that add significance to this symbolic picture, namely: the golden candlestick, the table with the loaves of proposition, the altar of perfumes, the Ark of the Covenant, the tables of the law, the propitiatory and oracle which reposed on the Ark, and the altar of holocausts.

3 Luke 2, 51.
4 1 Par. 28, 19.

Saint Epiphanius[5] and Saint John Damascene,[6] together with several other Doctors, tell us that the golden candlestick is a figure of the Holy Mother of God. Next to Jesus, her beloved son, Mary is the most luminous torch and the brightest light of the House of God. "O virginal candlestick," says Saint Epiphanius, "which enlightened those who sat in the shadow of death! O virginal torch, which dissipated the gloom of hell, and caused the brilliance of Heaven to shine in our souls! O radiant lamp, ever filled with the oil of grace and light, with the fire of divine love, lighting our minds and inflaming our hearts! This virginal light has spread its splendour throughout the world!"[7]

O admirable Virgin, thou art truly the golden candlestick of the chosen temple of God, which is His Church! With excellent reason does holy Church salute thee and recognize thee as the portal through which the light came into the world, "Hail, gate of morn, whence the world's true light was born."[8] But this parallel can best be applied to thy most holy heart, and especially to thy spiritual heart, which comprises the three faculties of the superior part of thy soul. Thy shining heart is the seat of light, of the light of reason, of the light of faith, and of the light of grace. It is the throne of the eternal sun and is itself a sun filling Heaven and earth with its radiance.

The remarkable table in Solomon's temple, described in the twenty-fifth chapter of Exodus, was made by divine command from the wood of Setim, not common variety of cedar, but according to the Septuagint, a most rare and altogether incorruptible wood. The table was completely covered with gold plate and edged with a gold plated cornice or border surrounding it like a crown while two additional golden crowns embellished it. It was designed to hold the loaves of proposition that were offered to God daily by the priests, and were thus named because they lay in the temple as a perpetual sacrifice proposed or exposed to the divine majesty. Afterwards they were consumed by the priests.

The Fathers of the Church all agree that the loaves of proposition were a figure of Our Lord Jesus Christ, the royal bread that came down from Heaven. Christ is the bread of the Angels, the bread of God, the bread of the children of God, a bread which is the nourishment and life of the Christian soul, and all Christians are called priests in Sacred Scripture: *Fecisti nos Deo nostro sacerdotes*.[9] Some are priests by office and bear the special character of consecrated priesthood; others share it by participation.

5 *De laudib. B.M.V.*
6 *Orat. 1 de Dorm. Deiparae.*
7   Saint John Eudes does not give the reference for this quotation.
8 Words taken from the hymn *Ave Regina caelorum*.
9 Apoc. 5, 10.

What is the table bearing this divine bread, prefigured by the table carrying the loaves of proposition? Saint Germanus, Patriarch of Constantinople, answers that it was the Blessed Virgin Mary[10] and Saint Epiphanius confirms his words.[11]

Is not the table designed to receive the bread and food laid on it? Is it not true that the heart of the Mother of God was the first to receive Our Lord as He came forth from the bosom of the eternal Father? Did she not receive Him in order to give Him to us? Is it not true that the eternal Father carries His beloved Son in His all-glorious heart from all eternity and that the Blessed Virgin will carry her son in her heart for all eternity? God the Father has revealed that His paternal heart gave us His well-beloved Son, the divine Word, in the Incarnation, and still gives Him to us daily in the Eucharist: Eructavit or according to another version, *Effudit Cor meum Verbum bonum*. "My heart hath uttered a good word."[12] In like manner, the Blessed Virgin refers to her maternal heart, and Holy Church often represents her as speaking in unison with the eternal Father: *Eructavit Cor meum Verbum bonum*. Hence we hear the words which the Holy Ghost puts on Mary's lips, "I was with him," that is, with the eternal Father, "forming all things."[13] In the Hebrew version this passage reads, "I was with Him and near Him as a nurse," which reveals Mary's role as the Mother who gives nourishment to mankind.

Our Lady says, "I was intimately united to almighty God in will, mind and heart, possessing only, as it were, one will, mind and heart in common with Him, and a heart ablaze with love for men. This love induced God to give mankind His well-beloved Son; a similar love urged me to give this same son, who is my own as truly and really as He is the Son of God, so I gave our divine son, the fruit of His Father's heart and of my own, to be the bread of men's souls and the life of their hearts."

Several learned interpreters of Sacred Scripture teach us that the altar of perfumes of the Mosaic temple represents the hearts of the faithful, which are symbolized as altars on which each one should offer a perpetual sacrifice of prayer and praise to God. Now if the hearts of the children of God were figured by this altar, how much more truly does it symbolize the heart of the Mother of God, which is after the heart of Jesus, the first and holiest of all altars? It is "the golden altar, which is before the throne of God," mentioned in the eighth chapter of the Apocalypse.[14] On this altar the Mother of the Saviour offered to God a sacrifice of love, adora-

10 *Orat. in Nativit. B. Virg.*
11 *Maria est fidei mensa intellectualis, quae vitae panem mundi suppeditavit. In serm. de laud. Virg.*
12 Ps. 44, 2.
13 Prov. 8, 30.

tion, praise, thanksgiving and prayer far more to His divine majesty than all the sacrifices that ever were or ever shall be offered on all other altars.

If we consult the Fathers of the Church we learn particularly from Saint Ambrose that the Ark of the Covenant was a figure of the Blessed Virgin Mary, and therefore of her most holy heart, the holy heart, the first and noblest part of her person. "Yes," exclaims the seraphic Saint Bonaventure, "the Ark of Moses was merely a reflection of the Virgin's heart. Her heart is the true ark containing within itself the secrets of the divine Word and the treasure of the law of God."[15] A holy Abbot[16] of the Cistercian Order calls Mary the Ark of Sanctification, containing revelations written by the hand of God. She is the holy Ark of the Covenant, the Covenant by which God reconciled us with Himself and pledged His alliance with us forever.

What more shall we say of the Ark of Moses? We may regard it as an image of the Blessed Virgin's most holy heart inasmuch as it contained the essential treasure, the chief glory and the holy joy of the Jewish people, the principal mystery of their religion, the bulwark of their defence and the terror of their enemies, even as the Admirable Heart of our Queen is the glory, treasure and joy of Christendom. Next to God, Mary's heart should be the first object to which we look when we pray. Her heart is an impregnable stronghold, *turris fortissima Cor Mariae*, for the true children of this heavenly Mother. This tower is strong, so well fortified with defensive and offensive weapons that the soldiers fighting under the banner of Mary, leader of the armies of the Most High, find there a mighty defence against the heaviest assaults of hell. Yes, her mighty heart is more formidable to the enemies of her children than any army terrible in battle. *Terribilis ut castrorum acies ordinata.*[17]

Let us, then, withdraw into this invincible fortress; let us entrench ourselves in the impregnable tower of Mary. May we ever dwell there, and never depart from its walls.

But let us remember that the heart of Mary is a tower of ivory, *turris eburnea*, which does not suffer within its precincts anything defiled and unclean. It is the tower of David, open only to those who follow the meekness of Jesus Christ, the true David. It is a tower built and adorned with all kinds of precious stones: *Turris Jerusalem gemmis aedificabuntur,*[18] that is, with perfections of every kind. He who seeks to dwell therein must renounce sin and imperfection; he must undertake wholeheartedly the practice of every Christian virtue.

14 Apoc. 8, 3.
15 *In Exposit.* cap. 2 Lucae.
16 Nicolaus Salicetus in *Antidotario animae*.
17 Cant. 6, 3.
18 Fifth antiphon of Vespers and Lauds for the Office of the Dedication of a Church.

Saint Gregory of Nyssa states that the *Tables of the Mosaic Law* kept in the temple of Solomon were a figure symbolic of the hearts of the saints.[19] Hence, Saint John Chrysostom affirms that the heart of Saint Paul was the table of the Holy Spirit and the book of charity, a living book in which divine charity inscribed with letters of gold the evangelical law of love and charity.[20]

Now, if the hearts of the saints are real tables of the evangelical law, what shall we say of the holy heart of the Queen of Saints, who is the Mother of the Saint of Saints? Her glorious heart is the first and holiest table of the Christian law. It is not made of stone, but of gold, or better still, of diamond; it is not dead but living; not breakable like the tables of Moses but indestructible. On it the Holy Ghost, the finger of God, has written and engraved in golden letters, not merely the will of God and His laws, but all the counsels, maxims and truths of the gospel as well. They are so deeply engraved that the united forces of hell and of earth could more easily snatch the sun from the sky and destroy the world than remove a single iota or tarnish a single letter of this sacred writing.

Mary's incomparable heart is not only the true table of God's law, but also a living and admirable book in which the Holy Ghost has stamped all the mysteries of the Deity, all the secrets of eternity, every Christian law, each maxim of the gospel and all the truths drawn by the Son of God from the heart of the almighty Father and poured forth abundantly in the heart of His Immaculate Mother. Saint Augustine[21] assures us that the books mentioned in the twentieth chapter of the Apocalypse represent the hearts of the saints, in which are engraved God's will and His laws; how much more truly must this be said of the most holy heart of the Mother of Him who is holiness personified?

The *Propitiatory*[22] is regarded as another figure symbolic of the glorious Virgin because by her intercession the flame of God's wrath was extinguished, His divine majesty was turned to look upon mankind with favor and His infinite mercy moved Him to compassion for our infirmities. For this reason Saint Ildephonsus calls the Mother of Grace: *Propitiatio humanae salutis*, "The propitiation of man's salvation."[23] Saint Andrew of Crete styles Mary: *Universi mundi commune propitiatorium*, "The universal propitiatory of the entire world."[24] Lastly, Saint Epiphanius proclaims her: *Admirandum propitiatorium*, "Admirable propitiatory."[25]

19 Homil. 14.

20 In cap. 16 *Epist. ad Rom.* Homil. 23.

21 Lib. 10 *de Civit.* Dei, cap. 14.

22 Cf. Saint Germanus of Constantinople, *Orat. in Nativ. Virg.*; Saint Ildephonsus, *Serm. I de Ass.*; Saint Andrew of Crete, *De dormit. Virg.*; Saint Antoninus, Part. 4, tit. 15, Cap. 14, 4; Richard of Saint Lawrence, Lib. 12 *de laud. B. Virg.*

23 *Serm. 1 de Ass.*

Now this qualification applies most properly and principally to her merciful heart. It is this gentle heart which is the admirable propitiatory. Whence does her compassion for sinners spring, if not from her heart full of mercy? What urged Mary to become our advocate before the throne of divine justice, if not the loving kindness of her heart? What could be more symbolic of Our Lady's holy companionship with the angels than the golden cherubim designed to guard the propitiatory?

Saint Augustine,[26] Saint Gregory the Great,[27] and several other Fathers say that the Altar of Holocausts also symbolized the hearts of all the saints, who are the real altars on which God is honored by the spiritual sacrifices offered day and night to His divine majesty. Yet much more truly can this be said of the holy heart of Mary. "Her heart is the true altar of holocaust," says the illustrious John Gerson, "and on it the sacred fire of divine love blazed day and night."[28]

The Mother of the Sovereign Priest constantly offered to God sacrifices of love, praise, thanksgiving, expiation for the sins of the world and every possible sacrifice. On the altar of her heart Mary sacrificed to God all the things of the world and every creature of the universe as so many different victims. She sacrificed her being, life, body, soul, all her thoughts, words and actions, the employment of her senses and faculties, and in general, all that she was, all that she possessed and every power of her soul. She offered to the divine majesty the very sacrifice that her son Jesus Christ offered on Calvary. Our adorable Saviour offered Himself to the eternal Father only once on the altar of the Cross, but His holy Mother immolated Him ten thousand times on the altar of her pure heart.

What veneration is then due to this sacred altar! Be thou blessed, O God of my heart, for having consecrated this most worthy altar to the glory of thy most adorable majesty. Deign to transform our cold hearts into glowing altars on which we may offer Thee an unremitting sacrifice of praise and love.

24 *De Dormit. Virg.*
25 *Serm. de laud. Deiparae.*
26 *Serm. 255 de temp.*
27 *Homil. 22 in Ezech.*
28 *Tract. 9 sup, Magnif. partit. 1.*

88

Chapter Five

MARY'S HEART, THE FIERY FURNACE OF BABYLON

Another symbolic picture of the Admirable Heart of the most Holy Mother of God is the miraculous furnace described in the third chapter of the prophet Daniel. Saint John Damascene and many other holy Doctors affirm that the fiery furnace was a figure of the sinless heart of the fire in the holy breast of the Mother of Fair Love. Here are Saint John Damascene's words, "Is it not true," he says, addressing Our Lady, "that this furnace, filled with a fire at once burning and refreshing, was a faithful image of thee and an excellent picture of the divine and eternal fire dwelling within thee?"[1]

But you may well ask how anything so noble and holy as the heart of the Queen of Heaven could be represented by the furnace of Babylon, an instrument of torture designed by the wickedness and cruelty of King Nabuchodonosor? Remember that the three young men, Sidrach, Misach and Abdenago, thrown into the furnace to be burnt to ashes, belonged to the people of Israel, and everything that happened to the Israelites was a figure and a foreshadowing of the great miracles that were to be fulfilled in Christianity, and in the Father and Mother of Christians. "All these things happened to them in figure."[2] Remember also that Saint Augustine[3] and Saint Gregory the Great[4] tell us that Sacred Scripture mentions many objects which, though profane and wicked in themselves, are nevertheless a representation of good and holy thoughts.

What can be more profane than a malodorous he-goat or a venomous snake? Yet the Holy Ghost employs them both to represent the Lamb of God laden with the sins of the world.[5] What could be worse

---

1 *Annon te fornax illa praemonstravit cujus ignis roridus simul ei flammeus erat, quae divini ignis in te habitantis figuram praeferebat? Orat. 1 de Dormit. B. Virg.*
2 1 Cor. 10, 11.
3 *Contra Faustum,* lib. 22, cap. 83.
4 *Moral.* lib. 3, cap. 21.
5 Lev. 16, 7–9.

and more reprehensible than the sensual and inordinate love of King Solomon for strange women or the immoral marriages he contracted, which were absolutely forbidden by God's law? The Holy Spirit makes of them, nevertheless, a figure of the adorable love of the King of Angels for sinful souls, and of the divine union His infinite goodness seeks to contract with the hearts of men.[6] What resemblance can we find between an Egyptian woman, dark like all those of her race in contrast to the Jews, as she herself admits, "I am black,"[7] and the peerless Queen of all women? The Egyptian woman springing from a barbarous and heathen people, was the daughter of an infidel and idolatrous king, and the spouse of one who recognized the disorders of his dissolute life, confessing himself to be the most foolish of men;[8] Mary was fair as the moon, bright as the sun, born of God's chosen people, the daughter of King David, the spouse of the King of Kings, the Mother of God Himself. Nevertheless, the Sacred Canticle, written under the inspiration of the Spirit of God, presents the Egyptian queen to us as an image and likeness of the Virgin Mother.[9]

A passionate lover delights to write the name of his beloved and sketch her image wherever he happens to be, not only on paper or canvas, but also on trees, stones and whatever else comes under his hand. Similarly, the incomprehensible love of God, Father and spouse of the most perfect and lovable Virgin Mary, causes Him to take pleasure in picturing her heart even in the burning furnace of Babylon.

Certainly that furnace was the product of Nabuchodonosor's impious rage, but divine providence, without whose order and permission nothing can happen, designated it to show the extent of the power of God and the marvels of His goodness, through the miraculous protection given to His faithful friends. God also willed that the fiery furnace should give us a glorious picture of the ardent heart of the Queen of Heaven, which is indeed a furnace of love and charity.

In the furnace of Babylon we behold many marvels wrought by God's omnipotence. Consider that in the midst of the furnace filled with fire and flame there should be a refreshing wind, likened to fragrant dew. "The angel made the midst of the furnace like the blowing of a wind bringing dew."[10] What a marvel it is to behold a burning furnace whose flames protect those inside its crucible, while they destroy those who remain outside! What a miracle to see fire comforting and refreshing those cast into the sevenfold heat of its flames, while burn-

6 Cant. 6, 7–8.
7 Cant. 1, 4.
8 Prov. 30, 2.
9 Cant. 6, 9.
10 Dan. 3, 50.

ing to death those standing at a safe distance! How miraculous for three young men to survive in a furnace whose flames leapt to a height of forty-nine cubits, not suffering injury, but walking about with joy as in a place of delight! The three gladly sang the praises of almighty God and emerged from their ordeal with greater strength and vigor than before while the fire could not so much as singe a single fibre of their clothing. Great indeed are the marvels to be found in Babylon's furnace; yet they merely foreshadow the miracles which we find in the furnace of the glowing heart of the Queen of Angels.

It is a great miracle to witness fire and water subsisting side by side in the furnace of Nabuchodonosor. The fire did not turn the cooling water into steam nor did the water quench the burning heat of the fire. What manner of fire is this? It is the fire of divine love burning in the virginal heart of Mary. What is the cooling dew? It is the water of tribulation, which so often flooded the holy heart of the Mother of Sorrows. The fire of love did not dry up the waters of affliction; and the waters of tribulation were unable, I shall not say to extinguish, but even to diminish in the least degree the divine ardor of that heavenly fire, "Many waters cannot quench charity."[11] On the contrary, the excess of love produced the abundance of affliction and the waters of tribulation were like inflammable liquids that augmented still further the fire of her love.

Is it not a great miracle to see a fire possessing at once the virtue of fire and the properties of water? Love has the virtue of fire, that it may unceasingly inflame the Virgin Mother's purest heart with its sacred ardor, and also the properties of water, as it extinguishes entirely the fire of self love and of attachment to vain and perishable things.

Is it not a great miracle to behold a fire refreshing, consoling and filling with joy the children of the Mother of God, while it pursues, burns, devours its enemies? Her virginal heart, which is ablaze with love for her true children, directs the fire and flame of its anger against those who injure or scandalize her loved ones.

Only three Hebrew boys were thrown into the furnace of Babylon, but all children of the admirable Mother of God can enter the furnace of her heart and dwell there as in a paradise of delights where they praise and glorify God forever in company with their heavenly Mother, and their hearts are filled with joy and consolation. "The dwelling in thee is as it were of all rejoicing,"[12] O holy Mother of God.

Three Hebrew children walked safely in the first furnace; yet the prophet saw there four, and the fourth was like the Son of God. "The

11 Cant. 8, 7.
12 Ps. 86, 7.

form of the fourth is like the Son of God."[13] Actually it was an angel, representing, according to Daniel, the only begotten Son of God in the Babylonian furnace, but this same Son of God resides and dwells in person in the glowing heart of His most holy Mother. He is all fire and flame of love and charity. "The Lord thy God is a consuming fire."[14] He possesses a throne of fire. "His throne like flames of fire,"[15] and a "fiery chariot."[16] In like manner, He wills to have a dwelling of fire and flame in the heart of His most worthy Mother. This dwelling place was depicted in the words, "The house of Jacob shall be a fire, and the house of Joseph a flame,"[17] which means that the abode of Jesus Christ, prefigured by Jacob and Joseph, shall be an abode of flaming fire.

We also notice that the three young men were bound hand and foot when thrown into the furnace, but immediately their bonds were consumed by the fire and they were freed within the furnace. Come, come, poor slaves of sin and of the world! Come, slaves of passion, of self-love and self-will, chained in the irons and fetters of Babylon! Fear not to plunge into our sacred furnace!

These flames will not harm you; instead they will destroy your fetters and establish you in the holy liberty of the children of God and of His loving Mother. They will inflame your hearts with the fire of heavenly love, they will transform them into divine fire itself. Your hearts will become holy furnaces heated seven times with the fire and flames that leap from the heart of your heavenly Mother. Your hearts must become furnaces of eternal love, if they would avoid being ranked with the miserable hearts of the wicked against whom the terrible sentence was uttered, "Thou shalt make them as an oven of fire, in the time of thy anger."[18]

What dost Thou will to do, O Lord, with the ungrateful wretches whom Thou didst create to love Thee, whose obligations to love Thee are boundless, yet who have loved everything but Thee, and have even kindled fires of insult and heaped outrages upon Thee? Thou shalt make of them furnaces of wrath, in the time of Thy terrible vengeance. Thou shalt hurl them into the eternal fire prepared for Satan and his minions, where they will be swallowed, burned and penetrated by the infernal fire. In life these souls would not permit the sweet and radiant flames of Thy holy love to burn within them, so they shall be yielded to the eternal torments of devouring fire in endless Hell.

13 Dan. 3, 92.
14 Deut. 4, 24.
15 Dan. 7, 9.
16 4 Kings 2, 11.
17 Abdias 1, 18.
18 Ps. 20, 10.

Would you avoid this tragedy, the greatest of all misfortunes? Then give your hearts to your admirable Queen, imploring her to offer them to her beloved son with the prayer that He may kindle in them the fire He came to spread on earth; the fire He so greatly desires should be lighted. On your part, correspond by removing every obstacle from your hearts, and if this sacred flame is already burning there, make every effort to increase it more and more by the practice of Christian virtues, the meditation of the gospel and especially the exercise of divine love and charity.

Be not satisfied with doing simply this. Seek to share actively in the ardent desire of the Son of God that the entire world should be illuminated with heavenly fire and to cooperate with him in spreading it everywhere. Nothing could be more agreeable to His divine majesty. All Christians who would please God should exert themselves towards this end but more especially should those whom He has chosen to be His cooperators in the salvation of souls. Take, then, a torch in your hand and, if possible, set the entire world afire with love.[19]

If you ask me what this torch should be, I shall answer that it is yourself. Each one is a torch. Have you not heard the Holy Ghost say of the prophet Elias that he rose up like fire, and that his words were like a burning torch? "And Elias the prophet stood up, as a fire: and his word burnt like a torch."[20] And does the Son of God describe Saint John the Baptist as "a burning and a shining light"?[21] When speaking through Zacharias of the time at which He shall work great wonders in His Church and in the entire world, God describes the leaders of Juda, namely, the Apostles and the other participants in the fulfillment of His desire to enkindle the earth with the fire of Heaven, stating that they shall be like a furnace of fire and a burning torch, consuming and devouring peoples to the right and to the left like fire which devours wood and hay. This means that His disciples will enkindle everything, fusing earthly and carnal-minded men into heavenly and spiritual beings, aglow with love of God and charity towards their neighbor. "In that day I will make the governors of Juda like a furnace of fire amongst wood, and as a firebrand amongst hay; and they shall devour all the people round about, to the right hand, and to the left."[22]

This is what you must become if you profess a particular obligation to work for the salvation of souls. You must be made of fire like Elias, and of flame like Saint John the Baptist. Each of you must be a burning furnace,

---

19 This thought is expressed in the symbolic picture, Our Lady of Hearts, which Saint John Eudes distributed among the faithful.
20 Ecclus. 48, 1.
21 John 5, 35
22 Zach. 12, 6.

a fiery, radiant torch; aglow within, shining without; ardent before God, and shining before men: ardent in prayer and brilliant in action; ardent with the love of God, and luminous with charity for your neighbor.

But where will you light your torch and obtain the fire which you must kindle in the hearts of men? It must be in the furnace of the holy heart of the Mother of Fair Love. To this end, approach the holy furnace of her heart more frequently with respect and veneration. Concentrate upon the divine fire inflaming her heart; imitate its all-glowing love and charity and humbly beg of our Mother most merciful that she may kindle in your hearts sparks of the celestial fire which burns in her own.

Having lighted and seized your torch, you will set everything on fire to the right and to the left; that is, you will inflame the hearts of the just and at the same time set fire to the hearts of sinners through the ardent example of your actions, the bright fervor of your prayers and the light of your teaching.

O divine fire that burns in the noble heart of our glorious Mother, come, come into the hearts of all men! Extinguish every other fire, destroying whatever would resist Thee. Burn, inflame, set on fire, transform into Thyself the hearts of men that they may become all fire and flames of love for Him Who created them that they might love Him and Him alone! Grant that we may say with Saint Augustine and in as holy a frame of mind, "O sacred fire, how sweet and pleasant is thy heat! How intimate and penetrating thy light, how amiable and desirable thy burning coals! Woe to them on whom thou shinest not, to them whom thou dost not burn!"[23] Happy they who are illuminated by the light and burned with thy sacred flame!

Come, then, most holy fire; come, heavenly flames; come divine furnace, come torrents, come flaming floods of the adorable fire of eternal love! Sweep over us and over every rational creature in the world! Burn everything, set all things on fire, that everything may be melted and fused into an eternal fire of love and charity towards Him Who is all love and charity towards us. Saint Augustine adds these words, "O fire ever burning and never dying out! O love always ardent and never weakening, inflame my entire being that I may love thee with all my heart."

23 *Soliloq.* cap. 24.

Chapter Six

MARY'S HEART, THE HILL OF CALVARY

Last in my series of symbolic pictures of the holy heart of the spot-less Virgin I show you Calvary, as it reveals the sorrows of the crucified heart of Mary at the time of her son's passion.

What is Calvary? It is a mountain, the most important and notable mountain the Holy Land. What is the heart of the Mother of God? Is it not also a mountain, the most illustrious mountain of that blessed land referred to in these words of Sacred Scripture, "Lord, thou hast blessed thy land."[1] This land is the Blessed Virgin Mary, and her heart is the noblest and highest peak of her body and of her soul.

What is Calvary? It is Mount Moriah on which God commanded Abraham to slay his son, Isaac. The Hebrew rendition of the twenty-second chapter of Genesis reads, "Go into the land of Moriah," instead of the usual version, "Go into the land of vision."[2] It is the place where King David raised an altar and offered sacrifice that God might stop the plague that ravaged his people, and also the site on which Solomon erected the Temple of Jerusalem, for Mount Sion is the same as Mount Moriah, and Calvary is part of the same chain of hills.

We have already seen that Christ, the true Solomon, established His foremost temple and holiest altar in the heart of the most worthy daughter of Abraham and of David. In this temple, on this altar she immolated, not merely in desire like Abraham, but in very truth, Her dearest and most adorable son, her Isaac.

What is Calvary? It is the place where the Cross of Jesus was raised. And was the Cross of Salvation not raised first of all in Mary's holy heart? What is Calvary? It is the place stained with the Precious Blood of Jesus Christ. But Mary's heart was bathed with It through love and compassion and the Precious Blood of her beloved son penetrated and impregnated His Mother far more than it soaked the soil of Calvary.

1 Ps. 84, 2.
2 Gen. 22, 2.

On Calvary, we behold the thorns that wounded the adorable head of our Saviour, the nails that pierced His hands and feet, the lance that opened His heart, the ropes that bound Him, the gall and vinegar He was given to drink, and the wounds which covered His body from head to foot. We can see the same wounds in the maternal heart of His saintly Mother. "The Cross and the nails which crucified the son's body, crucified the Mother's heart as well."[3] Saint Jerome quotes Saint Sophronius, Patriarch of Jerusalem, as saying, "All the wounds which covered the body of Jesus, had their counterpart in Mary's heart. The whips, the thorns, the nails which pierced and tore the Saviour's body, ran through His holy Mother's heart and shattered it. Every blow rending the body of the son had its cruel echo in the heart of His Mother."[4]

"O my Queen," exclaims Saint Bonaventure, "Thou art not only standing near the Cross, but thou art with Thy son on the Cross; Thou dost suffer, thou art crucified with Him, the only difference being that while He suffers in His body, thou dost suffer in thy loving heart. All the wounds scattered over His body are united in thy heart, because the sword of sorrow has pierced thy very soul. Thy virginal heart, O my sovereign Lady, is wounded by the lance, pierced by the nails and thorns, heaped with opprobrium, ignominy and imprecations, saturated with vinegar and gall. Why wouldst thou, most honored Lady, be immolated for us? Is not our Saviour's passion sufficient for our salvation? Must the mother also be crucified with her son? O sweetest heart, so full of love, must thou then be changed into bitter sorrow? I seek to behold thy loving heart, my dearest Mistress, but it seems to have vanished and in its place I find only the bitterness of gall, myrrh and absinth. I seek the Mother of God and I find only thorns, nails, a lance, a sponge and vinegar. I look for Mary on the Cross, and I see only spittle, insults, lashes and wounds, so truly has she been overwhelmed by outrages."[5]

I see my Redeemer crucified, suffering, agonizing, dying and finally dead on Calvary. I also behold His sorrows, suffering, agony and death in His Blessed Mother's heart. "She had lived of her son's life, and when He died on the Cross, she died with Him," says a holy Premonstratensian Abbot.[6] "Both Mother and son were nailed to the Cross, the son in the body, the Mother in her heart," exclaims Saint Lawrence Justinian,[7] the sainted Patriarch of Venice. "Could not Mary die in her heart, as Jesus died in His body?" asks Saint Bernard.[8]

3   Saint Augustine, *Serm. de Passione Dom.*
4   In *Epist. ad Paulam et Eustochium*, de Assumpt. B.V.
5   *Stimulus amoris*, lib. 1, cap. 3.
6   Philipp. Abbas Bonae Spei, in *Epist.* 14 ad Radulphum.
7   *Lib. de triumphanti agone Christi*, cap. 21.
8   *Serm.* in Signum, Magnum.

Among the great miracles wrought by Our Saviour on Calvary the most remarkable, according to Saint Augustine, was the miracle of goodness and charity on behalf of His executioners, when He besought His Heavenly Father to forgive them. At the same time, living in His holy Mother's heart, He communicated to her the charity which filled Himself, inducing her to imitate His sublime example of mercy. We hear His kind voice pleading with the all-just Father, and then we seem to hear the echo of His words in the heart of His holy Mother repeating, "Father, forgive them, for they know not what they do."[9]

On Calvary, the only son of Mary gave us an inestimable gift when in the excess of His incomprehensible goodness He addressed Himself to each one of us in the person of Saint John and speaking of His holy Mother, said to us, "Behold thy Mother."[10] And from Calvary, the Mother of Jesus, whose sentiments and will are one with those of her beloved son, gives herself to us to be our Mother with the same heart and with an equal love. Having enshrined the words of her son in her maternal heart, she echoes them again and adopts each one of us in particular. Thus both Jesus and Mary say to us, "Behold thy Mother."

On our part, we should unite with Jesus in saying to this supremely good Mother, "Behold thy son." Yes, O Mary, each one of us is thy child, who desires to love, honor and imitate thee as His Mother. Vouchsafe to look upon us, O most amiable Mother, and to love, protect, guide and treat us as thy children in spite of our extreme unworthiness.

We also behold on Calvary the author of life grown cold in death and we see the gloom of the sepulchre in the garden of Joseph of Arimathea, a part of Calvary's hill. But we can behold Him buried in the heart of His loving Mother more truly than in the tomb. Her marvelous heart is a living and life giving tomb. Having cooperated in the Incarnation of the Son of God by the ardor of her love, the fervor of her desires and the power of her prayers, Mary's heart also contributed to His resurrection, as we shall explain further on. Jesus arose in the sepulchre, but left it immediately. He likewise came back to life in Mary's heart, but there He remained and will remain forever. Of this living sepulchre, rather than of the inanimate tomb, can we say with good reason, "And his sepulchre shall be glorious,"[11] in the sight of angels and men, for time and for all eternity.

Finally, it was on Calvary that our Redeemer accomplished and consummated the work of our salvation, in which His Mother's heart cooperated so faithfully.

9 Luke 23, 34.
10 John 19, 27.
11 Isa. 11, 10.

You see therefore that Calvary is a most excellent picture of the Admirable Heart of the Mother of our crucified Redeemer. Do you wish your own heart to bear some faint resemblance to the heart of your heavenly Mother? Then plant in its center the Cross of Christ, her son: or better still, implore her to obtain for you the grace that Our Lord Himself may fix it there, and engrave on your heart a great love for His Holy Cross. May His love make you embrace, cherish and bear all the crosses that will be sent to you, in a spirit of humility, patience and submission to the divine will, and all the holy dispositions with which the son of Mary and the Mother of Jesus carried their heavy cross.

These symbolic pictures are but twelve of the many figures by which the eternal Father has illustrated for us the glory of the Admirable Heart of Mary. I have chosen them to reveal how unmistakably is the divine heart of God the first author and origin of devotion to the virginal heart of the Mother of His beloved Son. Almighty God enriched the heart of Mary with surpassing beauty and incomparable treasures so that our hearts would be stirred to venerate and love her with fitting devotion. Having begun to study the tributes of the Most High to His immaculate handmaid, how can we possibly refrain from pouring out our admiration and honour of Mary, and our humble praise of God for the countless favours He has heaped upon her Admirable Heart?

O divine painter, grant us the grace to praise and thank Thee for having, in these twelve pictures, portrayed the heart of our glorious Queen and Mother in symbols so colorful, rich and expressive, that even such as we can learn to understand, to love and to imitate her. We implore Thee now to take our hearts and make each one of them yet another symbol to depict forever some measure of the love, humility and purity of the other virtues of Thy infinite glory as they are manifested so magnificently in the heart of Mary, Mother Most Admirable.

Part Four

SECOND FOUNDATION OF THE DEVOTION:
THE HEART OF GOD THE SON

DIVINE PERFECTIONS MIRRORED IN THE
ADMIRABLE HEART OF MARY

Chapter One*

Our Lord Jesus Christ, Teacher of the Devotion to the Admirable Heart of Mary

We have every reason to consider the adorable heart of Jesus as the second foundation of the devotion to the Admirable Heart of Mary. The supremely ardent love for the heart of His dearest Mother, burning in the Sacred Heart of Jesus, makes Him the herald of this devotion, which He teaches to us both by word and example.

Would you know how the only begotten Son of God, who is also the son of Mary, exhorts us to venerate His glorious Mother's loving heart? Listen to what He revealed in 1300 to Saint Mechtilde, one of the most glorious daughters of Saint Benedict, whose writings have been approved by learned and devout doctors. One day during Advent, as the Saint sought to salute the Mother of God in a most pleasing manner, Our Lord Himself deigned to instruct her as follows:

"Thou shalt salute my holy Mother's virginal heart as an ocean replete with heavenly grace and a treasure filled with myriad blessings for mankind.

"Thou shalt honor it as the purest heart after mine own because she was the first to take the vow of chastity.

"Thou shalt hail it as the humblest heart of any simple creature, for her humility drew me from my Father's bosom and rendered her worthy to conceive me in her chaste womb by the power of the Holy Ghost.

"Thou shalt reverence her heart as supremely devout and most ardent in its desire for my Incarnation and birth on earth, because the fervor of her desires and of her longing attracted me to her and became the cause of man's salvation.

"Thou shalt honor her heart as most glowingly inflamed with love for God and man. Thou shalt salute it as the wisest and most prudent, for she kept in her heart the memory of each event of my childhood, youth, and adult life and made a most holy use of this remembrance.

---

* Comprising Chapters 1 and 2 of the original edition.

"Thou shalt greet her heart as the most faithful, for she not only consented to permit me, her only son, to be sacrificed, but she also offered me to my eternal Father as a sacrifice for the redemption of the world.

"Thou shalt salute her heart as the most vigilant and most zealous for the interests of the nascent Church, for the care she took to pray unceasingly could not be disregarded.

"Thou shalt glorify her heart as raised to the highest degree of uninterrupted contemplation, for no tongue can worthily speak of the graces and favors that men owe to the power of her intercession."[1]

Thus did Our Lord speak to Saint Mechtilde, revealing clearly how pleasing to His divine majesty is the devotion to His Blessed Mother's holy heart and how profitable to those who practice it.

But if we shall further lend our ears to Jesus, the great teacher of the devotion to Mary, Mary's august heart, He will impart to us many other edifying and consoling truths. Let us listen.

"I alone," Our Lord tells us, "can worthily proclaim the devotion which the hearts of all who love me shall cultivate towards the heart of my holy Mother, for I am the source and principle of all the great and marvelous qualities to be found in this abyss of wonders, and I alone have a perfect knowledge of the eminent perfections of her heart."

"I am the eldest son of this maternal heart and am therefore filled with the most tender and filial love for it. I am the firstborn of my most worthy Mother's incomparable heart, as I am the first fruit of the adorable heart of my eternal Father. My admirable Mother formed me and carried me in her heart more holily, longer and sooner than in her womb.[2] For the sanctity of her blessed bosom has its origin in the charity and purity of her most holy heart, and she became worthy to form and to bear me in her womb because by humility, purity and love she first formed and carried me in her heart. She bore me in her bosom for nine months only, but she always held me and will forever hold me in her heart. I am, therefore, in a way, more truly the fruit of her heart than of her womb.

"O admirable mystery! Her incomparable heart is, among created beings, the masterpiece of my almighty goodness; yet by an unfathomable miracle I am myself the excellent product of her humility, whereby she drew me from my Father's adorable bosom, where I was born before all ages began, that I might be born of my virginal Mother in the fullness of time.

"I have always been and shall forever be the most singular object

1 *Lib. spec. gratiae*, lib. 1, cap. 2.
2 *Prius et felicius in Corde quam in ventre concepit.* S. Leo, *Serm. de Nat. Dom.* See also S. Aug., *Lib. de Sancta Virginitate*, c. 30.

of all the affections of her holy heart, as she herself has always been and will forever be, after my eternal Father, the first object of my love.

"All who truly love me must, therefore, be particularly zealous in honoring and teaching others to honor the heart that I love more and that gives me greater glory and love than the hearts of all the angels and men together.

"For all these reasons I myself have willed to be the teacher of this devotion practiced by many of my saints during the past centuries, a devotion still observed in many churches today; and I personally taught the first principles of this devotion to Saint Mechtilde.

"It is I, my dearest children, who have made it flourish again in your hearts. I am now addressing those who have a special venera-tion for the most worthy heart of my virginal Mother. I myself have rooted in your hearts your ardent desire of honoring her heart as I wish it to be honored.

"I know that, as her heart is the first object of the love of my heart, after the eternal Father, it is likewise, after God, the first object of your most tender and holy affection. Therefore have I given it to you to be an inexhaustible fountain of blessings in your midst.

"I have given my Mother's heart to you as a divine sun to enlight-en you through the darkness of the world, to warm you in the frosts of mortal life, to gladden and to comfort you in the sorrows, pains and miseries of earth, and to vivify and strengthen you against the decline and weakness of human frailty.

"I have given her heart to you as a beautiful mirror, into which you should often gaze in order to see the stains that tarnish your souls, so that you may cleanse them. With the aid of this celestial mirror, you should array your souls with becoming ornaments that they may become pleasing in the sight of my divine majesty.

"I have given the heart of My Mother to you as an unshakeable tower and impregnable stronghold in which you may take refuge and seek shelter against the machinations of the enemies of your salvation.

"I have given it to you as a burning furnace of divine love into which you are to throw yourselves and be consumed that you may turn into fire and flames of love for Him who is all fire and flaming love for you.

"I have given her heart to you as a perfect pattern of the respect, love and obedience that you must entertain for those who hold God's place on earth. I have given it to you as a fountain of wine, milk and honey, whence you may draw the charity, kindness and meekness with which you should treat one another.

"I have given her heart to you as a heavenly chronicle and book of life, that you may study its pages unceasingly, and learn to know perfectly and to love ardently the ravishing beauty of those Christian virtues whose faithful practice gives eternal life. But what you should learn above all from this book are the marvelous merits of holy humility and the means to practice it, so as to crush in your hearts the cursed serpent of pride and vanity that wreaks such havoc, not only in the souls of children of perdition, but in my own children's hearts as well.

"I have given the heart of my incomparable Mother to you as a holy rule that will enable you to become saints if you faithfully observe it. It is the rule of the divine life you should lead, of the high qualities and habits you must assume, of the evangelical teachings you are to follow. By this rule you must measure the holiness that should permeate all your actions, the sentiments and affections that should fill your hearts. It is the rule of the love and hatred, the joy and sorrow, the desires and fears that must be yours, if you are to please me and sanctify yourselves.

"I have given her heart to you as a vast ocean of graces of every kind from which you must draw the graces you need at every hour, every moment, every place and every occasion, to avoid the manifold snares of Satan, which cover the entire earth, and to be able to serve God in justice and holiness all the days of your lives.

"I have given her heart to you as a precious vessel filled with manna from Heaven and the nectar of paradise to nourish your hearts with the meat of the angels, even in this world, and so to inebriate them with heavenly wine that the things of the earth and time may be forgotten entirely and the sole delight of your hearts rest in those things which are heavenly and eternal. Such was always the life of my holy Mother, who is also your beloved Mother, and such were the affections of her holy heart.

"I have bestowed upon you the royal heart of your great Queen to be regent of your hearts; to rule and govern them according to the most adorable will of my heavenly Father that you may be entirely fashioned according to His heart.

"I have likewise given you the Admirable Heart of my most worthy Mother, which is identified with my own heart, that it may be your true heart as well; that my children may possess only one heart with their Mother, and my members the same heart as their Head. Thus you may serve, adore and love God with a heart worthy of His infinite goodness: *Corde magno et animo volenti;*[3] that is, with an immense and measureless heart, with a heart all pure and holy, so that you may sing His divine praises and accomplish all your actions in the spirit, love, humility and all the holy dispositions of her Admirable Heart. But in order to make this come true you must renounce entirely your own

3 2 Mac. 1, 3.

heart, that is, your mind, your will and your love of self. Strive, there-fore, to rid yourself of your earthly heart that is depraved and wicked, and you shall receive an entirely heavenly, holy and divine heart.

"I have finally given this marvelous heart as an inestimable treasure containing every possible blessing. It is for you, beloved children, to engrave in your hearts a high esteem, a profound respect and a particular affection for so rich a treasure, and to preserve it jealously by the contin-uation and increase of your veneration for a heart so holy and amiable.

"It is to encourage you to do so that I have said these things. Set down my words in your hearts and practice them faithfully. In this way, you will become the true children of my holy Mother's heart, and you will live according to my own. My eyes and my heart shall ever watch over your necessities. I will carry you in my innermost heart. You will yourselves be my heart, my joy and my delight. I will love you as my own heart, and I will prepare a glorious habitation for you throughout eternity in my heart and in the heart of my Blessed Mother, which is one with my own. You shall abide forever in our hearts and live by their life, you shall possess all the treasures enclosed in our hearts, and be immersed and buried in their joys. Our hearts shall be your paradise, the life of your life, the heart of your heart.

"In the love of these hearts, or rather, this one heart, you will eter-nally love, bless and glorify my holy Mother and the sovereign monarch of all hearts, which is the adorable heart of the most Holy Trinity. May it be forever praised, adored and loved by all the hearts of angels and of men!"

After listening to the divine words of our divine Saviour encourag-ing us to love and honor the most amiable heart of His Blessed Mother, we shall now contemplate the operations of His adorable heart towards the maternal heart of Mary, whereby He teaches us even more effec-tively than by His eloquent words. Oh, who could worthily describe the least spark of the divine heart of Jesus, that furnace of love, towards the heart of His admirable Mother?

Our Lord has so loved and honored her maternal heart that He has exalted it above all the hearts of the universe and made it the most august empire of His glory and the glorious triumph of His love. He has so loved and honored her heart as to constitute it a Heaven higher and more brilliant than all the Heavens in which He is glorified and loved more ardently than in the empyrean Heaven.

God has loved and honored His Mother to such an extent that from the first instant in which He gave her blessed heart its being, He worked in it countless great miracles, imparting the most abundant communication of His own divine perfections and rendering it most worthy, noble, perfect, mighty, wise, holy, just, merciful, kind, liberal. He has made it the richest, happiest, most glorious, most amiable and most admirable of all hearts.

To understand this perfectly, you must recall that Saint Dionysius teaches us that divine love reflects the divine attributes in the hearts of the angels as in so many beautiful mirrors, according to the nine orders of the blessed Spirits.[4]

Now what Divine Love accomplishes in angelic hearts, Mary's only son, so filled with love and tenderness for His beloved Mother, has certainly accomplished in her heart also but in a far more excellent manner. He gathers all the perfections of His divinity, divided as it were among the Orders of the angels, and brings them together in the heart of the august Queen of all angels. It is fitting that, having chosen Mary to be His Mother and having become her son, Our Lord should establish such a perfect resemblance between Mother and son. The divine son seeks to render her similar to Himself in His divinity, just as His exalted Mother caused Him to resemble her in His humanity. As the eternal Father unceasingly communicates all the divine attributes to His only begotten Son with such fullness that He is called the figure and type of His substance and the image of the invisible God, similarly the Son makes His Mother's virginal heart participate in all the perfections He Himself received from His heavenly Father with such plenitude that her most blessed heart bears a marvelous resemblance to all the excellent qualities found in our adorable Saviour.

Yes, the incomparable heart of Mary, Mother of our Redeemer, is a most precious and radiant mirror in which Jesus, the eternal sun, reflects Himself in perfect manner with all His beauties and perfections, and thereby renders her holy heart so admirable, so amiable and so praiseworthy that it should be, next to the God-Man, the principal object of our devotion on earth, even as it is the first object of veneration for the happy inhabitants of Heaven.

4 *De Caelesti Hierarchia*, cap. 3, § 1.

Chapter Two

SOME ESSENTIAL DIVINE PERFECTIONS[1]
MIRRORED IN THE ADMIRABLE HEART OF MARY

Among His countless words in praise of the most Blessed Virgin Mary, the Holy Ghost honors His spotless bride with the glorious tribute of proclaiming that she is clothed with the sun, "A woman clothed with the sun."[2] What is this sun? It is the sun of divinity and of the divine perfections, according to the explanation of several holy Fathers. Our Lady is not merely clothed with and surrounded by this sun; she is completely filled and penetrated by it. Saint Andrew of Crete praises the incomparable Virgin Mary with appropriate dignity when he calls her "the compendium of God's incomprehensible perfections."[3]

Now if this is true of the Blessed Virgin's sacred person, it is still more true of her holy heart, the noblest part of her being, the source and sanctuary of the virtues of humility, obedience and charity which elevate her to the sublime and divine state that she personally revealed to Saint Brigid.[4] Her glowing heart is the perfect expression and marvelous compendium of all the attributes of the divine essence. It is the beautiful mirror in which the ardent love of Jesus Christ for His most amiable Mother reflects so excellently all the perfections of His divinity and His humanity.

In the first place, His divine love most perfectly draws its own image in His Mother's amiable heart. Next to the infinite love burning in the immense furnace of the adorable heart of Jesus, there never was and never shall be a love so strong, exalted, extensive, ardent and pure, as the love which always possessed, filled and inflamed the virginal heart of His Mother. This all-compassing love in turn stamps upon her a perfect image of all the other divine attributes.

---

1 The essential perfections or attributes of God are those which belong to the integrity of the divine essence or nature. Other attributes expressing a relation between creatures and God, such as Creator, Redeemer and Rewarder, are not essential because these relations are not in God but outside Him. Cf. Wilhelm-Scannell, *A Manual of Catholic Theology* (London, 1890), p. 179.

2 Apoc. 12, 1.

3 *Compendium incomprehensibilium Dei perfectionum. Orat. 2 de Assumpt.*

4 *Revel.* lib. 1, Cap. 42.

Her Admirable Heart is, first of all, a living image of divine unity. God is alone and unique in the infinite eminence of all His grandeurs. He is the only mighty,[5] the only good,[6] the only wise,[7] merciful,[8] just,[9] immortal and blessed Being, the King of kings and the Lord of lords.[10] Likewise there is in the whole universe only one heart of the one Mother of God, unique in dignity, excellence and perfections. It surpasses in power, wisdom, goodness, mercy, piety, love, charity and every other virtue and eminent quality the most perfect heart of any angel or saint.

The unique heart of Our Lady never knew any love other than the purest love of God. It never suffered from the multiplicity of superfluous thoughts, aimless desires and vain affections which usually fill and divide the miserable hearts of the children of Adam. Her heart held one thought, one purpose, one will, one intention, one single affection and one desire only: to please God and to fulfill in all things and everywhere His adorable will. Thus did this heavenly spouse wound, ravish and possess completely the heart of her adorable Bridegroom, as He Himself declares, "Thou hast wounded my heart, my sister, my spouse: thou hast wounded my heart with one of thy eyes, and with one hair of thy neck,"[11] that is, by loving and seeking me in all things, and in having in thy heart but one thought, intention and affection, to do everywhere and at all times the things that are most pleasing to me.

The Admirable Heart of our great Queen bears a true resemblance to divine simplicity. Duplicity, disguise, deceit, falsehood, curiosity, singularity, worldly wisdom, mundane prudence, the self love which prompts so many faulty thoughts and reflections concerning ourselves and our actions, these and all other things contrary to holy simplicity never had the least part in the heart of the heavenly Dove. She was always filled, possessed and animated by the spirit of truth, sincerity, candor and simplicity, that her son bade us follow when He said, "Be ye . . . as simple as doves."[12]

The incomparable heart of the Mother of God enjoys marvelous participation in and resemblance to the infinity and incomprehensibility of God Himself, because the almost infinite dignity of the Mother of God ennobles and raises to the highest degree even the smallest details concerning her. This is particularly true of her incomparable heart, the source of innumerable blessings and the principle of all that

5 1 Tim. 6, 15.
6 Luke, 18, 19.
7 Rom. 16, 27.
8 Apoc. 15, 4.
9 2 Mach. 1, 25.
10 1 Tim. 6, 15–16.
11 Cant. 4, 9.
12 Matt. 10, 16.

is great in her, loaded with numberless gifts and heavenly graces. Saint Bernardine of Siena tells us that when Our Lady became the Mother of God she was raised to an almost infinite dignity, which rendereth her like unto God, as she is the Mother of the son whose Father is almighty God. This miracle was accomplished by the well-nigh infinite graces, and perfections bestowed upon her, graces so excellent and sublime that only God can know perfectly their boundless extent.[13]

Mary's Admirable Heart also received an abundant communication of the immensity of God, a singular faculty to express His immeasurability. Let us listen to Saint Bonaventure. "O Mary," says the seraphic Doctor, "I behold in thee an immense grandeur and capacity. *Tu Maria immensissima.* I see in thee three kinds of immensity. The first is the immensity of thy blessed womb, which enclosed Him who is immense and infinite, whom the Heavens and the entire universe cannot contain. The second is the immensity of thy mind and heart, for thy virginal heart is more vastly immense than thy sacred womb. The third is the immensity of thy grace and charity, because thy heart being immense, replete with grace and charity, the charity and grace that fill it must necessarily be immense."[14]

Yes, Mother of Fair Love, thy charity knows no bounds or measure; it not only reaches all ages, all places and everything that God has made, but it is so vast and great that it would encompass a countless number of worlds!

The most constant heart of the Queen of Angels is likewise an excellent representation of divine stability and immutability. It remained always steadfast, firm, unalterable and resolute in its perfect love of God and all the holy dispositions which render a heart entirely pleasing to God.

O my Jesus, I beseech Thee, by the invariable love which the Immaculate Heart of Mary has always borne and will forever bear to Thee, deign so to establish and strengthen our hearts in Thy holy love that we may truly say with Saint Paul, "Who then shall separate us from the love of Christ? . . . Neither death nor life . . . nor any creature shall be able to separate us from the love of God which is in Christ Jesus our Lord."[15]

The holy heart of our great Princess is a beautiful representation of the eternity of God, not only because her affections were always entirely

13 *Per quamdam quasi infinitatem perfectionum et gratiarum. Tanta fuit perfectio ejus, ut soli Deo cognoscenda reservetur. Serm. 5 de Nativ. B. Virg. cap. 12; and Serm. 4 de Conceptione B. Virg.* art. 1, et 31.

14 *Tu ergo immensissima Maria, capacior ex caelo: quis quem caeli capere non poterant, tuo gremio contulisti. Tu capacior es mundo: quia quem totus non capit orbis, in tua se clausit viscera factus homo. Si ergo Maria tam capacissima fuit ventre, quanto magis mente? Et si capacitas tam immensa fuit gratia plena, oportuit utique quod gratia illa quae tantum implevisse potuit capacitatem, essa immensa. In Speculo,* cap. 5.

15 Rom. 8, 35, 38 and 39.

free from temporal attachments and securely fixed upon eternal things, but also because Mary was filled with the spirit of prophecy, which is a participation in the eternity that renders all things present in the sight of the divine majesty of God. God communicated this divine perfection to many saints, so we cannot doubt that the Queen of all Saints also participated highly in this privilege, as she possessed eminently all the gifts and graces that God has bestowed on other saints. Saint Albert the Great[16] says that whoever loves the most amiable Mother of God, must hold it for an infallible rule that whatever there is of goodness and beauty in all the other saints is to be found in Our Lady in a still higher degree; nay, that it is through her intercession that the other saints have received their great endowments. Therefore does the Holy Ghost give Our Lady the name and title of Prophetess saying, "I went to the prophetess."[17] Saint Basil[18] and many other saints refer these words to Mary.

The blessed heart of the Queen of Heaven displays a perfect imitation of the plenitude and self-sufficiency of God, who bears the name of *Saddai*, meaning precisely self-sufficient.[19] Almighty God has need of nothing, being filled with every good. The Son of God, speaking to His Father, exclaims, "Thou art my God, for thou hast no need of my goods."[20] In like manner, the virginal heart of the Mother of God, loving God alone, being always free and empty of every alien affection, was constantly filled with God much more perfectly than the Ephesians, to whom Saint Paul wrote that he bowed his knees to the Father of Our Lord Jesus Christ to obtain for them the grace that they might "be filled unto all the fullness of God."[21]

The blessed heart of Our Lady never desired, sought or found any delight or satisfaction outside of God. Her heart always enjoyed imperturbable rest and peace because being filled to capacity with the plenitude of God, it remained always fully satisfied and incomparably happier and content than the heart of a man possessing a million possible worlds.

Consider well, dear reader, how perfectly the Admirable Heart of your Queen fulfills the mandate to "seek but one thing" and to make God her portion and her heritage forever. To be happy, give and offer your heart constantly, exclaiming with Mary, Saint Thomas and Saint Francis, "My God and my All."

---

16 Pro infallibili regula debemus habere, qui Mariam diligimus, quod quidquid unquam bonitatis in aliquo Sancto fuit, vel pulchritudinis, hoc in ipsa per excellentiam excreverit, et per ipsam per eos. In Bibliis B. Mariae, ad cap. 1 Cantici Canticorum.

17 Isa. 8, 3.

18 In cap. 8 Isa.

19 See Meditations on Various Subjects (New York, 1947), p. 114.

20 Ps. 15, 2.

21 Eph. 3, 19.

Chapter Three

PURITY AND SANCTITY OF GOD
MIRRORED IN THE ADMIRABLE HEART OF MARY

In this chapter I shall show how Mary's heart bears a striking resemblance to divine purity and sanctity. The most pure and holy heart of Our Lady is a living image of those two adorable perfections which are one and the same, for Saint Dionysius tells us that sanctity is perfect purity;[1] purity meaning freedom from the slightest imperfection.

The most holy heart of Mary is indeed an excellent image of divine purity and holiness. Not only was her most pure and holy heart always far removed from every kind of sin, but it was entirely free from attachment to created things and intimately united to God by its pure and holy love for Him together with the eminent practice of all the other virtues which Mary's heart possessed in so high a degree. The Queen of Virtues is called by Saint John Damascene "the abode and the sanctuary of all virtues."[2] Even though Our Lady dwelt for years in this world full of filth and abomination, poisoned by the venom of sin, and among wicked and perfidious Jews, her most holy heart never contracted the least stain or blemish, was never attached by an inordinate affection to any creature nor even to God's gifts and graces. The Blessed Virgin remained always intimately united to God, as though nothing else existed save God and herself. Thus were the divine words most perfectly fulfilled in Her divine heart, "Let my heart be undefiled in thy justifications;"[3] that is, let my heart be immaculate by its union and adherence to Thy divine will, which justifies, sanctifies and even deifies the hearts that love it and perfectly follow it.

The most holy heart of the Queen of all Saints remained forever immaculate, preserved in eminent purity and holiness, and entirely filled with the purity and sanctity of God Himself. Her being was transformed and submerged in divine purity and holiness, to the surpassing

---

1 *De divinis Nominibus*, cap. 12, sect. 2.
2 *Virtutum omnium domicilium*. *De fide orthodoxa*, lib. 4 Cap. 15.
3 Ps. 118, 80.

extent that her heart merited to obtain the world's salvation. As Saint Anselm expresses it, "The pure sanctity and holy purity of Mary's devout heart, surpassing by far the purity and sanctity of all other creatures, merited for her the sublime dignity of becoming the restorer of the world wrapped in perdition."[4]

If you would find a place in the sanctuary of Mary's Admirable Heart, which so perfectly mirrors the purity and sanctity of the Most High, you must purify your heart and realize the meaning of the words, "This is the will of God, your sanctification."[5] These words are not meant just for souls specially consecrated and set apart. You must apply them to yourself, you who bear the name and imprint of Christ and membership in His Mystical Body. The sanctification of your spirit, heart and body is more than a commandment; it is a privilege, a participation, granted to you through the purity and sanctity of the heart of Mary, Mother of the Redeemer and your own Mother.

---

4 *Pura enim sanctitas et sanctissima puritatis piissimi Pectoris ejus, omnem omnis creaturae puritatem sive sactitatem transcendens, incomparabili sublimitate hoc promeruit, ut Reparatrix perditi orbis benignissimi fieret. De excell. B. Virg. Cap. 9.*
5 I Thess. 4, 3.

Chapter Four

STRENGTH AND POWER OF GOD
MIRRORED IN THE ADMIRABLE HEART OF MARY

The principal and most common appellations given to God in Sacred Scripture are the words "strong" and "mighty". He says of Himself, "I am the most mighty God"[1] and "I am God Almighty."[2]

If you should ask how these two attributes differ from each other, I would answer that in God, power and strength are one and the same perfection; yet there is some difference between their effects. It belongs to all-powerfulness to work great and admirable wonders and the characteristic of strength is to accomplish all things easily without pain or fatigue.

Let us now see the strength and power operate in the heart of our august Queen. I visualize their image engraved on her pure heart most perfectly. Consider the power which the heart of the Mother of the almighty exerts over Him Who has chosen to obey her as His Mother, "And he was subject to them."[3] The maternal authority and power God has given Mary over Himself will never be separated from her divine maternity, for the son of Mary will never relinquish the nature He assumed in His beloved Mother's womb and never will He withdraw the privileges He once conferred upon her.

If the heart of the faithful Christian, who believes in Jesus Christ, finds everything possible according to His holy word, "All things are possible to him that believeth,"[4] what can be impossible for the maternal heart of Mary who conceived the Son of God in her sacred womb, gave Him birth, nourished Him, took care of Him in childhood, accompanied Him in all labors and sufferings, and loved Him more than all the hearts of Heaven and earth put together?

"If all things are possible to him who believes, how much more must this be true of her who loves Him?" says Gerson. "And of her who bore Him," adds Saint Bernardine of Siena.

1 Gen. 46, 3.
2 Ibid., 35, 11.
3 Luke 2, 51.
4 Mark 9, 22.

If the Apostle Saint Paul says that he can do all things "in him who strengtheneth me,"[5] what must be the power of the maternal heart of the Queen of Apostles bearing eternally within itself Him who is called in Sacred Scripture, "Christ, the power of God?"[6] Her heart is filled and animated by the power and strength of the Most High. Cannot we then say that her virginal heart is all-powerful in Him who is her strength and power, as He is her soul and her spirit?

Hers is the heart of the valiant woman spoken of by Solomon, always inspired with vigorous and manly virtue, through which she accomplished all things with sovereign perfection and without the least defect. This valiant woman's heart bore the sharpest pain and the most violent anguish with marvelous constancy and unshakeable fortitude. Her intrepid heart crushed the infernal dragon's head, that is, sin, prefigured by Holofernes, and the powers of hell fear the Immaculate Heart even as an army in battle array[7] because Our Lady fought courageously against all God's enemies and obtained a glorious victory.

But what is more, she vanquished, so to speak, the Almighty Himself. For I hear an angel saying to Jacob, "Thou shalt no longer be called Jacob, but thy name shall be Israel," which means according to Saint Jerome and the Septuagint "strong against God."[8] This interpretation agrees with the Angel's own explanation, for after having said, "Thy name shall be Israel," he adds, "for if thou hast been strong against God, how much more shalt thou prevail against men?" Jacob had overcome only an angel, but that angel represented God; hence he was told he had overcome God Himself.

Jacob's holy daughter, the worthy Mother of Christ, has, in a way really overcome God Himself. How often has she not, through the efficacy of her prayers and merits, and by the power of her love, disarmed the anger of God and arrested the torrent of His indignation which would otherwise have flooded and destroyed the world because of its innumerable crimes? How many times has Our Lady besought divine vengeance to lay aside the thunderbolts ready to be hurled against criminal mankind? How often has her heart's incomparable charity clasped the hands of God's terrible justice and stopped Him from punishing men as they deserve? "How powerful is her love," says Richard of Saint Victor, "since it overcomes the Almighty."[9] Yes, the love and charity of Mary's heart are powerful, and have as it were vanquished God Himself!

5   Phil. 4, 13.
6   1 Cor. 1, 24.
7   Can. 6, 3.
8   Gen. 32, 28.

History is filled with instances where Our Lady has shown her incomparable power on behalf of those who invoke her protection, manifesting publicly to armies and nations the strength that she also extends to each Christian in his own inner struggle against sin. But her strength is for those who invoke, love, honor and venerate her heart.

O Glorious Queen of the World, make us sharers in the divine power which fills thy holy heart and give us strength against the enemies of thy divine son, who is all and does all in thee!

---

9 *De gradibus Caritatis. O quam potens est amor ejus, qui vincit Omnipotentem.* Saint John Eudes does not give the complete reference.

Chapter Five

WISDOM AND TRUTH OF GOD
MIRRORED IN THE ADMIRABLE HEART OF MARY

Divine wisdom and truth are communicated to the holy heart of the Blessed Virgin Mary in no lesser degree than divine power and strength.

If the Holy Ghost assures us that the soul of the just man is the seat of divine Wisdom, we can well say that the heart of Mary, Mother of Jesus, is the throne of this same Wisdom, the highest and most magnificent throne that it ever had or shall have on earth and in Heaven.

The heart of Mary is not merely the throne of Wisdom, but its living image, for it is the heart of the Mother of Him whom Sacred Scripture calls "the Wisdom of God."[1] In Christ are all the treasures of the wisdom and knowledge of God, and He certainly dispensed them in an incomparably higher manner to His Mother than to King Solomon and all the sages and wise men of the universe.

Mundane prudence and the wisdom of the flesh never found admittance into her wise heart, which was and still is an inexhaustible treasure and bottomless abyss of angelic prudence, holy science, heavenly light and wisdom divine, because her luminous heart always was and ever shall be the abode of the eternal and of uncreated Wisdom, Who has always dwelt therein. It is the city mentioned by the prophet Isaias, "One shall be called the city of the sun."[2]

Saint Bernardine of Siena expressly states that Our Lady was so completely filled with the light of divine wisdom from her mother's womb that from the initial moment of her existence she possessed a perfect general knowledge of the Creator and of all irrational, rational and intellectual creatures.[3] Our Lady knew all these things in God, as in their first and universal cause, for God was the single object of her gaze as well as of her love. She saw God in all things, and all things in God. She beheld God in all creatures as the principle, end, center, exemplar,

1 I Cor. 1, 21–24.
2 Isa. 19, 18.
3 *Serm. 13 de Exalt. BV. in gloria.*

author and preserver of every created being, and she saw every creature in God as participating in His sovereign Being and divine perfections; God loves all that is, and hates nothing that He has made, according to the divine word, "Thou lovest all things which thou hast made;"[4] so also the holy heart of the Mother of God was always filled with affection and even respect for all God's creatures. She looked upon the reasonable and intellectual beings as images and semblances of God; she considered the irrational and insentient beings as marks and vestiges of God; in a word, she saw in all creatures the expression of the wisdom of God and participations in His Divinity. If the heart of the Mother of the eternal sun was thus bathed in divine splendors from the beginning of her life, judge of her progress and her end. As her heart ever grew in grace and love, so also it increased in light and wisdom.

"Mary is rightly represented as clothed with the sun," says Saint Bernard, "for she has penetrated into the profound abyss of divine wisdom more deeply than we can think or believe possible; to such an extent, indeed, that she seems to have become immersed in that inaccessible light, beyond what is possible for a creature who does not have a hypostatic union with God."[5]

Since our incomparable Mother is in Heaven, entirely absorbed in the ocean of eternal wisdom and knowledge, and as God has made her partaker of His empire and associated her in His divine kingship, establishing her Queen and Empress of Heaven and earth, and communicating to her His own dominion over every creature, so has God filled her heart with the light of His adorable wisdom, that she may know all the subjects under her authority, and rule and govern every creature according to the necessities of each and the dispositions of the divine will.

Our Lady possesses a special knowledge of those who are most devoted to her; she knows God's designs concerning them, the road they should follow to reach God, the state and dispositions of their souls, all the accidents that befall them, all their possible perils, the pains they suffer, interiorly and exteriorly. She knows the temptations that assail them, the evil schemes of their enemies and all their corporeal and spiritual needs, so that she may assist, protect, defend and strengthen her faithful followers, obtain from her divine son the help they need most, and be herself the best of mothers to them. From this you can estimate the happiness and advantages enjoyed by those who make themselves worthy to be numbered among the true children of Our Lady's loving heart.

4 Wis. 11, 25.
5 *Jure ergo Maria sole perhibetur amicta, quae profundissimam divinae Sapientiae, ultra quam credi valeat, penetravit abyssum: ut quantum sine personali unione creaturae conditio patitur, luci illi inaccessibili videatur immersa. Serm. in Signum Magnum.*

Such are some of the effects wrought by divine wisdom in this Admirable Heart. We shall now contemplate in it the workings of the eternal truth of God.

Divine veracity stamps its image most excellently on the Blessed Virgin's heart. As God is paramountly the God of all truth and calls Himself the Holy and True One,[6] so is the heart of the Mother of God filled with truth. Only of the heart of Mary can it be said, speaking of simple creatures, that truth always filled it, because it was the only heart ever completely faithful to its divine rule and exemplar, the heart of God Himself. Give me all the hearts of the children of Adam, and I shall repeat of them all the words of the Holy Spirit, "Their heart is vain",[7] for none will be found who were always truthful and faithful to God. Only of the heart of the Mother of Him who is essential and uncreated Truth, could it be said from the first to the last moment of her life, "The heart of Mary is holy and truthful," because it always conforms to God's eternal decrees. "Whatever was done in her," says Saint Jerome, "was all purity and simplicity, sanctity and truth."[8]

Furthermore, as God is infallible in His judgments and knowledge and can commit no error, knowing and judging all things in His own truth,[9] so also He gave the Blessed Virgin Mary a knowledge of the truth which enlightened all her judgments. Her heart was ever filled and possessed by the spirit of truth, which guided her with the infallible light of faith that can truly be called a participation of divine truth.

Finally, as all the actions and words of God are imbued with truth itself, in like manner were the words and actions of God's Mother always truthful, that is, they were always conformable to the holiness, perfection and truth of the deeds and words of God. This was because they stemmed from a heart most holy, perfect, and truthful, and the Son of God Himself teaches us that man's heart is the principle of all his thoughts, words and actions, be they good or bad.[10]

All these considerations make us understand that the holy heart of Mary is a living portrait of the wisdom and veracity of God, given to us that we may invoke her guidance against the folly, deceit and falsehood of the flesh and of the world.

6 Apoc. 3, 7.
7 Ps. 5, 10.
8 *Serm. de Assumpt. B. Mariae.*
9 Ps. 95, 13.
10 Luke 6, 45.

Chapter Six

GOODNESS AND PROVIDENCE OF GOD
MIRRORED IN THE ADMIRABLE HEART OF MARY

Sacred theology distinguishes in God three kinds of goodness, which are fundamentally one and the same: natural goodness, moral goodness and goodness of benevolence or bounty, which is sometimes called benignity. Natural goodness is none other than the perfection and beauty of divine nature, containing the infinite excellences of the Godhead. Moral goodness comprises all the moral virtues that God possesses so eminently and in so high a degree that they are infinitely beyond what a created spirit can think or express.

The goodness of benevolence or bounty is God's infinite inclination to communicate Himself and it proceeds from His natural goodness. As a vessel brimming with a precious liquor tends to overflow, so a being filled with perfection has a natural inclination to communicate its fullness. God is an immense ocean, filled to overflowing with infinite good and divine perfections, and He possesses an unutterable and incomprehensible propensity to communicate them. This He does in two ways, with an outpouring of liberality worthy of His divine magnificence, within and outside Himself. Within Himself His perfections flow in a natural and necessary communication of the divine nature and all its inherent marvels from the Father of His beloved Son, and from both to the Holy Ghost. Outside Himself this benevolence is a free communication, whereby God confers, not indeed His nature and His essence, but His image, semblance, shadow, or mere reflection of His being on all creatures in the order of nature, of grace and of glory.

In the order of nature God communicates His being to all existing things, His life to all living things, whether their life be rational or merely sensitive and vegetative. His power is communicated to all things possessed of power, His wisdom to all intellectual beings, His goodness to all things good and kind. The beauty of God is transfused to things that are beautiful, His light to luminous bodies, His firmness and stability to things firm and stable, His immortality to immortal souls; God also imparts His happiness and felicity to such as possess not only being, but well being, which consists in a measure of natural enjoyment or satisfaction. God communicates Himself and His divine perfections in general to all things pertaining to the natural order, through His creation, preservation and government of all beings according to their nature.

In the order of grace almighty God communicates Himself much more abundantly to rational and intellectual creatures, through the adorable mystery of the Incarnation and all the other mysteries of His divine Son, Jesus Christ, Our Redeemer. Through the Sacraments He has instituted in His Church, especially the Holy Eucharist, and all the other spiritual channels, He pours grace into our souls, provided there be no obstacle on our part.

In the order of glory God communicates Himself most fully and perfectly to all the souls in heavenly bliss, clothing them in His radiant glory, surrounding them with His felicity, enrapturing them with His holy joys, and making them partakers of all the goodness He Himself possesses.

Finally, as the sun, to quote Saint Dionysius,[1] enlightens everything that can participate in its light, which is marvelously diffused, unfolding throughout the world the glittering of its rays, in the highest as well as in the humblest spheres, so that nothing visible can escape the sovereign grandeur of its brightness, so too does the divine essence extend its beauty to all beings, as their principle, preserver and end, as the universal cause, the common and infinite good, whence all things derive their being and well being, wherein they are established, enclosed and preserved.

The superlative Goodness communicates Its adorable perfections to the holy heart of Mary with much greater abundance and plenitude than to all other creatures put together. Next to the heart of God, there never was and never shall be a heart so good, liberal, benevolent, magnificent and so replete with kindness as the most Admirable Heart of Mary.

The heart of Mary is so full of goodness that Saint Bernard thus speaks of her, "Why does a human weakness fear to come unto Mary? Nothing in her is austere, nothing frightful, for she is filled with sweetness. Go over the Gospel story with the greatest attention; if you find therein the least mark of harshness or severity on Mary's part, the least sign of indignation, you may well fear to appear before her. But if, on the contrary, you find (as you surely will) her virginal heart full of love, piety, sweetness and goodness, then give thanks to Him who in His infinite mercy has provided such a mediatrix for us."[2]

"Her heart is so alive with pity that she never rejects any suppliant coming to her with humility and confidence," says Raymund Jourdain.[3]

1 *De divinis Nominib.* Cap. 4, sect. 4.
2 *Serm. de verbis Apoc. Signum Magnum.*

120

It is this loving confidence that we express as often as we recite that beautiful prayer, attributed by many annotators to Saint Bernard, and by others to Saint Augustine, "Remember, O most gracious Virgin Mary, that never was it known that anyone who fled to thy protection, implored thy help and sought thine intercession, was left unaided."[4]

Her heart is so filled with bounty that she readily grants whatever we ask of her. Saint Bernard says, "O Blessed Mary, whoever loves thee honors God; who serves thee pleases God; who invokes thy holy name with a pure heart, will infallibly receive the object of his petition."[5] "Who has ever invoked Mary without being heard?" says Pope Innocent III.[6] The venerable Abbot Blosius adds, "She rejects no one but lends a favorable ear to the petitions of all."[7] "Heaven and earth would sooner perish, than Mary refuse her help to such as invoke her seriously and with affection," reiterates Saint Bernard, adding, "Let him be silent in praise of thy mercy, O most Blessed Virgin, who having invoked thee in his necessities, should remember not having received thy help."[8]

Her heart is so good and merciful that she extends her kindness not only to the good but also to the wicked, no not only to the faithful but to sinners as well. "In this life, thou art a help to the just and unjust," says Raymund Jourdain. "Thou dost aid the just man and the sinner; the former by keeping him in the state of grace, wherefore the Church calls thee the Mother of Grace; the latter by bringing them back to divine mercy, for which thou art named the Mother of Mercy."[9]

Our Lady's heart is so kind and gentle that she helps not only those who implore her aid, but even the careless souls who neglect to invoke her. Listen again to Saint Bernard, "Why should we marvel to see her stretch a helping hand to such as beseech her, if she assist even them who do not pray to her?"[10]

The holy Abbot Blosius has written, "Mary spurns no one; to nobody does she refuse her aid. She comforts and relieves all who seek her assistance; she opens her bountiful heart to all who implore her intercession; she readily succors all who have recourse to her charity and, by an excess of goodness, she often shows her kindness to persons who do not think of her and have no devotion, gently and effectively drawing them to God

---

3   Raymund Jourdain was provost of Uzes in 1381 and later Abbot of Celles in the diocese of Bourges. This passage is taken from his *Contemplations on the Blessed Virgin*.
4   The *Memorare* is usually attributed to Saint Bernard.
5   Saint Bernard quoted by Pelberto, lib. 4, part 1, art. 2.
6   *Serm. de Assumpt.*
7   *In Speculo Spirit.* cap. 12.
8   *Serm. 4 de Assumpt.*
9   *Contempl. B.M.* Part 5. cont. 2.
10 *Serm. 4 de Assumpt.*

by means of the graces she obtains on their behalf. Thus did divine bounty constitute Our Lady as a supreme gift to mankind, that all might have recourse without fear and with complete confidence."[11]

Her heart is so merciful that she loves even those who hate her. Mary always renders good for evil because she willingly sacrificed her own beloved son to save the reprobates who crucified Him.

Other Fathers of the Church express the same thoughts and assure us that the almost boundless charity of the heart of Mary extends to all places, times and things in general, through a most abundant communication and eminent participation of God's infinite goodness and likewise of His divine providence.

As this adorable providence governs and regulates all things created, from the greatest to the least, both in general and in particular, so also does God's most powerful and merciful Mother, Queen of the Universe, bestow the affections and care of her royal heart on all things within her realm and subject to her rule. She leads all created things to the last end for which God made them, namely the glory of His divine majesty. But her special care is the guidance of rational beings, above all, of Christians, and most particularly of her own devout children, who strive faithfully to honor, serve and imitate her.

Her maternal heart protects and cherishes her devotees in a unique manner, having her eyes ever intently fixed upon them. She preserves and guards them as the apple of her eye and assumes the guidance and conduct of their entire life and actions. She leads them by the hand in all their ways, removing from their path the obstacles and hindrances which might make them stumble or retard their progress. She obtains the assistance and the means whereby they will receive strength and advance more rapidly. She bears their soul in her arms and on her virginal breast through the dangerous crises where their peril is greatest. She assists them most lovingly in the dark passage from this life into the next world, protecting them valiantly from the efforts and snares of the enemies of salvation. She receives their souls in her sweet and gentle hands at the moment of death and lovingly folds them in her most charitable heart. She finally bears them upward to Heaven with unutterable joy and presents them with all-surpassing kindness to her beloved son.

If such is the miraculous goodness of Mary to those who love and venerate her, how can there possibly be any Christians who hold back from devotion to the center and principle of her benignity, her Admirable Heart?

Praise, honour and glory be forever to the Most High, who has thus caused the heart of this incomparable Mother to reflect to mankind the perfect image of His goodness and all-merciful providence!

11 *In Paradiso animae*, cap. 18.

Part Five

FURTHER DIVINE PERFECTIONS
MIRRORED IN THE ADMIRABLE HEART OF MARY

Chapter One

MERCY OF GOD MIRRORED IN THE ADMIRABLE HEART OF MARY

Divine mercy is a perfection directed towards the miseries of creatures, tending to alleviate them and even to free them from created things when such a liberation enters into the designs of divine providence, which does all things with measure, number and weight.[1]

This adorable mercy extends, like goodness itself, to all God's works, "His tender mercies are over all His works."[2] God's mercy overshadows the works of nature, the works of grace and the works of glory.

Mercy supervises the works of nature, because God has created out of nothing all things contained in the natural order. It overshadows the works of grace, because man had fallen into the horrible abyss and divine mercy not only drew him from its depths but reestablished man in a state of grace so Godlike and noble that from being a member of Satan (as he was by his crime) he became a member of Jesus Christ.

God's mercy permeates the works of glory because God was not content simply to raise man to the supernatural and sublime state of Christian grace, making him thus partaker of the divine nature. The Creator further designed to withdraw man from the baseness, miseries, imperfections and perils which surround him here below, and to elevate him to Heaven, even to the throne of God, to grant participation in His everlasting glory and the enjoyment of His eternal happiness. God has willed to share all His possessions with man, His creature.

Among the effects of divine mercy we must enumerate three principal realities, which in turn embody numberless effects. The first is the Incarnation of the God-Man; the second, His Mystical Body, namely Holy Church; the third is the Mother of the God-Man, namely the most Blessed Virgin Mary. These constitute three admirable masterpieces of divine mercy.

1 Wis. 11, 21.
2 Ps. 144, 9.

In order to save us from the deepest possible abyss of misery and male-diction, and to raise us to the highest conceivable degree of happiness and grandeur, God willed that His divine Son should become man, mortal and capable of suffering like ourselves; that He should descend to earth, to abide and converse with us and teach us a heavenly and divine doctrine by His own sacred lips. God willed His Son to give us a most excellent and holy law and to teach us to observe it by His own divine example. God willed that His only begotten Son should suffer and perform great mira-cles for our sake while in this world; that He should die on the cross, be buried, rise again the third day and remain forty days longer on earth; that He should found a Church, establish therein a sublime priesthood, an admirable sacrifice and seven divine sacraments; that, having ascended into Heaven, He should send His Holy Spirit to govern His Church, to rule her in all things and to abide with her forever.

All this, namely the numerous episodes and mysteries of the God-Man, His thoughts concerning our salvation, the words He spoke in preparation for this great mission, the thanksgiving He offered, the sufferings He endured, every drop of blood He shed, the sacrifices He offered and continues to offer daily and hourly in His Church, all the Sacraments established by Him, all the enlighten-ment and sanctification that He accomplished in human souls, under the Old as well as under the New Law, by virtue of His mysteries, sac-rifices and sacraments, and whatever other graces communicated to men, all this, I repeat, emanated from the manifold operations of the divine attribute of mercy.

Beyond this, God not only willed to become man that men might become partakers of the divine nature, but He willed that His only Son should become the son of Man that men might become sons of God. God willed that His Son come into this world by being born of the seed of Adam and of a daughter of Adam that we might have the God-Man for our brother and the Mother of God for our mother. Thus we have the same father and the same mother as the Son of God Himself. We are His brothers, and as He is our mediator with His Father, so His heavenly Mother is a mediatrix between Himself and us.

In order to render His admirable Mother paramountly able to exer-cise her double office of Mother and mediatrix, so that she might pro-tect, favor and assist us with greater efficacy in all our needs, Divine mercy constituted her, first of all, most agreeable and holy. Secondly, mercy gave her dominion over everything in Heaven and on earth. Thirdly, it gave her the mildest, sweetest and most loving heart save that of the God-Man. To the heart of Mary God communicated in great abundance His merciful inclinations and established in it the throne and reign of His mercy more gloriously than in the heart of any other creature, save the sacred humanity of Christ.

Divine mercy reigns so perfectly in Mary's heart that she bears the name of Queen and Mother of Mercy. And this most loving Mary has so completely won the heart of God's mercy that He has given her the key to all His treasures and made her absolute mistress of them. St. Bernard says, "She is called the Queen of Mercy because she opens the abyss and treasure of divine mercy to whom she chooses, when she chooses and as she chooses."[3]

Divine mercy holds such complete sway over Mary's heart and fills it with so much compassion for sinners and for all persons in need that Saint Augustine addresses her thus, "Thou art the sinner's only hope,"[4] after God. "My dearest children," says Saint Bernard, "her heart is the ladder by which sinners go up to Heaven; this is my reliance, this the only reason of my hope."[5] Euthymius, one of the ancient Fathers who lived over seven centuries ago, adds, "O most merciful Virgin, deign to cast thy pitiful eyes on thy poor servants, for, after God, we have placed all our hope in thee who are our life, our glory, and, as it were, our substance and our being."[6]

Holy Church, animated and guided by the Spirit of God, exhorts us to salute and honor this prerogative of Mary in that admirable prayer, "Hail, holy Queen, Mother of Mercy, our life, our sweetness and our hope, all hail!" And the same divine Spirit puts into Mary's mouth the words which Holy Church repeats in her Office, "In me is all grace of the way and of the truth; in me is all hope of life and of virtue."[7] Saint John Damascene tells us that Our Lady is the only relief of the afflicted, the sovereign comforter of anguished hearts;[8] and Saint John Chrysostom declares her to be a boundless ocean of mercy.[9]

Would you know in what further manner divine mercy lives and reigns in the heart of the Mother of Mercy? Listen to Saint Bonaventure, "Great was Mary's mercy towards the wretched while she was living in exile here below; but immeasurably greater still now that she is happily reigning in Heaven. She manifests this greater mercy through innumerable benefits, now that she possesses a clearer insight into the numberless woes of mankind. She does not require past merits, but grants the petitions of all men, out of charity, and opens the bosom

3 Serm. 1 super Salve.
4 Serm. 18 de Sanctis.
5 Serm. de Aquaeductu.
6 In Adoratione venerandae Zonae Deip. cap. 8.
7 Ecclus. 24, 25.
8 Orat. 2 de dorm. Deip.
9 In Horto Ani.

of her clemency to everyone. She relieves every need and necessity with an incomparable affection and tenderness of heart."[10]

Her gentle heart is so filled with mercy that it overflows on all sides and spreads itself in Heaven, on earth and even in Hell. Let us again listen to Saint Bernard proclaiming this truth, "Who can comprehend, O Blessed Virgin, the length, the width, the height and the depth of thy mercy? Its length extends to the last day in the life of those who invoke thee; its width encompasses the whole world; its height reaches to Heaven, there to repair the losses of the heavenly Jerusalem; its depth has penetrated hell to obtain the deliverance of them that sit in the darkness and shadow of death."[11]

The virginal heart of the Mother of Grace is filled with such exceeding mercy that she exercises it not only in favor of sinners who wish to be converted, but also towards many persons who never think of their eternal salvation. She implores her Blessed son to inspire them, to excite in their hearts sentiments of fear of God and terror at the thought of His judgments. She asks Him to chastise them in divers ways, to raise in their midst persons leading holy and exemplary lives, whose example will draw them to Himself, and to use all other means of obtaining their conversion, or at least, if they will not mend their ways, to prevent them from multiplying their sins that their damnation may be less terrible.

But what is even more, the heart of Mary is so full of mercy that, using the extraordinary privileges God has granted to her alone, and out of her incomparable goodness, she often saves from eternal perdition souls who in the ordinary course of divine justice would have been cast into Hell. Such is the mind of that ancient and excellent author, Raymund Jourdain, who succeeded in hiding his name, but not the extent of his learning and holiness, "The Mother's mercy often saves many whom the justice of the Son would have otherwise condemned."[12]

Hence Saint Germanus, Patriarch of Constantinople, addresses these beautiful words to Mary, "O purest, best and most merciful Lady, help and relief of the faithful, powerful comforter of the afflicted and assured refuge of sinners, forsake us not, but keep us ever under thy protection. If thou forsake us, to whom shall we have recourse? What would become of us without thee, most holy Mother of God, who are the spirit and life of Christians. Even as respiration is an infallible sign of life in our bodies, so is thy holy name, when it is constantly on the lips of thy servants, on all occasions, at every time and in all places, not only a sign, but a veritable cause of life, happiness and protection."[13]

10 *In Spec. B.V.* lect. 10.
11 *Serm. 4 de Assumpt. B.V.*
12 *Contempl. B.V.* in Prologo.
13 *Orat. in ador. venerandae Zonae B.V.*

Chapter Two

MEEKNESS, PATIENCE AND CLEMENCY OF GOD MIRRORED IN THE ADMIRABLE HEART OF MARY

God's meekness, patience and clemency are three divine perfections which are joined with mercy to form one and the same perfection, although their effects are different.

Mercy regards the misery of creatures in general, to relieve and to deliver them from its fetters. The first and greatest of miseries, the source of all wretchedness, is sin. When man is so unhappy as to offend God mortally, he at once becomes the object of God's wrath which would crush him the very instant he consents to sin, as he infinitely deserves to be. But divine meekness prevents the destruction and arrests the torrent of God's just anger, ready to pour upon the sinner. If man perseveres in his crime, he deserves to be cast upon divine vengeance, but divine patience interposes and persuades God to suffer the sinner and await his repentance with admirable goodness.

These are the effects of divine meekness and patience. God's clemency is manifested by remitting entirely or in part the punishment due to sin.

Whoever is in mortal sin deserves the eternal punishment of Hell, but divine clemency often sends temporal affliction to those who are in that miserable state, to oblige them to struggle out of it and thus become delivered from eternal suffering. If they will be converted at the very instant they feel sentiments of true remorse, divine mercy effaces the guilt of sin from their souls.

Although the actual guilt is thus effaced, it remains true that divine justice still pursues the sinner to exact the penalty his offences have deserved, but divine clemency commutes first of all the eternal penalty into a temporal punishment.

Furthermore, God's marvelous clemency seeks to deliver the sinner from even this temporal punishment, or at least to diminish it, and sends further afflictions, by means of which sinful man may satisfy divine justice.

This sweetest clemency offers him still other means of paying his debt to the justice of God, for example, jubilees and indulgences. It induces the repentant sinner to assist with devotion at the Holy Sacrifice of the Mass, the supreme means of satisfying all our obligations to God, and at the same time it urges him to receive the Blessed Eucharist frequently with holy dispositions and to perform various other good works.

If the sinner dies before he has rendered full satisfaction, his imperfectly purified soul is sent to Purgatory to complete its purification, which is yet another effect of divine mercy.

If it is true that the sufferings of Purgatory are greater than we can describe or imagine, divine clemency has nevertheless found several means of mitigating and shortening them. It hastens the deliverance of suffering souls by the application of indulgences, and by the prayers, fasts, alms and sacrifices of the faithful on earth, as well as the suffrages of the saints in Heaven.

These are some of the effects of the meekness, patience and clemency of God.

Now these three divine perfections live and reign in the heart of the Mother of Mercy, communicating their own divine inclinations most excellently. After the heart of God Himself there never was and never shall be a heart so full of meekness, patience and clemency as the noble heart of Mary.

While she dwelt on earth she beheld the world filled with idols and idolators. With the exception of a very small number, men generally were armed against God, trying, if possible, to dethrone Him, to put Him under their feet and annihilate Him. They would set His enemy in His place and sought to procure for the usurper the adoration and honor which belong to God alone. As the most Blessed Virgin Mary loved God with a love so great that we cannot describe it, she experienced an indescribably great sorrow at the sight of the crimes committed against His divine majesty.

But who can appreciate her greater grief over the atrocious torments inflicted on her beloved son by the perfidy of the chosen people? She knew Him to be Innocence and Sanctity incarnate; yet she saw Him persecuted and tormented as though He were the greatest of criminals.

She watched Him bound and tethered like a thief, dragged through the streets of Jerusalem like a scoundrel, beaten, bruised, mocked, spit upon, clothed in the white garment of a fool, given up to the mockery, insults and outrages of a band of insolent soldiers, reviled, spurned in favor of Barabbas, scourged and torn with whips from head to foot, crowned with thorns, exposed to the gaze of an enraged crowd crying, "Away with him; away with him: crucify him."[1] She saw her dear son condemned to a cruel death, carrying the heavy

Cross to be the instrument of His torture, stripped, nailed and fastened to the Cross with great nails that pierced His gentle hands and feet. She watched His adorable lips, in the torment of thirst, given gall and vinegar to drink, His sacred ears filled with curses and blasphemies, all the members of His body dislocated so that one could count His very bones, "They have numbered all my bones."[2] She beheld the body of the God-Man, her son, covered with wounds, experiencing inconceivable pain, His blessed soul lacerated with anguish and torment. Finally, she watched Him die the cruelest and most shameful death that ever happened.

Now what did she do, the Mother of Sorrows, as she beheld her treasure, her most innocent Lamb torn, flayed and slain? She loved Him with a peerless love. Did she cry out against His pitiless murderers? Did she lament of the wrong and injustice wreaked upon Him? Did she implore the eternal Father's justice? No. She remained silent; not a word was heard from her lips; only her stifled sighs, her tears alone were seen. Her most gentle heart fought against the entry of any sense of injury or movement of impatience, or aversion or bitterness towards her cruel tormentors. Her heart abounded with meekness, patience and clemency, so that she imitated her son, Jesus, and sought to excuse the men who with such distorted rage were killing Him, repeating in her heart the words He uttered with His lips, "Father, forgive them, for they know not what they do."[3] She offered for their salvation the very blood they shed, the sufferings they inflicted upon Him, the cruel death they perpetrated. She was prepared, if necessary, to sacrifice herself together with her son, to obtain mercy for those wicked men.

Nor is that all. The glorious Virgin now reigning in Heaven can see much more clearly the numberless multitude and frightful enormity of the sins committed against God. She sees this earth of ours which should be a paradise since the God of Heaven honored it with His presence and made it His dwelling place; yet it is filled with sinners and enemies of God, who blaspheme and dishonor Him without ceasing, even more than the devils and the damned in Hell. For the devils, being deprived of liberty, cannot add to their sins, whereas living sinners heap crime on crime, impiety on impiety, murder upon murder, abomination upon abomination, "Blood hath touched blood."[4]

Our Lady knows that her son, the Son of God, came into the world to save all men; that salvation cost Him infinite labor, ignominies, tears

1 John 19, 15.
2 Ps. 21, 18.
3 Luke 23, 34.
4 Osee 4, 2.

and blood to deliver mankind from the bondage of the devil and hell and reconcile them to His Father. And yet she sees men turning their back on God, denying and forsaking Him, to side with Satan and cast themselves headlong into Hell. She sees innumerable atheists and blasphemers making every effort to exterminate the Holy Church founded by her Jesus Christ through the shedding of the last drop of His Blood, and to render His sacred name despicable, abominable and odious to the entire world, "They have set me an abomination to themselves."[5]

Our heavenly Mother perceives all these crimes and all the wickedness most clearly, and her inconceivably great love for God and for her son is wounded beyond anything we can imagine, even though she is glorious and incapable of suffering. She is Queen of Heaven and earth and God has given her sovereign power over all created things; therefore she would not lack the power, if such were her will, to avenge most justly the many atrocious insults offered by men to their God and Saviour. But far from doing this, she permits herself to be induced by her very patient and gentle heart to use the power of her merits and intercession in order to halt the just fury of divine vengeance and to arrest the torrent of God's wrath ready to burst on the hapless heads of sinners. She obtains from His divine majesty that He punish them not as enemies but as children, not like a severe judge but as a merciful father, not to exterminate them but to correct and convert them.

True the Blessed Virgin Mary does not entertain the same sentiments for all sinners, nor does she treat them all alike. She distinguishes between those in Hell, whom she knows to be irreconcilable enemies of God, and those on earth, whom she considers still capable of being reconciled to His divine majesty. Hence her heart is filled with very great and just indignation towards the wretched creatures in Hell, for she is most perfectly united to God, and therefore shares in all His adorable inclinations. She loves what God loves and hates what He hates, approves what He approves, and condemns what He condemns. As the damned will forever be the object of God's wrath, "They shall be called the people with whom the Lord is angry forever,"[6] so shall they forever be the object of the anger of God's Mother. Her love and charity for God and the friends of God are greater than the ardor of all angels and saints together; so also is her hatred of God's irreconcilable enemies greater than that of all the denizens of Heaven.

But towards sinners who are still in this world, which is a place of mercy where our all-bountiful Mother has established the throne and

5 Ps. 87, 9.
6 Mal. 1, 4.

empire of her mercy and clemency, her heart is so filled with sweetness and benignity that the venerable and holy Abbot Blosius declares, "The world does not hold any sinner so detestable that this pious Virgin should not be disposed to open to him the arms of her clemency and her most merciful heart. Provided he seek her assistance, she will always have the power and the will to reconcile him to her son."[7] Blosius says further, "As long as the time of grace endures, this merciful Mother cannot avert her eyes from miserable sinners who invoke her with a sincere desire of conversion. With the heart of a Mother and a sister, she continually offers up her prayers to God on behalf of men and takes special care of their salvation. No one who shall invoke this Mother of grace with devotion and perserverance can possibly perish forever."[8]

O sweetest and most holy Virgin, look down with the eyes of thy mercy on all the afflictions and all the afflicted that fill the earth. Behold the many poor people, the many widows and orphans, the sick troubled with so many diseases, the captives and prisoners, the thousands who are cursed and persecuted by the malice of men, the defenceless persons oppressed by the strong and the mighty, the seafarers and pilgrims struggling against perils on sea and land, the missionaries exposed to countless dangers in their task of saving endangered souls. Look down upon the number of afflicted minds, of anguished hearts, of souls tormented by manifold temptations, and of souls suffering the frightful penalties of Purgatory. But above all, have pity on the countless souls that are in the state of sin and perdition and are groaning under the tyranny and the bondage of hell.

Finally, O gentlest of Virgins, take pity on the great number of wretches who people the universe, whose innumerable miseries are so many voices crying to thee: O Mother of Mercy, comforter of the afflicted, refuge of sinners, open the eyes of thy clemency to see our desolation, the ears of thy bounty to hear our supplications. "To thee do we cry, poor banished children of Eve; to thee do we send up our sighs, mourning and weeping in this vale of tears." Yes, Eve's miserable children, banished from the house of their heavenly Father, groaning and weeping in this valley of tears, have recourse to thine incomparable benignity. Hear our sighs and our cries; behold our weeping and our tears. "Turn then, O gracious Advocate, thine eyes of mercy towards us, and after this our exile show unto us the blessed fruit of thy womb, Jesus."

7 In Sacell. anim. cap. 51.
8 Blosius, loc. cit.

Chapter Three

JUSTICE OF GOD MIRRORED IN THE
ADMIRABLE HEART OF MARY

Mercy and justice resemble two sisters, inseparable and holding each other by the hand. Wherever mercy is, there also is justice; where justice goes, mercy follows. Hence King David sang to God, "Mercy and judgment I will sing to thee, O Lord."[1] He mentions them together and does not separate these qualities.

We have studied how divine mercy reigns and triumphs in the gentle heart of Mary; we shall now contemplate divine justice establishing therein the throne of its glory. "In this perfect heart," says Richard of Saint Lawrence, "mercy and justice gave each other the kiss of peace."[2]

In God there are two kinds of justice: the first is distributive; the second, vindictive justice.

"Distributive justice," says Saint Dionysius, "gives to each one what belongs to him, according to his rank and merit. It allots and dispenses to each thing the proportion, beauty, arrangement, good order and all other things proper to it within the bounds and limits that are just and equitable."[3]

The chief characteristic of vindictive justice is infinite hatred of sin and a desire to destroy it in the souls of men, thereby delivering them from its cruel tyranny.

Now these two types of justice have ever held sovereign sway in the most just heart of the Blessed Virgin Mary. In the first place, she always rendered to God and to all God's creatures, in a most faithful and perfect manner, what she owed to them. To God, she accorded adoration, fear, dependence, gratitude, honor, glory, praise, love and the sacrifice of all she possessed and of her very self. She observed all the Mosaic laws very devotedly and with exact obedience. She exercised respect, veneration and humility towards her parents, Saint

---

1 Ps. 100, 1.
2 *De divin. Nomin.* Cap. 8, § 7.
3 *De laudib. B.M.*, lib. 2, part 2.

Joachim and Saint Anne, towards the persons who had charge of her while she dwelt in the Temple of Jerusalem, and towards Saint Joseph, her most worthy spouse. She punctually obeyed even the edicts of Emperor Augustus, though he was a pagan idolator. She held her own self in very low esteem and in great contempt, knowing she was a creature drawn from nothing and a daughter of Adam, who would have come under the curse common to all his children, if God had not preserved her from it. In a word, she faithfully practiced the words of the Holy Ghost even before they were spoken by Saint Paul, "Render therefore to all men their dues. Tribute, to whom tribute is due; custom, to whom custom: fear, to whom fear: honor, to whom honor. Owe no man anything, but to love one another."[4] This last is a debt which no one can ever finish paying.

In the second place, divine justice had so completely filled her heart with such an unfathomable hatred for sin that this holy Virgin was always ready to undergo the sufferings of as many Hells as God's omnipotence could create rather than commit the least venial sin.

What is still more admirable, however, is that, having the same heart and mind as the eternal Father, according to the inspired words, "He who is joined to the Lord, is one spirit,"[5] Our Lady united her will to His concerning the passion of her son and gave her consent to the painful death of her dearly beloved so that He might destroy sin. This sacrifice demonstrates a hatred of sin greater than suffering the torments of all imaginable Hells to cooperate in its destruction; for it cannot be doubted that if Our Lady had given her choice, she would have preferred all such sufferings for herself rather than see the treatment inflicted on her beloved son at the time of His cruel and ignominious passion.

If the holy heart of Mary is filled with such terrible hatred of sin that she consented to the cruel death of her beloved son, because she saw Him loaded with the sins of men; if she readily sacrificed Him to divine justice in order to crush the mortal enemy of God and men, who can doubt that she still hates the infernal monster wherever she finds it? She hates sin to the point of sometimes uniting herself to divine vengeance in order to destroy it in souls, especially in those souls who are their own enemies to the extent of supporting evil and opposing its destruction. They force their sweet Mother, as it were, to relinquish the tenderness of her maternal love and to participate in the severity of divine justice in order to punish the obduracy of a rebellious soul hardened in malice.

O most holy Virgin, since thou hast but one heart and one spirit

4 Rom. 13, 7–8.
5 1 Cor. 6, 17.

with thy divine son and since thou hast no other sentiments save His, thou dost love what He loves and thou dost hate what He hates. Hence, as Christ has an infinite hatred for sin, thou also dost hate it beyond all thought and words. Thy hatred for the infernal monster is equal to the love thou hast for God.

O Blessed Mother, thy love of thy heart for God is infinitely greater than that of all the hearts of the angels and saints. Consequently, there is in thy heart more hatred against God's enemy, sin, than in the hearts of all Heaven's citizens. Make us sharers, O Mary, in this love and hatred so that we may love our Creator and Saviour as thou hast loved Him, and that we may hate sin as thou hast hated it.

Chapter Four

ZEAL OF GOD MIRRORED IN THE
ADMIRABLE HEART OF MARY

Everything in nature, grace and glory, all the effects of power, wisdom, goodness, mercy and justice of God, all the mysteries, actions and sufferings of the God-Man, all the sacrifices, sacraments and functions of God's Church, in a word, all things in Heaven, on earth and even in Hell, are like so many voices proclaiming God's ardent zeal for His own glory and for the salvation of souls.

In the first place, God does everything for Himself and for the glory of His divine majesty, "The Lord hath made all things for himself."[1] Being the first principle and the last end of all things, it were impossible for Him to act otherwise. This zeal for His own glory fills Him with an infinite hatred of everything that is contrary to it, that is, every kind of sin, especially vanity, presumption and pride. Whereas the humble render honor and glory to God in all things, the proud are like thieves who would take for themselves the honor and glory which belong to God alone. This same zeal for His honor leads God to derive His glory from all created things, even from the greatest evils. He would never permit such evils to exist if He did not have the power to turn them to His greater glory. As Saint Augustine expresses it, "He has deemed it preferable to derive good from evil, than to prevent evil altogether."[2] Finally, the zeal of the Son of God for His Father's honor induced Him to assume human nature, to be born in a stable, to live thirty-four years on earth amidst tribulations and sufferings, and to die on the Cross, that He might atone for the insults offered by sinners to God the Father and to glorify Him in a manner worthy of His infinite majesty.

In the second place, God's ineffable goodness and immense love for all the souls created to His image and likeness enkindles in His heart a most ardent zeal for their salvation. It is this zeal that induces Him to avail Himself, in order to save souls, of His divine essence, His power,

---

1 Prov. 16, 4.
2 *In Enchiridio*, cap. 26 and 27.

wisdom, goodness, love, charity, mercy, justice and all His other perfections. The three Divine Persons, their thoughts, words and actions, the
life, passion, precious blood and death of the Son of God, the angels,
the saints, the entire Church with the sacraments she administers, all
God's works, all He is, everything He has, everything is employed to
procure the salvation of souls.

Now this divine zeal likewise inflames the virginal heart of the
Mother of God in a wonderful manner. The holy heart of Mary was
ever on fire with such zeal for the glory of God and the salvation of
souls that she never allowed anything contrary to the honor of the
divine majesty to come near her. Not only were her actions performed
with sovereign perfection for God's glory alone, not only did she
employ all the powers of her soul and body to serve and honor Him, but
she was ever ready to sacrifice to this end her life and her very being,
and to suffer all conceivable torments.

What is more, she sacrificed her well beloved son. Why did she
offer Him up to God? For His glory and the salvation of souls. She
immolated Christ Her son to destroy everything contrary to the honor
of the divine majesty and the eternal salvation of men, to render to
God a glory worthy of His infinite grandeur, to repair the offence given
to God by the sins of the children of Adam, to deliver all souls from the
tyranny of hell and to enable them to glorify God eternally in Heaven.

Saint John Chrysostom, Theophilactus, Oecumenius, Saint
Bernard and Rupert comment on these words of Moses in the thirty-
second chapter of Exodus, "Either forgive them this trespass or strike
me out of the book of life," by explaining that this holy prophet, Moses,
inflamed with zeal for the salvation of his brethren, asked God to
deprive him of eternal felicity and to impose this penalty on him forever that the people might be delivered from damnation.[3]

Explaining the words of Saint Paul, "I wished myself to be anathema from Christ, for my brethren,"[4] Saint John Chrysostom and many
other holy doctors say also that we must understand this text to refer to
the eternal torments, but separated from sin. In other words, the zeal of

3   Saint John Eudes is here the echo of Cornelius a Lapidé who, in his commentary on Chapter 32
    of Exodus, 31, 32, after having quoted Rupert's commentary on this passage, adds, "Therefore
    Chrysostom commenting on Rom. 9, teaches that Moses and Paul, going beyond the Heavens
    and the very angels, despised all invisible things, and, out of love for God not only requested, but
    really and seriously desired to be deprived of the enjoyment of God and ineffable glory." *Unde S.
    Chrysost, in c. (ad Rom. Docet Moysen et Paulum . . . caelos et Angelos supergredientes, omnia invisi-
    bilia sprevisse, ac pro Dei amore ab ipsa Dei fruitione, beatitudine et ineffabili gloria excidere non tan-
    tum petisse, sed revera et serio optasse.* Thus Saint Chrysostom, Theophil., Oecumen, on chapter 9
    of the epistle to the Romans; Cassian, *Collot.* 32, chapter 6; Bernard, *Serm, 12 in Cant.* These are
    precisely the references given here by Saint John Eudes.
4 Rom. 9, 3.

the holy Apostle for the salvation of his brethren was so ardent that he desired for their sake to suffer the eternal punishment of Hell, provided there was no sin on his part. "He wishes to be lost forever," says Chrysostom, "that many, nay all, may love and praise Christ." "He desires to suffer eternal torments," says Cassian. "Because we are so far removed from such charity," adds Chrysostom, "we cannot understand these words." "We should not marvel," observes Origen, "to see the servant desiring to be anathema for his brethren, since the Master deigned to become malediction for his servants, 'being made a curse for us.'"[5]

Cornelius a Lapidé, in his commentaries on this thirty-second chapter of Exodus, relates that Blessed Jacopone, of the Order of Saint Francis, possessed the most ardent desire of suffering in this world all imaginable sorrows, afflictions, pains and hardships, and after this life he would fain have been thrown into Hell to suffer eternal torments out of love of Our Lord and in satisfaction for his own sins and to atone, if possible, for the sins of all mankind, including the damned and the demons.[6]

We read in the tenth chapter of the life of Saint Mary Magdalen de Pazzi, a Carmelite nun, that God showed her a place (which she calls the Lion's Lake) where she saw a numberless multitude of demons having a most frightful appearance. She was told that she was to enter the lake and remain there five years, suffering atrocious pains, in order to help in the salvation of many souls. She readily consented, and actually entered this Lion's Lake, which was a veritable Hell. There the malice and rage of the demons inflicted the greatest torments on her, both interiorly and exteriorly, during the space of five years.

These prayers, desires and sufferings of Moses, Saint Paul, Blessed Jacopone and Saint Mary Magdalen de Pazzi are irrefutable proofs of a great love for God and a supernal charity towards men. But what is this compared to the peerless zeal of the most charitable heart of the Mother of God? It is but a spark compared to a burning furnace. Divine zeal is only the ardor of divine love, or divine love in its greatest ardor; therefore it follows that the measure of this holy love is likewise the measure of the zeal, and that a heart is filled with zeal in proportion to its love of God. Now it is certain that the heart of Mary, the Mother of God, was always filled with greater love of God and men than the hearts of all the prophets, patriarchs, apostles, martyrs and other saints whence it follows that her heart was inflamed with a zeal for the glory of God and the salvation of souls far greater than the hearts of all the saints put together.

5 Gal. 3, 13. Saint John Eudes is still echoing Cornelius a Lapidé.
6 Corn. a Lap. *loc. cit.*

Our Lady can well say with the prophet David and several other saints, but more truly and perfectly than any of them, "My zeal hath made me pine away; because my enemies forgot thy words. My eyes have sent forth springs of water: because they have not kept thy law."[7] "The zeal of thy house hath eaten me up,"[8] that is, zeal for the salvation of souls, created by God for His eternal indwelling.

So it is that the Mother of Fair Love accomplished more for the salvation of souls and the glory of God by sacrificing her beloved son to His heavenly Father when she stood at the foot of the cross, than was done or could have been done by all the saints together, even if each had suffered all the torments of Hell for that end.

We can now judge of our obligation to honor the maternal heart of our Mother most admirable so filled with affection and zeal for our interests. But do not say that we have a true devotion to this heavenly Virgin, if our hearts do not share the holy inclination of her heart, if we do not love what she loves and hate what she hates. Our Lady's love is the greatest for all things that contribute to the honor of God and the salvation of souls, and her hatred deepest for everything opposed to God.

Let us enter into these sentiments and employ our mind, heart, thoughts, affections, words, actions to glorify the divine majesty in every way, and to procure the salvation of souls, above all, our own. Consider that salvation as the great and only business of God, of the God-Man, of the Mother of God, of all the angels, of all the saints and of the entire Church.

7 Ps. 118, 139 and 136.
8 Ps. 68, 10.

Chapter Five

Divine Sovereignty Mirrored in the Admirable Heart of Mary

Among the several names given to God in Sacred Scripture, none occurs more frequently than that of *Lord*. It is the name His divine majesty constantly assumes when speaking to men. "I am the Lord."[1] He wishes to impress upon our minds and in our hearts a most high esteem, a profound respect and a complete submission towards the supreme authority of His adorable Sovereignty.

What then is this divine Sovereignty? It is a perfection that gives God absolute and infinite power over all the works of His hands. He can give life or death when He pleases, in the place and manner He chooses; He can hurl us into the abyss of nothingness, or withdraw us therefrom. He can throw us into Hell and deliver us from it. "The Lord killeth and maketh alive, he bringeth down to Hell and bringeth back again."[2] In a word, God can dispose of all His creatures, from the least to the greatest, as He pleases, and no one may ask Him, "Why dost Thou act thus?"

Having chosen to make the Queen of Angels and men the most noble image and the most perfect picture of His divine attributes, God likewise chose to communicate to her His adorable Sovereignty in a very sublime degree.

God is called *Lord*, and He wishes Mary to be called *Lady*. He is universal Lord of all things, and He wills her to be sovereign Lady of the universe. He is "King of kings and Lord of lords,"[3] and she is the queen of queens and sovereign of sovereigns. He has absolute power to do whatever He wishes; and having given Mary a Mother's authority over His Son, who is God Himself, He has consequently given her marvelous power over everything that is subject to her son. In other words, God possesses the dominion of a God over all things created by Him,

1 Exod. 29, 46; Lev. 19, 32.
2 1 Kings 2, 6.
3 Apoc. 19, 16.

and can dispose of them as He pleases. Mary, on the other hand, has the power of the Mother of God over all things that depend on her son and she can do with them what she chooses.

I hear Jesus Christ, the son of Mary, saying, "All power is given to me in Heaven and in earth,"[4] and I hear Mary, the Mother of God, exclaiming, "My power is in Jerusalem."[5] God has given me power over the great city of Jerusalem, its suburbs, villages and dependencies, that is, over the entire Church, Triumphant, Militant and Suffering, as well as over all the other parts of the world, which are, as it were, the suburbs, villages and appurtenances of this marvelous city. "In every people and in every nation I have had the chief rule."[6]

But let us listen to the voice of the holy Fathers, or rather to the Holy Ghost speaking through their lips. "When Mary became the Mother of the Creator, she was established sovereign Lady over every creature," says Saint John Damascene.[7] And he adds, "The son of Mary put all things under the sway of His Blessed Mother."[8] "O most Holy Virgin," exclaims Saint Anselm, "God Almighty has wished to make all things possible to thee, as they are to Himself!"[9] "Having made her the Mother of His Son," says the commentator Eusebius Emissenus, "God raised her to the dignity of Queen of Angels and men, and gave her sovereign authority, after Himself, in Heaven and on earth."[10] "Nothing is capable of resisting thy power," observes Saint Gregory, Archbishop of Nicomedia, "nothing can withstand thee. All things comply with thy commands, all things obey thy sway; thy sovereignty is over everything."[11] "God has given her absolute power in Heaven and on earth," remarks Saint Bernard. "He has placed our life and our death in her hands."[12]

Other writers assure us that the power of the Blessed Virgin Mary has no limits when she wishes to help those who invoke her with good dispositions. "Her help is omnipotent."[13] Her intercession with her son possesses never failing virtue. Saint Peter Damian says that when she appears before the dread tribunal of the divine majesty, her son does not regard her as His servant, but as His Mother, having all power over Him. He therefore receives her prayers, not as petitions, but as commands.

4 Matt. 28, 18.
5 Ecclus. 24, 15.
6 Ibid. 24, 9–10.
7 Maria rerum omnium conditarum Domina effecta est, cum Creatoris Mater extitit, et super omnes creaturas primatum tenuit. De fide orthod. lib. 4, cap. 115.
8 Orat. 2 de Assumpt.
9 De excel. Virg. cap. 12.
10 Homil. in fer. 5, 4 Temp. Advent.
11 Orat. de Oblat, B.V. in templo.
12 Serm. 1 in Salve.
13 Cosmae Hierosolymit. Hymn. 6.

"For how would it be possible, O Blessed Virgin," adds the Saint, "that He whom thou didst bring forth, even though He is almighty, should resist the maternal authority He has given thee over Him?"[14]

Another Father of the Church[15] says, "The son of Mary is pleased exceedingly to have His Mother ask for anything on our behalf, for He desires to give her whatever He vouchsafes to grant us through her intercession. He is most happy to be able thus to show her some gratitude for all He has received from her in His Incarnation." Saint Bonaventure tells us that the very name of Mary is, after God, all-powerful.[16]

We should not marvel at this. The Archangel Gabriel said to her, "The Lord is with thee,"[17] and Mary contracted a new alliance with the Son of God, who thus became her own. Their union is so intimate that they have but one flesh, one mind and one will. "One is the flesh of Mary and of Christ, one their mind, their will and their energy." Mary's son is the sovereign Lord of Heaven and earth; the Mother of Jesus Christ is the absolute mistress of earth and Heaven, and her sway is over all things. "Christ is the Lord, Mary the Lady; she has been placed over every creature." "Whoever prostrates himself before the Son to adore Him, bends the knee to honor the Mother and implore her help." Thus speaks the learned and devout Arnold of Chartres, who lived in Saint Bernard's time, being his disciple and friend.[18]

Let us listen again to Saint Peter Damian, "He who governs all things with sovereign authority subjected Himself to His Mother. A simple maid can give orders to Him whom all things obey."[19]

"All things," says Saint Bernardine of Siena, "are subject to the divine power, even the Virgin Mother. All things and God Himself are subject to Mary."[20] For it is written that her son obeyed her, "And he was subject to them."[21]

"Behold two great prodigies," writes Saint Bernard, "which must fill Heaven and earth with admiration. It is a marvelous thing to witness God's supreme majesty lowered and humbled to the point of obeying a woman; there is no other example of such a prodigy of humility. And it is most admirable to behold a woman raised to such greatness that she is endowed with the right to command God Himself; so marvelous a dignity knows no peer."[22]

14 *Serm. de Nativ. Mariae.*
15 Theoph.
16 *In Cantico 4.*
17 Luke 1, 28.
18 *Tract. de laud. B. Virg.*
19 *Homil. 46, de laud. B.V.*
20 *Serm. 61 art. 4, cap. 36.*
21 Luke 2, 51.
22 *Serm. 1 sup. Missus.*

"Every creature" says Saint Peter Damian, "should remain profoundly and respectfully silent, trembling at the sight of so wonderful an object, and not daring to look up to the sublime height and immensity of such great dignity and so exalted a power."[23]

By all these pronouncements see that we have a Queen and a Mother who, after God, is all-powerful in her person, in her name and in her prayers. She holds sovereign sway over every creature, and wields a marvelous power over the Creator Himself.

Thus does the Sovereign Lord of all things communicate His adorable Sovereignty to the great Queen of the Universe, and consequently to her royal heart. For if she be Queen, her heart is King; if she be Sovereign, her heart is Sovereign like unto herself; if she have all power in Heaven and on earth, so does her Immaculate Heart.

O Admirable Heart of my Queen, what honor is due to the eminence of the exalted dignity! What praise thy profound humility commands, when it caused God to exalt thee so high! Thou didst humble thyself beneath all things, and God not only raised thee above every creature, but conferred on thee a marvelous power over Himself. May He be blessed forever!

O most amiable heart of my Mother Mary, I am filled with joy, and I give thanks to God for having so abundantly communicated His divine Sovereignty to thee and having made of thee the sovereign of all hearts. But I feel unutterable sorrow in seeing that the hearts of the children of Adam usually prefer to be subject to Satan's horrible tyranny rather than to allow thee to reign over them. Whence comes this calamity? From sin, its cause. The enormous ingratitude and abominable wickedness of the human heart proclaim by their countless crimes that they refuse to be governed by thee, O detestable sin, how frightful must thy malice be, if thou canst withstand the omnipotent heart of the world's sovereign Lady!

Mother of Mercy, take pity on such great misery. Thou seest, alas, that the earth is crowded with miserable hearts enslaved by Satan, hearts that do not feel the extreme misfortune in which they are plunged! Mother of Grace, I offer thee all these slaves of hell; by thy most compassionate heart, I beg thee to take pity on them. Break their chains asunder; implore thy beloved son, Who came into the world to enlighten all men, that He deign to give sight to the blind, and to remove from the sinners their hearts of stone, replacing them with hearts obedient to the inspirations of the Holy Ghost.

Mother of Fair Love, I also offer thee the hearts of those of thy children who are faithful, who love and honor thee as their cherished

23 *Serm. 2 de Nativ.*

Mother. Preserve and increase the precious treasure which is theirs, that they may love thee more and more, and become more worthy to be the true children of thy heart.

Queen of my heart, suffer me to offer my own miserable heart to thee. I beseech thee, by the ineffable goodness of thy Admirable Heart to employ the entire strength of the power God has given to thee, to crush and destroy in my heart at any and every cost all that displeases thy divine son. Establish in me the sovereign empire of His heart and thy own. May these two hearts, which are one and the same, reign within me unceasingly, sovereignly and forever, for the greater honor and glory of the most Blessed Trinity.

Chapter Six

PEACE OF GOD MIRRORED
IN THE ADMIRABLE HEART OF MARY

The peace of God is another divine perfection completely realizing its faithful image in the Admirable Heart of the most holy Mother of God. But before studying the reflection, let us gaze at the original and consider this adorable perfection of the peace of God Himself.

What is the peace of God? It is a divine perfection consisting, according to Saint Dionysius, in the ineffable union of God with Himself.[1]

God is unutterably united with Himself, first of all, by His incomprehensible love for His divine self. Secondly, by His infinite sanctity, which raises Him immeasurably above anything that could affect His peace, if this could ever be affected. Thirdly, by His admirable simplicity, which renders all His perfections one single united perfection, which is the equivalent of the divine essence itself.

Fourthly, the infinite peace of God is maintained by the union which reigns between the eternal Persons, who share one spirit, one heart, one will, one purpose, one power, one wisdom, one goodness, and the same essence. This essence is eternal, impassible, invariable; hence nothing that happens in Heaven, earth or Hell can ever trouble its peace. God's peace is God Himself, who is ever tranquil and unutterable. He is the first and sovereign principle of peace and entertains an unspeakable horror of discord and division. He sent His only Son, the Prince of Peace, into the world to extinguish all our enmities with His Precious Blood, "killing the enmities in himself,"[2] to reconcile us to His heavenly Father, as well as to our brethren and to ourselves, and to be Himself our peace, "For He is our peace."[3] Our Saviour accomplished this by destroying sin, the only source of division, and pacifying all

---

1 *De ipsa divina pace . . . quomodo Deus quiescat in se et intra se sit, et totus secum sic supra quam unitas . . . neque dicere, neque cogitare ulli eorum qui sunt fas est, neque possibile. De divin. Nominibus.* Cap. 11, 1.

2 Eph. 2, 16.

3 *Ibid.* 14.

creatures in Heaven and on earth, "He made peace through the blood of his cross, both as to the things that are on earth, and the things that are in Heaven."[4] Such is the peace of God which Saint Justus called the silence of God.[5]

Now this adorable peace of God has impressed an excellent image of itself on the heart of the Mother of Peace. In the first place, sin, the sole enemy of peace and the only cause of discord, never possessed the slightest power over the most holy heart of Mary.

Secondly, divine grace, which always reigned within her heart, kept the passions, senses, and all other faculties of the body and soul of the Mother of Grace under the rule of reason and the laws of God's spirit.

Thirdly, the most profound humility of Mary's heart endowed her with a passionate love of suffering and humiliation and enabled her to endure them in peacefulness.

Fourthly, the extraordinary love of her Admirable Heart for holy poverty induced her to bear with equanimity the sorrows and discomforts which invariably accompany it.

In the fifth place, her ardent love of the Cross made her find refreshment even in trials and tribulations. In the sixth place, the invincible patience which strengthened her in the troubles, tempests and changes of our miserable earthly life, gave her complete possession of the most profound peace.

In the seventh place, the inconceivable charity towards mankind, which filled her gentle heart, allowed no sentiment of aversion of enmity to sway her, even towards those who betrayed, sold and crucified her dearly beloved son. Nay more, she herself offered Christ to the eternal Father in expiation of their crime and to reestablish an everlasting peace between God and man. That is why the Holy Ghost inspires her to say that she "found the precious treasure of peace that man had lost through sin."[6]

In the eighth place, her virginal heart never having followed any will but the will of God, she always possessed God's own peace in a most eminent degree.

Finally, divine peace so completely filled and permeated this peaceful heart that it became a haven of peace and a source of tranquility for all who, troubled and shaken by the storm of adversity, passion and temptation, have recourse to her incomparable benignity with humility and confidence. O Queen of Peace, grant that our hearts may bear an image of the holy peace that reigns in thine!

4 Col. 1, 20.
5 Cf. Pachymer. *Paraphras, sancti Dionysii*. Migne, Patrol, gr. latine tant. edita, tom. 2, p. 579.
6 Cant. 8, 10.

Chapter Seven

GLORY AND FELICITY MIRRORED IN THE ADMIRABLE HEART OF GOD

The glory of God is a perfection consisting in His most clear knowledge of His divine perfections, the sum of which, being perfectly understood by His divine intelligence, constitutes the essential glory of His adorable majesty.

Felicity is another divine perfection, consisting partly in God's knowledge, partly in His love of himself. The union of these two spiritual activities constitutes the incomprehensible and ineffable bliss of His divine majesty. The divine eternity of God maintains Him at every moment in full possession of all the grandeurs, glories, joys and felicities He has ever enjoyed or ever will enjoy while the ages course along.

Now I not only find an image of these divine attributes in the heart of the Virgin Mother, but I behold therein this marvelous glory and incomparable felicity, in a certain sense, as they are in God Himself.

To understand this, we must remember that it is characteristic of love, more especially of supernatural and divine love, to transform the lover into the object of his love, as the fire changes iron into fire, leaving it its nature and essence of iron, but endowing it with the qualities and perfections proper to fire. As it is quite certain that there never was and never shall be a love equal to that which inflamed Mary's virginal heart, we cannot doubt that divine love so completely transformed her, even while she remained on earth, that she had but one mind, one heart, one will and one love with God Himself. She loved only what He loves, hated nothing but what He hates. She had no interests save His, no glory or honor, no contentment or happiness save only God's. Thus did the glory and felicity of God ever abide in her heart.

But did not all the ignominies and sorrows she suffered here below, especially at the time of her son's passion, bereave her of this bliss and glory? Nay, rather they increased it. Do you not know that the Holy Ghost, speaking of the passion of the Son of God, calls it the day of His heart's rejoicing, "In the day of the joy of his heart."[1] Speaking of His passion, Our Lord Himself calls it His Father's glory and His own. Thus Saint Ambrose,[2] Saint Hilary,[3] Saint Augustine and other doctors explain the words spoken by Our Saviour on the eve of His death, "Father, glorify thy Son, that thy Son may glorify thee."[4] The passion of the Son of God represents, in fact, the greatest glory of God, for it most abundantly repaired the injury done to God by all the sins of the world, and glorified the Creator in a manner worthy of His infinite grandeur. When the Church sings, "We give thee thanks for thy great glory," she means to thank God for the passion of His divine Son as well as for His own essential glory.

Now we know that the Mother of Jesus had no sentiments other than those of her son, and she realized that nothing in the world can give greater glory and honor to God than sufferings and humiliations endured for the sake of His love. Hence, just as her son calls His ignominious and most bitter passion His glory and joy, so did she find her greatest glory and most perfect joy in supreme humiliation and the most poignant sorrows, for her honor and happiness consisted in the things which give the greatest honor to God and please Him best.

We should not believe, however, that this contentment of hers prevented her from suffering. Not in the least, for it is certain that no one on earth, after her beloved son, suffered as much as she. But in Christ, joys and sorrows were joined together in such fashion that the joys possessing the superior part of His soul did not destroy the sorrows that ruled the inferior part. So when the Mother of Jesus was crucified and reviled with her son, the bitter anguish and inconceivable torments she endured in her senses and in the inferior part of her soul did not prevent her from enjoying in her spirit and in her heart, a profound peace and an unutterable contentment, for she knew that such was God's will and His good pleasure.

Thus did the glory and felicity of the Most High dwell in the blessed heart of the glorious Virgin while she was on earth, but in Heaven, her incomparable heart is so completely lost and absorbed in the infinite glory and boundless joy of the Divinity, that this divine joy and immortal glory transform it entirely and fill it with greater glory and happiness than the hearts of all the angels and saints put together.

O most holy Mother, my heart is transported with joy to contemplate thine own heart so overwhelmed with grandeur and unspeakable

---

1 Cant. 3, 11.
2 *Hexameron*, cap. 2.
3 *De Trinitate*, lib. 3.
4 John 17, 1.

felicity, which never shall end. I would dare to say with the grace of thy beloved son, that if my heart possessed all these gifts instead of thine, I would, if possible, strip my heart and give them to thee. Yes, I would sooner be annihilated forever than to see thy holy heart lose any of the treasures wherewith divine goodness has so profusely adorned it.

Chapter Eight

THE ADMIRABLE HEART OF MARY:
COMPENDIUM OF THE LIFE OF GOD

Life and vision, in a Christian soul, constitute the same principle. According to God's Word, Christian life and vision are one and the same thing, since faith, which is the light and vision of the just man, is also his life, as it is written, "The just man liveth by faith."[1] Eternal life consists in knowing God, as His Son Jesus Christ teaches us when He addresses His heavenly Father, saying, "Now this is eternal life: That they may know thee, the only true God."[2] Since the life of God abides in His knowledge and love of Himself and of His divine perfections, so the life of the children of God consists in knowing and loving the eternal Father. Those who know God by the light of faith, and love Him with a supernatural love, are alive with God's own life, and God is living within them. He is the life of their hearts and of their souls.

God always lived thus in the heart of the Blessed Virgin Mary, and her Immaculate Heart always lived in God and partook of God's life in a much more excellent manner than any other human heart.

The life of God consists in the very sublime and clear knowledge that His boundless wisdom gives Him and in the infinite love He bears Himself. Now the Blessed Virgin's heart is filled with God's wisdom and love more than all other hearts; consequently it expresses and represents God's life better than any of them.

Two kinds of life exist in God: the interior life known only to Himself, and the exterior or visible life, which manifests itself in the humanity of His Son, in His saints, especially while they are still on earth, and in all living creatures. In like manner, there are two kinds of life in the heart of the Mother of God: the interior life, hidden in God and visible to Him alone, and the exterior, visible life, manifested in the body and external actions of Our Lady, having its origin in her heart. Both these lives are entirely holy and deserving of eternal honor.

1 Rom. 1, 17.
2 John 17, 3.

To this we must add that God is not only life, but the source of life, animating the natural and the supernatural life of all living creatures, and therefore the heart of the Mother of Life is not only alive with God's life, in which it participates in an eminent degree which knows no equal, but it is itself a principle of life.

God, however, lives in our hearts with different degrees of perfection; He does live in those who love Him tepidly, and serve Him with weakness, cowardice and negligence, but His life in these souls is imperfect, languishing and half dead.

God also lives in those who love Him more ardently and serve Him with greater fervor. Here His life is nobler, more vigorous and more perfect. If these hearts remain firm and stable in the ways of divine love, they shall be numbered among those of whom it is written! "Their hearts shall live forever and ever."[3]

In other hearts God not only lives but reigns perfectly. Who are these souls? They are those who have destroyed self love and self will, those who in this world and in the next are desirous only of pleasing God in all things. Their sole satisfaction and joy consists in doing His adorable will at all times and in all places.

Such is the virginal heart of the Queen of Heaven, in which God always lived and reigned most sovereignly, to which He granted so perfect a resemblance to His own life. For so great a gift, may His divine majesty be eternally praised and blessed.

O most holy Mother, how my heart rejoices to contemplate thy heart living so noble, holy and perfect a life, a life never in the least impaired by sin, a life most admirably united with the life of the adorable heart of Jesus. Would that all hearts and tongues would cry with me: Hail Jesus and hail Mary! Glory to the amiable hearts of Jesus and Mary! Live all hearts who love and honor these admirable hearts! May their hearts live forever and forever!

O Mother of my life, let my heart die to every life and live of thy life. Let my life be animated by the spirit and inflamed with thy love, that together with thee, it may forever bless, love and praise Him Who is life essential, the first and sovereign principle of all life, whose infinite desire it is to communicate it to all men!

3 Ps. 21, 27.

Part Six

THIRD FOUNDATION OF THE DEVOTION:
THE HEART OF GOD THE HOLY GHOST*

INSPIRED TEXTS REFERRING TO
THE ADMIRABLE HEART OF MARY

* This section has been considerably shortened.

Chapter One

"ALL THE GLORY OF THE KING'S DAUGHTER IS WITHIN"

Infinite goodness compels God the Holy Ghost to disclose to us the inestimable treasures hidden in the marvelous heart of Mary and to proclaim them through Sacred Scripture, the inspired word of God. The first significant text that I shall point out is taken from the forty-fourth Psalm, "All the glory of the king's daughter is within", (*Ps. 44, 14*) where the Holy Ghost reveals that the Admirable Heart of Mary is a source of benefactions without number and of every kind.

To explain this truth, I shall stress three thoughts that are most glorious for the magnificent heart of our great Queen and founded on these divine words, "All the glory of the king's daughter is within," and from her heart.

Who is this daughter of the King? We know full well that she is the Queen of Heaven and earth, the daughter of the King of kings. But why does all her glory proceed from her heart? It is because her heart is the source and principle of all the grandeur, excellence and prerogatives that adorn her, of all the eminent qualities that exalt her above every creature, namely her position as eldest daughter of the eternal Father, as Mother of the Son, as spouse of the Holy Ghost, as the Temple of the most Holy Trinity, as Queen of Angels and men, as the Mother of Christians, and as Empress of the Universe. It also means that this most holy heart is the source of all the graces that accompany the privileges bestowed on her, of the holy use she made of those graces and of all the sanctity of her thoughts, words, works, sufferings and of the other mysteries of her life. It means, finally, that her heart is the source of the eminent virtues she practiced on earth, of her perfect exercise of the faculties and powers of her soul and of her body, and of the glory and felicity she now enjoys in Heaven.

How is her heart the source of all these things? In the following ways. We know that the humility, purity, love and charity of her heart have rendered her worthy to be made Mother of God, and consequently have enriched her with all the advantages and privileges that belong to so high a dignity. We know further that the heart is the seat of love and charity, and that love and charity are the principle, rule and measure of all the sanctity on earth, and therefore of all glory in Heaven. Hence, God, eternal Truth, tells us in the Gospel that, as the heart of man is the origin of all evil, so it is also the source of every good. The Son of God teaches us that from the heart proceed evil thoughts, homicides, and blasphemies,[1] Our Saviour further tells us that the heart of the good man is a treasure from which He draws all sorts of good things, and the heart of the wicked man a treasure from which He draws all evil things.[2] We may conclude therefore that the supremely good heart of God's most loving Mother is the source of all that is great, holy, glorious and admirable in her.

I say further, and this is the second of the three thoughts I promised you, that Mary's heart is the source, after God, of all the excellence, sanctity, glory, felicity and other great and precious marvels to be found in the Church Militant, Suffering and Triumphant.

The reason of this is clear. We all agree that every grace and blessing possessed by the Church, all the treasures of light, holiness and glory that abide in her, on earth as well as in Heaven, are due to the intercession of the Blessed Virgin Mary. "All graces," says the learned and devout Abbot Rupert, "every gift that the world has received from Heaven, are as streams which issue from that sacred fountain, as fruits belonging to that holy tree."[3] "It was decreed by God in His eternal counsel," writes Saint Bernard, "to give nothing to anyone except through Mary's hands.

"Through her He was pleased to give us every good. Yes, indeed, because through her He gave the first principle of every good, Jesus Christ, Our Lord."[4]

But how did Mary make herself so holy and so pleasing to the divine majesty, that He should choose her to be the intermediary of this infinite gift, from which are derived all the other gifts ever made to His Church? It was by the sanctity of her most humble, pure and charitable heart.

Let us acknowledge, then, that her heart is the origin of everything noble, rich and precious in all the holy souls which form the universal Church in Heaven and on earth. We can therefore say of her marvelous heart, and with greater reason, what Saint John Chrysostom says of the

---

1 Matt. 15, 19.
2 Luke 6, 45.
3 *Emissiones tuae paradisus. In illa verba Cant.*
4 *Totum nos habere voluit per Mariam. Serm. de Aquacductu.*

heart of Saint Paul, when he calls it the fount and principle of number-less graces: *Fons et principium innumerorum bonorum.*[5]

Shall we stop here? No, we must go further and explain the third truth that I promised you, which is that the heart of the Mother of the Saviour is, in a certain sense, the fountain and source of all that is holy, and admirable in the life and the successive mysteries of our divine Redeemer himself.

Was not this represented by the river described in the second chapter of Genesis, which came out of the fountain created by God at the beginning of the world.[6] This fountain is a figure of the holy heart of Mary, and Jesus, the son of Mary, is designated by the river springing from the fountain. Do we not hear eternal Wisdom, that is, the Son of God, saying, "I came out of paradise," out of the virginal heart of Mary, which is the true paradise of the new Adam, "like a channel of a river,"[7] that is, like the river that flowed out of the earthly paradise.

Let us acknowledge, then, that her Admirable Heart, being the fountain from which that great river originated, is the miraculous source of all the treasures and of the great and priceless wonders contained in that divine stream. We must conclude that Our Lady's heart is the fountain and principle of numberless goods: *Fons et principium omnium bonorum.* Saint Irenaeus, asking why the mystery of the Incarnation did not take place without Mary's consent, answers that it was because God sought her to be the principle of every good.[8] What does he mean by that, if not that the Son of God wished the heart of His Blessed Mother to be the source and origin of all the blessings and graces derived from the Incarnation, and that He wished to become man only by her consent? "She is the perennial fount of every good," declares Saint Andrew of Crete.[9]

O most loving heart of Mary, O abyss of miracles, who can tell the unfathomable marvels that God has worked in and through thee! O boundless Sea, God alone can know the inestimable riches hidden in thee! O heart most holy, thou art Heaven's own Heaven, for, after the heart of the eternal Father, thou are the most magnificent and glorious abode of Jesus, who is Himself the highest Heaven, "The Heaven of Heaven is the Lord's."[10] Next to the heart of Jesus, thou art the highest throne of glory and majesty of the Blessed Trinity. What honor and

5 *In Act. 22,* homil. 55; et in Rom. 14, homil. 32, in fine.
6 See Part 11, chapter 5.
7 Ecclus. 24, 41.
8 *Quia vult illud Deus omnium bonorum esse principium.* S. Irenaeus citatus apud Salazar, *in cap. 31,* Proverb. vers. 29. num. 179.
9 *In Ser. de Dorm. B. Virg.*
10 Ps. 113, 16.

praise should be rendered unto thee! Oh, may every human and angelic heart recognize and honor thee as its sovereign after the adorable heart of our Saviour!

Dearest Jesus, what thanks we owe thine infinite goodness for having given thy Blessed Mother to us, and for having endowed her with a maternal heart so full of love and tenderness towards her most unworthy children! Grant, dear Saviour, that we may have truly filial affection for so good a Mother, and may the hearts of her children bear the image and likeness of the love, charity, humility and all the other virtues that reign in the heart of their most loving Mother!

Chapter Two

"A Bundle of Myrrh Is My Beloved to Me"

"A bundle of myrrh is my beloved to me; he shall abide between my breasts."[1] These words are taken from the first chapter of the Canticle of Canticles, which is referred entirely to the Blessed Virgin Mary by many serious and learned authors. We can therefore say that it is the book of the virginal heart of Mary and of her ardent love. It is a book filled with inspired words, revealing that her incomparable heart is ablaze with love of God and filled with charity for men.

"My beloved is like a bundle of myrrh to me: he shall abide between my breasts," and in my heart. Who utters these words? The most Blessed Virgin Mary. Who is the beloved of whom she speaks? It is her only son, her well beloved. Why does she call Him a bundle of myrrh? Because she beholds Him crucified and plunged in an ocean of contempt, insults, ignominies, anguish, bitterness and most atrocious torments. This fills her maternal heart with so much bitterness, pain and suffering that she can truly call her desolate heart a sea of anguish and tribulation according to the words which can be applied to both Jesus and Mary, "Great as the sea is thy desolation."[2] Thy sufferings, O Jesus, are immense, boundless and bottomless like the sea. And thy dolors, O Mother of Christ, are so exceeding great that all the afflictions and desolations of the world are as nothing compared to thine, as the waters of all fountains and rivers seem but a drop beside the boundless ocean.

To understand this truth perfectly, one would have to comprehend the immense and ardent love of her son that constantly inflamed the ineffable heart of our Saviour's Mother. For a mother's sorrow over the sufferings of her son exists in proportion to her love for Him, and the love of our Redeemer's Mother was, in a sense, measureless. The eternal Father had made her share in His divine paternity and chosen her to be the Mother of His own Son; He therefore communicated to her

1 Cant. 1, 12.
2 Lam. 2, 13.

something of His own inconceivable love, a love befitting the sublime dignity of her divine maternity.

How great is the love of the incomparable Mother for the most perfect of Sons. This Mother holds the place of father as well as mother towards her son, and her heart is miraculously filled with paternal as well as with maternal love towards Him. Her love is so great, that if the love of all the human fathers and mothers that ever have been or shall be were concentrated in a single heart, it would be but a small spark compared to the furnace of Mary's love for her beloved son. He is an only son, the sole object of His Mother's affection. He is an infinitely lovable and loving son and she loves Him without measure. He possesses all that is beautiful, rich, desirable, admirable and lovable in time and eternity. This son is everything to His mother; He is her son, her brother, her father, her spouse, her treasure, her glory, her love, her delight, her joy, her heart, her life, her God, her Creator, her Redeemer and her all.

From this we may fathom the love of such a mother for such a son, and consequently the most torturing and painful martyrdom of her maternal heart when she sees Him bathed in blood, covered with wounds from head to foot, and so filled with pain in body and soul, that the Holy Ghost, speaking through Isaias, calls Him the "Man of Sorrows,"[3] the man entirely transformed into sorrow.

We shall therefore not be surprised to hear Saint Anselm thus addressing the Mother of Sorrows, "All the torments which the martyrs underwent are as nothing, O Virgin, when compared to the immensity of the dolors, which transpierced thy soul and thy most loving heart."[4] "O sweetest heart of Mary," exclaims Saint Bonaventure, "heart transformed by love, how art thou now changed into a heart of sorrow, satiated with gall, myrrh, and absynth?"[5] "O admirable prodigy," he adds, "thy heart and mind are plunged in thy son's gaping wounds, while thy crucified Jesus dwells and lives in thy inmost heart."[6]

We should not be surprised, therefore, at the revelation to Saint Brigid, that the Blessed Virgin would have died of sorrow during the passion of her son, if He had not miraculously preserved her. And Mary herself, speaking to the same Saint Brigid, says, "I can presume to

3 Isa. 53, 3.

4 *Quidquid crudelitatis inflictum est corporibus Martyrum, leve fuit, aut potius nihil comparatione tuae passionis, O Virgo, quae nimirum sua immensitate transfixit cuncta penetralia tua, tuique benignissimi Cordis intima. De excell. Virg. cap. 5.*

5 *O suavissimum Cor Amoris, quomodo conversum es in Cor doloris, in quo nihil nisi fel, acetum, myrrha et absynthium. Stimul. Amor. cap. 3.*

6 *O mira res, tota es in vulneribus Christi, totus Christus crucifixus est in intimis visceribus Cordis tui. Ibid.*

say that my son's sorrow was my sorrow, because His heart was my heart."[7] "O my Queen," says Saint Bonaventure, "thou art not only standing by the cross of thy son, *juxta crucem*, but thou art on the cross suffering with Him: *In cruce cum Filio cruciaris*. He suffered in His body and thou didst suffer in thy heart, and the wounds scattered over His body were gathered together in thy heart."[8]

Finally, just as the love of Mary's maternal heart for her son Jesus Christ is past all that can be imagined, so the most painful martyrdom of her amiable heart is beyond what thought can conceive or words express.

> Nullus dolor crudelior,
> Nam nulla proles charior.
> Non est amor suavior,
> Non moeror est amarior.[9]

---

7 *Revel.* lib. 1, cap. 35.
8 *Stimul. Amor.* cap. 3.
9 "No sorrow is more cruel than hers, for no son could be more dear than hers. If her love is most sweet, so is her pain the bitterest of all."

Chapter Three

"I Sleep and My Heart Watcheth"

"I sleep, and my heart watcheth."[1] It is the glorious Virgin Mary who speaks, or rather the Holy Spirit, who utters these words through her virginal lips and reveals to us five mysteries most gloriously perfected in her blessed heart.

The first of these mysteries is the death of Our Lady's heart to whatever is not God, through self-denial. This is signified by the words "I sleep." The second mystery expressed by the words "I sleep," is the admirable contemplation of her blessed heart. The third mystery contained in the same words is the most intimate and perfect union of the most holy heart of Mary with the adorable will of God, whose commandments were so dear to her, that not only did she desire everything He wanted, not only did she shirk from whatever He forbade, but she found her entire rest, contentment, felicity and joy in observing the commandments of God.

Blessed are the hearts who strive to imitate this entire and perfect conformity of the Admirable Heart of the Mother of God to His divine will. This adorable will being our end, our center and our sovereign good, those who obey it with all their hearts shall never fail to find in it peace, rest, felicity, and a real paradise for their souls. Outside of God's will one experiences only anguish, troubles, embarrassment, torture and a veritable hell.

The fourth mystery designated by the words "My heart watcheth," contains a truth according the highest honor to Our Saviour's Mother; namely, that her son Jesus is her true heart, for it is of Him that she speaks when she says, "My heart watcheth." It is as though she said, "While I devote myself to contemplating and to loving the grandeurs of God and His adorable mysteries, and while I perform the duties and obligations of my divine maternity, my son Jesus, being my heart, is ever occupied in

1 Cant. 5, 2.

watching over all that concerns my body and my soul. His infinite love for me makes Him take unceasing care to protect me from the snares of the enemies of my soul. He enlightens me with His own divine light; He guides my steps along the path to Heaven; He grants me all the graces I need to lead a life worthy of the Mother of God, and He constantly inflames me with the sacred fire of His divine love."

The fifth mystery marked by the words "My heart watcheth," embodies the vigilance of the most holy heart of the Blessed Virgin Mary. What is watchfulness? If we consider it first in God, before considering it in her marvelous heart, we shall find that watchfulness is a perfection which constitutes, as it were, the strength and vigor of the divinity of God and makes Him incapable of experiencing weakness or fatigue. It is like the torch of His divine essence, in whose radiance He forever contemplates Himself. It is the eye of His bounty, mercy, justice, zeal, and all His other divine perfections. The royal prophet, David, indeed proclaims the watchfulness and care of divine providence when he says, "Behold he shall neither slumber nor sleep, that keepeth Israel,"[2] but he remains ever watchful and attentive to protect His people.

Now this adorable vigilance has established its throne and its reign most excellently in the noble heart of the Mother of God. Consider that the Holy Ghost causes her to say, "I sleep, and my heart watcheth."

These words teach us that even when her virginal body was taking its necessary sleep and rest, her heart never slept but kept constant vigil. Yes, her heart, so full of love for God, watched day and night to study His adorable will, and to accomplish it most perfectly. Her heart, filled with tenderness for her divine son, attended faithfully to His every need and necessity, providing for Her all-precious child, with the utmost care fulfilling all the duties of a loving Mother to so perfect a son. Her heart, filled with esteem and peerless veneration for each successive event unfolding in the admirable life of the Redeemer, watched over His development, His miracles and mysteries, His actions, sorrows, words and gestures, so that she might gratefully adore and praise the manifestations in the name of all mankind, and preserve them as an infinitely precious treasure which would one day enrich the Church and encompass her true children with numberless blessings.

The heart of Our Lady, inflamed with love towards men, was always attentive to fulfill the obligations of charity, the queen of virtues, and was ever watchful so as not to miss one single occasion of practicing it.

Finally, the holy Virgin's heart exercised perpetual vigilance over her own thoughts, words and actions, over her passions and inclinations, over all her interior and exterior senses, and over all the powers

2 Ps. 120, 4.

163

of her soul, that she might drive far away from herself anything that could possibly displease God and to use her faculties as perfectly and as virtuously as possible.

O most charitable Mother of God, by thy powerful intercession, grant that we may imitate the most holy watchfulness of thy faithful heart so that we may be numbered among those who merit the happiness to see the face of God in blissful eternity, to behold the glory of the God-Man and the grandeur of His Mother in that blessed company of souls who never weary of praising, loving and glorifying the most Holy Trinity together with Jesus, Mary and all the angels and saints. To the Triune God be honor, glory and empire for all eternity.

Chapter Four

"My Beloved to Me and I to Him"

"My beloved to me, and I to him."[1] "I to my beloved, and my beloved to me."[2] "I to my beloved, and his turning is towards Me;"[3] with His mind, His heart, His affection and His whole being.

It is not without mystery that the Blessed Virgin Mary repeats the three foregoing verses under the inspiration of the Holy Ghost, speaking in the sacred Canticle, which is so mysterious and full of eternal verities. The preceding three verses admit of nine explanations, each revealing to us the incomprehensible love of the Almighty for the peerless Virgin and the ardent love of her virginal heart for God, Her Creator.

1. The all-surpassing love of God for Mary causes Him to become entirely hers, "My beloved to me," by His thoughts, words and actions. By His thoughts, because she has been from all eternity the first object of His love, after the sacred humanity of His Word, and the first and worthiest subject of His thoughts and designs, "The Lord possessed me in the beginning of his ways."[4] By His words, because Saint Bernard declares that the whole of Sacred Scripture was written "for Mary, about Mary and on account of Mary."[5] By His works, because everything that God has done in the world of nature, grace and glory, and everything He has accomplished in the God-Man and through Him is more for the sake of this admirable Virgin than all other creatures together as He loves her alone above all His creatures.

Similarly, the ardent love of Mary's privileged heart obliges her to belong entirely to God, "I to my beloved," by her thoughts, words and actions. By her thoughts, she never entertained a single thought which was not centered in God or for God. All her thoughts were so holy and so inflamed with divine love that they became like so many fiery darts

1 Cant. 2, 16.
2 *Ibid.* 6, 2.
3 *Ibid.* 7, 10.
4 Prov. 8, 22.
5 *De hac, et ob hanc, et propter hanc omnis Scriptura facta est. Serm. 1 in Salve.*

wounding the heart of His divine majesty. As we have seen already, this is the explanation given by many great authorities to the words, "Thou hast wounded my heart . . . with one hair of thy neck."[6] By her words, she carried out most perfectly what Saint Peter the prince of the Apostles says, "If any man speak, let him speak as the words of God."[7] By her actions, the Blessed Virgin Mary performed all things for God's glory, in faithful obedience to the inspired counsel, "Whether you eat or drink, or whatsoever else you do, do all to the glory of God."[8]

2. The ineffable love of God the Creator for Mary causes Him to belong entirely to her, "My beloved to me," by His power, His wisdom and His goodness. He is hers in a much nobler and more glorious manner than His possession by all creatures together, for the Father communicated His power to Mary so fully that she alone is mightier than every other power in the universe.

The divine son makes her participate in His wisdom with such plenitude that, next to His own Sacred Humanity, His Mother possesses all the treasures of God's knowledge and wisdom more excellently than every other human or angelic intellect.

The Holy Ghost pours His love and charity into Mary's virginal heart with such abundance that He makes of it a boundless and bottomless ocean of mercy, liberality and benignity, flooding Heaven, earth and Purgatory with its sweet graces and comforts.

On Mary's part, the inconceivable love of God flaming in her heart, consecrates her entirely to His divine majesty by holy use of her memory, her intellect and her will under its inspiration. From the first instant in her life she gave and consecrated her whole memory to the divine person of the eternal Father, her intellect to the adorable person of her son, and her entire will to the most lovable person of the Holy Ghost. From the first moment until the end of her mortal life she never used the three faculties of her soul except for the honor and service of her Creator.

3. Mary belongs to Jesus, "I to my beloved," as to her Creator, Preserver and Redeemer, who saved her, not by delivering her from sin, which never had any part in her, but by preserving her from every sin, original and actual. Jesus belongs to Mary, "My beloved to me," because she formed Him in her blessed womb with her own pure blood. She preserved, nourished and brought Him up, and when Herod's fury sought to destroy the Holy Child, she saved and delivered Him.

4. The Son of God is Mary's son from all eternity, in the fullness of time, and for all eternity, "My beloved to me." From all eternity, He

6 Cant. 4, 9.
7 1 Pet. 4, 11.
8 1 Cor. 10, 31.

regarded her as His chosen Mother; in the fullness of time, because she became the instrument for the accomplishment of the ineffable mystery of the Incarnation; for all eternity, because Christ will forever regard, honor and love her as His most worthy Mother. For the same reason Mary is the Mother of her beloved son from all eternity, in the fullness of time and for all eternity, "I to my beloved."

5. Mary belongs to Jesus, "I to my beloved," according to nature, grace and glory because everything she possesses in nature, grace and glory comes to her from her divine son; and Jesus belongs to Mary, "My beloved to me," according to nature, grace and glory, because, in the Incarnation, she gave Him His nature as man. She gives Him daily the life of grace in His members, "Mother of grace; life is given to us through the Virgin." *Mater gratiae; vitam datam per Virginem.* She has also given Him the life of glory in His members, because after Him she is the source of all graces upon earth and of all glory in Heaven.

6. The eternal Father belongs to Mary, "My beloved to me," as the only creature to whom He communicated, so to speak, His divine paternity, that she might become the Mother of His own Son. The son belongs to Mary, as to the only one He has chosen to be His Mother. The Holy Ghost belongs to Mary as to the bride He chose that He might work in her His admirable masterpiece.

Mary, on her part, belongs to the eternal Father, "I to my beloved," as to Him with whom she is one, in a certain admirable manner, as she shares with Him the virtue of His divine and adorable fecundity, being the Mother of the only begotten Son whose Father He is. She surrendered to the Almighty her heart and her will, her most pure blood and her virginal substance, to bring forth the God-Man, of whom it can truly be said that He was begotten of His Father's substance before all ages and born of the substance of His Mother in the fullness of time.

Mary belongs to the Son of God, as the only one who gave herself to Him to be His Mother, when she uttered the words, "Behold the handmaid of the Lord, be it done unto me according to thy word."[9]

Mary belongs to the Holy Ghost, for she gave herself to be His bride, that she might become the Mother of God made man without ceasing to be a virgin, after hearing the divine words spoken by the angelic Messenger, "The Holy Ghost shall come upon thee."[10]

7. The intellect of the eternal Father belongs to Mary, "My beloved to me," for he produces His Word, he engenders the Son in his adorable bosom and gives Him to Mary, to cause Him to be born

9 Luke 1, 38.
10 *Ibid.* 1, 35.

167

of her chaste womb, to make of Him the flower and fruit of her virginal bosom and of her holy heart.

The will of the only begotten Son belongs to Mary, because together with His Father, the Son generates the Holy Ghost, and gives the divine Spirit to Mary, that He may, in a most excellent manner, become her Spirit and her heart, and that she may, in a certain sense, have but one Spirit and one heart in common with the Father and the Son.

The charity of the Holy Ghost belongs to Mary, for in her only, from her, with her and through her, has He performed the most stupendous miracle of His love, the incarnation of the love of all loves, who is Jesus Christ.

On the other hand, just as the eternal Father imparts to the incomparable Mary the first and unique fruit of His intellect and of His adorable bosom, so also, as soon as this ineffable fruit has been formed in her virginal womb, does she offer, give and sacrifice Him to the Creator who gave Him to her, "I to my beloved."

As the Son endows Mary with the fruit of His will, who is the Holy Ghost, so does she give Him all the inclinations and desires of her will, so perfectly and entirely that He always disposes of them absolutely and in the manner most pleasing to Himself, for the Mother of God never possessed the slightest will other than that of her all-glorious son.

And as the Holy Ghost accomplishes in her alone the greatest wonder of His love, namely, the Incarnation of Jesus Christ, so also did this Spirit of love and charity establish in her heart the empire of the holy love and divine charity so perfectly that they have ever reigned and will reign there more absolutely than in all other hearts save that of Christ.

8. The Mystical Body of Christ belongs to Mary, "My beloved to Me." By this is meant that the Church Triumphant, Militant and Suffering belongs to Mary, or better still, Jesus Christ combating against hell on earth, Jesus Christ triumphant in Heaven, and Jesus Christ suffering in Purgatory in His members, belongs to Mary because our divine Saviour gave His holy Mother all things together with Himself.

Mary likewise belongs to the Church Militant, Triumphant and Suffering, "I to my beloved," for this son Jesus Christ has given her to the Church Militant, that she might be the general of her armies. He has given His Mother to the Church Triumphant as a resplendent sun filling the hearts of the blessed in Heaven with incredible joy, second only to the joy they experience from the Beatific Vision of the face of God. Christ has given her to the Suffering Church as a mother of mercy and comforter of the afflicted, who is ever spreading comfort and refreshment among those scorching flames of divine justice. Mary her-self assured Saint Brigid that every pain suffered in Purgatory was rendered more bearable by her intervention.

9. The heart of the divine Father belongs to Mary, as the heart of the most loving of fathers to the most devoted of daughters, "My beloved to me." The heart of the Redeemer belongs to Mary, as the heart of the most affectionate of sons to the worthiest of all mothers. The heart of the Holy Ghost belongs to Mary, as the heart of the most perfect spouse to the most dearly beloved of all bridegrooms. The heart of Mary likewise belongs to the Father of Mercies, "I to my beloved," as the heart of the peerless daughter to the best of fathers. The heart of Mary belongs to the Son of God, as the heart of the most loving mother to the incomparable son. Finally, the heart of Mary belongs to the Holy Ghost, as the heart of a bride, who is a furnace of the holiest and most ardent fire that ever existed, to a spouse who is Himself uncreated and essential love, a God of love, infinite, eternal and immense.

Thus does Mary's beloved belong entirely to her and in every way, and thus does Mary belong to her beloved. Immense and infinite thanks we render to thee, O my God, for all the marvels of Thy love towards Thy beloved daughter, Mother and Bride! Everlasting praise to thee, beloved Daughter of the Father, most worthy Mother of the Son, dearest spouse of the Holy Spirit, for all the love and all the glory that thy Admirable Heart has rendered and will forever render to the most Blessed Trinity.

O Mother of fervent love, deign to obtain by thy holy prayers, that, as the Father, Son and Holy Ghost have given themselves to us in an excess of unspeakable love, they may also take full and irrevocable possession of our bodies, our hearts, our souls and of all that is in us, to the end that there may remain in us nothing that is not totally consecrated to their love and glory, alone and forever!

Chapter Five

"PUT ME AS A SEAL UPON THY HEART"

Christ gave all Christians this command, "Put me as a seal upon thy heart, as a seal upon thy arm;"[1] that is, impress upon yourself inwardly and outwardly the image of my interior and exterior life. "For love is as strong as death, jealousy as hard as hell," which means, as I have died a most cruel death to turn your love back to me, so if you love me, you must likewise die to sin, to yourselves, to the world and to all things, in order to live only in me and for me. As my infinite love for you would have made me suffer even greater torments if such had been necessary to save you from Hell, so also, if you love me, you must be ready to suffer the pangs of hell rather than offend me!

Such is the command of the Son of God to every faithful soul, but no one has ever kept it perfectly except the Blessed Virgin Mary.

Would you see how she observed this command of her son? Notice that our Redeemer does not tell her, "Put my seal on thy heart and on thy arm;" but He says, "Put me, myself, as a seal upon thy heart and upon thy arm. As I am the perfect image of my heavenly Father and the divine character of His substance, make thy heart also a living image of myself; make it live of my life; make it be animated by my spirit, filled with my sentiments, inflamed with love and charity for me, and adorned with all virtues. Put me also as a seal on thy arm, which means, let thy exterior person be an image and likeness of my own exterior, of thy modesty, humility, meekness, affability, mortification of my senses and holiness of all my outward bearing."

The Blessed Virgin Mary accomplished all these things most excellently and with an inconceivable love. "Love is as strong as death," and stronger still, for it vanquished the Almighty Himself and caused the Immortal One to die, Him who is beyond the scope of death. The heart of the glorious Virgin Mary was so filled with love for God that she

1 Cant. 8, 6.

would rather have suffered every conceivable torment and death, than to do, say or think anything displeasing to His divine majesty.

"Love is as hard as hell." Witness the infinite love our Saviour bears us, a love so admirable that He revealed to Saint Brigid, "I am charity itself; and if I could endure as many deaths as there are souls in Hell, I would do it most willingly and with perfect charity. I am ready to suffer for a single soul the very passion and death that I suffered for all mankind."[2] I read in a trustworthy author[3] that, when our most merciful Redeemer is obliged, by His justice, to chastise sinners, His infinite love for His creatures would make Him endure pain comparable to those of Hell, if He were still capable of suffering.

So also was the Blessed Virgin Mary filled with love for her Creator and with charity towards souls, that she would gladly have suffered the pains of a thousand Hells rather than consent to the least sin, and that she would willingly have undergone even more sorrow and suffering, if possible, in this world or in the next, in order to cooperate in the salvation of a single soul. We have also seen many saints inspired with this same readiness.

With much reason, therefore, does the Holy Ghost say, speaking of the love and charity of the Mother of God, "The lamps thereof are fire and flames."[4] All her thoughts, words and actions were like fiery flames leaping from the furnace of her heart and flaring up to highest Heaven, where they kindled an even greater love in the hearts of the seraphim themselves.

But let us return to the divine words of the only son of Mary to His Blessed Mother, "Put me as a seal . . ." and let us see how they show us a most glorious privilege of our admirable Mother. What greater favor can a ruler bestow on one of his subjects than to entrust his seal to him, saying, "Behold my seal; I place it in your hands together with my entire governing power, that you may use it as you see fit in sealing letters of every sort and kind."

This is the signal favor with which the King of kings honors His glorious Mother when He says to her, "Put me as a seal upon thy heart, as a seal upon thy arm," as though He were saying, "Thou hast had a very great share indeed in the sufferings and ignominies of my passion; in like measure do I now wish to make thee participate in my dignity and kingly power.

Jesus speaks thus to the Admirable Heart of Mary, "I give myself to thee, O my peerless Mother, not as a lifeless and material seal, but like

2 *Revcl.* lib. 1, cap. 48.
3 Ghisler. in cap. 8 *Cant.* in Expostio. 2 versus sexti.
4 Cant. 8, 6.

one that is living and divine. Put me as a seal, yet, put me myself as a seal on thy heart and on thy arm, that all thoughts, intentions, desires and affections emanating from thy heart may have the same virtue and effect as those proceeding from my own heart; as also that thy hand and arm may possess, in a way, as much strength and vigor as my own, to sustain, defend, protect, assist and favor thy children and all who shall have recourse to thee. I place my seal and my regal power in thy hands, that thou mayst dispose of them as thou wishest and as I would dispose of them myself, namely, to grant petitions, to make liberal gifts, to dispense graces for whatever end thou mayest choose. It is I who shall do whatever thou dost, and wherever thou dost place thy seal, I shall place mine."

After all this, do not be surprised if the Fathers of the Church declare that the admirable Mother of our Saviour possesses all power in Heaven and on earth, and that God grants her every request. "All power is given to thee in Heaven and on earth," says Saint Peter Damian.[5] "The all-merciful and almighty God hath raised thee so high," asserts Saint Anselm, "that thou art become all-powerful with Him."[6]

Infinite and eternal thanks be given to thee, my dearest Jesus, for having granted thy holy Mother so great a power. We are bound to express as much gratitude to thy infinite goodness, as though thou hadst granted the power to each one of us in particular, for thou hast given it to Mary that she may help, defend and assist us in all corporeal and spiritual necessities.

O Mother of perfect love, behold my miserable heart, together with the hearts of all my brethren; take full and entire possession of them; destroy whatever is displeasing, unite them to thine and make them, after the example of thy Admirable Heart, glow as ardent lamps of fire and flame.

---

5 *De excel. Virg.* cap. 12.
6 *Te pius et omnipotens Deus ita exaltavit, ut tibi secum omnia possibilia esse donaret.* Saint John Eudes does not give the reference to the works of Saint Anselm.

Chapter Six

"Mary Kept All These Words, Pondering Them in Her Heart."

Devotion to the Admirable Heart of Mary is by no means new, for it springs from the adorable heart of the most Holy Trinity, and it is as old as the Christian religion and the Gospel itself. Saint Luke the Evangelist bears witness to this in one chapter of his Gospel by making twice a particular mention of her most holy heart. In the nineteenth verse of chapter two he says, "But Mary kept all these words, pondering them in her heart," and in the fifty-first verse, "And his mother kept all these words in her heart."

The devotion, therefore, has its origin and foundation in the holy Gospel itself. The Holy Ghost inspired the Evangelists and willed that one of them should speak with such particular honor of the virginal heart of the Saviour's Mother, representing it as the sacred depository and faithful custodian of the ineffable mysteries and inestimable treasures contained in the life of Our Lord. This must have been written that we might likewise honor her august heart, so worthy to be honored forever.

To incite us to this devotion, let us consider this inspired text, "But Mary kept all these words, pondering them in her heart." To understand the full significance, we must remember that, according to God's language, *verba* does not signify *words* only, but *also deeds* as will be seen in the following passages: *Ecce ego faciam verbum in Israel;*[1] *Quia postulasti verbum hoc;*[2] *Videamus hoc verbum quod factum est.*[3] In like manner, we must understand the words: *Maria conservabat omnia verba haec.* Mary kept all these words, that is, all these things, for there is a great difference between the words of men and the words of God. The words of men are gone with the wind, and usually produce no

1 1 Kings 3, 11.
2 3 Kings 3, 2.
3 Luke 2, 15.

effects, "They say, and do not."[4] But God's words are facts, "He spoke and they were made."[5]

Mary kept all these *things* in her heart, that is, all the marvelous events of our Saviour's life. "This holy Virgin," writes Saint Ambrose "always carried in the depths of her heart the mysteries of God and the passion of her son and whatever else He did."[6]

She kept these things as wonderful tokens of the love of her dear son for His heavenly Father and for mankind. She kept them as sacred relics preserved and cherished for most special veneration. She kept all these things as a store of precious fuel to augment divine fire brought upon earth by her divine son and to inflame the hearts of men with fresh love. She kept them because they were the foundation stones on which our adorable Saviour willed to build His Church.

Mary kept these things in her heart as living miracles and incomprehensible works of the all-powerful goodness of God with which evangelical history was to be filled. She kept them as precious mysteries and secrets consoling and divine, representing the new alliance of God with men under the covenant of the New Testament. She kept them also as the precious inheritance and rich share of God's chosen children, joint heirs with the Son of God.

Our Lady kept all these words in her heart as the source and foundation of the divine graces to be spread throughout the world and of the immortal glories which were to shine forever in Heaven. She guarded them as the boundless treasure of divine mercy with which she could enrich all the denizens of Heaven and earth. She kept them to be the bread and wine placed on the table of the heavenly Father to His children, as a priceless manna brought down from Heaven by her beloved son that mortal men might feast on the Bread of Angels.

Mary, the general of the great King's army, kept these words as celestial weapons for her to place in the hands of her soldiers and thus help them to overcome the enemies of God and of their own salvation. She kept them also as sacred torches to lighten the path of mankind shrouded in the gloom and shadows of death.

She kept them as medicine to heal our souls from all types of evil and as a powerful remedy to fill mankind with all kinds of good. She kept them as inexhaustible records of divine wisdom, in which we might find the divine lore of the saints. She kept them as the very heart of Jesus, her son, and therefore, as her own heart. The heart of man is the source of his life, and the treasury of his secrets, plans and aspira-

4 Matt. 23, 3.
5 Ps. 32, 9.
6 *In ista verba:* Tuam ipsius animam.

tions, so likewise Sacred Scripture, containing as it does the word of God is the source of the life Our Saviour wills to have in His members, and the treasury of His designs and secrets. Saint Augustine[7] and Saint Gregory[8] both refer to Holy Writ as the heart of God.

Our Lady kept all these words, not merely in her memory and her intellect, but in her heart, *in corde suo*, in that heart which is the most worthy sanctuary of all virtues, and the ocean of grace and holiness; in that heart that is a furnace of love and charity and the Paradise of the most Blessed Trinity. In that heart she kept all the mysteries, marvels and every event of the life of her beloved son, our Redeemer, to be the object of her love and of all the sentiments, aspirations and affections of her soul.

She kept them, not in part, but entirely, *omnia*. In the first place, Our Lady knew that no part of the Saviour's life could be termed small, that everything in Him was great, divine and admirable and that each one of His footsteps, each breath, each flutter of his eyelids, each very least thought of His, deserved the eternal adoration of angels and men. In the second place, Mary knew that the love of her son Jesus Christ for mankind is so great that He counts every hair of their heads, "The very hairs of your head are all numbered;"[9] all their thoughts, all their steps, "Thou indeed hast numbered my steps;"[10] and that He takes into account the least action performed for love of Him, in order to reward each deed with an eternal glory. He keeps them in His heart as a precious treasure and guards them as the apple of His eye, according to the divine words, "The alms of a man is as signet with him, and shall preserve the grace of a man as the apple of the eye,"[11] which means, "As a man having a purse full of diamonds would guard each stone jealously, so does God keep the alms given or the favor shown to a poor man, even if it were only a glass of water."

Hence the eyes of the Blessed Virgin Mary were constantly fixed on her beloved son, and she was ever vigilant and attentive to the smallest detail of His life. Not one of these heavenly pearls and divine diamonds was lost, for she understood their infinite value, and that they would be the focus of the eternal happiness, praise and adoration of all the denizens of the heavenly Jerusalem. She hid there these treasures and preserved them in her virginal heart, where, after the adorable heart of the eternal Father, they were more worthily, holily and gloriously guarded than in the hearts of Seraphim, and they worked hidden

7 *In Ps. 21.*
8 *In 1 Reg.*
9 Luke 12, 7.
10 Job 14, 16.
11 Ecclus. 17, 18.

effects of light, love and sanctification more admirable than in the breadth of the empyrean Heaven. Those inestimable treasures shall forever remain in Mary's heart; there angels and saints shall contemplate, adore and glorify them throughout eternity.

But why did the glorious Virgin keep all these things so worthily and so holily in her heart? Why? Because of her ardent love for her divine son and for us. She kept these mysteries in her heart to adore and glorify them incessantly in the name of all men for whom they were fulfilled, men who nevertheless remained indifferent. She kept them that they might one day be adored and glorified throughout the world, and become like so many inexhaustible fountains of grace and blessings for all the souls belonging to the household of God.

She kept all these words so that she might reveal them to the Evangelists to be written in the holy Gospel and thus they would become the center of the faith and religion of all Christians. She kept these words, finally, to repeat them to the holy Apostles, who were to make the treasures of Mary's heart known and reverenced throughout the entire world.

Let us now see what is meant by the words: *Conferens in corde suo.* Mary kept all these things, comparing them one with the other. Saint John Chrysostom and several other Fathers say that the Blessed Virgin Mary, having read what the Prophets had foretold concerning the Saviour, compared their prophecies with the events that were happening before her own eyes, admiring and honoring the marvelous conformity of the latter with the former. Saint Bernard is of the opinion that the comparison concerned the admirable parallel of prediction and fulfillment of the angelical salutation, the conception of the Son of God in her chaste womb, her painless childbirth, the adoration of shepherds and kings, the flight into Egypt, and all the other mysteries of the Redeemer which occurred in His Blessed Mother's presence. Thus did Mary keep in her heart and compare everything she saw in her beloved son and whatever she learned from His divine lips in their familiar intercourse. It was revealed to Saint Brigid that while the adorable Infant Jesus lived with His holy Mother, He manifested many divine secrets, not merely to enlighten and guide her, but also to enable Mary to teach and enlighten others. Hence the martyr Saint Ignatius, in a letter addressed to Our Lady calls her *Apostolorum doctricem*, "Teacher of the Apostles."[12] Other writers call her heart the "library of the Apostles," the treasury of wisdom "where they learned," says Saint Jerome, "many things they would never have known otherwise."[13]

---

12 Only one letter of Saint Ignatius the Martyr is extant. The expression *Apostolorum doctricem* is not found in it. Cf. Migne, *Summa aurea*, vol. 2, col. 694, and vol. 10, col. 928.

13 *Serm. de Assumpt.*

After all this, what should be our gratitude to our heavenly Mother's most loving heart for having preserved such great treasures for us? Should we not reverence it as a sacred depositary and faithful guardian of the infinite riches Our Saviour has acquired for us by His blood? Ought we not to honor her heart as a living and eternal Gospel, containing the admirable heart of our Redeemer written in letters of gold by the Holy Ghost Himself? How great should our veneration be for this holy ark of the New Testament, containing a heavenly manna unknown to the children of the world, the bread of life, which can be found and tasted only by those whose hearts are consecrated to the love of Jesus, the son of Mary, and of Mary, Mother of Jesus.

Part Seven[1]

INSPIRED CATHOLIC TRADITION
CONCERNING THE ADMIRABLE HEART OF MARY

1 Part Seven is an abridged translation of Parts Seven and Eight of the original French work.

Chapter One

TESTIMONY OF THE FATHERS AND ASCETICAL WRITERS

Having listened to the Holy Ghost, whose divine heart is the third foundation of the devotion to the Immaculate Heart of the Mother of God, revealing to us through Sacred Scripture many marvelous truths which should inspire us to render fitting honor and praise to Mary's Admirable Heart, we must next hearken to the Spirit of God promulgating this devotion through the writings of the Fathers and authoritative writers of the Church.

First, there are twelve Fathers and ascetical writers: Saint Augustine, Saint Leo the Great, Saint John Chrysostom, Saint Anselm, Saint Peter Chrysologus, Saint John Damascene, Saint Bernard (who with other members of the Cistercian Order received most signal favors from Our Lady), Saint Bonaventure and Saint Bernardine of Siena, two illustrious sons of Saint Francis, Saint Lawrence Justinian, Richard of Saint Lawrence, and Venerable Louis of Grenada (son in religion of the great Saint Dominic, who preached so extensively the devotion to the Holy Rosary).

Our first quotation is from the pen of Saint Augustine. In a sermon on the Annunciation he brings out our great obligation to the loving heart of Mary in return for her admirable consent to the Angel's request.

"O most happy Mary, who can render thee adequate thanks for the help thou hast given to a lost world *by thy consent*[2] to Gabriel's demand? What praise can be presented by our fallen nature, which found the beginning of deliverance through thee? Accept, we beseech thee, our thanks, humble and weak though they be; accept our resolutions and excuse our sins by thy prayers. Receive what we offer thee, give us what

---

2 The significance of these words of Saint Augustine may be inferred from the words of Richard of Saint Lawrence: *Ex Corde beatae Virginis processerunt fides et consensus, per quae duo initiata est salus mundi.* "From the Heart of the Blessed Virgin came the two things that marked the beginning of the salvation of mankind, namely faith and consent which Mary gave to the mystery of the Incarnation." *De laud. B.M. lib. 2, partit. 2.*

we ask thee, pardon what we fear, thou who art the sole hope of our happiness."[3]

Another testimony of the ardent devotion of Saint Augustine to the Admirable Heart of Mary is found in his book on the Mother of God: *Materna propinquitas nihil Mariae profuisset, nisi felicius Christum Corde, quam carne gestasset.* "The divine maternity would not have profited Mary if she had not first borne Jesus Christ in her heart more happily and advantageously than in her womb."[4]

Saint Leo the Great, who lived in the same century as Saint Augustine, also speaks of the holy heart of Mary. He preached the glory of Mary's virginal heart in the city of Rome, as is proved from the following words from his sermon on the birth of Christ; "A royal virgin, of the race of David, is chosen to be the Mother of the Infant God and to conceive Him in her heart before bearing Him in her womb."[5]

Saint Anselm, the illustrious Archbishop of Canterbury and worthy son of Saint Benedict, clearly reveals his love and devotion to the Mother of God in his writings, especially in a book called: *The Excellence of the Blessed Virgin Mary.* One passage in this work makes a special mention of the loving heart of Mary. After the saintly Archbishop has pronounced a beautiful eulogy on the glorious Assumption of Our Lady, he speaks thus; "What praise and thanksgiving do men and all other creatures owe the Blessed Virgin Mary! The most pure holiness and the most holy purity of her pious heart, which surpasses incomparably the holiness and purity of all other creatures, merited that God choose her to be the restorer of the world which was lost."[6]

Saint Anselm is right in attributing the resurrection and restoration of man and of all things to the most pure and holy heart of the Mother of the Sovereign Restorer. It was by the purity and holiness of Mary's heart that she drew God the Son into her holy womb so that we might have a redeemer.

Saint Peter Chrysologus, Bishop of Ravenna, to console and strengthen his flock in the midst of the many disasters and calamities of war, strove to imprint in their hearts devotion to the Blessed Virgin Mary, exhorting them to have recourse to her mercy and to supplicate her to be their shelter and refuge in the misery that encompassed them. Those who followed the saint's advice felt the effects of the inconceivable goodness of Mary, of whom this holy Bishop speaks beautifully in a sermon on the Incarnation. Here are his very words:

3 *Serm. 2 de Annunt.*
4 Cap. 3.
5 Serm. de Nativ. Domini.
6 *De Excell. Mariae,* cap. 9.

"He who is not surprised and amazed in considering the perfections of Mary's soul, ignores the greatness and wonder of God. Heaven is filled with awe at the sight of the majesty of God; the angels tremble with respect, all nature is overwhelmed at the brilliance of this power. Yet a virgin receives this God of infinite grandeur *in her heart,* where she gives Him a holy and worthy dwelling place. And in return for so pleasing a lodging He wills that she exact from His goodness peace for the earth, glory for Heaven, life for the dead and salvation for all who are lost."[7]

Can anything more glorious be said of the heart of the august Mother of God? The heart of Mary is the sacred palace of the sovereign monarch of the universe. It is the holy house of the eternal Wisdom which the Holy Ghost expresses in these words; "Wisdom hath built herself a house, she hath hewn her out seven pillars. She hath slain her victims, mingled her wine, and set forth her table. She hath sent her maids to invite to the tower, and to the walls of the city. Whosoever is a little one, let him come to me. And to the unwise she said: Come, eat my bread, and drink the wine which I have mingled for you."[8]

What is this house that eternal Wisdom, the Son of God, has built to dwell in? It is the heart of the Blessed Virgin Mary. What are the seven columns? They are the seven gifts of the Holy Ghost, which support and sustain this heart and render it unshakeable to all the assaults of the devil. The victims are Mary's thoughts, affections, desires, which she sacrificed to His divine majesty. The wine that divine wisdom mingled with water is the divinity of the Son of God and His humanity, united in the womb of Mary by the holiness of her heart, which drew Him from the eternal bosom of the Father.

Saint John Damascene, the great defender of holy images against the impious Emperor Leo and the iconoclasts, wrote several excellent essays on the devotion to the Mother of God from which the following lines are taken:

" . . . Thy lips were fashioned only to praise Jesus Christ and to be pressed against His. Thy mouth and thy tongue cannot taste anything but the heavenly bread and wine of the words of God, whose sweetness can fill and inebriate thee. Thy pure and immaculate heart is always turned towards thy beloved, and is applied only to contemplate Him, to desire Him, to seek Him and to aspire after Him . . ."[9]

Saint Bernard, the glory and ornament of the Cistercian Order, expresses his ardent love for Mary's maternal heart in these beautiful words:

7 *Serm. 140 de Annunt.*
8 Prov. 9, 1–5.
9 *Orat. 1 de Nativ. B. Virg.*

"Open, O Mother of Mercy, open the door of thy merciful heart to the prayers that we offer to thee with sighs and tears. Thou dost not reject the sinner even when he is corrupt with sin, if he comes to thee and begs thine intercession with a contrite and humble heart. It is no wonder that thy heart is filled with the greatest compassion, since the incomparable work of mercy ordained by God was accomplished in thy sacred womb in which God hath been pleased to dwell. He hath built a house of the immaculate substance of thy virginal flesh, a house supported by seven silver columns, a house in which He placed a golden bed, thy holy heart, on which He took His peaceful rest. The seven columns are the seven gifts of the Holy Ghost, and thou art the unique and holy woman in whom the Saviour of the world finds perfect and pleasing repose. In thy pure womb and in thy loving heart He pours all the treasures of his power and love. Hence the Holy Spirit derives unfeigned pleasure from thee, O admirable Mary, when He wills to consecrate thy womb by the fulfillment of His divine mysteries. This adorable Spirit is a consuming fire, which inflames thy most holy soul, and consequently the loving heart, which is filled with the splendor of His divine majesty."[10]

The virginal heart of His heavenly Mother so charmed his soul that Saint Bernard expresses a loving complaint in one of his works, "O ravisher of hearts, thou hast ravished my heart; when wilt thou give it back to me?"[11]

The Order of Saint Francis has always counted sons outstanding for their writings and sermons on the doctrine of Mary's Immaculate Conception. Among these sons, Saint Bonaventure was most prominent for the fervor of his devotion to the Queen of Heaven. His special love for Mary is shown in the psalter composed in her honor, containing 150 psalms modeled on the psalms of David, in one of which he calls the heart of Mary the source of salvation. *Omnis salus de Corde Mariae scaturizat.*[12]

Saint Bonaventure in other treatises on the devotion to Mary portrays the symbolic pictures of her august heart. In his commentary on the second chapter of Saint Luke, he calls Mary's heart the Ark of the Covenant. As the Ark contained a portion of manna which God sent down from Heaven, so the heart of the Saviour's Mother kept all the mysteries of her divine son, all the words of life and the sacred truths

---

10 *Serm. panegyric.*
11 *In medit. sup. Salve.*
12 *Psal. B.V. Ps. 79.*
13 *Virginis fuit arca continens divinorum eloquiorum arcana. Et ideo per arcam Moysis designatur, de qua dicitur quod continebat tabulas legis divinae. In cap. 2 Luc. Unde Cor.*

that He brought down from Heaven to be the sweet and precious manna of our souls.[13]

Saint Bernardine of Siena was another son of the seraphic Saint Francis. So ardent and tender was Saint Bernardine's devotion to the Mother of God and to her amiable heart that it is difficult to find his equal.

In a sermon on Mary's Immaculate Conception Saint Bernardine shows the wonders of Our Lady's Admirable Heart which will be an object of rapture for all the denizens of Heaven. One marvel of the heart of Mary is that it is the focus of a mirror towards which all the rays of the sun converge. In this mirror he sees a fire so ardent that it inflames everything placed in front of it. "Similarly," says the Saint, "all the vehement desires of all the hearts of Patriarchs, Prophets, and the other saints of the Old Testament concerning the coming of the Redeemer, united in the holy heart of Mary as in their center, kindle therein such ardent desires that no mind can conceive them and no words express them."[14]

Saint Lawrence Justinian, Patriarch of Venice, gave manifest marks of his very special devotion to the Blessed Virgin Mary. His book, *De triumphanto agone Christi*, "The Triumphant Agony of Christ," represents Mary's sorrowful heart as a clear mirror of Our Lord's passion and as a perfect image of His death: *Clarissimum passionis Christi speculum et perfecta mortis ejus imago*. This implies that he who could see the maternal heart of the sorrowful Mother, as the angels see it, would also see the cords, the thorns, the nails, the spear, the wounds, the pain and all the torments that the beloved son suffered in His soul and body.

Richard of Saint Lawrence, zealous penitentiary of Rouen, four hundred years ago, wrote a work in twelve parts called *The Praises of the Glorious Virgin*, in which he mentions six things concerning Mary's heart.

The Admirable Heart of the Mother of God is the source of salvation.[15] It is the first of all hearts, which was worthy to receive in itself the Son of God, who came out of the bosom of the Father into this world.[16] In the meek and humble heart of Mary, mercy and justice gave each other the kiss of peace.[17] The amiable heart of Mary received the same wounds as our loving Redeemer suffered in His body.[18] The heart of our Mother was the armory and treasury of Sacred Scripture for the Old and New Testaments.[19] Lastly, Mary's Admirable Heart is the book

---

14 *Serm. 4 de Concept B.V.* art. 3, cap. 1.
15 *De Laud, B.V.* lib. 2, partit. 2, p. 104.
16 *Ibid.*
17 *Ibid.*
18 *Ibid.*

of life in which the life of Jesus Christ was written in gold letters by the Holy Ghost, the finger of God.[20]

The white habit of the sons of Saint Dominic shows that they belong in a special way to Mary, the Queen of Angels. After the principal aim of the Order, the glory of God, Saint Dominic founded it to teach by word and example the devotion to the Blessed Virgin Mary as a powerful means of salvation.

From among the writings of Saint Dominic's spiritual sons I have chosen a few excerpts from the Venerable Louis of Grenada on the loving heart of the Saviour's Mother.

"The holy Gospel ends the account of the sweet birth of the Redeemer by a very expressive sentence in which it mentions the heart of Mary thus: 'Mary kept all these words, pondering them in her heart.' The story of this Gospel is truly a royal banquet and a table which God has set for the elect and has covered with thousands of kinds of delicious food. The Child, the Mother, the birth, the crib, the angels and the shepherds, all details are filled with miracles distilling drops of honey. Everyone may take what pleases him and eat what he likes. As for myself I confess that the last dessert, I mean the last sentence in that Gospel story, which pictures the heart of Mary, is a dish of unspeakable deliciousness . . .

"O Queen of Heaven, O Gate of Paradise, Lady of the world, Sanctuary of the Holy Ghost, Throne of Wisdom, Temple of the Living God, guardian of the secrets of Jesus Christ, and witness of all His works, what didst thy heart feel in all these mysteries. . . . Who can understand what was in thy heart? She was astonished to behold the Word of God, a babe without speech, to see the Almighty wrapped in swaddling clothes and lying in a crib. She was enraptured by the goodness of God, His generosity, His humility and His extraordinary devotion. She was astonished to see how greatly He loved man, how much He cherished them, did them honor, longed for their salvation, ennobled and lifted them up to such a height by the mystery of His sacred humanity."[21]

Further testimony is found in the writings of four learned writers, who are almost like four Evangelists in teaching us the devotion to the Admirable Heart of Mary. I cite Joseph de la Cerda, Benedictine monk and professor of theology at the University of Salamanca; John Gerson, Chancellor of the University of Paris and French delegate to the Ecumenical Council of Constance; Nicolas

19 *Ibid.*, lib. 10, p. 593.
20 *Ibid.*, lib. 4, p. 309.
21 This excerpt is taken from the *Addition to the Memorial.*

Salicet, Abbot of the Cistercian Order; and Bartholomew de los Rios, of the Order of Saint Augustine, whose works are entitled *Hierarchia Mariana,* "Hierarchy of Mary."

Listen to the salutation to the most Holy Heart of Mary, taken from the *Antidotarium animae,* "Antidotarium of the Soul"[22] of Abbot Nicolas, whose assurance that he garnered the prayers and salutation from the writings of the Fathers demonstrates the antiquity of the devotion to the Admirable Heart of the Mother of God.

"I shall speak to thy heart, O Mary, mirror of angelic beauty. I shall speak to thy most pure heart, O Mistress of the world, I shall prostrate myself before thy holy temple and thank it with all the powers of my soul. I shall salute thy Immaculate Heart from the inmost recesses of my soul, thy heart which was found worthy to receive the only begotten Son of God coming out of the bosom of His eternal Father.

"Hail, unique sanctuary, which God consecrated by the unction of the Holy Ghost. Hail, Holy of Holies, which the Supreme Pontiff dedicated for his admirable and ineffable entrance on the day of His Incarnation. Hail, Ark of Sanctity, which kept within itself the Sacred Scripture engraved by the finger of God.

"Hail, Golden Urn, filled with celestial manna. In thee is found a delicious banquet, in thee are all delights, in thee are the remedies and sources of grace.

"Hail, Virginal Heart, inviolable sanctuary and noble dwelling place of the Blessed Trinity, in which Divinity met humanity in a kiss of love. Rejoice with an eternal joy.

"O Emerald Cup, whose brilliance will never fade, thou hast offered to our King, thirsting for our salvation, the delicious nectar of refreshing faith, at the blessed moment when thou didst answer the salutation of the Archangel: 'Behold the handmaid of the Lord: be it done unto me according to thy word.' May thy soul exalt, O Mary, Mother of sweetness, and may every creature praise the happiness of thy most holy heart from which comes the source of our salvation.

"O Furnace in which the Seraphim are inflamed! O Paradise of Delights! Oh, what pulsations of love, O Blessed Virgin Mary, did thrill thy heart, when the vivifying Spirit of God, like a burning wind, breathed on thee and drew thee to Him with thy whole soul.

"May thy most noble heart be forever blessed, O Mary, thy heart adorned with the gifts of celestial wisdom and inflamed with the ardor of charity. May thy heart be blessed, in which thou didst meditate and

---

22 This salutation is in Latin in the original edition of the *Admirable Heart.* Cf. *Oeuvres Completes,* v. 7, p. 295 ff.

cherish the sacred mysteries of our redemption, keeping them to reveal to us at the opportune time. Praise and love to thee, O most loving heart; honor and glory from all creatures forever and ever. Amen."

Among the Religious Orders existing in Holy Church, none has shown more zeal and ardor in the veneration and service of Our Lady than the illustrious Society of Jesus, whose constant work in this regard falls into three classes.

Firstly are the Sodalities of Our Lady, established in all Jesuit colleges, which are schools of Christian virtue as well as learning, blessed schools teaching the science of eternal salvation, which can never be wanting to those who cherish heartfelt devotion to the Mother of God.

Secondly, by their apostolic preaching the sons of Saint Ignatius have spread the knowledge and exaltation of the Admirable Mother of God throughout the world.

Thirdly, many of the members, who number over three hundred authors of note in this one Society, have devoted their pens to proclaiming the glorious perfections of the Admirable Heart of Mary.

I have no intention of setting forth here all that these writers have penned concerning the august heart of the Queen of Heaven, for it would make this work too long. I shall merely mention twelve whom I consider to be as twelve apostles of the perfections of Mary's incomparable heart. Here are their names: Francis Suarez, Osorius, one of the first disciples of Saint Ignatius, Saint Peter Canisius, Sebastian Baradius, Father John Eusebius of Nieremberg, Father John Baptist, Saint Jure, Father Stephen Binet, Father Francis Poiré, Father Paul Barry, Christopher de Vega, Cornelius a Lapidé and Father Honorat Nicquet.

If you ask me where these remarkable writers learned the science of the saving devotion to the heart of Mary, I can only reply that it sprang from the zealous heart of their illustrious father, Saint Ignatius, who bore constantly from the day of his conversion to the end of his life the image of the Admirable Heart of the Mother of our Saviour, which is preserved as a precious relic in the Jesuit College at Saragossa.

May almighty God vouchsafe that the example of this great Saint inspire the hearts of the readers of this book to imitate his devotion to the most holy heart of the Glorious Virgin Mary!

Chapter Two

ECCLESIASTICAL APPROBATIONS

The Holy Ghost has inspired and approved this devotion by specific ecclesiastical approbations. Pope Julius II,[1] memorable for his particular devotion to Our Lady of Loreto, promulgated three invocations to be recited at the sound of the Angelus bell, the second being in honor of the heart of Mary.

"O most glorious Queen of Mercy, I salute thy virginal heart, whose most perfect purity was never stained by sin."

Pope Clement X[2] solemnly authorized devotion to the Admirable Heart of the Blessed Virgin Mary in six formal bulls granted to the Congregation of Jesus and Mary in 1674. The Pontiff dedicated every church and chapel of the Congregation to the Holy Heart of Jesus and Mary and also gave permission to institute Confraternities or Societies under the same name with special indulgences for the members.

Cardinal Louis de Vendôme,[3] legate of His Holiness Clement IX in Paris gave his approbation to the devotion to the holy heart on two separate occasions. Both acts of the legate were confirmed by the Apostolic See and by Pope Clement IX.

Cardinal Peter de Berulle,[4] Founder of the French Oratorians, has left us a wonderful treatise, *Grandeurs of Christ*, in which I have found deeply inspired passages in praise of the Admirable Heart of the Mother of our Saviour. In one paragraph the saintly Cardinal speaks thus:

" . . . The state of the Mother of God gives Mary by nature and by grace the privilege to possess Jesus within herself and to possess the

---

1 Julius II was supreme pontiff from 1503–13.
2 Clement X, elected pope at the age of 80, sat on the pontifical throne from 1670 to 1676.
3 Cardinal Louis de Vendôme (1612–69) was appointed legate *a latere* to France by Clement IX. He died at Aix-la-Chapelle in 1669.
4 Cardinal Peter de Berulle (1575–1629) founded the Oratory of Jesus in 1611. The French Congregation of the Oratory was modeled on the one formed a few years before by Saint Philip Neri at Rome. Saint John Eudes was a member of the French Oratory from 1623 to 1643 when he left to found the Congregation of Jesus and Mary.

noblest part of Christ's being; to possess the spirit, the heart and the life of Christ so intimately that He is the spirit of her spirit, the heart of her heart, and the life of her life. O excess! O abyss! O excess of grandeurs! O abyss of marvels! O Mary, thou dost give life to Jesus Christ, and thou dost receive the life of Jesus Christ. Thou dost give life to Jesus, animating the heart and spirit of Jesus by thy heart and spirit. Thou dost receive from the heart and the body of Jesus living and dwelling in thee, life in thy heart and body and spirit together."

Another of Cardinal de Berulle's books entitled *Oeuvres de Dévotion* contains these very significant words on the mystery of the Incarnation.

" . . . It is the mystery of the two noblest and most closely united hearts that ever existed in Heaven and on earth. When Jesus Christ dwelt in Mary and was part of her being, the heart of Jesus was very close to the heart of Mary. When Mary was living in union with Jesus, He was her all, and the heart of Mary is very near the heart of Jesus and influenced her life. At that moment Jesus and Mary were but one living person. The heart of the one did not live nor beat but by the heart of the other . . ."

"O heart of Jesus living in Mary and by Mary! O heart of Mary living in Jesus and for Jesus! O sweet union of these two hearts! Blessed be the God of love Who united them together! May He unite our hearts to these two hearts, and may He make these hearts live in unity in the honor of the sacred unity which exists in the three divine Persons."

Here are other words from this holy Cardinal on the same subject:

"We should always seek the Son of God, and we should always find Him; for he who seeks Christ will find Christ: *Qui quaeret invenit*. There are three dwelling places in which to seek Him. First is the bosom of the eternal Father! Oh! what an august abode! Oh! what a celestial repose! The second dwelling is His sacred humanity. The third is the heart and the chaste womb of the Blessed Virgin."

In addition to the foregoing, no less than fifteen archbishops and bishops have authorized the devotion, the office and the celebration of the special feast in honor of the most Admirable Heart of the Mother of God.

Those granting formal approbation are: Archbishop Peter d'Hardivilliers of Bourges, Archbishop Francis Harlay de Champvalon of Rouen, Bishop Claude de la Madeleine de Ragny of Autun, Bishop Simon Le Gras[5] of Soissons, Bishop Henry de Baradat of Noyon, Bishop Leonor Goyon de Matignon of Coutances, Bishop James du Perron of Evreux, Bishop Henry de Maupas of Puy, who endorsed the devotion in his dual capacity of Bishop and Doctor of Theology, Bishop Andrew du Saussay of

---

5 Bishop Le Gras was a relative of Mademoiselle Le Gras, foundress of the Daughters of Charity.

Toul, also prince of the Holy Roman Empire and Royal Councillor, Bishop Francis de la Pallu of Heliopolis and Bishop Ignatius Cotolendi of Metellopolis, both Vicars Apostolic of China and Indo-China, where Bishop Cotolendi died in 1662, Bishop Francis de Nesmond of Bayeux and finally Bishop Francis de Montmorency-Laval, Bishop of Petraea and Vicar Apostolic of the whole of Canada, known as New France.

Bishop Laval's approbation reads as follows:

"Francis, by the grace of God and of the Apostolic See, Bishop of Petraea, Vicar Apostolic of the whole of Canada, called New France. The Holy Ghost has taught by Sacred Scripture and by the mouth of the Fathers the excellence of the holy heart of His worthy spouse, the Blessed Virgin Mary, and has by the same means exhorted all the faithful to have a particular devotion and veneration for her heart. This book,[6] written to enkindle in the hearts of its readers the devotion to the Admirable Heart and the Holy Name of Mary, has no need of our approbation, since it is in perfect conformity with the designs and intentions of the Holy Ghost. Hence it is not our will to grant approval when writing this, but rather to give public testimony of the particular esteem we feel after having read it carefully and to express the desire that this devotion be profoundly engraved within the hearts of all Christians. May the most lovable heart of the Mother of God, which is all aflame with love for His divine majesty, and with charity towards mankind, together with her most august name, be praised and honored by all men. May the Feasts, with the Offices and Masses contained in this book, be celebrated with fitting solemnity and devotion. This is the opinion that we hold of the book which we deem most worthy of being published. In witness thereof we have this testimony written by our own hand and sealed with our coat of arms."

Paris, this 23rd day of December 1662.

Francis, Bishop of Petraea

Furthermore, seven esteemed doctors of the Sorbonne have granted theological approbation to the devotion to the Admirable Heart of Mary in a joint submission.

"All the true children of the most holy Mother of God should be convinced that her most holy heart was never stained with any kind of sin; that it was always full of divine grace and animated, possessed and guided by the Holy Ghost; that it never existed for a moment without

---

6   This book is *Dévotion au très saint Coeur de la bienheureuse Vierge Marie* written and published by Saint John Eudes in 1648. The Saint had given a complimentary copy to his personal friend, Bishop Laval.

loving God; that its love for the Almighty exceeded that of all the hearts of men and angels; that the heart of Mary was perpetually filled with charity, zeal and vigilance for our salvation as well as with mercy and compassion for our miseries; that it was inebriated a hundredfold with the gall and myrrh and transpierced with a thousand arrows of sorrow because of us. We have been most willingly led to grant our approbation to this book entitled *Dévotion au trés saint Coeur de la bienheureuse Vierge Marie* containing a proper Office and Mass in honor of her heart, and the other prayers and exercises of devotion on the subject, which we the undersigned, Doctors of the Faculty of Sacred Theology in Paris, have read and in which we have found nothing that is not in conformity with Holy Scripture, the teaching of the Church and of the Fathers, and consider it capable of exciting those who read it to honor and imitate the most holy and most worthy heart of Mary.

Given at Paris, this 31st day of January 1661.

M. Grandin
C. Gobinet
Anthony Raguier de Pousse
J. Desgardiers de Parlages
Saussoy
Blouet de Than
L'Amy

Chapter Three

Example of Saints and Religious Orders

The Holy Spirit has also inspired many saints to show forth by word and example a most special devotion to the Immaculate Heart of the Blessed Virgin Mary.

It is true that every saint belongs to the court of the Queen of all Saints; nevertheless, there are certain ones who stand out as being very closely associated with the royal heart of Mary, their sovereign Lady. First, of course, is Saint Joseph, her most chaste spouse, incomparably dear to her holy heart. Even her parents, Saint Anne and Saint Joachim, cannot dispute the first place of Saint Joseph in her heart, having conceded it during their lifetime, when they entrusted the Virgin Mary to his care. Then comes Saint John the Baptist, truly the eldest son of Mary in the life of grace. Saint Gabriel the Archangel had the inestimable privilege of being the Guardian Angel of the immaculate Mother of God. And what can we say of Saint John, the disciple most dear to the heart of Our Lord, to whom Our Saviour entrusted the life and heart of His beloved Mother from the cross? Saint Luke the Evangelist also belongs to the heart of Mary because he was chosen by her to reveal the sublime secret to mankind, that "she kept all those words in her heart."

There are many saints who have consecrated themselves under the special designation of spouse of the Queen of Angels. Among these I name as examples: Saint Edmund of Canterbury, Saint Robert, Saint Stephen, Saint Alberic, Founder of the Cistercian Order, Saint Bernard, Saint Dominic and his disciple Blessed Alanus, Blessed Herman the Premonstratensian, Saint Francis of Assisi, Saint Bernardine of Siena, and so many others whose names are inscribed in the Book of Life.

Saint Mechtilde and Saint Gertrude, noted daughters of Saint Benedict, in the revelation of their surpassing devotion to the Sacred

Heart of Jesus, have shown most clearly the beauties and mysteries of devotion to the loving heart of the Mother of Our Lord and Saviour.

Saint Thomas Becket, martyred Archbishop of Canterbury, had special devotion to the seven joys of the heart of Our Lady during her earthly life, seven joys that accompanied the unfolding of the mysteries of redemption: the Annunciation, the Visitation, the Birth of Our Lord, the Adoration of the Magi, the Finding of the Child Jesus in the Temple, the Resurrection of Our Lord, and finally her own glorious Assumption into Heaven.

The contemplation of these joys of Our Lady gave much joy and devotion to Saint Thomas of Canterbury; yet Our Lady appeared to him and revealed that she would extend special intercession, at the hour of death, to those who united to her seven earthly joys the seven additional joys of her holy heart in Heaven. Saint Thomas composed a hymn proclaiming these seven heavenly joys, an inspiring canticle which is still sung and recited in many places. Therefore this Saint well deserves to rank among those specially favored by Our Lady because of devotion to her Admirable Heart.

I have mentioned more than once the special tenderness of the heart of Mary towards the Cistercian Order. Also belonging particularly to the heart of Our Lady was Saint Teresa, together with the entire Order of Discalced Carmelites. In addition to the writings of Saint Teresa herself, I have seen a book published in Milan, by one of her followers, Venerable Father John of Saint Joseph, which gives a most beautiful exposition of the ardent love and union of the heart of the Mother of God with the heart of her Divine Child.

Saint Philip Neri, founder of the Oratorians at Rome, inspired in the members of his Order devotion patterned after his own signal love of Our Lady, devotion expressed in the writings of Dom Francis Marchese. His anthology of numerous devotional practices in honor of the Blessed Virgin Mary contains eight remarkably inspirational exercises for the Octave of the Feast of her most Admirable Heart.

Among other members of religious orders who have merited distinction as votaries of the heart of Mary because of their writings in her honor are John Tauler of the Dominican Order, Blosius the Benedictine and Lanspergius the Carthusian.

In the life of Mother Mary Villani, a Dominican nun who died in Naples in the odor of sanctity on March 26, 1670, there is a signal proof of her devotion to the holy heart of the Blessed Virgin Mary. Mother Villani described how the Holy Ghost seemed to inspire her to recite three Hail Marys in honor of the hearts of Jesus and Mary. At the first Ave she offered the Immaculate Heart of Mary to the Sacred Heart of Our Lord; at the second Ave she honored the sweet heart of the Blessed Mother by presenting the heart of her beloved son in thanksgiving for the graces He bestowed upon the heart of Mary; at the third Ave she offered her own heart to the united hearts of Jesus and Mary. Mother Villani's life records that this practice was rewarded by a vision of Our Lady, in which the Blessed Virgin expressed the joy it imparted to her and promised special protection for those who practiced this devotion to her heart and that of her divine son.

Saint Francis de Sales is another great saint whose words glow with burning love for the heart of Our Lady, a love communicated to his devout daughters in religion, the Religious of the Visitation. We also see the Ursulines, and the Congregation of Our Lady, bearing in their lives the mark of the charity inflaming the heart of Mary, the Mother of Fair Love. There are many other religious and holy persons who celebrate every year, some on the eighth of February, others on the first of June, the Feast of the Heart of the Queen of Heaven, the most compassionate, most generous, most magnificent of all hearts, a heart that cannot fail to pour upon this world, and obtain in the next, the richest of blessings for those who persevere in its love and veneration.

The Priests of the Congregation of Jesus and Mary have a great cause for consolation and a very special obligation of thanksgiving to Our Lord and to His most holy Mother for being called and received into a Congregation belonging particularly to their most holy hearts. Five principal reasons emphasize this:

Firstly, the Congregation is wholly consecrated to this Admirable Heart, one of the chief objects of its establishment being to give special honor to this august heart, which is regarded and revered as its Patron, and as the model held up to its members, so that they may learn to conform their own hearts to its sublime pattern.

Secondly, all the churches and chapels of the Congregation are dedicated and consecrated to the honor of the same most holy heart. Our Holy Father Pope Clement X in his Bulls has named them "The Churches and Chapels of the Heart of Jesus and Mary."

Thirdly, this Congregation was the first to hold solemn celebration of the Feasts of the Admirable Heart of Jesus and Mary. It is not necessary to be concerned over the extreme unworthiness of him whom God has used to establish these feasts, who is the least of men, the first of sinners and the most unworthy of priests. Almighty God who created the world from nothing, and retrieved it without its having contributed to its own redemption, is wont to choose things most vile and low, which are nothing, to accomplish the designs of His will. Did not God use Saint Julian, a poor Cistercian, to induce Pope Urban IV to establish the Feast of Corpus Christi?

Fourthly, from the time Our Saviour and His Blessed Mother gave birth to this Congregation in Holy Church, it has experienced the extraordinary effects of love of the Admirable Heart. Those who have the happiness to be members of the Congregation should have holy confidence that the Blessed Virgin will cherish all of them in her maternal heart as she has so repeatedly proved. If they raise no obstacles by their sins and infidelities, they will have a secure place for the hereafter, in her loving heart, which is a Heaven more vast and extensive than all the Heavens, for it is the abode of Him whom the Heavens cannot contain.

Fifthly, if Saint Paul assures all his spiritual children that neither life nor death shall ever separate them from his heart[1], how much more strongly does Our Blessed Mother give the same assurance to her true children, for whom her love is incomparably greater than that of Saint Paul for his disciples. But, on the other hand, each one of us should strive to live so that we may exclaim like Saint Paul: "Who shall separate me from the loving heart of my adorable Father Jesus and my heavenly Mother Mary? Shall it be tribulation? or distress? or famine? or nakedness? or danger? or persecution? or the sword? No, I am sure that, with the grace of God, neither death, nor life, nor angels, nor principalities, nor powers, nor things present, nor things to come, nor might, nor height, nor depth, nor any other creature, shall be able to separate my heart from the holy heart of Jesus and of His most Blessed Mother, who is also mine."

As for the Religious of Our Lady of Charity, their very great obligations to the most holy heart of the all-glorious Virgin shall certainly prevent any one from surpassing them in the love they owe to her heart, after the heart of Jesus, the most lovable, loving and loved of all hearts. They dwell in an Order which originated at the same time as the Congregation of Jesus and Mary, and is likewise entirely consecrated to the Admirable Heart of the Mother of Fair Love. In token of this, the Sisters wear a silver heart bearing an image of the Mother of our Saviour, and are called Religious of Our Lady of Charity, because they have been founded to work for the salvation of derelict souls, and salvation is the greatest object of the charity that abounds in the heart of Mary. They should think most highly of their religious vocation and follow with the greatest care and affection the devotional exercises of their holy institute. They should often consider the very ardent love of Mary's heart for souls redeemed by the most Precious Blood of her

1 2 Cor. 7,3.

divine Son so that their own hearts may experience the sacred fire of charity with which they ought to exert themselves in the task of saving the souls entrusted to them by divine providence.

This chapter has presented a large number of saints and religious orders who belong very specially to the most august heart of the Queen of Saints. Through their example the Holy Ghost preaches eloquently the devotion to the holy heart of Mary. Let us offer to her Admirable Heart the honor rendered to it by all these saints and holy persons and cultivate an ardent desire to imitate their zeal and ardor. Let us beg them to make us sharers in their devotion and to associate us in the glory and praise that is rendered to the most powerful and merciful Queen of all Christian hearts that love almighty God.

Part Eight*

FOURTH FOUNDATION OF THE DEVOTION:
SANCTITY OF THE ADMIRABLE HEART OF MARY

EXPOSITION OF ITS EXCELLENCE

---

* Two chapters in the original work have been omitted in this edition.

Chapter One

HEART OF MARY, IMMACULATE AND SINLESS

With good reason does Sacred Scripture call Mary the "Valiant Woman," for she is the marshal of the armies of God Himself and the principal enemy of the infernal serpent. The battalions of Hell fear Mary far more than a small, weak body of foot soldiers would fear a powerful mechanized enemy force in battle array. She is as "terrible as an army set in array."[1] She has completely crushed the serpent's head. God's words to Satan after the fall of man, "She shall crush thy head,"[2] mean that Our Lady would vanquish every kind of sin, mortal, venial, actual and original, the last being especially designated by the infernal monster's horrible head.

Mary would sooner have suffered all the torments of earth and of Hell rather than to consent to the least venial sin, and a thousand times less to mortal sin. Thus did she completely overcome actual sin.

Concerning original sin, the holy Fathers, famous Doctors, learned theologians and sacred Councils have defended the honor of the Immaculate Conception and maintained that the almighty God preserved Mary from original sin. I cannot understand how there are today so many Catholics and even devout persons who seem to want to place this most worthy glorious Virgin on a level with the other children of Adam, waging war against their Creator from the first moment of their existence. It is impossible to understand why anyone would maintain that the most holy Mother of God, purer than the sun, was tainted in her conception with the stain of original sin.[3]

---

1 Cant. 6, 3.
2 Gen. 3, 15.
3 Saint John here inveighs against Catholics of his day who refused to believe in the Immaculate Conception of the Blessed Virgin Mary. He builds up a veritable thesis, adducing proofs from Scripture, the Councils, the Fathers, the Religious Orders and the liturgical feasts kept in honor of Mary Immaculate. This chapter is of special interest because the dogma of the Immaculate Conception was not then defined as an article of the faith.

To deny the Immaculate Conception of Our Blessed Lady is to accuse of error the infallible word of eternal Truth, Sacred Scripture, which calls Mary the one "dove"[4] without sin or rancor, the "all fair"[5] and the "immaculate one" in whom "there is not a spot."[6]

To hold that Mary was not preserved from original sin is to oppose the divine pronouncements of the Holy Ghost, the councils of the Catholic Church, especially the holy Council of Trent, which declared manifestly that there is no question of Mary being included in the decree of original sin.[7]

To assert that the Mother of God was conceived in sin is to prefer private opinion to that of the Apostles, in particular, Saint Andrew, Saint James the Less and Saint James the Greater. The glorious Apostle Saint Andrew at the hour of death, expressed himself as follows, "As the first Adam was formed out of the earth before it was cursed by God, so the second Adam was formed from the virginal flesh never sullied by the malediction of Heaven."[8] The Apostle Saint James the Less makes a special mention of the Mother of his divine master, calling her "most holy, immaculate, blessed above all creatures, more honorable than the Cherubim, more glorious than the Seraphim, always blessed and altogether irreproachable.[9] Saint Thesiphon, disciple of Saint James the Greater, called the "mouth" of the great Apostle, has left us the doctrine taught by the Apostles themselves, "This Virgin, this Mary, this holy one has been preserved from original sin from the first moment of her conception. Never would the Angel have said to Mary, 'Hail, full of grace,' if she had been conceived in original sin."[10]

To refuse to believe in Mary's exemption from original sin is to show a lack of respect and submission to the Sovereign Pontiffs Alexander VI, Julius II, Leo X, Paul V, and Gregory XV, who authorized the doctrine of Mary's pure conception, by recommending that a Feast be kept in its honor, and by approving its office. Some of these pontiffs even went so far as to forbid under pain of excommunication any opposition to this teaching either by word of mouth or in writing, in public or in private.

To uphold that Mary was not conceived immaculate is to believe that one has more light than the many Cardinals, Patriarchs, Archbishops and Bishops from all parts of the world, who favored the

---

4 Cant. 6, 8.
5 Cant. 4, 7.
6 Ibid.
7 Sessio 5, De Peccato Orig.
8 Abdias in gestis D. Andriae, 1, 4. Cf. Marraccius, Apostoli Mariani, cap. 4 in fine.
9 Liturg. S. Jacobi in Bibliotheca Patrum, tom. 1.
10 Cf. Vega, Theol. Mar. Paul. 3, cert. 5, no. 258.

doctrine of the Immaculate Conception. It is to place oneself above the Fathers of Holy Church and all the Religious Orders of Saint Anthony, Saint Basil, Saint Benedict, the Orders of the Cistercians, the Carthusians, the Franciscans, the Dominicans, the Society of Jesus, the Barnabites, the Theatines, and others that testified great zeal and ardor in defending the Holy Mother of God from the stigma implied in fact that she was numbered among the children of wrath and malediction.

To contradict the belief of the Catholic Church is to condemn the famous universities of Paris, Cologne, Maintz, Valencia, Salamanca, Coimbra, Barcelona, Seville, Cracow, and nearly all the other universities of Christendom, that refused to grant the degree of Doctor of Theology until the candidate bound himself by oath to sustain the innocence of Mary's conception.

To withhold one's assent to Mary's privilege is to give the lie to five hundred doctors in France, Italy, Spain, Germany, England, Scotland, Poland, Portugal and Flanders, who asseverated to this truth by numerous beautiful and learned books. The Society of Jesus alone employed more than sixty of its members to defend the honor of their heavenly Mother in this matter by their erudite and pious writings.

To maintain that Mary was not spotless in her conception is to ridicule the many miracles wrought by almighty God, many of which are mentioned in the letters of Saint Anselm. It is to show no fear of the terrible chastisements which divine justice will inflict upon those who oppose this doctrine as may be seen in a book written by John of Carthagena, a Franciscan.[11] It is to give preference to the impiety of the detestable Calvin, so full of hatred for the Mother of God, rather than to the devotion of the Christian world to the holiness of Mary's conception. It is to give more favor to the demons who were created in the state of grace than to the Queen of Angels. It is to elevate Adam and Eve, the first man and woman, who were the cause of the loss of countless souls, above their daughter Mary, the mediatrix of Salvation and the restorer of grace.

Lastly, to impugn the dogma of Mary's preservation from original sin, is to reject the wisdom of the Catholic Church, which solemnizes the Feast of the Immaculate Conception with so much fervor throughout the world, setting oneself against a fact authorized by the Church and stated by Saint Augustine in the following words: *Quod per universum orbem commendat Ecclesia, hoc quin ita faciendum sit disputare insolentissimae insaniae est.* "To question anything that is done throughout the whole world by the order and recommendation of the Church is the most insolent folly imaginable."[12]

11 Homilia de sacris arcanis Deiparae, Lib. 1, Hom. 19, Sec. 4.
12 Epist. 118.

O Blessed Virgin Mary, I humbly beseech thee, by thy immaculate conception and through thy pure heart, to take full possession of my heart. Give it completely to thy divine son and beg Him to banish from it all sin and to establish in it forever the perfect reign of His divine love.

Chapter Two

HEART OF MARY, OCEAN OF GRACE

It is in the heart, that is, in the very depth and substance of the Christian soul, that sanctifying grace resides and exercises its powerful influence. There grace establishes the throne of its power, extending to the memory, the intellect and the will, affecting all the higher and lower faculties, and all the internal and external senses.

Granting this, I say that the Admirable Heart of Mary is an ocean of grace. Yet it is not I who make this statement, it is the Archangel Gabriel, sent by God from Heaven to announce to the Queen of Angels that the divine majesty had chosen her to be the Mother of His divine Son. The Archangel greets Mary by telling her first of all that she is "full of grace."[1] Notice that he does not say she will be, but that she is full of grace.

Would you know how it is that Mary was full of grace even before the Son of God became Incarnate in her womb? You must consider two truths taught by several distinguished theologians.

The first is that Mary was filled with such eminent grace at the moment of her Immaculate Conception that, according to many learned divines, she already surpassed the chief of Seraphim and the greatest of saints. From the beginning of her existence she possessed more grace than they enjoyed at the time of their greatest perfection.

The second truth is that the heavenly Virgin was never idle, but remained constantly turned towards God, ever exercising her love for His divine majesty. She loved Him with her whole heart, her whole soul and all her strength, according to the full extent of the grace that was in her, so that grace was doubled in her soul, if not from moment to moment, at least from hour to hour, and perhaps more often. She had therefore attained to an inconceivable and unutterable degree of grace when the Archangel Gabriel saluted her as being full of grace.

1 Luke 1, 28.

Now if this most Blessed Virgin was so full of grace before conceiving the Son of God, what must have been the abundance and plenitude of grace poured by the Holy Spirit into her heart and her virginal bosom, to make her worthy to give birth to the Son whom the eternal Father begets from all eternity in His own adorable bosom; to make her worthy to be the true Mother of His Son? Surely, the dignity of Mother of God being infinite, the grace bestowed on the Blessed Virgin to prepare her to give being and life to God Himself must also in a way be infinite, for Saint Thomas assures us it was proportioned to her sublime dignity.

If it is a great privilege to be Mother of God, and if no grander destiny can be conceived than for a mere creature to form the Son of God of her own substance, what shall we say of the glory of having Him in her womb and making Him live by her virginal blood for a space of nine months! What abundance of grace did the Holy Ghost pour into her heart to make her worthy thus to continue her office of motherhood towards such a Son! Who could fathom what the adorable Infant, infinitely rich, generous and grateful, gave in return to the Mother from whom He constantly received during those nine months a new being and a new life, a life incomparably more precious than all the lives of angels and of men? To this we must add all the love and praises Mary incessantly rendered Him then. If Jesus bestows an eternal kingdom upon those who give a glass of water to the poor for love of Him, what gifts, what treasures, what graces did He constantly pour into Mary's pure heart, in which He did not encounter the least obstacle to the inexhaustible blessings which He ardently wished to communicate to her.

Mary performed the duties of a mother towards her son Jesus not only when she conceived and gave birth to Him in Bethlehem; but also when she nourished Him, carried Him in her arms and on her bosom, clothed Him, delivered Him from the fury of Herod, brought Him to the Temple of Jerusalem, led Him back to Nazareth and cared for Him as every good mother cares for her child.

If, according to Saint Bernardine,[2] Mary merited by her consent to the Incarnation of the Son of God more grace than all the angels and saints together by all their acts of virtue, what graces and merits must our Saviour's most worthy Mother have acquired when she so often carried Him on her virginal bosom. What blessings she received during her familiar conversations with her son, when she possessed Him on earth and listened to His divine discourses; but above all when, in the Temple on the day of His presentation, as well as on Calvary at the time of His

2 Plus meruit gloriosa Virgo in suo consensu, scilicet conceptionis Filii Dei, quam omnes creaturae, sive Angeli, sive homines, in cunctis suis actibus, motibus et cogitationibus. Serm. 5 pro festivitat B.M.V.

death, she offered Him to the eternal Father as a sacrifice for the salvation of mankind.

If the Holy Ghost poured into this admirable Mother's heart torrents of almost infinite grace to render her worthy of giving Him birth, what must He have done to dispose her to sacrifice her beloved son in spite of so great sorrow and love? We can certainly state that as her heart was then turned into an immense sea of sorrow, so did it also become an unfathomable and boundless ocean of grace and holiness.

Who could conceive the almost infinite abundance of graces that filled the loving heart of the Mother of the crucified Saviour when He visited her after His Resurrection? Measure, if you can, the extremity of this desolate Mother's sorrow when she beheld her beloved son actually die amid frightful torments and you will understand the immense graces she thus merited, which Jesus Christ bestowed upon her after His Resurrection and on the day of His Ascension.

What treasures of grace enriched the most holy heart of the Mother of God through the divine Sacrifice of the Altar at which she daily assisted with unutterable devotion, and by her daily communions made with inconceivable love during the fifteen years she remained on earth after her son's Ascension!

After all this, be not surprised if I say that the Blessed Virgin's heart is an ocean of grace, and if the mouthpieces of the Holy Ghost proclaim the grace of this glorious Virgin to be immense, even as the capacity of her heart. "The grace of the Holy Virgin is immense," says Saint Epiphanius.[3] "When I desire to contemplate the immensity of thy grace and of thy glory, my mind fails me and my tongue is dumb," writes Saint Anselm.[4] "The sacred Virgin is a treasure of life and an immense abyss of grace," exclaims Saint John Damascene.[5] "The grace wherewith Mary was filled," asserts Saint Bonaventure, "was certainly an immense grace."

For an immense vessel cannot be filled unless its contents are likewise immense. Now Mary is a most immense vessel, having contained Him whom the Heavens cannot contain. If she encompassed God in her bosom, how much more truly in her heart? And if the immense capacity of her heart was filled with grace we must necessarily conclude that the grace which filled such a capacity was itself immense."[6]

Immense and eternal thanks be to the sovereign Author of grace, who gave His Blessed Mother so great and vast a heart and filled it with

---

3 *Gratia sanctae Virginis est immensa. In Orat. de laud. Virg.*

4 *Immensitatem gratiae tuae et gloriae considerare cupienti, O Virgo, sensus deficit, lingua fatiscit. Lib. de Excell. Virg.*

5 *Virgo, vitae thesaurus, gratiae abyssus immensa. Orat. 2 de dorm. Virg.*

6 *Specul. B.V. Lect. 5.*

such riches that it became an ocean of grace and a sea of blessings for all true children of her most sweet and loving heart! O Admirable Heart, thou wast ever closed to sin of every kind and filled with the highest sanctity of which a human heart is capable; behold I now offer thee my heart. Deign to take full and eternal possession of it, suffer not that anything displeasing to God may enter my heart but implore His Divine Majesty to establish in it the perfect reign of His grace and of His love.

Not only is the Admirable Heart of the Saviour's Mother an ocean of grace, containing and almost infinitely surpassing all the graces of the Church, triumphant and militant, but it is also their source and origin. As the eternal Father chose Mary from all eternity that through her we might receive Him who is the first author and principle of all grace, so did God likewise choose her, that through His handmaid we might receive all the graces proceeding from that first source. As God deigned to give us a Saviour only with the holy Virgin's consent, so also did He eternally decree to grant any gift or grace only through Mary. "God wishes us to have everything through Mary's hands," says Saint Bernard.[7] "None is saved but through thee, O holy Virgin," says Saint Germanus of Constantinople. "None is delivered from evil but through thee; through thee alone do all receive the gifts and grace of God."[8] Hence does the Church salute and invoke her as Mother of Grace: *Maria Mater gratiae*. "It is no wonder," exclaims Saint Bonaventure, "that the graces of all the saints overflow in Mary as the rivers flow into the sea, for the grace of graces was to be communicated to the whole Church by her, according to the saying of Saint Augustine: 'Thou art full of grace, O Mary, of the grace thou didst find in the Bosom of God, which thou wast found worthy to spread over the whole earth.'"[9]

Finally, Saint Bernard,[10] Saint Fulgentius,[11] Saint Bonaventure,[12] and many other Fathers agree that it was necessary for the Mother of our Saviour to contain in herself all graces necessary and useful for her state, because every grace is given to men through her intercession.

O my God, how admirable is Thy goodness towards the children of men! Under what obligation are we to serve Thee, to praise Thee and to love Thee in return for all the abundant and most excellent graces wherewith Thou hast enriched the glorious Virgin! We are as much

---

7 *Nihil nos Deus habere voluit quod per Mariae manus non transiret. Serm. de Nativ. B. Virg.*

8 *Nullus est qui salvus fiat. O Sanctissima, nisi per te: nemo est qui liberetur a malis, nisi per te, O purissima; nemo est cui donum concedatur, nisi per te, O charissima. Specul. B.M.V. lect. 3.*

9 *Quid mirum est si omnis gratia in Mariam confluxit, per quam tanta gratia ad omnes defluxit? Ait enim Augustinus: Gratia es plena, Maria, etc.*

10 *In Serm. de Aquae ductu.*

11 *In Serm. de laud. Mar.*

12 *In Spec. lect. 3.*

compelled to gratitude as if Thou hadst granted these graces to each one of us in particular, for Thou didst give them to Mary, not for herself alone, but for each one of us, that she might be made worthy to become the Mother of the only begotten Son, and to give Him to us as our saviour, our brother, our father, our head, our soul, our heart, our life and our all. May Heaven and earth and every creature therein bless, praise and glorify thee for ever!

O Mother of perfect grace, thou wast the woman chosen to find the grace that all mankind had so unhappily lost. Through thee the God of grace and goodness restored to us what we had lost. To thee, after Jesus Thy divine son, must we have recourse in order to find the graces we need to serve Him and to assure our own salvation. Thy maternal heart is the treasure and the treasurer of all these graces. In thy most loving and ardent heart we cannot fail to find them. Hence dare we say to thee, with the beloved of thy heart, Saint Bernard, "O Mother of Mercy, open the door of thy most tender heart to the prayers and sighs of the children of Adam, thou who dost not despise the sinner however horrible his condition, if he but cry to thee and implore thy aid with a penitent and contrite heart."[13]

---

13 *Aperi itaque tu, Mater misericordiae, benignissimi Cordis tui januam suspiriosis precatibus filiorum Adam . . . Tu peccatorem, quantumlibet foetidum, non horres, non despicis, si ad te suspiraverit, tuumque interventum poenitenti corde flagitaverit. In Deprec. B.V.*

Chapter Three

HEART OF MARY, MIRACLE OF LOVE

Sanctifying grace is a great queen who never walks alone, but is always accompanied by the three theological virtues, the four cardinal virtues, the seven gifts and twelve fruits of the Holy Ghost and the eight evangelical beatitudes.

All these virtues and graces are found within the most august heart of the Mother of God. As her heart is the abode of sanctifying grace, it is likewise the palace of the virtues, gifts and beatitudes, these heavenly princesses who can never be separated from their queen. Her most holy heart is an ocean of grace, encompassing all the grace merited for us by the Precious Blood of Our Saviour. As grace raises the holiness of her blessed heart above all the sanctity of Heaven and earth, so all the virtues reigning in her heart shine more brightly by far than in all other hearts of the Church Triumphant and Militant.

It would give me great pleasure to describe the marvelous perfections of each virtue, but lack of space obliges me to speak only of her most ardent love for God, her surpassing charity towards us, her most profound humility, and her perfect submission to the divine will.

Let us begin with love, and say boldly that the Admirable Heart of the Mother of our Saviour is a living miracle of love. My intention is to show you the principle and origin of the love of God which consumes the Blessed Virgin's heart, the qualities and perfections of that love, and its marvelous effects.

Would you know the origin and principle of this peerless love? Then raise the eyes of faith to the adorable heart of the Father of all goodness, to the ineffable heart of the Holy Ghost, who is the essential and uncreated love. There you shall behold the primal and eternal source of the greatest love that ever was or shall be in the heart of any creature save that of Christ.

The eternal Father, having willed to communicate His divine paternity to the Blessed Virgin by making her the Mother of His only begotten Son, made her participate in His own paternal love, that she might love His Incarnate Son with a love worthy of the Mother of God-made-Man.

The Son of God, on His part, united His most holy Mother to Himself so intimately that, after the hypostatic union, there never was or can be a union so close as that which binds our Saviour to His Blessed Mother. Undoubtedly, He communicated to her His love for His heavenly Father and thus prepared her to cooperate with Him in fulfilling that divine Father's will concerning the great work entrusted to Him, the work of the redemption of the world.

Then the Holy Ghost, having chosen this Virgin of virgins to be His spouse, must have inflamed Her virginal heart with a love worthy of so exalted a privilege; namely the love which the chosen bride of God must experience for His divine spouse, who is Himself all love, and has transmuted her with love, so that the bride may become like unto the Bridegroom.

Such is the principle, such the source of the divine love burning in the heart of the Queen of Heaven for the Father, the Son and the Holy Ghost. Let us now mention the rare perfections that enrich the heart of Mary. Here are twelve principal characteristics that impart a marvelous lustre to the sublime love of Mary's heart. Hers is a love most holy, most wise, most prudent, most strong, most ardent, most zealous, most constant, most vigilant, most patient, most faithful, most joyful and most pure.

As for the effects of the love that reigns in the heart of the Queen of Heaven, it would be easier to count the stars of the firmament than to number them. Count, if you can, all the moments Our Lady spent on earth, and you will be counting as many operations of Mary's love for God, for she never ceased to love Him a single moment during the entire course of her life. Count all her thoughts, words and actions, the exercise of every faculty of her soul, and of all her interior and exterior senses, and you will likewise be counting as many effects of her love, for she obeyed most perfectly the command of her divine spouse. "Put me as a seal upon thy heart, as a seal upon thy arm."[1] Hence all her interior and external actions were stamped with the seal of divine love. Count all the acts of faith, hope, charity, justice, prudence, fortitude, temperance, humility, obedience, patience and all other moral virtues which she practiced during the years of her life and you will again be counting as many manifestations of her love, because that love was the principle, the soul and the life of all her virtues. Count all the services she so lovingly rendered to her dearest son at His birth, during His

1 Cant. 8, 6.

childhood and throughout His entire life; all the steps she took in her journeys with Him and for Him; all the burdens, pains and anguish she bore for Him on account of her incredible love for Him; all the tears so abundantly shed for Him and you will still be counting further effects of her incomparable love.

But, to say much in few words, you should understand that perfect love possessed, filled and penetrated so completely the heart, soul, and all the faculties of the Virgin Mother that it constituted the soul of her soul, the life of her life, the mind of her mind and the heart of her heart. Thus love inspired and accomplished everything in her and by her. If she prayed, love prayed in and by Mary, if she adored God, love adored and praised Him in her and through her; if she spoke, love spoke by her lips; if she was silent, her silence stemmed from love; if she worked, love motivated her action; if she rested, love caused her repose; if she ate or drank, it was in obedience to the words of the Holy Ghost, who is essential love, "Whether you eat or drink, or whatsoever else you do, do all to the glory of God."[2] If she mortified herself, her decision was moved and guided by the same love which kept her in a state of constant mortification.

Finally, the virginal heart of Mary became so completely transfigured by love, that Suarez[3] boldly affirms that the effects and acts of its love were innumerable. Now if Saint Bernardine writes that the seven words spoken by the Blessed Virgin, as related in the holy Gospel, were seven flames of love, what shall we say of all the acts and effects of love which sprang from that glowing furnace, except that they were as many fires and flames of divine love, which would be capable of kindling all the hearts in the universe, if no obstacles were raised by the frigidity of sin? To this we must add the further words of Saint Bernardine, "The Blessed Virgin's love for her son was so great that she would have been willing to die for Him times without number."[4] Furthermore, it is quite certain that Our Lady's love was almost without limit or measure. Hence one must not hesitate to say she would have been ready to suffer as many deaths and as many infernal torments for her son's sake as there are atoms in the air and grains of sand on the seashore. Now count all the acts of love mentioned by Suarez and by Saint Bernardine, as well as all the deaths and infernal torments she would gladly have suffered, and you will count the effects of the love that consumes the marvelous heart of the Mother of Fair Love.

2   1 Cor. 10, 31.
3   *In 4 Part. disput.* 18, sect. 4, 5.
4   The Saint does not give the reference for this quotation.

Nor is this all. You must also count the numberless acts and the myriad effects of love that were ever produced in Heaven and on earth by the hearts of all the Seraphim and other angelic Spirits, of all the holy Confessors, of all the holy Virgins and of all the saints, and you will still be counting as many effects of the ineffable love that burns in the heart of our Saviour's Mother. It is undoubtedly true that *Quod est causa causae, est causa causati*, that the effects proceeding from a cause must be attributed to the principle and origin of that cause. Now it is a doctrine of faith that Mary is the Mother of the God of love. We must conclude, therefore, that the love which burns in the hearts of all the angels and saints, and all the acts and effects of love ever produced by them, having proceeded from the adorable heart of that God of love, are to be reckoned among the effects of the Admirable Heart of His holy Mother. This is what Saint Bernard has in mind when he tells us that God had decreed that we should receive everything through Mary.[5] And another holy Doctor adds, "Without Mary's petition and intercession, nothing comes down to us from Heaven."[6]

This is also signified by the words of Raymund Jourdain, "Whatever good and precious things the world possesses has come to it through Mary, in Mary, with Mary and from Mary."[7] And have we not heard Saint Irenaeus explain that God accomplished the mystery of the Incarnation only with the consent of the glorious Virgin because He willed that she should be the principle of every good for mankind?[8]

O Jesus Christ, God of love, may all the hearts and tongues of angels and of men love and glorify thee infinitely and eternally for having established such a furnace of love in thy peerless Mother's divine heart. O God of my heart, I offer thee all her love to atone for the icy coldness of my miserable heart. O Mother of love, send into our hearts some living sparks from the divine fire that burns in thy virginal heart, and be pleased to associate thy unworthy children with thee in all the love and glory thou dost forever render to the most adorable and amiable Trinity.

---

5 *Totum nos Deus habere voluit per Mariam. Serm. de Nativ. B. Virg.*
6 *Sine negotiatione et sine petitione Mariae nihil descendit de caelo.* The reference for the text is not given in the original work of Saint John Eudes.
7 *In Prol. Contempl. B. Virg.*
8 *Quod vult illam Deus omnium bonorum esse principium.* Quoted by Salazas in *cap. 31 Prov.* versus 29, num. 179.

Chapter Four

HEART OF MARY, MIRROR OF CHARITY

Among the innumerable blessings we have received from the liberal hand of our heavenly Father, there are three very important favors which seem to pass unnoticed by the majority of men. They are three special graces wherewith His immense goodness honored us when we were given the first two commandments, "Thou shalt love the Lord thy God with all thy heart . . . and thy neighbor as thyself."[1]

The first of these favors consists in the fact that it pleased God to command us to love Him. What goodness! How great a favor! To understand this commandment accurately we would have to measure the infinite distance that separates God from man, the Creator from the creature, the All from the nothingness, the Saint of Saints from the most miserable sinner, God Who is the sovereign good and the source of all good from man who is a dark pit of evil and miseries. If we but knew who God is and what we are, we would certainly be amazed by His divine majesty's command to love Him, for we should clearly see that God confers tremendous privileges by merely allowing us to think of Him, and that it would be a signal honor if He simply permitted us to adore Him as our Creator and Sovereign Lord. But this does not satisfy His infinite goodness towards us; He therefore commands us to love Him as our Father.

The second favor manifested is that God is not content with loving us as His children, but publishes an explicit commandment to all men on earth, whatever their condition, enjoining them to love each other as they love themselves, under penalty of incurring His eternal wrath and indignation. He forbids them, with the threat of hellfire, to harm their brethren in any way, whether by deed, word, intention or even thought, in their bodies, their souls, their reputation or anything that belongs to them. O ineffable goodness! O admirable love!

1 Luke 10, 27.

The third favor, even greater than the others, is that God commands all men to love each other not only as they love themselves, but as they love Him. Saint Augustine, Saint Thomas and all theologians teach us that the love or charity with which we must love God and our neighbor is but one and the same virtue, namely, the third theological virtue. Hence our Saviour declares in the holy Gospel that the second commandment, obliging us to love our neighbor, is like unto the first, which enjoins us to love God. The reason is that, in order to love our neighbor as God wills, we must love him in God and for God. This means that we must love our fellow man with the love wherewith God loves him, not for our own interest and satisfaction, but for the love of God, and because God wants us to love him. Now to love God in this way is to love Him in our neighbor, and to love our neighbor with love similar to our love for God. Hence the second commandment is like unto the first.

Thus does the Blessed Virgin love us with a most great and ardent love. In the first place, she loves us with the same love she has for God, seeing and loving God in us. The third theological virtue in Mary's heart is not of another nature than the one in the hearts of the rest of the faithful which has as its sole object God and neighbor. It is true that this divine virtue is, in a sense, indescribably more ardent in the Blessed Virgin's heart where its object is God instead of ourselves; nevertheless, it is substantially the same charity (though different in degree), and the Mother of Fair Love truly loves us with the same love wherewith she loves God Himself.

I maintain, in the second place, that the most glorious Virgin loves us with a supremely ardent love, because she loves us with the very same love with which she loves the God-Man, her divine son Jesus Christ, for she knows that He is our Head and we are His members, that we are therefore one with Him, as members are one with their head. She thus considers us her children and loves us, in a way, even as her own son. We are her children for two reasons: first, because as Mother of our Head, she is mother of His members as well, and second, because our merciful Saviour, when He was suspended on the Cross, out of an excess of inconceivable goodness gave us to His Blessed Mother to be her children. We had nailed Him to the Cross by our sins, we had made Him suffer the most ignominious and cruel death; yet at the very hour when we were thus unworthily and cruelly treating Him, He conferred upon us the most signal favor, the gift of His most admirable Mother. Christ gave her to us to be not only Our Queen and Our Lady, but Our Mother as well, saying to each of us in the person of the beloved Disciple, "Behold thy

Mother."[2] He gave us to her, not as servants and slaves (which in itself would be a great honor for us), but as her children, "Behold thy son." Thus did Christ speak of each one of us as though He were saying, "Mother, behold all my members: I give them to thee to be thy children. I put them in my place, that thou mayest consider them as being myself, and may love them with the same love as thou lovest me. Thou dost see, by my horrible torments and cruel death, how much I love them; do thou likewise love them as I do."

Mary's heart is a burning furnace whose flames reach everywhere, generating more fire and warmth of love for us than ever existed in the hearts of all fathers and mothers towards their children, of brothers for brothers, of friends for their friends; in one word, more ardour than ever burned in all the hearts of Heaven and of earth.

This love is like a dazzling sun illuminating all things. It lightens the darkness of those who approach its glow; it reveals our faults and weaknesses, that we may detest them; it shows us our nothingness and our misery so that we may become humiliated in our own eyes. The glow of Mary's love reveals to us the malice and snares of the enemies of our salvation, in order to save us from them; it shows us the illusion and deceit of the folly and conceits of the world, teaching us to despise them; and it manifests to us the marvels of the greatness and goodness of God, that we may serve Him with fear and with love.

The charity of Mary is a most vigilant love, ever watching over us and our actions, in order to protect, assist and guide us in all things.

This most holy love, or rather this most holy heart of the Mother of Uncreated Love, is Heaven's oracle for all who have recourse to it in their doubts and anxieties. It is an oracle full of incredible goodness which resolves our difficulties, enlightens our doubts, and always imparts salutary and helpful answers, if we have recourse to it with humility and confidence.

Of this love one can truly say that it is a mighty tower and an impregnable bulwark for all the friends of God who would choose to die rather than deliberately offend Him; especially for humble souls, for pure persons (as everyone loves most those who resemble him), and for those who have vowed in a particular manner to serve and honor the beloved of God, namely, Mary Most Amiable, the Mother of Jesus; for she also loves most dearly those who love and imitate her.

Mary's love is swift to help them that invoke her. "Remember, O most pious Virgin," says Saint Bernard, "that never was it known from the beginning of the world that any of those who fled to thy protection

2 John 19, 27.

and sought the help of thy prayers, was left unaided." "O most amiable Mary," adds the same Saint, "we cannot pronounce thy name without being comforted; no one can invoke thee without being heard or without feeling the effects of thy assistance."[3]

Mary's is a love that is mild and meek, and knows not how to be severe or terrifying. "She is full of sweetness," says Saint Bernard, "her heart and mouth are filled with milk and honey."[4] "Milk and honey are under thy tongue."[5] "Her heart is manna," writes Saint Ambrose, "containing all the delights of paradise."[6] "It is a promised land," observes Saint Augustine, "flowing with milk and honey."[7]

The love of the Admirable Heart of the Mother of God is a paradise of delights for all hearts who, being truly detached from all earthly things, strive to serve, honor and love only Jesus and Mary, the King and Queen of Heaven.

Mary's is a most liberal love, which has given us an immense and infinite treasure encompassing all the riches of Divinity and whatever is rare, precious, desirable and lovable in Heaven and on earth, in time and eternity. Indeed Mary has given us the treasure of all treasures, because the love of her virginal heart gave the Son of God, drawn from the adorable Bosom of His heavenly Father, a resting place on earth; and through her love He entered the hallowed womb of Mary for our sake.

Mary's charity is a love most zealous for the salvation of souls. This zeal gave the Blessed Virgin, from the beginning of her life, a most ardent desire to see the Son of God come into the world to save mankind from universal perdition of sin. This zeal made her offer so many prayers, practice such mortifications and shed so many bitter tears to obtain the grace that the eternal Father might send His Son into the world to deliver us from the bondage of hell. This zeal induced Mary to give her most willing consent to the mystery of the Incarnation. It caused her to give us the Saviour and to preserve, nourish and educate Him for us with the greatest imaginable care and affection. It obliged her to offer Him on Calvary at the cost of the greatest suffering and anguish ever experienced.

The love of Mary is a most perfect love, than which none is more perfect or more excellent.

It is most constant and firm, for the Mother of all charity loves us with an invincible love: *Amore invincibili*, says Saint Peter Damian.[8] All

3 *Deprecat. ad V. Mariam.*
4 *Serm. 4 de Assumpt.*
5 *Cant. 4, 11.*
6 *In Psal. 35.*
7 *Serm. 100 de Temp.*
8 *Serm. 1 de Nativ. Virg.*

the torrent of our ingratitudes, infidelities, negligences and cowardice in her service, all our imperfections and innumerable offenses are not able to extinguish Mary's love, for it is stronger than death and hell. This love perseveres in its goodness and care until our last breath and exerts all its power, wisdom and mercy to protect us from the malice and snares of the enemies of our salvation.

O Mother of Love, make us sharers in thy boundless charity. Obtain for us the grace of doing all things for the pure love and glory of God.

Chapter Five

HEART OF MARY, ABYSS OF HUMILITY

Consider the words of the Holy Ghost, "Deep calleth on deep."[1] What do they mean? They mean that the Holy Ghost sets before us the image of a twofold or dual abyss.

The first is the humble heart immersed by profound humility in the realization of its own nothingness, an abyss that engulfs the humble man, preventing him from seeing in himself anything but nothingness and making him love the lowliness and abjection of such nothingness.

The second is the abyss of graces and celestial blessings that everywhere surround and accompany the truly humble heart.

The first depth calls for the second, "Deep called on deep,"[1] because the prayer of the humble heart has such power with God that it is always heard. Divine Goodness can refuse it nothing. It is the profundity that summons and attracts all the graces of Heaven; God showers them into the lowly soul with open hand and without reserve. Humility is the guardian of all other graces and virtues and they are safe where it abides, according to the words of Saint Basil, "Humility is the safe treasury of all virtues."[2]

All the greatness of the Blessed Virgin was accomplished by the humility of her most holy heart. From the first to the last moment of her life, her humility never ceased to invoke and draw upon her grace after grace, perfection after perfection, holiness upon holiness, until it brought her to the summit of the grace and holiness that next to that of Christ ever was or shall be greatest among men. As Saint Bernard puts it, "It was just that she who considered herself the least of creatures, even though she was above all others, should have been honored as the worthiest and holiest of all."[3]

---

1   Ps. 41, 8.
2   *In Constitut.* cap. 17.
3   *In Serm. Super Signum Magnum.*

Would you observe the admirable effects of such prodigious humility in the heart of the Queen of the humble? Consider Mary throughout the course of her life and you will see that, just as the life of Jesus was a constant exercise of humility, so the life of His Blessed Mother constituted a perpetual practice of the same virtue. As humility is our Saviour's own spiritual virtue which He constantly preached by His example and earnestly recommended with the words, "Learn of me, because I am meek, and humble of heart";[4] so can we say that humility is also the most beloved virtue of His dearest Mother. She urges us to practice it by her example and does not cease to tell us with her divine son, "Learn of me, my dearest children, for I am meek, and humble of heart." This is the constant message of her marvelous humility which I shall now describe in its twelve principal manifestations.

The first manifestation was the complete self annihilation with which she adored God from the very beginning of her life as her Creator and Sovereign Lord.

The second manifestation of the humility of the glorious Virgin's most holy heart was the uneasiness she felt on hearing the salutation of the Angel Gabriel. Whence this perturbation? Was it from beholding the Archangel? "No," says the Angelic Doctor, "for Our Lady was accustomed to visits from angels."[5] The holy Gospel says that she was troubled not by the presence of the Angel, but by his words, "She was troubled at his saying,"[6] because he greeted her as full of grace, as one having the Lord with her in a special manner and as being blessed among all women. That salutation is what troubles her most humble heart which cannot listen to such exalted praises without trembling.

The third effect produced by the humility of Mary's Admirable Heart was that, after hearing Saint Gabriel proclaim that God had chosen her to be the Mother of His divine Son and consequently the sovereign lady of the universe, she answered the Angel with the words, "Behold the handmaid of the Lord; be it done unto me according to thy word."[6] Saint Bonaventure exclaims, "How wonderfully deep is Mary's humility! An archangel salutes her; she is called full of grace; she is told the Holy Ghost will overshadow her; she becomes the Mother of God Himself; she is raised above all creatures; she is appointed sovereign lady of Heaven and earth; and yet instead of becoming filled with pride, she humbles herself most deeply, saying, 'Behold the handmaid of the Lord.'"[7]

4 Matt. 11, 29.
5 *Summa theol.* 111, Q. 30, a. 3, ad 3.
6 Luke 1, 29.
7 *In Speculo B.V.* Cap. 4.

The fourth effect of the humility of the Blessed Virgin's most holy heart was that after she had conceived the only begotten Son of God in her blessed womb, she revealed to no one, not even to her spouse, Saint Joseph, the tremendous mystery which exalted her to the highest pinnacle. She would not have mentioned the sublime dignity that raised her above the Seraphim and put the entire world under her feet if the Holy Spirit had not revealed it to her cousin, Saint Elizabeth. This stupendous silence, caused by the marvelous humility of our Saviour's Mother, excites the admiration of Saint Thomas of Villanova and makes him exclaim: "O marvelous modesty, peerless humility! O admirable severity, prudence and constancy! What shall I say to thee, most sacred Virgin? Here thou art Mother of God, lady of the universe, Queen of Heaven and earth, the greatest mystery, the most incomparable marvel, has been wrought in thee by the divine power, and thou dost tell no one. No human being knows the vital miracle, so jealously dost thou guard thy secret! Thou dost remain in profound silence, until, in the house of thy cousin Elizabeth, beholding that God Himself has revealed this miracle of miracles, then only dost thou breathe thy blessed silence, and raise to Heaven the sublime canticle of praise and adoration for the author of all these marvels: 'My soul doth magnify the Lord.'"[8]

The fifth effect of Mary's humility was accomplished during her visit to her cousin Saint Elizabeth, concerning Saint John the Baptist.

Its sixth effect was manifested in her relationship with Saint Joseph, whom she regarded and honored as her husband. "Behold a marvelous thing!" says Saint Thomas of Villanova. "See the Queen of Virgins, the Mistress of the world, the very Mother of God, not disdaining to serve a poor carpenter, to prepare his meals and to obey him like a dutiful wife! But what exalts her humility above all admiration is that she prefers to endure an unspeakable humiliation rather than reveal to Joseph the admirable mystery wrought in her by God and her newly received rank of Mother of the promised Messias. O prodigy of humility! Never has its like been seen before and never shall it be seen again."

The seventh effect of the humility of the royal heart of Mary was revealed at the birth of her divine son in a stable at Bethlehem. The sovereign Empress of the universe went to lowly Bethlehem to give birth to the King of men and angels, the Redeemer of all mankind. Yet she found no lodging there and being turned away from every house, was obliged to seek the lowly abode of animals. There she brought forth the only Son of God the Father, the King of Glory, the sovereign Lord

---

8 Luke 1, 46—Saint John Eudes does not give the reference for this quotation from the works of Saint Thomas of Villanova.

of all things. And she sustained these humiliations without a complaint and with most perfect humility.

The eighth effect of the admirable humility of the Mother of God became apparent when she subjected herself to the Hebrew law of Purification.

The ninth effect of the humility of the blessed heart of Our Saviour's Mother was the virtue she practiced during the forty days' penance of her divine son in the desert. Remember what we have said above; namely, that our Saviour's incomparable love for His Blessed Mother made Him desire her to resemble Him as closely as possible, and caused Him to engrave in her heart a perfect image of all the states and mysteries of His most holy life.

The tenth effect of the humility of Mary's all-pure heart became manifest at the wedding of Cana in Galilee, where she obtained from her beloved son the miracle whereby He changed water into wine. But how did she induce Him to perform that miracle? Was it by exerting her authority as His Mother? By no means. Was it by pressing Him with repeated entreaties to show her power over Him and the reality that she was indeed His Mother? No, for she did not even presume to entreat Him, but merely made plain to Him, with the greatest modesty and humility, the need for additional wine. Mary left it entirely to His divine will to act as He thought best.

The eleventh effect of the humility of the Admirable Heart of the Mother of Jesus was that she suffered with her beloved son all the contempt and insults He endured during His public ministry from His enemies, who offended and affronted Him in a thousand ways, seeking to bind Him as a madman, to stone Him like a blasphemer, and even to hurl Him from the top of a mountain. She likewise endured with her son all the humiliations and ignominies of His passion when He was treated as a criminal, bound and throttled like a thief, torn with whips, crowned with thorns, reviled by the shocking preference of the mob for Barabbas, and nailed to a cross between two bandits. Yes, my Jesus, Thy most worthy Mother bore with Thee all this shame and humiliation! As Thy glory is now her glory, so were Thy ignominies her very own, which she bore with such humility that she never uttered a complaint to God or man. O prodigious humility! Most humble Mary, pray to thy dear son that He may grant us the grace to learn from Himself and from thee how to suffer insults and humiliations patiently and with humility and never to complain.

The twelfth effect of the humility of the Admirable Heart of Mary is recorded in the first chapter of the Acts of the Apostles where it is written that, after the Ascension of Christ into Heaven, Saint Peter,

Saint John and the other disciples withdrew to the Cenacle of Jerusalem. There they remained until the coming of the Holy Ghost, united in prayer with the holy women and Mary, Mother of Jesus, whom Saint Luke the Evangelist mentions last, not only after the holy Apostles, but even after the sinner from whom our Saviour had driven seven devils. How can it be that she who is the first in dignity, in merit and in sanctity should be put in the last place? It is that her most profound humility compelled her scribe, Saint Luke, to name her thus in the last place, according to the lowliness of her self estimation, considering and treating herself as the least and most unworthy of creatures. What peerless humility! The Queen of Heaven and earth, the Mother of the King of kings, among whose ancestors fourteen kings are numbered, treats herself and wishes to be treated by others as though she were nothing at all.

Such, then, are twelve effects or manifestations of the humility of the incomparable heart of Mary, Mother of God. But that is not all, for we must count, if we can, all the moments of her life and we shall be counting as many acts and effects of her humility, for her entire life constituted, in fact, a constant exercise of that holy virtue.

O Queen of the humble, thou seest how remote we are from the practice of true and perfect humility. Obtain from thy beloved son the pardon of all the sins we have committed against this great virtue; offer to Him thy very humble heart in reparation and satisfaction for our misdeeds; and entreat Our Lord to grant us the graces we need to enable us to imitate carefully and faithfully the most holy humility of the amiable heart of Jesus and Mary.

Chapter Six

HEART OF MARY, EMPIRE OF THE DIVINE WILL

After the most amiable heart of Jesus there never was nor will be, in Heaven or on earth, any heart where the adorable will of God reigns so perfectly and gloriously as in the Admirable Heart of the Blessed Virgin Mary.

In the first place, the glorious Virgin always esteemed and revered the divine will as her origin and principle, the source of her being and her life, to which she constantly referred her use of these gifts as to their first cause.

Secondly, she considered and honored the divine will as her last end and as the center of her existence, knowing full well that she existed in the world only to accomplish and do the Creator's will in all things. To this end all her thoughts, words and actions were directed, and in this amiable center her pure heart exclusively sought and found its sovereign contentment and complete rest.

Thirdly, Mary considered and respected the divine will as ruler and sovereign, whose every order was so dear and precious, that she would have preferred a thousand deaths to the slightest disobedience.

Fourthly, Our Lady considered and loved God's holy will as her true paradise, where she found sublime delights, because not only did she desire everything that God ordained, but she willed her acceptance in the manner most pleasing to Him. Hence, as God Himself derives infinite pleasure from the operation of His decrees, so did our heavenly Virgin receive the greatest joy and happiness from her faithful fulfillment of the divine will.

Fifthly, Mary considered God's holy will not only in itself but also manifested in the will of Saint Joseph, her most worthy spouse, in the edicts of the pagan emperor Augustus, in the whole Mosaic law, and in every disposition of divine providence towards her divine son, herself and all other creatures. She loved the most holy will of God in all these aspects and subjected herself as lovingly as when she considered it directly in its essence.

The sixth illustration of the perfect reign of the divine will in Mary's heart is shown by the fact that, although this incomparable Virgin owed obedience to none save God Himself, and while as Mother of God and Queen of Heaven and earth she held sovereign sway over all creatures, she nevertheless practiced very faithfully what the Holy Ghost was to teach later on through Saint Peter, "Be ye subject therefore to every human creature for God's sake."[1] Mary was, in fact, always ready to yield not only to her superiors, but to her equals and even her inferiors, preferring the will of others to her own, whenever it was not contrary to the good pleasure of almighty God.

What else shall I say? I may add that the most pure Virgin's love for the sweet will of God was so intense that it truly constituted the soul of her soul, the spirit of her spirit and the heart of her heart. This spirit and heart caused her to live a heavenly life, animated every power of her soul and all her interior and exterior senses, was the principle of all her actions and inspired her to loving acceptance of all her afflictions.

I hear my Saviour tell us, "I came down from Heaven, not to do my own will, but the will of Him that sent me." and "My meat is to do the will of him that sent me, that I may perfect His work."[2] The Blessed Mother can indeed truly repeat after Him, "I am in the world only to do the will of my Creator and I find my supreme pleasure in its constant fulfillment."

We read in the works of Saint Gertrude that one day she made the following request of her divine spouse, "I ask, dear Lord, and I desire with all my heart that thy most praiseworthy will be accomplished in me and in all thy creatures, in the manner most pleasing to thee."[3] If Saint Gertrude possessed such great love for the will of her divine spouse, what shall we say, what can we think of the Queen of all Saints, whose love for the will of Him who is her God, her creator, her saviour, her brother, her son, her father and her spouse, was greater than the love of all angels and men together?

We can certainly say that Mary's incomparable love of the divine will formed her and identified her with it. Hence God could well say to her first of all what He says of His Church through the prophet Isaias, "Thou shalt be called my pleasure"[4] which is equivalent to saying: Thou art my heart, my love, my bride, my beloved in whom I am delighted and well pleased; because thy love for my divine will is so great that thou art identified with it.

---

1   1 Peter 2, 13.
2   John 6, 38; 4, 34.
3   *Legat. div. piet.* lib. 3, cap. 11.
4   Isa. 62, 4.

Finally, the adorable will dwelt in the Blessed Virgin's holy heart as in its own home, holding its keys as uncontested Master. God's Holy will dwelt there as in its kingdom, enjoying complete and sovereign sway. Mary's blessed heart was the triumphal call of the divine will bearing a triumph over all its enemies. It was the Heaven of the glory of God's eternal will, a paradise where everything was subject to its orders, nothing contrary to it, and all things were consecrated to its praise and worship.

Mary's obedience to God's adorable will caused Mary to utter the divine *Fiat*, more admirable, in a way, than the *Fiat* whereby God created the universe. God's *Fiat* created the world, but Mary's *Fiat* was the occasion by which God became man, and man, God. St Bernard says, "We were all created by God's eternal word, and behold we die; in thy brief answer, namely, *Fiat*, we find a new being and are called back to life."[5] "I dare affirm of the Blessed Virgin," writes Saint Anselm, "what Saint John has said of the eternal Word; namely, that as nothing was made without Him, so also nothing was made without her. The great God accomplishes more through the Blessed Virgin's *Fiat* than through His own. Why? Because God's *Fiat* was a *Fiat* of command, whereas the Blessed Virgin's *Fiat* was a *Fiat* of obedience."[6]

What greater praise could be pronounced concerning the obedience to be the glorious Mother of our Saviour? How admirable! "Nothing is made save through Mary's hands," says Saint Bernard, "and God Himself became man only after that admirable Virgin had said *Fiat*."

Let us harken also to Saint Andrew of Jerusalem, who says, "God ordered light to be, and all things are made. The Blessed Virgin says: Be it done unto me according to Thy word, and the greatest of all things was accomplished. God's *Fiat* is a *Fiat* of command; the *Fiat* of the Mother of God is a *Fiat* of obedience. By God's command Heaven and earth were made. By the Blessed Virgin's obedience, the admirable Incarnation of the eternal Word followed."[7]

The final act of submission and obedience to the divine will that sprang from holy Mary's maternal heart was her consent to that adorable will concerning the passion and death of her beloved son. This consent she gave with such wonderful obedience, that if such had been the eternal Father's will, she would have been as ready to crucify and sacrifice Christ with her own hands, even as Abraham prepared to sacrifice his

5 *Homil. 4 sup. Miss. est.*
6 *De Excel. Virg. cap. 11.*
7 *Dixit Deus: Fiat lux et facto est lux, fiat firmamentum, caeteraque et facto sunt. Dixit Virgo: Fiat mihi secundum verbum tuum, et factum est opus omnium maximum. Dei fiat secutum est caelum operaque reliqua, quae caeli ambitus complectitur. Obedientis Virginis fiat secuta est admiranda divini Verbi incarnatio. Serm. de Assumpt. B.V.*

only son Isaac, yet with incomparably greater love and obedience.

Thus the divine will ever reigned in the most holy heart of the Queen of Heaven and thus will it ever be. May we not truly say, therefore, that the adorable will of the Almighty possesses her Admirable Heart more mightily, more magnificently and more gloriously by far than all other hearts that ever were or shall be in Heaven and on earth? It possesses absolute authority and power over Mary's heart where it will reign forever, where it will eternally receive the veneration, homage and adoration of all the angels and saints.

Infinite and eternal glory, then, to that adorable will for all the marvels it has ever wrought in the pure heart of the Mother of God! Unending praise and thanksgiving be to her most Admirable Heart for all the love and honor that its most perfect submission and obedience have ever rendered and shall forever render to the adorable will of the heavenly Father!

Chapter Seven

HEART OF MARY, TREASURE-HOUSE
OF GRATUITOUS GRACES

The Immaculate Heart of the Blessed Virgin is the sanctuary of gratuitous graces, by which are meant graces imparted by the Holy Ghost not so much for the sanctification of the recipient as for the instruction, comfort and benefit of other souls.

Saint Paul enumerates nine such graces: the gift of speaking wisely; the gift of speaking with knowledge; the gift of faith; the power of healing the sick; the gift of miracles; the gift of prophecy; the gift of speaking in diverse tongues; the discernment of spirits; the gift of interpreting Scripture.[1]

What is the gift of wise speech, or the word of wisdom? The gift of wise speech is a grace of the Holy Ghost that enables us to expound with clarity the truths of faith, while the word of knowledge is a gift of the Holy Spirit which imparts facility in explaining truths that concern morals.

What is the gift of faith? It is, according to Saint Chrysostom, the special confidence necessary to perform miracles, or, according to Saint Ambrose, a grace of the Holy Ghost which provides strength to preach the Gospel boldly and fearlessly. Other theologians define it as the heavenly light which must enlighten in a special manner the minds of those who preach the Gospel.

What are the graces of healing and the gift of working miracles? These two graces can really be combined because the grace of healing the sick has the effect of restoring bodily health through miracles, while the gift of working miracles manifests the power of God through miraculous works.

What is the gift of prophecy? It is a grace of the Holy Ghost by which we know future events and secret things that cannot be known in a natural way. This gift likewise includes the grace of revelations.

1 Cor. 12, 8–10.

What is the discerning of spirits? It is a light of the Holy Ghost, whereby are known the thoughts, desires, movements and interior affections proceeding from a good or evil principle.

What is the gift of speaking diverse tongues? It is the gift bestowed by the Holy Ghost on the Apostles at Pentecost and includes the special facility in making heavenly truths understood by those to whom they are taught.

What is the gift of interpretation of Scripture? It is a grace of the Holy Spirit enlightening the intellect to understand the sense of Holy Writ and animating the will to extend this understanding to others.

Did the Blessed Virgin possess all these graces? Yes, without doubt. Such is the opinion of Saint Albert the Great,[2] Suarez, and many other great theologians who offer several substantiating proofs. First of all, since Our Lady was full of grace, according to the declaration of Saint Gabriel, she must therefore have possessed all graces. Secondly, her incomprehensible dignity as Mother of God must necessarily have been adorned with the highest and most perfect gifts of the Holy Ghost. Thirdly, being after her divine son the universal dispenser of all graces in the Church, Mary must necessarily have possessed the totality of the graces that she was to obtain for mankind.

We may therefore say, first, that the Holy Ghost gave the Blessed Virgin a most penetrating and clear understanding of Sacred Scripture, together with a great facility in explaining its truths concerning faith and morals.

Secondly, Mary possessed in the highest degree the special confidence necessary to work miracles.

In the third place, Our Lady possessed more perfectly than any saint the gift of actually working miracles, because apart from the miracle of miracles wrought by her cooperation with the Father, the Son and Holy Ghost in the ineffable mystery of the Incarnation, we have every reason to believe that she worked many other wonders, though they have not been recorded.

In the fourth place, many proofs could be adduced to reveal that Our Lady enjoyed the gift of prophecy. Be it enough to mention the prophecy expressed in the Magnificat, "Behold from henceforth all generations shall call me Blessed,"[3] for it includes all the honor and homage that will ever be paid to Mary in Heaven and on earth, while endless ages run and throughout eternity.

In the fifth instance, having received the gift of prophecy, the most Blessed Virgin likewise possessed the grace of revelations in a much more excellent degree than all the other saints.[4] Throughout her life,

2 Apud Vega. *Theol. Mar.* n. 1342.
3 Luke 1, 48.

says Saint Andrew of Crete,[5] she was enlightened by countless divine revelations. How many mysteries did not the Holy Ghost reveal to her, even from the moment of her Immaculate Conception? How many wondrous secrets did she not hear from the adorable lips of her beloved son during the rich hidden years He spent at her side? How many lights did she not receive from her familiar conversations with the angels? Finally, Saint Ambrose[6] and many other holy Doctors have testified that Saint John the Evangelist owed his intimate knowledge of the divinity of Christ and the revelations contained in the Apocalypse to his special relationship to Mary and his filial services to her.

In the sixth place, the holy Virgin possessed the gift of discerning spirits more perfectly than the greatest saints, as this gift is contained in that of prophecy.

In the seventh place, she received on Pentecost with the Apostles the gift of speaking in diverse tongues. Saint Albert the Great, Saint Antoninus and Saint Athanasius assert that Mary received it with greater plenitude than the Apostles themselves, for the instruction and consolation of many of the faithful, who came from every part of the world to seek and to consult her as an oracle of the Holy Spirit.

In the eighth place, being endowed with the gift of wisdom and of faith and the spirit of prophecy, Mary likewise possessed the grace of interpreting Scripture with much more perfect clarity than was ever granted to anyone else.

But what relation do all these graces bear to the most holy heart of our heavenly Mother? They are related to it as effects are to their cause, as streams to their source, as lines to their center, as the solar rays to the sun. For is it not true that the love and humility of the amiable heart of Mary, having drawn the Holy Ghost to take up His abode, likewise attracted the complete plenitude of all His gifts and graces? Hence do we justly term her virginal heart the sanctuary of the graces of the divine Spirit. This being so, it is only fitting that Heaven and earth, men and angels, and every creature be employed in blessing, praising and glorifying the thrice Holy One, who has enriched the incomparable heart of Mary with so much grace, so much sanctity and so many marvels.

I do not exhort you, dear reader, to imitate the graces just described, for these sublimities are admirable rather than imitable, but I adjure you to take care not to fall into the sentiments of Luther, Calvin and other sectarians, who seek to snatch from the Church some of its greatest and most signal jewels, by attempting to deprive it of the

4 Cf. Suarez, In 3 part. disp. 19, Sect. 4.
5 Serm. de Assumpt.
6 De Instit. Virginis, cap. 7.

grace of revelations[7] and the gift of miracles.

Throughout the history of the Church there have been such manifestations of the power of God. The Spirit of Light operated marvelously and powerfully in certain chosen and faithful souls. The spirit of darkness, who is the ape of God, tries to counterfeit these works, in order to discount their value, making them seem to be like his own, full of falsehood and deceit. The world brings forth many more thorns than roses; fool's gold is far more abundant than true ore. In the time of Achab, King of Israel, the deceitful spirit spoke through more than four hundred false prophets, while the Spirit of Truth spoke only through the prophet Micheas. It is indeed with strong reason that Saint John the beloved disciple cries out to us, "Believe not every spirit, but try the spirits, if they be of God."[8]

There are in this confused world persons too credulous, believing too easily, and there are others to whom belief is too hard. These two extremities are dangerous and the wise will avoid both of them. To accept every revelation or supposed miracle is the mark of a weak, imprudent spirit; to reject every revelation is the mark of a rash, unreasoning spirit. Tell me, do sensible men destroy all currency because much of it is counterfeit? Satan had always had diviners and false prophets, from the earliest days, but God has also had His chosen mouthpieces, and He always will have them, in fulfillment of His divine promise, "I will pour out my spirit upon all flesh: and your sons and your daughters shall prophesy: your old men shall dream dreams, and your young men shall see visions."[9]

God has many ways to lead souls to Heaven, and as Master of Life, He leads as He wills; some souls by ordinary paths, others by extraordinary paths. The way of faith is the great highway built to guide men to eternal life; yet is not faith founded upon revelation? And is it not by revelation that we hold the mystery of our creation?

It is true that the fundamental revelations of our faith are authorized and ratified by Holy Church; yet it is a mark of faith to treat with respect anything which suggests the shadow of almighty God, so long as no error appear, and with prudence to refrain from attributing to the devil what may perchance come from God. That is why it is wise to withhold judgment in such matters. Those, who by reason of their office or by order of their superiors must investigate these manifestations, should never rely on their own knowledge or experience, but,

---

7   Saint John Eudes probably added these concluding paragraphs to justify his belief in the visions and revelations of Mary Des Vallés, a saintly woman of Coutances.

8   1 John 4, 1.

9   Joel 2, 28.

seeking counsel and careful theological study, they should humbly seek the aid of the Holy Ghost and invoke the Mother of Truth and of the eternal light, so that thus they may fulfill the words of Saint Paul; "Extinguish not the spirit. Despise not prophecies. But prove all things; hold fast that which is good."[10]

10 1 Thess. 5, 19–21.

Chapter Eight

HEART OF MARY, INESTIMABLE TREASURY OF RICHES

The immense liberality of divine goodness has granted us possession of four great treasures here on earth.

The first is the most Holy Eucharist, containing all that is richest, most precious and most admirable in time and in eternity, in all the angels and all the saints, in the Queen of saints and angels, in the sacred humanity of the Son of God and His divinity, in the divine essence and in the three eternal Persons.

The second treasure is Sacred Scripture, which epitomizes all the truths, all the revelations, all the mysteries and every revealed secret of the Godhead, for which reason Saint Augustine[1] and Saint Gregory[2] call Sacred Scripture the heart of God.

The third treasure is the relics of the saints, which the Church possesses, cherishes and honors as the dowry of her divine spouse.

The fourth treasure is the Admirable Heart of the glorious Virgin, whose riches are unfathomable.

In the first place, the holy heart of Mary is "the treasure of the love of the eternal Father," says Saint Methodius,[3] Bishop and martyr, "because in her Immaculate Heart the adorable Father placed His love;" that is, His only and well beloved Son, when He sent Him for the world's salvation into the virginal womb and maternal heart of holy Mary. This beloved Son, the heart and treasure of His most loving Father, was enclosed for nine months in the sacred bosom of the most pure Virgin and He shall forever dwell in her maternal heart; hence her virginal heart must be honored as the precious treasure of the love of the Father of all goodness.

Secondly, the Queen of Heaven's most august heart is the treasure of the only Son of God. In her marvelous heart He hid and preserved

1 *In Ps.* 21.
2 *In 1 Reg.* cap. 2.
3 *In Orat. de Hypapante.*

all the mysteries and all the wondrous manifestations that took place in Him while He dwelt on earth, according to the divine text, "and his mother kept all these words in her heart."[4]

Jesus poured into the heart of His Mother the plenitude of the treasures of wisdom and knowledge that are hid in His own heart. Beyond that He has enriched it with all the treasures of grace and mercy acquired for us by His Precious Blood and His saving death. Christ imparted to Mary the power of distributing these treasures "to whom she pleases, when she pleases and as she pleases," says Saint Bernard. "In thy hands, O Mary," says the pious and learned Dionysius the Carthusian, "are all the treasures of the multitudinous mercies of God."[5]

The most august heart of the Queen of Angels is not only the treasure of the Father's love and of the Son's goodness; it is also the treasure of the charity of the Holy Ghost. Into this treasure chest the Holy Spirit poured immeasurable wealth of graces: all the graces of the holy patriarchs and prophets, of the holy apostles and martyrs, of the holy priests and Levites, of the holy confessors and virgins, all the graces granted to every saint and all gratuitous graces. In the treasury of her heart the divine Spirit has enthroned all the theological, cardinal and moral virtues to an incomparably higher degree than they are to be found in the hearts of all the angels and saints. In Mary's heart the adorable Spirit has concentrated the plenitude of His sevenfold gifts, His twelve fruits and the eight evangelical beatitudes. We may therefore say with Saint Andrew of Crete that her most Admirable Heart is itself "the most holy treasury of all sanctity."[6]

Let us add with Saint Epiphanius that her most holy heart is "the admirable treasure of the Church."[7] It is the storehouse of glory, felicity and jubilation for the Church Triumphant. Saint Bernard exclaims, "By thee, O holy Virgin, Heaven was peopled, Hell emptied, and the ruins of the heavenly Jerusalem were rebuilt."

Our Lady's heart is likewise a treasury of graces and mercies for the Church Militant, for Saint Germanus of Constantinople pronounced that "no man is delivered or preserved from the worldwide snares of Satan save through Mary; and God grants His graces to no one except through her alone."[8]

Our loving Mother's heart is a treasury of solace and comfort for the Church Suffering because, as has been shown, the pangs of

---

4 Luke, 2, 51.
5 *Opuscul*. de Laud. vitae solitariae.
6 *Orat de Assumpt*.
7 *Orat de Laud Deip*. Serm. 94.
8 *Nemo liberatur a malis, nisi per te, O Sanctissima! Nemo est, cui donum concedatur, nisi per te, O Purissima. De Zona B. Virg.*

Purgatory are constantly diminished, hour by hour, thanks to the marvelous charity of Mary's heart. Finally, no grace or favor ever comes to us from the lofty throne of almighty God without passing through the merciful hands of Mary, Mother of Charity.

Let us join with Saint Cyril, Patriarch of Alexandria, to salute our most lovable Mary with our whole heart, saying to her, "Hail, O holy Mother of God, thou art the most precious treasure of the entire universe."

O incomparable treasure! O Admirable Heart! O ineffable goodness of the most adorable Trinity, to give us this marvelous maternal heart and inestimable treasure, or rather, these most holy hearts and very rich treasures! Actually we possess four hearts and four treasures: the adorable heart of the eternal Father, which is His Son Jesus Christ, whom we possess in the Holy Eucharist; the loving heart of Jesus Christ Himself in the relics of the passion; the divine heart of the Holy Ghost, in Sacred Scripture; and the most tender heart of Mary, Mother of God. What respect for the sacred relics! What veneration for Holy Writ! What devotion and tender affection for our dearest Mother's most excellent heart!

How rich are we not rendered by the possession of these four great treasures, especially the first and the last, which are the divine heart of Jesus and the most holy heart of Mary! We surely thus possess the means to pay off all our debts and satisfy all our obligations. And indeed we are encumbered with three great debts, as well as three great obligations.

First of all, we are obliged to adore and glorify the most Holy Trinity in all Its grandeurs and in all that It is, in Itself and in Its creatures. To meet this obligation, we shall offer to the three divine Persons all the adoration, honor and glory that have been and ever shall be rendered to the Blessed Trinity by the most worthy heart of Jesus and Mary.

Secondly, we are bound to love God with our whole heart, our whole soul and with all our strength, as much for His own sake as because of His great love for us. Yet we have not even begun to love Him as we should. To pay this debt and to make up for our deficiency, let us offer to the eternal Father the divine heart of His only begotten Son, whose burning love for the almighty Father is truly worthy of Him; and let us offer to Jesus the most holy heart of His Blessed Mother, whose love immeasurably surpasses that of all the angels and saints together.

Thirdly, we are obliged to satisfy divine justice for our innumerable offenses, negligences and sins. To discharge this obligation, let us offer all the sorrow, anguish and sufferings endured by the all-perfect heart of Jesus and Mary out of love for us, and let us offer ourselves to them that we also may endure, for their sake, whatever sufferings it may please them to make us bear.

Whenever we experience any spiritual or temporal necessity, let us beg the eternal Father, with deep humility and greatest confidence, to grant our requests through the most loving heart of His divine Son. And let us implore the Son, through His Mother's tender heart, to grant us the assistance we need in the manner most pleasing to Mother and son; thus we shall certainly obtain our desire.

When we are sad and desolate, let us remember that we possess a treasury containing inestimable riches, the Blessed Virgin's most holy heart, a heart that holds more love and affection for us than the hearts of all the devoted fathers and mothers that ever were, are, or shall be; nay, than the united hearts of all the angels and saints. What a subject of joy and comfort this should be for us! If we but realized the wealth of love and tenderness stored for us in the Admirable Heart of our good Mother, we would surely die of joy.

Chapter Nine

Heart of Mary, Sanctuary, Censer and Altar of Divine Love

The hearts of all the angels and saints of Heaven constitute, according to the different degrees of love possessed by those same hearts, as many diverse sanctuaries of divine love, where almighty God is adored, glorified and loved forever. The divine heart of our most amiable Saviour, however, is the Sanctuary of sanctuaries and the Love of loves. As from all eternity, ever shall it adore, glorify and love God in a manner infinitely worthy of divine grandeur and sublime goodness.

The most holy heart of the peerless Mother of our Saviour is the second sanctuary of divine love, a sanctuary fashioned by the Holy Ghost Himself, Who is love essential and uncreated, a sanctuary never defiled by sin, but always adorned with the highest degree of every virtue. Mary's heart always was, and shall forever remain, the glorious abode of the Saint of Saints. In it there always existed and ever shall exist greater honor, glory and love for the most Holy Trinity than in all material and spiritual sanctuaries that ever were, are or shall be in Heaven and on earth.

This adorable sanctuary comprises several features that we shall now have to consider.

The first is its perpetual sacrifice ceaselessly offered to God, a sacrifice of love and praise. Mary offered the sacrifice of love, for during her pilgrimage on earth and still much more since her Assumption into Heaven, her virginal heart constantly made a perpetual exercise and sacrifice of love towards God, a love never surpassed, except by the love of the deified heart of Jesus.

She also offered the sacrifice of praise, for her heart is a perpetual host of praise and adoration, of glorification, of thanksgiving to the most Holy Trinity, which is more worthily praised, more perfectly adored and more highly glorified by Our Lady than by all human and angelic minds and hearts in Heaven and on earth.

Mary's is the heart represented by the golden censer held in the hand of the angel mentioned at the beginning of the eighth chapter of the Apocalypse.[1] It is a golden censer, to show that Mary's Immaculate Heart is unmixed love as typified by pure gold. The Angel in whose hand it is held is the Angel of the great counsel, namely, our Blessed Saviour Himself, to show that the holy heart of Mary always belonged to God alone and that it was ever possessed and guided by the Angel of the great counsel. If the heart of an earthly sovereign is in the Lord's hand, to be ruled as He wills, how much more truly the heart of the Queen of Heaven? The Angel of the great counsel fills the censer with fire from the altar, adding great quantities of incense, which are the prayers of the saints, to signify that the Son of God filled His holy Mother's heart with the sacred fire He had come to bring upon earth, and that all the adoration, praise and prayers of her virginal heart proceed from the adorable heart of Jesus.

The prayers of the saints are placed in Mary's heart, represented by the golden censer, to make us understand that the saints place their prayers and all their praise and adoration rendered to God, in the Admirable Heart of the incomparable Mother of their Saviour, that being united to her prayers, their own may become more acceptable and efficacious in the sight of the divine majesty.

So much concerning the nature of the sacrifice of love offered in the august sanctuary of Mary's most pure heart. The victims of love there offered are threefold:

First is her divine son, the adorable victim offered by the Blessed Virgin with all her heart and love unspeakable in the Temple of Jerusalem and on Calvary. She still continually offers Him to God in Heaven and in each of the sacrifices being daily celebrated throughout the world. If all Christians possess the right to offer to the divine majesty the same sacrifice that is offered by those who are honored with the sacerdotal character, how much more truly must not the Mother of the sovereign Priest enjoy that right and power? I do not claim that Mary is corporeally present at the sacrifices offered on earth, but she does assist at each Holy Mass in spirit, heart and affection.

John Gerson, the pious Chancellor of the Paris University, says, "If Mary did not receive the character of the sacerdotal office on the night of the Lord's Supper, nevertheless, both then as well as before and after, she was anointed with the interior grace of the faithful. She was not to consecrate, but to offer a pure, holy and spotless Host on the altar of her heart."[2]

The second sacrificial victim is the Saviour's Mother herself. As our adorable Redeemer immolated Himself for the glory of His eternal Father

---

1 Apoc. 8, 3.
2 *Tract. 9 super Magnif.* alphab. 49, lit. B.

and for the salvation of mankind, so too His most holy Mother, wishing to imitate Her son as far as possible, likewise sacrificed herself for God's greater glory with a heart burning with love for His divine majesty. Thus Mary lived on earth in a state of perpetual sacrifice of her whole being.

The third victim comprises countless souls that have been sacrificed to God in the marvelous sanctuary of Mary's virginal heart. To understand this, we should remember that if the eternal Father gave us all things when He gave us His beloved Son,[3] this gift applies still more truly to her to whom He gave the divine Word to be her own son. Hence the Queen of Heaven and earth, knowing full well that all things in the universe belonged to her and wishing to employ all of them for the greater glory of Him from whom she received them, offered and sacrificed as victims of His divine majesty every creature in the world. She knew that sacrifice is the greatest honor that can be rendered to God, and that we therefore cannot make a holier use of anything that belongs to us than to offer, give and sacrifice it to the sovereign Lord of all things, provided it be done in accordance with His holy will.

These, then, are the three types of victims that were offered to God in the sanctuary of the Immaculate Heart of the Mother of our sovereign Priest. Mary will forever continue to offer these victims in Heaven, just as her son Jesus Christ continues the perpetual offering of Himself and His possessions to the almighty Father.

Let us, in turn, give ourselves unreservedly to the Son of God and His Blessed Mother, that we, and all that we have, may be joined in their sacrifices and united to them in the ardent love of their offering.

The true identity of the High Priest who offers all these sacrifices in the sanctuary of Mary's virginal heart is none other than her heart itself, which is therefore the sanctuary of divine love and, in part, the victim of love offered therein, as well as the officiant who offers it with peerless love.

Another adornment of our admirable sanctuary is the altar of divine love, on which all the foregoing sacrifices have been and will forever be offered. It is again the most loving heart of the Mother of Fair Love. Let us listen again to the saintly and illustrious doctor John Gerson, who wrote, "After the divine sacrifice offered by Our Lord Himself on the altar of the Cross, the one most pleasing to God and most useful to mankind, is the sacrifice offered to the divine majesty by the most holy Virgin on the altar of her heart, when she so often and with so great a love, offered her beloved son as a living Host. Here is the true altar of holocausts whereon the sacred fire of divine love was

3 Rom. 8, 32.

continually burning without interruption day or night. It is the golden altar seen by Saint John before the throne of God in Heaven."[4]

Of this altar of the glorious Virgin's ardent heart, united as it is with the divine heart of her son Jesus, do we say at the beginning of Holy Mass, *Introibo ad altare Dei*. "I shall go up to the altar of God." These two hearts being only one heart, as we have often said, they are likewise but a single altar. On this altar the sacrifice we are about to offer has been offered time and again by both mother and Son. Therefore does Holy Church put those words three times on the lips of the priest at the beginning of Mass, to admonish us that we should offer our sacrifice on that divine altar and not merely on the material and visible altar, which is only a shadow of the former. Having therefore to offer our sacrifice on so holy and divine an altar, we must offer it in union with the love, charity, humility and holiness of the Admirable Hearts of Jesus and Mary who are in a sense but one heart and one altar. We also designate it as the Holy of Holies when, on ascending to the altar, we pray God to deliver us from our iniquities "*ut ad Sancta Sanctorum puris mereamur mentibus introire*," that we may be worthy to enter with pure minds into the Holy of Holies."

Holy Church refers again to the heart of Mary when we are made to say during the wonderful sacrifice, "We humbly beseech thee, almighty God, command these to be carried by the hands of thy holy angel (the Angel of the great counsel) to thine altar on high, in the presence of thy divine majesty, that as many of us as shall, by partaking at this altar, receive the most sacred Body and Blood of thy son, may be filled with all heavenly blessing and grace."

Notice that when the priest says: *Ex hac altaris participatione*, he kisses the material altar as being the figure of the true mystical and spiritual altar; namely, the heart of Jesus and Mary. This reveals the intimate union our own heart should have with that most amiable heart at all times and in all places, but more especially during the oblation of the divine sacrifice.

O Admirable Heart, O heart most loving, thou art the foremost sanctuary of divine Love, the holiest earthly victim, the golden thurible offering perpetual incense of prayer and sacrifice, the altar of sacrifice. Thou art the Saint of Saints and the queen of all those privileged to offer the Holy Sacrifice of the Mass.

O reader, priest of God, think of the august sanctuary of Mary's heart, and the holy love, purity and fervor with which you must offer the same sacrifice every day. In the name of God I counsel you to realize the words: *Introibo ad altare Dei*, remembering that you go in to the

4 *Tract. 9 sup. Magnif. Partit. 1.*

altar of God, which is the heart of Jesus and Mary. And when you mount the altar steps, give yourself yet again to Jesus and Mary, that you may be united to their immaculate purity and to a holiness higher than that of the Seraphim.

Those of you, O readers, who are not priests, when you enter a church to assist at the Holy Sacrifice, or to say your prayers, hearken to the heavenly voice that strikes your ears: *Pavete ad sanctuarium meum.*[5] "Reverence my sanctuary." Tremble because you are sinners coming before your Judge, and having humbled your heart, beg pardon and implore of Him the grace of perfect repentance.

O Mary, Mother of Mercy, O mother of loving grace, hide us in thy blessed heart, draw us to share in thy constant sacrifice and immolate our hearts forever in thy sanctuary and in thy altar, to the eternal glory of Thy beloved son.

5 Lev. 26, 2.

Chapter Ten

HEART OF MARY, CENTER OF THE CROSS AND CROWN OF MARTYRS, DOCTORS AND VIRGINS

With much reason we may call Mary's most holy heart the center of the Cross through which salvation came to us. The profundity of Mary's love did not prevent her from experiencing most poignant sorrows. Saint Albert the Great,[1] Saint Bernardine[2] and many other saints affirm that Our Lady would have died of sorrow at the foot of the Cross had not divine power imparted to her extraordinary strength as she shared the passion of her beloved son. Hence the Fathers of the Church consider her to have been in truth a martyr and more. Many doctors boldly proclaim that Mary suffered more than the combined sufferings of all martyrs. No one ever could or ever can understand the depths of the sorrow of her most loving heart.

O Mother of my Saviour, thy well beloved son has exalted thee with a crown more glorious and shining than the crowns of all the martyrs. Not only hast thou suffered more than they, therefore making thy sorrow more glorious, but also the holy martyrs have revered and honored thee as their queen and their mother, through whose intercession they have obtained the grace to merit the palm and eternal crown of martyrdom. They lay their glorious crowns at thy feet, O Mary, for to thee, after God and thy divine son, they owe their triumph and everlasting bliss.

Among the countless martyrs, I shall cite three who hold special obligations to the heart of the Blessed Virgin. First is John Travers, an Irish theologian, imprisoned and burned at the stake by King Henry VIII of England. It is recorded that he prayed particularly to Our Lady for the grace of martyrdom, which she promised to him. When the tribunal of judges asked if he had written a book in defense of the Primacy of the Pope, he cried out, showing his hand, "Here are the three fingers with which I wrote the book, and I shall never retract."

1 Sup. Missus est.
2 Serm. 2 de Nom. Mariae, art. 2, cap. 4.

Although his body was burned, those three fingers remained intact, nor was it possible to burn them.

Secondly, I cite Saint Andrew of Sic, in Greece, sustained by Our Lady through most terrible and prolonged martyrdom at the hands of the Mohammedans in 1463. His mangled remains were found to have been miraculously restored in the grave, so that his body, when disinterred by the faithful, appeared whole and incorrupt, because of his constant invocation of Our Lady.

The third martyr, chosen because of the extent of his sufferings and his prayers while being dismembered, is Saint James Intercis, a Persian who obtained his crown under the Emperor Theodosius the Younger.

Now if you would derive benefit from these thoughts of Our Lady's heart considered as the center of the Cross of Christ and as Queen of martyrs, you must not doubt the great love of her heart for the countless souls who are crucified in this life. It will be most pleasing to her if you will commend to her special protection all afflicted persons everywhere, but particularly those held captive by the Mohammedans, and likewise those Christians who are destined to suffer the greatest of human tribulations, the persecution of Antichrist at the end of the world. Implore the Mother of Mercies that she may be the Comforter of the Afflicted and obtain from her divine son the grace that all their sufferings may be turned to eternal and holy profit.

Offer to Mary all your own pains of mind and body, begging her to offer them to her Crucified son, uniting your tiny crosses to the tremendous crosses, for the Glory of God.

In addition to the crown of martyrdom, the Blessed Virgin also is called by many theologians the teacher of the Apostles and Doctors and is crowned with a diadem of learning and virtue beyond that of saintly doctors and confessors. Therefore, you must invoke her specially on behalf of those souls suffering in the darkness of paganism, heresy and sin. Have recourse to the heart of Mary in all your doubts and worries, begging her to grant you the light to avoid the snares of error in this world.

Her third crown is that of Queen of Virgins, which she possesses far more excellently than any saintly exponent of the virtue of purity, far beyond any perfection that can be written or described. Beg Mary to imprint in your soul a great love for chastity and an inconceivable hatred for impurity.

Chapter Eleven[1]

HEART OF MARY, WORLD OF WONDERS

From the beginning of time the three divine Persons have cherished a most ardent love for the glorious Virgin, upon whom They have showered such inestimable favors, even to the communication of Their adorable perfections.[2]

In addition, think of the numberless churches which, in every century since the time of the Apostles, God has caused to be built all over the world in honor of the incomparable Mary where her praises are chanted night and day. Among these churches there are more than sixty in Rome alone, sixty-six in the city of Naples, eighty thousand in Spain, and an uncountable number in France. At Avignon not only is the main altar of the Cathedral dedicated to the Mother of God, but every one of the many other altars in the edifice are likewise dedicated.

Consider the feasts of the universal Church, which include seven principal feasts of Our Lady, not to mention fifteen others celebrated in special localities or churches. Also, every Saturday of the year is dedicated by Holy Church to Our Lady.

Add to the great number of Orders, Congregations and Sodalities the processions and pilgrimages made wherever Christianity prevails in honor of the Blessed Virgin with the approving sanction of Holy Church. Together with these are the miracles performed by God through veneration of the Mother of God and the blessings poured by Our Saviour upon those who honor and cherish pictures and images of His beloved Mother.

Then consider the number of books that have been penned in praise of the Queen of Angels, in such quantities that one noted bibliographer counts more than five thousand, composed by persons of importance: popes, cardinals, bishops, theologians, emperors, rulers, princes, lords, canons and religious. There is scarcely a nation which

---

1   This chapter is an abridgment of chapters 13 and 14 in the original work.
2   Saint Chrysostom calls Mary *abyssus immensarum Dei perfectionum. In Hor. ani.*

has not produced literature in praise of Mary, for among these writers are men of Ethiopia, Africa, Arabia, Dalmatia, Sardinia, Syria, Hungary, Scythia, and of the West and East Indies. Others are Irish, Scottish, Polish, Portuguese, Sicilians, English, Flemish, French, German, Greek, Spanish, Italian.

No less than forty-six Popes have written treatises concerning the Mother of God; fifty-seven Cardinals; thirty-four Patriarchs; two hundred and fifty-nine Bishops; twelve Emperors, six Kings and Queens, princes and lords, eighteen, not to count the many works of members of religious orders.

Imagine for yourselves the innumerable panegyrics and sermons which have been pronounced in every part of the world at all times by successive saintly Fathers in praise of the Mother of Our Saviour, together with the praises chanted forever by the blessed in Paradise.

Even thus has the majesty of God proclaimed His love for Mary. *Omnis gloria Filiae Regis ab intus.* All the glory and all the splendours of the peerless daughter of the Most High spring from within, from her Admirable Heart.

Mary's heart is truly a world of wonders because it is the principle and source of everything great and admirable in the peerless Virgin. We have already listened to the Holy Ghost preaching the grandeur and marvels of His most worthy spouse, but let us open the ears of our heart to hear again the words of tradition throughout the centuries of history, inciting our zeal for devotion to the admirable Virgin Mary.[3]

In the first century, there stand out the Twelve Apostles, and in the second, Saint Irenaeus, Saint Ignatius and Saint Justin Martyr. From the Fathers of the third century I chose, writing in praise of Mary, St. Gregory Thaumaturgus, Bishop of Neocaesarea, and of the fourth, Saint Athanasius, renowned Patriarch of Alexandria, together with Saint Ephrem, Father of the Eastern Church, whose invocations to Mary constitute a most beautiful litany.

In the fifth century there is the great Saint Augustine, and Saint Eucher, Archbishop of Lyons. From the sixth I cite Saint Fulgentius, who, while defending the Divinity of Christ so ardently against the Arians, had signal devotion to proclaiming the praises of the Mother of our Saviour.

In the seventh century, Pope Saint Gregory extolled Our Lady as "the mountain towering above all creation in dignity,"[4] while Saint Ildefonsus, Archbishop of Toledo, vehemently cursed the Helvidians and other heretics who dared to deny the perpetual virginity of Mary.

---

3 In this concluding chapter Saint John Eudes summarizes the history of the devotion to the Blessed Virgin Mary in Catholic Tradition. Cf. *Oeuvres Completes*, V. 7, pp. 607 ff.

4 *Expos. in 1 Reg.* lib. 1 cap. 1, n.45.

In the eighth century, Saint Germanus, Patriarch of Constantinople stands out particularly for his writings and sermons in praise of Our Lady, having special recourse to her most merciful heart.

From the writers of the ninth century I have most frequently quoted a religious of the Augustine Order who sought to conceal his name by calling himself by the extraordinarily humble title, "The Idiot."[5] Nevertheless, God Who exalts the lowly saw that he became known by his true name, Raymund Jourdain. His writings reveal exceptionally profound devotion to the Mother of God.

I wish to mention a few other writers of subsequent centuries, particularly Saint Anselm, Archbishop of Canterbury, whose love for the glorious Virgin Mary, his princess, shines particularly in his treatise on her excellence.[6] I quote from his panegyric, which should suffice to warm even the coldest hearts, the following words, "O woman admirably unique, and uniquely admirable, grant me the grace that thy love may be constantly in my heart, and that thou wilt bear me forever within thy heart."

In the twelfth century the great Saint Bernard, expounding the symbolism of the twelve stars in the crown of the woman envisioned in the Apocalypse, says that they represent the mysteries and virtues of her life, while the twelfth star signifies the "martyrdom of her heart."[7]

Saint Bonaventure, Saint Albert the Great, Thomas a Kempis, Saint Thomas of Villanova, Arnauld of Bonneval, all have written eloquently on the prerogatives and privileges of the incomparable Mary. The revelations and writings of Saint Brigid, including the vision of the Admirable Mother of Our Saviour,[8] have been approved by Holy Church.

In conclusion, if we were to recount everything written by the Doctors of the Church and all that God has caused to become known through His saints concerning the privileges, excellence and perfection of Our Lady, it would fill an almost countless number of large volumes.

Mother Most Admirable, what great and glorious things have been said, thought and written in praise of thee and of thy loving heart! To me it seems incontestable that thy heart is the center of all these wonders, having drawn down the munificence of the Most High by its humility, purity and love. That is why I regard, hail and honor the virginal heart under so many titles and symbols. Infinite and everlasting praise be to God, the Sovereign of all hearts, for having filled thy Admirable Heart with such miracles of wonder and grace!

5   Saint John Eudes follows the opinion of Salazas and other writers who assigned the works of "The Idiot" to the Ninth Century. But Theophilus Raymund, the editor of Jourdain's works, discovered that this learned writer was Abbot of Celles and lived about 1381.

6   *Alloquia Caelestia.*

7   *Serm. in Signum Magnum.*

8   *Revel.* lib. 1. cap. 31.

O Queen of my heart, I have testified many times already, but I shall repeat thousands of times again, imploring all the inhabitants of Heaven to repeat with me and on my behalf, that all sublime prerogatives are thine, and that if the least of thy perfections were wanting, and it could be given thee by the complete destruction of myself, I should consent to it with all my heart.

Part Nine

PRACTICE OF THE DEVOTION TO
THE ADMIRABLE HEART OF MARY

Chapter One

TWELVE REASONS FOR HONORING THE HEART OF MARY

The truths contained in the eight preceding parts oblige us to honor the Admirable Heart of the Mother of God, but there are additional reasons compelling us to do so, among which the twelve principal motives are these:

1. We ought to honor and love the things that God loves and honors, and through which He is loved and glorified. Now, after the most adorable heart of Jesus, there is no heart in Heaven or on earth which has so loved and honored God, or has rendered Him so much glory and love, as the most worthy heart of Mary, the Mother of the Saviour.

2. Who could possibly describe the ardent flames of love in the incomparable heart of the Mother of God toward her beloved son Jesus? Count, if you can, all her thoughts, all her words, all her actions, labors, anxieties and vigilance in feeding, clothing, protecting and rearing our divine Saviour, and you will count so many reasons obliging us to love and praise her most amiable heart.

3. Count also all the thoughts, feelings and affections which filled her motherly heart with regard to our salvation, and you will count so many obligations on our part to love and honor Mary.

4. Picture yourself the means employed by the Mother of Mercy to cooperate with her beloved son our Saviour in the great work of the Redemption of the world; that is, her prayers, fasts, mortifications, tears, sufferings and her most poignant sacrifice of her dear son at the foot of the cross, her heart utterly consumed with love and charity, and you must realize that all these facts are just so many additional obligations on our part to revere and love her most worthy heart.

5. The holy name of Mary has always been so highly honored in the Church, that, according to Surius, Saint Gerard, Bishop of Pannonia, ordered the people of his diocese to prostrate themselves on the ground at the mention of her holy name. Blosius[1] reports that in his

1 *Serm. de Assumpt.*

251

time it was the universal custom in the Church that, whenever the holy name of Mary was pronounced, everyone knelt and all the faithful prayed, sighed and wept with most extraordinary devotion and fervor. This devotion is not dead, because the feast of the Holy Name of Mary is celebrated in a number of churches, especially in the Order of the Redemption of Captives, where the office of her holy name is recited on all Saturdays not assigned to an office of nine lessons. If the venerable name of Mary be worthy of such great veneration, what honor should we not render to her Admirable Heart?

6. Holy Church never ceases to sing daily, in addressing the only son of Mary, "Blessed is the womb that bore Thee, and the paps that gave Thee suck,"[2] because we can never sufficiently praise and revere the consecrated womb in which she bore the Son of the eternal Father, nor the blessed breasts at which she nursed Him. What honor and praises should be given to her most worthy heart?

7. According to the aspirations of Saint Paul, the hearts of the faithful become the abodes and dwellings of Jesus Christ,[3] and Christ Himself assures us that the Father, the Son and the Holy Spirit reside in the hearts of all who love God;[4] so who can doubt that the most Blessed Trinity dwells perpetually in a most admirable and ineffable manner in the virginal heart of her who is the Daughter of the Father, the Mother of the Son and the spouse of the Holy Spirit; Mary who alone loves God more than all other creatures combined? This being the case, with what devotion should we not honor her Immaculate Heart?

8. If we are indebted to the holy Evangelists for having left us the written records of the life of our Redeemer and the mysteries of our Redemption, how much more do we owe to our most holy Mother for having preserved for us this precious treasure in her maternal heart?

9. Is it not we miserable sinners who pierced this most innocent heart of Mary at the time of the passion of the Saviour, with countless thousands of shafts of sorrow by our innumerable sins? How greatly are we obliged, then, to render all the honor within our power in order to make some reparation for the most bitter anguish that we caused her loving heart to suffer.

10. The Admirable Heart of Mary is the perfect image of the most divine heart of Jesus. It is the pattern and model for our own hearts; and all our happiness, perfection and glory consists in striving to transform them into so many living images of the sacred heart of Mary, just as her holy heart is a consummate likeness of the adorable heart of Jesus.

2 Luke 11, 27.
3 Ephes. 3, 17.
4 John 14, 23.

Therefore it is most useful, good and beneficial to exhort Christians to practice devotion to the most august heart of the Queen of Heaven. The sovereign devotion is to imitate what we honor, says Saint Augustine;[5] so who can fail to perceive that, in encouraging the faithful in devotion to the most amiable heart of the Mother of God, we are also exhorting them to imitate the most eminent virtues that adorn it, to engrave its likeness on their own hearts and to render themselves worthy children of such a Mother?

11. Not only is the heart of the Mother of Our Saviour the prototype and model of our own hearts, but her heart, after the adorable heart of Jesus, is also Sovereign Ruler of all the hearts that have been created to love God, since she is Queen of the universe. For that reason all hearts should look upon and imitate the heart of Mary as their model, but in addition they are obliged to render it all the homage that they owe to it as to their Sovereign.

12. Finally, consider all the attributes and perfections of the incomparable heart of the Mother of Fair Love, and you must realize that there are just that number of reasons compelling us to praise, honor and love this most praiseworthy and lovable heart.

---

5 *De Civit.* lib. 8, cap. 17.

Chapter Two

Twelve Methods of Practicing the Devotion

All that has been said in the foregoing pages demonstrates that the devotion to the most holy heart of the Blessed Virgin is most firm and well established and that we are obliged by a countless number of reasons to render special honor and veneration to this heart. Therefore we must now seek proper and suitable methods of doing so. Here are twelve principal recommendations:

1. If you wish to afford extreme happiness to the virginal heart of Our Lady, so zealous for the salvation of your soul, hear and do what our Lord tells you in these words, "My son, give me thy heart;"[1] and "Be converted to me with all your heart."[2] To that end make a firm and true resolution to fulfill your solemn promise to God in Baptism: to make a complete renunciation of Satan, of the works of Satan which are synonymous with sin and of the pomps of Satan which are synonymous with the world; and to follow our Lord in His teaching, example and virtues. And in order to be converted to God not only in heart but with all your heart, cultivate an ardent desire (and ask Him for the grace to fulfill it) to transform all the passions of your heart and turn them toward His divine majesty, placing them at the service of His glory. For example, the passion of love should be directed towards loving only God and one's neighbor in God and for God; the passion of hate, towards hating only sin and all that leads to sin; the passion of fear, towards fearing nothing in the world except offending God; the passion of sadness, to the end of letting nothing sadden us except the sins we have committed against God; the passion of joy, towards seeking all our joy in the love and service of God and in doing His most holy will everywhere and in all things; and so on with the other passions.

2. In order that our Saviour may perfectly possess each heart, listen to these holy words and practice them: *Hoc sentite in corde vestro, quod*

1 Prov. 23, 26.
2 Joel 2, 12.

et in Corde Mariae, "Keep in thy heart the feelings which are in the heart of Mary, the Mother of Jesus." These principal feelings are:

i. Horror and abomination for every kind of sin.

ii. Hatred and scorn for this corrupt world and everything pertaining to it.

iii. The lowest possible esteem, and even of scorn and hatred, toward self.

iv. Profound esteem, respect and love for all the things of God and His Church.

v. Veneration and love for the Cross, that is, for privations, humiliations, mortifications and sufferings, which are one of the richest treasures that a Christian soul can possess in this world, according to the oracle from Heaven, "My brethren, count it all joy, when you shall fall into divers temptations,"[3] so that you may say with Saint Paul, "God forbid that I should glory, save in the cross of our Lord Jesus Christ."[4]

3. One of the most useful and important ways of honoring the most worthy heart of the Queen of virtues is to strive to imitate and to implant in your heart a lively image of her holiness, meekness and forbearance, humility, purity, devotion, wisdom and prudence, patience, obedience, vigilance, faithfulness, love and all its other virtues.

4. Offer your heart frequently to the Queen of all hearts consecrated to Jesus and implore her to take full and complete possession of your heart so that Mary may give it entirely to her son, fill it with supernatural sentiments to adorn it with virtues, and mould it according to the heart of the divine son and His Blessed Mother.

5. Assist the poor, widows, orphans and strangers, protect the helpless, console the afflicted, visit the sick and imprisoned, and perform other similar works of mercy. All these acts are most highly pleasing to the most merciful heart of the Mother of Grace.

6. The greatest joy that we can afford the Admirable Heart of Mary, all aflame with love for the souls which cost the Precious Blood of her son, is to work zealously and devotedly for their salvation. If the hearts of the angels and saints in Heaven rejoice for each conversion of a sinner on earth, the Queen of Angels and saints derives infinitely more joy from it than that of all the denizens of Heaven combined because her heart possesses more love and charity.

7. Cultivate particular devotion to all the saints who enjoyed some special relationship with the most lovable heart of the Mother of God; for example, those mentioned in Part Seven, Chapter Three.

---

3 James 1, 2.
4 Gal. 6, 14.

8. Remember what has been said above: that Our Saviour has given us His own divine heart, along with the most holy heart of His Blessed Mother, to be the model and rule of our lives. Make a careful study of this divine rule, therefore, in order to follow and keep it faithfully.

9. Our Saviour has given us His divine heart, together with the holy heart of His Blessed Mother, not only to be our rule, but also to be our very heart, so that as members of Jesus and children of Mary we may share but one heart with our adorable Head and our incomparable Mother. This privilege should help us to perform all our actions with the heart of Jesus and Mary, that is, in union with the holy intentions and dispositions that motivated Jesus and Mary in all their actions. To this end strive earnestly, at least at the beginning of your principal activities, to renounce yourself entirely and to give yourself to Jesus so that you may become united with His divine heart, which is one and the same with the heart of His Holy Mother; thus may you enter into its love, charity, humility and holiness, so that you may do all things in the holy dispositions which have always filled it.

10. Pay some special honor daily to the royal heart of the sovereign Lady of the universe. This may be done through an act of devotion or a prayer offered for that intention, in imitation of Blessed Herman of the Order of Saint Dominic, who each day used to recite an *Ave Maria* in greeting to the most amiable heart of Mary.

Even though, following the example of this holy religious, you were to say only one *Ave Maria* each day in honour of the Admirable Heart of the Mother of God, you would be doing something highly pleasing to her and most advantageous to your own soul, since the great Suarez, that wonder of learning and piety, said that he would rather lose all his knowledge than lose the merits of a single *Ave Maria*.

11. In all your affairs, necessities, perplexities and afflictions, have recourse to the most benign heart of Mary, regarding it as your refuge in every need, and as a refuge, fortress and safeguard which God has given you as a shelter in the midst of all the miseries engulfing man in this valley of tears, this place of exile and banishment. Yes, the most bountiful and gentle heart of Mary is truly *solatium exilii nostri*, "The solace and comfort of our exile." Whoever has recourse to it with respect and confidence will feel the marvelous effects of its incomparable goodness. There glows in the maternal heart of our most charitable Mother more love than in all the hearts of the fathers and mothers of all time past, present and yet to come.

Mary's heart is constantly mindful of us and the little things that concern us. Her heart is so filled with kindness, meekness, mercy and generosity that never has anyone been known to invoke this Mother of Goodness in humility and confidence without receiving comfort in her presence.

It is a heart full of wisdom and enlightenment which possesses a perfect understanding of all our needs and of all that is most fitting for us to have. It is a most generous heart, strong and mighty to fight our enemies, to repulse and crush whatever oppresses us, to obtain from God whatever it asks of Him and to shower us with all kinds of blessings.

Finally, it is the heart of our great Queen, our most bountiful sister and our most amiable Mother, to whom all power is given in Heaven and on earth and who holds in her hands for distribution to men all the treasures of her beloved son, *cui vult, quando vult et quomodo vult*, says Saint Bernard; "to whomever she wills, whenever she wills and however she wills."

12. The twelfth means of honoring the Admirable Heart of the Mother of Our Saviour is to celebrate its feast, or rather its feasts, with particularly marked devotion. I say "feasts" for there are several feasts of the most august heart of our heavenly Queen.

The first is celebrated in the Congregation of Jesus and Mary and in several other places on February 8th, and in a number of other communities and churches on the first day of June.[5]

The second is the feast of the most ardent longing of the virginal heart for the birth of our Saviour, which is called the feast of the Expectation, and is observed on December 18th.

The third is the feast of the Sorrows of the Pure Heart of the Mother of Jesus, which is celebrated on the Friday following Passion Sunday.

The fourth is the feast of the Resurrection of the Heart of Mary which was restored to life by the Resurrection of her divine son, "(Her) spirit (was) revived,"[6] and overwhelmed with the greatest joy imaginable when this beloved son visited her after His Resurrection. For that reason this feast is observed under the name of the Apparition of the Risen Jesus to His Most Holy Mother, on the first free day after the octave of Easter.

The fifth is the feast of the Joys of the Heart of Mary on July 8th.

There are in addition many others, for all feasts of the Blessed Virgin are really feasts of her Admirable Heart.

The feast of the Immaculate Conception, celebrated on December 8th, is the feast of the creation or formation of her most holy heart, which was fashioned by the almighty hand of God and filled with grace and love from the very first of its creation.

5 The Congregation of Jesus and Mary and the Order of Our Lady of Charity, founded by Saint John Eudes, still solemnize the Feast of the Holy Heart of Mary on February 8th. In the Universal Church the Feast of the Immaculate Heart of Mary is now celebrated on August 22nd.

6 Gen. 45, 27.

The feast of the Nativity of Mary is the feast of the birth of her heart, which on that day began to live a life more holy than any other life.

The feast of the Presentation of Mary in the Temple commemorates the solemn and public dedication of her heart to eternal Love, which is God Himself.

The feast of her angelic marriage[7] with Saint Joseph is the feast of the divine betrothal of the two purest of hearts, two virgin hearts so closely united that they form but a single heart which loves God more than do all the hearts of the Seraphim.

The feast of the Annunciation commemorates the greatest miracle of the marvelous heart of this admirable Mother, which on that day becomes an unfathomable depth of wonders, where greater and more prodigious things take place than have ever happened or ever will happen, no matter how great or worthy of admiration, in all centuries past, present and yet to come.

The feast of the Visitation is the feast of the *Magnificat* and of the inspired words that came forth on that day from her blessed heart so filled with the Holy Spirit.

Christmas is the feast of her divine and virginal childbirth, the feast of the delights of her heart, which is utterly suffused and exalted with joy and love for her lovable Infant upon beholding Him born before her eyes.

The feast of the Purification is the feast of the first public and solemn sacrifice which her heart made to almighty God of His Son, her dearest Child. It is also the feast of the humility of her heart, when she took her place in the temple among the ordinary mothers and joined the ranks of the poor in offering what the poor were accustomed to offer.

The feast of the Assumption commemorates the triumphs of her heart, the feast of its most perfect and intimate union with the heart of the most Blessed Trinity; the feast of the glorification and crowning of her heart as Sovereign ruler of all hearts.

Finally, all these solemnities are the feasts of the most holy heart of the Queen of every heart, because, as we said before, her heart is the source and origin of whatever is great, holy and admirable in each of these feasts. And thus, the feast of the Holy Heart of the Mother of God, which is celebrated on February 8th, encompasses all the other feasts of our holy Mother, for it is the feast of her heart strictly speaking—the feast of this heart which is the principle of all her holiness, all her holy virtues, all her holy mysteries, and all the glories and grandeurs that she will possess everlastingly in Heaven, "All the glory of the King's daughter is within."[8]

---

7   This feast is celebrated in some religious orders on January 23rd.

After that, judge for yourself how many great and marvelous things are honored by this holy solemnity of the Admirable Heart of the Queen of Angels and with what devotion it ought to be celebrated.

To all the above recommendations add meditation on the virtues, excellences and wonders contained in the Admirable Heart of the Mother of the Saviour, which is an excellent way to motivate yourself to love and honor it.[9]

---

8 Ps. 44, 14.
9 Two series of meditations on the holy heart of Mary will be found in another volume of The Selected Writings of Saint John Eudes entitled, *Meditations on Various Subjects*, New York, 1947. p. 231 ff.

Part Ten

THE CANTICLE OF THE
ADMIRABLE HEART OF MARY

EXPOSITION OF THE MAGNIFICAT,
TREATING ITS SIGNIFICANCE VERSE BY VERSE

Chapter One

Excellence of the Sublime Canticle

Sacred Scripture includes a number of inspired canticles that were composed by saintly women, for example, the canticles of Mary, sister of Moses and Aaron, of Deborah, of Judith, of Anna, mother of the prophet Samuel, all of which give thanks to God for outstanding favors received from His divine bounty. But the holiest and worthiest of all canticles is the *Magnificat* of the Mother of God, which stands unsurpassed because of the dignity and holiness of its author, as well as because of the great and admirable mysteries it contains. This is to say nothing of the miracles that God has performed by means of this canticle. While there is no record of any miracles having been performed through other canticles, Saint Thomas of Villanova,[1] the Archbishop of Valencia, points out that upon the recitation of this canticle the Holy Spirit wrought a number of wonders on behalf of Saint John the Baptist, the holy precursor of the Son of God, as well as in the person of his parents. Experience also has shown on more than one occasion that the *Magnificat* is an excellent means of expelling evil spirits from the bodies of those who are possessed by the devil. Several other esteemed writers report various miracles which have taken place through the recitation of this canticle.[2]

There is no evidence that the Blessed Virgin Mary ever sang or spoke it publicly more than once during her lifetime, but we cannot doubt that she recited it numberless times in private. Some writers report that Our Lady has often appeared in churches, during Vespers, surrounded by throngs of angels, and that she has been heard to sing her marvelous canticle with the angels and the priests so melodiously and enchantingly that no words can express the perfection of her participation.

1 *Concio. De Visit. B. Virg.*
2 Cf. Saint Anselm, *In lib. Miracul.*

Remember, too, whenever you sing or recite this virginal canticle, to surrender yourself to the Holy Spirit so that you become united to the devotion and all the holy dispositions with which it was sung or spoken by the Blessed Virgin Mary and by countless numbers of zealous saints.

Chapter Two

THE TRUE CANTICLE OF MARY'S HEART

I call the *Magnificat* the true canticle of the most holy heart of the Blessed Virgin Mary for several reasons.

First of all, it originated in her Immaculate Heart and its melody vibrated her heart strings before it found voice on her lips.

Secondly, the words were sung only through the impetus and inspiration flowing from her heart—from her corporeal, spiritual and divine heart. The corporeal heart of Mary, being filled with acute and extraordinary joy, impelled her most holy mouth to sing this *Magnificat* with extraordinary fervor and jubilation; her spiritual heart, being wholly delighted and enraptured in God, brought forth from her hallowed lips these ecstatic words, "And my spirit hath rejoiced in God my Saviour."[1] But her divine heart, that is to say, the divine child who was hidden in her blessed womb and dwelling in her heart, the soul of her soul, the spirit of her spirit and the heart of her heart, is the primary author of this canticle. It is this divine heart which inspired the mind of the holy Mother with the thoughts and truths contained in the canticle. It is the heart of Jesus who pronounces through her its prophetic utterance of praise.

Thirdly, the *Magnificat* is the canticle of the heart of the Mother of uncreated love, that is, the canticle of the Holy Spirit, Who is the spirit and the heart of the eternal Father and the divine Son. The Holy Ghost is also the heart and the Spirit of the Virgin Mother, pervading and possessing her so completely that her very presence and voice filled with the same spirit Saint Zachary, Saint Elizabeth and her unborn child, Saint John the Baptist.

Finally, it is the canticle of the heart and the love of Our Lady, because it is the divine love inflaming her utterly that inspired her to pronounce the words of this marvelous canticle—words which, accord-

1 Luke 1, 47.

ing to Saint Bernardine, are like so many flames of love darting from the ardent furnace of divine love burning in the Immaculate Heart of this incomparable Virgin.

O canticle of love, O virginal canticle of the heart of the Mother of love, having thine origin in the heart itself of the God of love, Who is Jesus, and in the heart of the personal and incarnate love which is the Holy Spirit, it is fitting only for the most blessed lips of the Mother of love to sing and pronounce thy message! The very Seraphim deem themselves unworthy to do so. How is it, then, that miserable sinners like us dare to repeat thy divine words and to pronounce with our worldly mouths the ineffable mysteries thou dost contain? Oh, with what respect and veneration should this most holy canticle be recited and sung! Oh, what should be the purity of the tongue and the holiness of the lips that intone it! Oh, what fire and flames of love should it kindle in the hearts of the ecclesiastics and religious who repeat and sing it so often! One should indeed be all heart and love in order to sing and recite this canticle of love.

O Mother of pure and tender love, deign to make us partakers of the holiness, fervor and love with which thou didst sing this admirable canticle here on earth, and as thou wilt sing it everlastingly in Heaven with all the angels and the saints. Obtain for us from thy divine son the grace to be numbered among those who will sing the *Magnificat* eternally with thee, that we may give immortal thanks to the most adorable Trinity for all the wonders wrought in thee and through thee, and for the countless graces bestowed on all mankind through thy blessed intercession.

Chapter Three

"My Soul Doth Magnify the Lord"

The first verse contains only four Latin words, *Magnificat anima mea Dominum*, but they are words imbued with great mysteries. Let us weigh them carefully and devoutly; let us consider them attentively, in a spirit of humility, piety and respect, in order that we may be inspired, like the Blessed Virgin, to magnify God for the great and marvelous things that He wrought in her and through her, on her behalf and for us as well.

Here is the first word: *Magnificat*. What does this word mean? What does it mean to magnify God? Is it possible to magnify one whose grandeur and magnificence are immense, infinite and incomprehensible? Not at all; such a thing is impossible—impossible for God Himself, Who cannot make Himself greater than He already is. We cannot magnify God, that is, make Him greater in Himself, since His divine perfections are infinite and therefore cannot be increased in themselves, but we can magnify Him in ourselves. "Every holy soul," says Saint Augustine, "can conceive the eternal Word within himself by means of faith. He can engender God in other souls by preaching the divine Word, and he can magnify his Creator by loving Him so truly that he too may say: 'My soul doth magnify the Lord.'"[1] "To magnify the Lord," continues Saint Augustine, "is to adore, praise and exalt His immense grandeur, His supreme majesty, His infinite excellence and perfections."

We can magnify God in several ways: first of all, by our thoughts, having a most exalted idea of God and the highest esteem for Him as well as for all things of God; secondly, by our devotion, loving God with all our hearts and above all things; thirdly, by our words, always speaking with the most profound respect of God and all things pertaining to Him, and by adoring and praising His infinite power, His incomprehensible wisdom, His immense goodness and His other perfections;

---

1 *Serm. De Assumpt.*

fourthly, by our actions, always performing them solely for the glory of God; fifthly, by practicing what the Holy Spirit teaches us in these words, "Humble thyself in all things, and thou shalt find grace before God, for great is the power of God alone, and He is honoured by the humble."[2] In the sixth place, we can magnify God by willingly bearing the crosses He sends us for love of Him; for there is nothing that honors Him more than suffering, since our Saviour found no means to glorify His Father more excellent than the torments and death of the Cross. Last of all, we can magnify God by preferring and exalting Him above all things through our thoughts, affections, words, actions, humiliations and mortifications.

But alas! How often do we do just the contrary! Instead of exalting God, we lower Him; instead of preferring Him to all things, we prefer the creatures to the Creator; instead of preferring His Holy will, His interests, His glory and His happiness to our own will, interest, honor and satisfaction, we do just the opposite, putting Barabbas before Jesus.

Such is not thy behaviour, O holy Virgin! Thou didst always magnify God most highly and perfectly from the first moment of thy life until the last. Thou didst always magnify Him most excellently by all thy thoughts, affections, words and actions, by the most profound humility, by the multitude of thy sufferings, by practicing all virtue in a sovereign degree and by making saintly use of all the powers of thy soul and of all thine interior and exterior senses. In a word, thou alone hast glorified God more worthily and magnified Him more highly than have all other creatures combined.

We come now to the second word of our canticle, which is *anima*, "My *soul* doth magnify the Lord." Notice that the Blessed Virgin Mary does not say "I magnify," but "My soul doth magnify the Lord," in order to show that she magnifies Him from the utmost depths of her heart and with her whole inner strength. Thus does she magnify Him not only with her lips and tongue, her hands and feet, but she also employs all the faculties of her soul—her understanding, memory, will and all the powers of the superior and inferior part of her soul, exhausting full inward and outward strength in order to praise, glorify and magnify her God. She does not magnify Him exclusively in her own name, nor to discharge her infinite obligations because of the inconceivable favors that she has received from His divine bounty; she magnified God in the name of all creatures and for the graces that He has bestowed upon all men, since He became man in order to render men God-like and save the whole human race, if men will but cooperate with the designs of His inconceivable love for them.

2 Ecclus. 3, 20–21.

Here is the third word: *mea*, "*my* soul." What is this soul which the Blessed Virgin calls her soul?

My first reply to this question is that I know a great author[3] who maintains that this soul of the Blessed Virgin is her son Jesus Christ, the soul of her soul.

Secondly, I answer that these words, *anima mea*, refer first to the individual and natural soul which animates the body of the immaculate Virgin, and second, to the soul of the Divine Infant whom she is carrying in her womb, Who is so closely united with her own soul that their two souls, in a certain sense, form but a single soul. In the third place, these words, *anima mea*, "my soul," indicate and include all souls created in the image and likeness of God who have ever been, are now, and ever will be in the whole world. Saint Paul assures us that the eternal Father has given us all things in giving us His divine Son,[4] so there can be no doubt that, in giving Christ to His divine Mother, He thus gave her all things and therefore all souls belong to her. Mary is not unaware of this, and she also knows full well her sacred obligation to make use of everything that God has given her, for His honor and glory. Consequently, when Mary pronounces these words, "My soul doth magnify the Lord," considering all the souls of the past, present and future as souls who belong to her, she includes them all in order to unite them with the soul of her son and her own soul, and in order to avail herself of every soul for praising, exalting and magnifying Him who descended from Heaven and took flesh in her own virginal bosom so that He might accomplish the great work of their redemption.

We come now to the last word of the first verse: *Dominum*, "My soul doth magnify *the Lord*." Who is this Lord whom the Blessed Virgin magnifies? It is He who is the Lord of lords, the sovereign and universal Lord of Heaven and earth. This Lord is the eternal Father; this Lord is the Son; this Lord is the Holy Spirit—three divine Persons who are but one God and one Lord, having but one single essence, power, wisdom, goodness and majesty. The most pure Virgin praises and magnifies the eternal Father for having associated her with His divine paternity by making her the mother of the very Son whose Father He is. She magnifies the Son of God for having deigned to choose her to be His Mother and Himself to be her true son. She magnifies the Holy Spirit for having willed to accomplish in her the greatest of His works; that is, the adorable mystery of the Incarnation. She magnifies the Father, the

---

3 Vigerius, *in suo Decachordo*, chord. 7.—Cardinal Mark Vigerius, a Franciscan, died at Rome in 1516.

4 Rom. 8, 32.

Son and the Holy Spirit for the infinite graces which They have grant-ed to her and intend to bestow on all mankind.

Let us learn from this canticle that one of the principal duties required by God, and one of our greatest obligations towards His divine majesty, is gratitude for His blessings, for which we must render thanks to Him with all our hearts and with most special devotion. Let us be eager, therefore, to imitate the glorious Virgin in her sublime thanksgiv-ing and to say frequently with her, "My soul doth magnify the Lord," in order to thank the most Blessed Trinity, not only for all the graces that we have received, but also for all the blessings that providence has ever bestowed on all creatures. And in saying the words *anima mea*, let us remember that the eternal Father, in giving us His only begotten Son, has given us all things. Consequently the holy souls of Jesus and His divine mother, together with all other souls in general, belong to us. For that reason we can and should profit by these souls for the glory of Him who has given them to us, through an ardent desire to praise and glori-fy God with our whole heart, our whole soul and all our strength. In these words we should include all the hearts and souls in the world, which are ours and which we wish to unite into one great heart and one single soul, to be employed to praise our Creator and Saviour.

Chapter Four

"My Spirit Hath Rejoiced in God My Saviour"

These divine words, uttered by the inspired lips of the Mother of our Saviour, reveal to us the ineffable and incomprehensible joy that enraptured her heart, her spirit and her soul, together with all its faculties, not only at the moment of the Incarnation of the Son of God within her, but during the time that she bore Him in her blessed womb; indeed, even throughout the remainder of her life, according to Saint Albert the Great and other doctors. It was such an excessive joy, especially at the moment of the Incarnation, that, just as her holy soul was separated from her body during the last moment of her life by the strength of her love for God and her superabundant joy upon beholding herself preparing to join her son in Heaven, so also, if her life had not been miraculously preserved she would have died of joy upon realizing the inexpressible bounty of God on her behalf and that of all mankind. History recounts numerous instances of persons who, hearing news of even temporal benefit, have died of joy; so it is most credible that the Blessed Virgin Mary would have died of joy if she had not been sustained by virtue of the Divine Child in her virgin womb, because hers was the greatest cause for joy that ever existed or ever shall exist.

Mary rejoiced in God, *in Deo*; that is, because God is infinitely powerful, wise, good, just and merciful; because He so admirably displays His power, goodness and all His other divine attributes in the mystery of the Incarnation and the Redemption of the world.

Mary rejoiced in God her Saviour, *in Salutari*, because He had come into the world to save and redeem her first and foremost, preserving her from original sin and overwhelming her with His graces and favors in such an abundance that He made her His mediatrix and cooperator in the salvation of all mankind.

Her heart was overcome with joy because God had regarded her favorably, that is, had loved and approved of the humility of His handmaid, in which He found a most singular happiness and pleasure.

"Herein," says Saint Augustine, "lies the cause of the joy of Mary—that He beheld the humility of His handmaid. It was as if she were saying, 'I rejoice because of the grace that God has granted to me, for it is from Him that I have received the reason for this joy; and I rejoice in Him because I love His gifts for love of Him.'"[1]

Mary rejoiced for the great things that God's omnipotent goodness had wrought in her, the greatest wonders that had ever come to pass in all the preceding centuries, the greatest that will ever take place in all the ages to come, as we shall see further on in the explanation of the fourth verse.

Mary rejoiced not only for the favors that she had received from God, but also for the graces and mercy that He had showered upon all men who were disposed to receive His priceless gifts.

Mary's heart rejoiced not only in the goodness of God toward those who place no obstacle in its way, but also in the manifestations of His justice toward the proud, who scorn His generosity.

In addition, the rejoicing of the Blessed Virgin sprang from another very special cause most worthy of her incomparable bounty. Saint Antoninus cites this reason[2] and I repeat it here so that it may encourage us to love and serve Mary whose love for us is so very great. Here it is. In explaining the words *Exsultavit spiritus meus*, the Saint says that we must interpret them as we do those spoken by our Saviour on the cross, "Father, into Thy hands I commend my Spirit,"[3] that is, Father, I commend to Thee all who will be united with my spirit through faith and charity. "But he who is joined to the Lord is one Spirit."[4] In like manner, the Mother of the Saviour being wholly delighted and ecstatically enraptured in God when she pronounces these words, "My spirit hath rejoiced in God my Saviour . . ." sees in spirit the almost countless multitude of those who will have special love and devotion for her, and be numbered among the predestined, from which she derives an inconceivable joy.

That being the case, who is it that will not be inspired to love this all-good and all-lovable Mother, who experiences such deep love for those who love her that she regards and loves them as her own spirit, soul and heart? Let us listen to what Lanspergius the Carthusian says to each one of us, that we may be made to realize that truth:

"I exhort you, my dear son, to love our most Blessed Lady and divine Mistress. If you wish to safeguard yourself against an infinite number of

1 *Sup. Magnificat.*
2 *Part. R.* tit. 15, cap. 2. § 29.
3 Luke 23, 46.
4 1 Cor. 6, 17.

dangers and temptations, of which there are so many in this life, if you wish to find comfort and never to be overcome by sorrow in your adversities, if, in short, you wish to be inseparably united with our Saviour, then cultivate special veneration and love for His most pure, amiable, meek, faithful, gracious and powerful Mother. If you truly love Mary and try conscientiously to imitate her, you will find that she in turn will be a most sweet and tender Mother to you, and that she is so filled with kindness and mercy that she despises no one and never ignores those who invoke her aid, because her greatest desire is to dispense to all sinners the treasures of the graces which her divine son has placed at her disposal. Whoever loves this immaculate Virgin is chaste; whoever honors her is devout; whoever imitates her is holy. No one loves her without feeling the effects of reciprocal love. Not one of those who love her can perish; not one of those who try to imitate her can fail to attain eternal salvation. How many wretched sinners has she taken to her merciful bosom when they were in despair and abandoned to all sorts of vices, with one foot in Hell, if we may use the expression; yet they were not rejected by Mary when they had recourse to her goodness. Rather were they snatched by her from the jaws of the infernal monster, being reconciled with her divine son and replaced on the path to paradise by the power of her intercession? It is a grace, a privilege and a power specially conferred upon Mary by her omnipotent son, that she is able to obtain penance for those who love her, grace for those who are devoted to her, and the glory of Heaven for those who strive to imitate her."[5]

Here is another joy of the Queen of Heaven which is indicated in these words, "My soul hath rejoiced . . ." a joy which surpasses all the others. Several holy Fathers and important Doctors write that this Virgin Mother, being ecstatically elevated to God at the moment of the Incarnation of her son within her, was filled with the same inconceivable joys which are possessed by all the blessed in Heaven, and that she was rapt to the third Heaven, where she had the happiness of seeing God clearly face to face. In proof of this, these holy writers advance the indisputable maxim that all the privileges with which the Son of God has honored His other saints were also bestowed by Him upon His divine Mother. Now Saint Augustine, Saint John Chrysostom, Saint Ambrose, Saint Basil, Saint Anselm, Saint Thomas and a number of others do not hesitate to assert that Saint Paul, while he was still on earth, saw the essence of God when he was transported to the third Heaven. Who can doubt, then, that the Mother of Our Saviour, who always lived in the most perfect inno-

5 Lansperigius, *Epist.* 23.

cence and who alone loved God more than all the other saints combined, enjoyed this same favor, not only on one occasion but on several, particularly at the happy moment of the conception of her son? This is the opinion of Saint Bernard, Saint Albert the Great, Saint Antoninus and many others. "O Blessed Mary," exclaims the holy Abbot Rupert, "it was then that a deluge of joy, a furnace of love and a torrent of heavenly delights burst upon thee, wholly absorbed and inebriated thee, and made thee experience what no eye has ever seen, no ear has ever heard and no human heart has ever understood."[6]

Let us learn from this that the children of the world are victims of very pernicious error, being gravely mistaken in imagining that there is no joy or happiness on earth, that there is only sadness, bitterness and affliction for those who serve God. O insupportable delusion! O hateful lie which can proceed only from him who is the father of all errors and falsehoods! Do we not hear the voice of eternal Truth crying out, "Tribulation and anguish upon every soul of man that worketh evil . . . but glory, and honor, and peace to every one that worketh good,"[7] and that the heart of a sinful person is like a sea that is always troubled, agitated and disturbed, "The wicked are like the raging sea";[8] that the fear of God changes the hearts of those who love Him into a paradise of joy, gladness, peace, happiness and "The fear of the Lord shall delight the heart, and shall give joy, and gladness, and length of days";[9] and that true servants of God possess a felicity that is greater, more genuine and more steadfast, even in the midst of the most overwhelming tribulations, than all the pleasures of those who espouse the cause of Satan? Do you not hear Saint Paul assuring us that he is filled with consolation and imbued with joy in the midst of all his tribulations?"[10]

Do you desire to learn these truths from experience? "O taste, and see that the Lord is sweet."[11] But if you wish to acquire this experience, you will have to renounce the false pleasures and misleading delights of the world.

O holy Virgin, implant in our hearts a share in the scorn, aversion and detachment which thy virginal heart always felt toward the false pleasures of earth. Obtain for us from thy divine son the grace to seek all our happiness, joy and delight in loving and glorifying Him; in serving and honoring thee with our whole heart and soul and with all our strength.

6 *In Cant.* 1.
7 Rom. 2, 9–10.
8 Isa. 57, 20.
9 Ecclus. 1, 12.
10 2 Cor. 7, 4.
11 Ps. 33, 9.

Chapter Five

"He Hath Regarded the Humility of His Handmaid"

In order to understand this verse appropriately, we must consider it in relation to the preceding verse from which it springs, "My spirit hath rejoiced in God my Saviour, for He hath regarded the humility of His handmaid; behold from henceforth all generations shall call me Blessed."

This verse contains two principal truths, the first of which is expressed in these words, "He hath regarded the humility of His handmaid." What is this humility of which the Blessed Virgin speaks here? The holy Doctors are divided in their opinions about it. Some of them say that among all the virtues, humility is the only one which never perceives or becomes aware of itself, for he who believes himself to be humble is really proud. Therefore, when the Blessed Virgin says that God has regarded her humility, she is speaking not of the virtue of humility but of her lowliness and abjection.

Other authorities maintain that humility in a soul consists, not in being ignorant of the graces that God has bestowed upon it and the virtues that He has granted, but in returning His gifts and keeping for oneself only nothingness and sin; and that the Holy Spirit, speaking through the mouth of the Blessed Virgin, wishes to teach us that among all the virtues He beheld in her, He loved her humility and approved of it most of all, because the Blessed Virgin had humbled herself beneath all things, and this humility persuaded His divine majesty to elevate her above all creatures by making her the Mother of the Creator. "O true humility," exclaims Saint Augustine, "which gave birth to God for the sake of men, and granted life to mortals! The humility of Mary is the heavenly ladder on which God descended to earth. For what is the meaning of *respexit*, if not *approbavit*, 'He hath approved?' There are many who appear humble in the eyes of men, but their humility is not beheld by God. For if they were truly humble, they would not find pleasure in the praises of men, and their spirits would not rejoice in the eulogies of this world, but in God."[1]

"There are two kinds of humility," says Saint Bernard. "The first is the daughter of truth; it is cold and without warmth. The second is the daughter of charity, and it inflames us. The first consists of knowledge and the second of love. Through the first we realize that we are nothing, and we learn this humility from ourselves and from our own wretchedness and weakness. Through the second we trample underfoot the glory of the world; and this humility we learn from Him Who annihilated Himself and fled when they sought Him out to offer Him the glory of royalty; but when they hunted Him down to crucify and plunge Him into the depths of opprobrium and ignominy, instead of fleeing He voluntarily offered Himself."[2]

The Blessed Virgin possessed in a sovereign degree these two kinds of humility, especially the second; and Saint Augustine, Saint Bernard, Saint Albert the Great, Saint Bonaventure, Saint Thomas and several other writers all maintain that the words which the Holy Spirit uttered through the mouth of the most humble Virgin, *Respexit humilitatem*, mean true humility.

If you ask why God regarded the humility of the most glorious Virgin rather than her shining purity or other virtues, seeing that she possessed them all in the highest degree, Albert the Great[3] will reply, together with Saint Augustine, that God preferred to look down upon her humility because it was more pleasing to Him than her purity. "Virginity is highly praiseworthy," says Saint Bernard, "but humility is necessary. The former is counselled; the latter is commanded. You can be saved without virginity, but there is not salvation without humility. Without humility, I dare say that the virginity of Mary would not have been at all pleasing to God. If Mary had not been humble, the Holy Spirit would not have descended upon her; and if He had not descended upon her, she would not have become the Mother of God. She pleased God with her virginity but she conceived the Son of God through her humility. Hence it must be inferred that it was her humility which rendered her virginity pleasing to His divine majesty."[4]

O holy humility, thou hast given us a God-Man and a Mother of God, and consequently thou art the source of all the graces, favors, blessings, privileges and treasures that we possess on earth and hope to possess one day in Heaven. Thou art the destroyer of all evil and the source of all good. Oh, how we should esteem, love and desire this holy virtue! With what fervor we ought to implore it of God! Oh, with what

1 *Serm. 2 de Assumpt.*
2 *Serm. 43 super Cant.*
3 *Serm. 2 de Nat. Dom*
4 *Homil. 1 super Missus est.*

ardor should we seek and embrace all the means necessary to acquire it! Whoever has no humility has nothing; and whoever does possess it has all the other virtues. Hence it seems, to quote the Holy Spirit speaking through the mouth of Holy Church, that the eternal Father sent His only begotten Son into the world to become incarnate and to be crucified only that He might teach us humility through His example. It is what Holy Mother Church proclaims in this prayer on Palm Sunday, "Almighty and eternal God, who didst cause our Saviour to take upon him our flesh and to suffer death upon the cross that all mankind may imitate the example of his humility, mercifully grant that treasuring the lessons of his patience we may deserve to have fellowship in his resurrection." "What the devil has destroyed through pride," says one of the holy Fathers, "the Saviour has reestablished through humility."[5]

O Jesus, King of the humble, grant us the grace, we beseech Thee, to learn well the divine lesson which Thou hast taught by these holy words, "Learn of me, because I am meek, and humble of heart."[6]

O Mary, Queen of the humble, it is thy privilege to crush the head of the serpent, which is pride and arrogance. Crush it completely, then, in our hearts, and make us partakers of thy holy humility, that we may sing with thee for all eternity, *Respexit humilitatem ancillae suae*, rendering thanks to the Most Blessed Trinity for having been so well pleased with thy humility that It deemed thee worthy, because of it, to become the Mother of the Saviour of the world, and to cooperate with Him in the salvation of all mankind.

5 Caesarius Arelat. *Homil*. 18.
6 Matt. 11, 29.

Chapter Six

"FROM HENCEFORTH ALL GENERATIONS SHALL CALL ME BLESSED"

This brings us to the second part of this verse, namely, "From henceforth all generations shall call me Blessed." We need not be astonished if the most holy Virgin says something here about herself which is highly favorable, and refers to her own glory and praise, for it is the Holy Spirit Who speaks through her lips. Here is one of the greatest, most celebrated and most important prophecies that was ever made or ever will be made, announcing to mankind the infinity of admirable things that God will accomplish everywhere on earth in every age and everlastingly in Heaven on behalf of the Mother of the Redeemer, in order to make her known, loved, served and honored throughout the world.

This great prophecy, informing us that all generations are to acknowledge and acclaim the Mother of the Blessed Saviour, applies to the whole universe, from the highest Heaven to the lowest depths of Hell. For not only has the Most Blessed Trinity sent the Archangel Gabriel, one of the first princes of Its empire, as ambassador, to announce to Mary that she was full of grace, and that the Lord was with her in order to accomplish in her the greatest wonder of all time, and that she is blessed forever among all women; this same Trinity also exalts Mary above all the angels on the highest throne of glory.

The eternal Father honors her as the most blessed of all women, making her eternally the Mother of the only begotten Son Whose Father He is, and granting her a power which surpasses all the powers of Heaven and earth.

The Son of God proclaims her Blessed among all the nations who hear His holy Gospel, which teaches the fullness of the grandeurs that He has bestowed upon Mary in choosing her to be His Mother.

The Holy Spirit renders her supremely blessed and glorious in choosing her as His most worthy spouse and endowing her with His holiness in such a high degree that she is Queen of all the saints.

All the hierarchies of angels acknowledge Mary to be blessed because in contemplating her on the day of her triumph and glorious Assumption they find the glorious Virgin so filled with wonders that they can speak of them only with admiration and transports of delight. *Quae est ista?* they ask, *Quae est ista?* Who is she? Who is she? And after the adoration that they continually render to God in Heaven, their foremost activity is to proclaim incessant praises of their Sovereign Empress.

Do we not hear the voice of holy Church Militant which perpetually sings all over the earth, "Blessed is the womb of the Virgin Mary which bore the Son of the eternal Father, and blessed are the breasts which nourished Him?"

Have we not already heard of the merciful Virgin once declaring to Saint Brigid that there is no pain in Purgatory which is not eased through her mediation? And do we not hear the voice of Holy Mother Church asking God to deliver the poor souls from that prison of divine justice through the intercession of Blessed Mary ever Virgin: *Beata Maria semper per Virgine intercedente?* It must convince us that the souls of the Church Suffering are not only relieved in their agony but also delivered from it through her mediation.

Is it not also true that the souls who were in Limbo from the beginning of the world until the death of the Son of God profited by the intercession of this incomparable Virgin, since it was she who gave them the Redeemer to free them from captivity?

Let us descend still lower to the utmost depths of Hell. If it is true, as Saint Thomas, the Angelic Doctor, says, that the miserable damned are punished *citra condign condignum*—that is to say, they do not suffer the full torments merited by their sins—it is certain that this is a concession of divine mercy. Now it is also true that for every effect of grace or mercy that proceeds from the adorable bosom of divine bounty our Mother of Mercy prays, and her prayers are effective. Therefore, all the souls in Hell ought to recognize and revere her as the most benign and sweet Mother of Mercy. But because they do not do so, let us compensate for their neglect, praying all the inhabitants of Heaven to do likewise.

What shall we say of the wretched demons? Is it not true that, in spite of the rage they directed against this most bountiful Virgin because of the souls that she frequently snatches from their claws, they are nevertheless constrained to acknowledge her inconceivable charity whenever they are forced to abandon their prey by virtue of her intercession? And that upon the pronunciation of the holy name of Mary, they are compelled to leave the bodies in their possession and flee to their infernal dungeon?

Thus it is that all the generations of Heaven, of angels, of saints, of the Church Triumphant, Militant and Suffering, and even of Hell itself, fulfill this prophecy of the glorious Virgin, "All generations shall call me Blessed."

Finally, there is no country in the world, no nation under the sun, either great or small, rich or poor, no religious or priest, no man or woman, not under the obligation to confess and proclaim that the Mother of the Saviour is the most blessed, powerful, generous, compliant, admirable and amiable of all creatures; for she seems to belong to the world and to think only about doing good to all who love and invoke her and to make them partakers of her own happiness and felicity.

"O many times blessed!" exclaims the holy Doctor John Gerson, "Blessed first of all because thou hast believed. Blessed secondly because thou art full of grace. Blessed thirdly because thou art blessed. Blessed fourthly because the Almighty hath wrought great things in thee. Blessed in the fifth place because thou dost possess the joys of motherhood together with the glory of virginity. Blessed last of all because thou art incomparable, having been and always to be without equal."[1]

Let us listen now to Saint Germanus, Archbishop of Constantinople, addressing Mary most admirable. "Who does not admire thee, who does not love thee, O most bountiful Virgin? Thou art our firm hope, our sure protection, our unshakable refuge, our most vigilant guardian, our perpetual safeguard, our most powerful help, our strongest defense, our unconquerable tower, the treasure of our joy, the garden of our delight, our impregnable fortress, our inaccessible bulwark, the port of those who are in danger of shipwreck, the security of sinners, the asylum of the abandoned, the reconciliation of criminals, the salvation of the lost, the blessing of the accursed, the general and public purveyor of every kind of blessing. In short, who could ever comprehend the effects of thy mercy? O Heaven! O Queen of Heaven! Blessed be thou amongst all generations! There is no place in the world where thy praises are not sung; and there is no race or tribe from which God does not receive some tribute and service through thy mediation."[2]

O holy Virgin, my heart is overcome with joy to see thee proclaimed blessed by all generations, past, present and yet to come; and I implore the most Blessed Trinity with all my heart to allow this divine prophecy to be fulfilled even more and more throughout the universe. Oh, would that every breath of mine, every pulsation of my heart and

1 *Super Magnificat*, Tract. 4, notula 1.
2 *Serm.* 2 de *Dormit.* B.V.

veins, every use of the faculties of my soul, and all my interior and exterior senses, were as so many voices continually singing, in company with all the angels and saints, with the whole Church and all creatures; "Blessed is the womb of the Virgin Mary which bore the Son of the eternal Father, and blessed are the breasts which nourished Him." O Blessed Mary, Mother of God, ever Virgin, temple of the Lord, repository of the Holy Spirit, who alone without rival hast been found most pleasing to Our Lord Jesus Christ, pray for thy people, intervene for the clergy, intercede especially for all devout women, and grant the help of thine incomparable goodness to all who honor thee.

Chapter Seven

"HE THAT IS MIGHTY HAS DONE GREAT THINGS TO ME"

In the preceding verse the Blessed Virgin prophesied that all generations shall call her Blessed; in this verse she reveals the reasons for this honor, namely the great things that God has done to her.

What are these great things? Let us listen to Saint Augustine. "It is a great thing," he says, "for a virgin to be a mother without the cooperation of man. It is a great thing for her to have borne in her womb the Word of God the Father, to have clothed Him with her own flesh. It is a great thing for her who characterizes herself as a handmaid to become the Mother of her Creator."[1]

"It is a great thing," says Saint Antoninus,[2] "to have created Heaven and earth out of nothing. It is a great thing to have brought manna down from Heaven in order to nourish the Chosen People in the desert for forty years. It is a great thing to have given the Israelites possession of the promised land after having exterminated all the kings and people who inhabited it. All the miracles that our Saviour performed in Judea, giving sight to the blind, driving out devils from the bodies of those who were possessed, curing the sick, restoring the dead to life, are great and marvelous things. But the mystery of the Incarnation, which the infinite power of God wrought in the Blessed Virgin, incomparably surpasses all these other things. It is what prompts her to say, 'He that is mighty hath done great things.'"

"Here are the great things," says Saint Thomas of Villanova,[3] "that God wrought in the most holy Virgin. He elevated her to such a high degree of grandeur that all the eyes of men and angels cannot scan that eminence. He transformed this granddaughter of Adam into the Mother of her own Creator, the lady of the world, the Queen of Heaven and the empress of all creatures. A new prodigy appeared in the world,

1 *In Magnif.*
2 *Summa theol.* Part 4, titul. 15, cap. 22.
3 *Concio 2 in Annunt. B.V.*

to the great wonderment of Heaven and earth: a God-Man, a Man-God; God become man, and man united with God. Prodigy of prodigies, miracle of miracles, after which there remains nothing on earth worthy to be admired!"

"It is quite true that all the wonders witnessed on earth are as nothing compared with this incomprehensible event. We admire the miracle that God performed when He allowed His people to pass dry shod across the Red Sea. That is a trifle. Here is something far greater: it is the immense ocean of the Divinity confined within the body of a young and mortal virgin. We admire the bush that burned without being consumed. That is a little thing; here is a virgin who brings forth a Child while preserving her virginity intact. We admire the prophet Moses lying in a tiny cradle of rushes. That is insignificant; let us rather admire the King of Heaven lying in a manger. We admire a column of fire and a pillar of cloud which guided the people of God in the desert. That is nothing; instead let us admire the essential fire of Divinity enclosed in a tiny cloud in order to guide and govern the whole world. We admire the manna sent from Heaven. That is a mere nothing; let us admire the Word of the almighty Father Who descends from Heaven into the bosom of the Virgin Mother. We admire the sun halted in its course by the command of Josue, or retreating at the prayer of Ezechias. That is unimportant; let us admire the God who voluntarily annihilates Himself. We admire the prophet Elias restoring a dead child to life. That is a small thing; let us admire the Son of God, co-equal and co-eternal with His Father, restoring Himself to life after having died on the Cross. We admire the same prophet Elias ascending into Heaven. That is nothing wonderful; let us admire the man who ascends to the throne of the Divinity and becomes God."

It is what Saint Cyprian[4] extols when he exclaims, "O Lord, how admirable is Thy name! Truly Thou art a God Who dost perform wonders. I no longer admire the marvelous construction of the world, nor the stability of the earth, nor the order and arrangement of the days, nor the course and brilliance of the sun; but I admire a God made man in the womb of a virgin; I admire the Almighty brought down into a cradle; I admire the Word of God united personally with the mortal and perishable body of a man."[5]

Finally, God wrought such great things to this chosen virgin that He could not have accomplished greater marvels. He could easily make a world larger than the one He did make, a sky more vast, a sun more brilliant; but He cannot make, says Saint Bonaventure, a mother

4 *Serm. de Nativ. Christi.*
5 *Serm. de Nativ. Christi.*

greater and nobler than the Mother of God. For if He could make a greater mother, He would have to give her a more excellent son. Now is it possible to find a son more worthy than the Son of God, whose Mother is the Blessed Virgin?

What more shall I say? I quote a great prelate distinguished for learning and piety, Rutilius Benzonius, Bishop of Loreto, who is not afraid to assert that God elevated this incomparable Virgin to such heights and granted her such extraordinary privileges that it may be said that she gave, so to speak, greater things to His divine majesty, in a certain sense, than the gifts granted to her. Everything that Mary received is finite and limited, confined within the bounds of created things, but the Queen of Heaven gave birth to the Son of God, the Creator and Sovereign Lord, the Saviour and Redeemer of the world. From God she received the privilege of being His creature, of being pleasing to Him, of being full of grace, of being blessed among all women. But she made it possible for God to be our Emmanuel, that is to say, God with us; to be the Redeemer of men through the Precious Blood that He received from her; to possess all power in Heaven and on earth as a man; to be the universal Judge of the whole world as a man; to be seated at the right hand of the Father as a man; to be the head of the whole Church as a man; to be the leader of the angels as a man; to forgive sins as a man.

If our Saviour gave His Apostles the power to perform miracles greater than those that He Himself performed, according to the testimony of the Gospel,[6] we need not be astonished that He granted to His most holy Mother the power to give Him gifts even greater than those she received from Him and this power is one of the marvels to which Mary refers when declaring that the Almighty "hath done great things to her."

After that, who will not admire the great and wonderful accomplishments of almighty God with regard to the glorious Virgin? And who will not acknowledge that it is the Holy Spirit Who was speaking through her: *Fecit mihi magna qui potens est?* Oh, what a wealth of prodigies and miracles is bound up in these words! Oh, what a great thing it is to be both virgin and mother, and to be a virgin and the Mother of God! Oh, what a great privilege it is to be associated with the eternal Father in His divine fatherhood, to be the Virgin Mother, in the fullness of time, of the very Son generated from all eternity without a mother! Oh, what a great thing it is to be clothed with the virtue of the Most High, to be a partaker of His adorable fecundity in order to be the Mother of the Son, who is consubstantial, co-equal and co-eternal with

6 John 14, 12.

God His eternal Father! Oh, what a great thing it is to give temporal birth from a virginal bosom to Him who was born before the beginning of time in the bosom of the Father of mercy! Oh, what a great thing it is for a mortal creature to give life to Him from whom she received her own life! Oh, what a great thing it is to be the worthy spouse of the Holy Spirit, associated with Him in the production of His adorable masterpiece, the God-Man.

Such indeed are the great and marvelous things that God wrought upon the Queen of Heaven, but lo! here follows the miracle of miracles. Great, holy and admirable as thou wert, O Virgin Mother, thou didst always look upon, demean and humble thyself as if thou wert the least and most insignificant of all creatures. "It is a great thing for the Queen of Angels to be a virgin," says a Holy Father of the Church,[7] "it is a great thing for her to be a mother, it is a greater thing for her to be a mother and virgin at the same time, and it is a very great thing for her to be a virgin and the Mother of God; but what surpasses all else is that, great as she is, Mary considers herself as if she were nothing."

Furthermore, Mary uses all these tremendous powers, her immense privileges, her sublime mercies, to help the humble, the wretched and even the most hopeless, if they will simply have recourse to her with humility and confidence. "All power," says the holy cardinal, Peter Damian, "is given to Mary in Heaven and on earth, and nothing is impossible to her who holds the power to restore the hope of salvation in the most despairing individuals."[8] "Yes," exclaims Saint Bonaventure, "because the almighty Lord is most powerfully with thee, O Mary, thou art therefore most powerful with God, most powerful through Him, most powerful in Him."[9]

O most powerful and benign Virgin, with all my heart do I give infinite thanks to the Almighty for having made thee so great, so powerful and so admirable. With all my heart do I also offer, deliver and abandon myself entirely and irrevocably to the great power that God has granted thee, imploring thee most humbly to exercise it on my behalf for the total destruction of whatever in me is displeasing to Him and to thee, and to establish in its stead the perfect reign of His glory and love.

The Blessed Virgin, having affirmed that the Almighty has wrought great things in her, then adds these words, "And holy is His name," words which contain six great mysteries.

---

7 Venerable Bede—*Magnum, quia Virgo; magnum quia Mater; majus, quia utrumque; maximum, quia Deiparens; sed majus, quia, cum tanta sit, putat se nihil esse.*
8 *Serm. 1 de Nativ. B. Virg.*
9 *In Spec. Virg. Cap. 8.*

The first is that the mystery of the Incarnation, being a mystery of love, is attributed to the Holy Spirit, who is personal love, as the masterpiece of His love and bounty, in fulfillment of the words of the angel: "The Holy Ghost shall come upon thee."[10]

The second mystery indicated in the words, "and holy is his name," is that the holy humanity of the Divine Infant whom the Blessed Virgin conceived in her womb is sanctified by His most intimate union with essential Holiness, the Divinity. This is further designated by these words of Saint Gabriel, "The Holy which shall be born of thee shall be called the Son of God."[11]

The third mystery is that the Infant God is thus sanctified and made the Saint of Saints in order to sanctify and glorify the name of the Thrice Holy One as much as it deserves, as well as to make it sanctified and glorified on earth, in Heaven and throughout the universe, thus fulfilling the proclamation, "Hallowed be thy name."[12]

The fourth mystery included in the words, "And holy is His name," is that the Saviour of the world, whom the holy Virgin bears in her most sacred womb, is divinely anointed with the unction of divinity, that is, He is sanctified and consecrated as a Saviour so that He may exercise the functions of Saviour, and of the Sanctifier of all men, a mission He commences at once with regard to His precursor, the Baptist, and His relatives, Saint Zachary and Saint Elizabeth.

The fifth mystery is that the Holy Spirit, by overshadowing Mary in order to accomplish in her the most holy work that ever was or will be done, and the Saint of Saints, holiness itself and the source of all holiness, by being conceived by her, filled and overwhelmed her with an ocean of grace and inconceivable holiness.

The sixth mystery indicated in these words, "And holy is his name," is that the ineffable mystery of the Incarnation is an inexhaustible source of all the grace and holiness that has ever been, is now and ever will exist in Heaven and upon earth.

Behold and admire how many wonders are contained in these few words pronounced by the hallowed lips of the Mother of the Saint of Saints, Whose holy name be praised, sanctified and glorified for all eternity.

For this intention let us repeat together with the seraphim, with all Paradise and with holy Church, "Holy, holy, holy, Lord God of hosts. Heaven and earth are full of thy glory."

10 Luke 1, 35.
11 Luke 1, 35.
12 Matt. 6, 9.

Chapter Eight

"HIS MERCY IS FROM GENERATION UNTO GENERATIONS, TO THEM THAT FEAR HIM"

We come now to the second part of our divine canticle, the true canticle of the most holy heart of the Mother of tender love, and a very precious relic of her Immaculate Heart.

Having magnified God for the infinite favors bestowed upon her and having made this admirable prophecy, "All generations shall call me Blessed," which includes a world of wonders which the Almighty has wrought and will continue to accomplish for all time and eternity to render this Virgin Mother glorious and venerable throughout the universe, she makes yet another prophecy that vibrates with rich comfort for all mankind, particularly for those who fear God. In it our peerless Mary affirms to us that the mercy of God extends from generation to generation to all those who fear Him, "And his mercy is from generation unto generations, to them that fear him."

What is this mercy? "It is our most bountiful Saviour," explains Saint Augustine.[1] The eternal Father is called the Father of mercy, because He is the Father of the Word Incarnate who is uncreated Mercy itself. It is this Mercy which the royal prophet David begged God, in the name of the whole human race, to send into the world through the mystery of the Incarnation, when he prayed: "Show us, O Lord, Thy Mercy, and grant us Thy salvation."[2] The Word Incarnate is all love and charity; therefore He must be all mercy. God is naturally and essentially all-merciful, says Saint Jerome, and always ready to save by His clemency those whom He cannot save according to His justice. But we are so wretched and so inimical to ourselves that when mercy is offered to us for our salvation, we turn our backs on it in scorn.

It is through the Incarnation that the Son of God exercised His mercy on our behalf, and His great mercy, according to these words of the prince

1 *Exposit. Sup. Magnif.*
2 Ps. 84, 8.

of the Apostles, "According to his great mercy (He) hath regenerated us."[3] All the effects of the mercy which our Saviour has wrought in men from the beginning of the world up to this moment, and will continue to produce for all eternity, have proceeded and will proceed from the adorable mystery of His Incarnation, as from their source and primary origin. That is why David, in asking pardon for his sins, prays in this fashion; "Have mercy on me, O God, according to thy great mercy."[4]

Three elements are necessary for mercy: the first is that it take pity on the miseries of others, for he is merciful who bears in his heart, through compassion, the miseries of the wretched; the second, that it possess the greatest will to help the outcast in their miseries; the third, that it pass from thought and will into effect. Now our most benign Redeemer became man that He might manifest His great mercy. First of all, having become man and assumed a body and a heart capable of suffering and sorrow, like ours, Our Lord was so filled with pity at the sight of our troubles and rendered so sad by carrying them in His heart that no words can express his suffering; because on one hand, He bore an infinite love for us, like the very best father for his children, and on the other hand, He kept constantly before His eyes all the misfortunes of body and spirit, all the anguish, tribulations, martyrdoms and torments which all His children would have to endure until the end of the world. His most tender and loving heart would have caused Him countless deaths had not His love, stronger than death itself, preserved His human life so that He might sacrifice it on the cross for our sake.

Secondly, all our tribulations were present to our most merciful Saviour at the very first moment of His life and He resolved so firmly, ardently and steadfastly at that time to help us free ourselves from them and He so faithfully preserved this intention in His heart from the first to the last instant of His life, that all the most atrocious cruelties and tortures that wretched men, to whom Christ was so wonderfully good, caused Him to suffer while He was on earth, as well as all His prescience of the ingratitude, outrages and crimes with which we would repay His adorable mercy, were not capable of cooling even slightly the ardor and strength of His will to show mercy to mankind.

Thirdly, what did He not do and suffer in order to deliver us effectively from all the temporal and eternal miseries into which our sins had plunged us? All the actions of His life—of a life of thirty-four years, of a life divinely human and humanly divine—all the virtues that He practiced, all His steps and travels here on earth, all the labors that He endured, all the humiliations, privations and mortifications that He

3   1 Pet. 1, 3.
4   Ps. 50, 3.

underwent, all His fasts, vigils, prayers and sermons, all His sufferings, wounds and sorrows, His most cruel and shameful death, His Precious Blood shed to the last drop—were not all these things, I repeat, employed not only to rid us of every kind of evil, but also to grant us possession of an eternal empire, filled with an immensity of glory, grandeur, joy, felicity, and inconceivable and inexpressible blessings? O bounty! O love! O superabundance! O incomprehensible and inexplicable mercy! O my Saviour, how well indeed art Thou called the God of mercy! O human heart, how frightful is thy hardness and stupidity if thou dost not love this God of love! Oh, what shalt thou love if thou dost not love Him Who has so much love and kindness for thee?

But what is the meaning of the following phrase, "From generation unto generations, to them that fear Him?" According to the explanation of holy Doctors, these words mean that, since our Saviour was made flesh and died for all men, He also pours the treasures of His mercy upon all those who do not oppose but rather fear Him. Being the inexhaustible fountain of grace and mercies, God also derives a sovereign pleasure from bestowing them continually upon His children, everywhere and at all times. Although, according to Saint Bernard, divine mercy is equally shared by the three divine Persons, together with all the other divine attributes, it is nevertheless attributed particularly to the person of the Son, as power is to the Father and bounty to the Holy Spirit. It is particularly the Incarnate Word who, through His great mercy, delivered us from the tyranny of sin, from the power of the devil, from eternal death, from the torments of Hell and infinity of evils and miseries, and acquired for us, at the cost of His Precious Blood and His divine life, the same eternal empire which His eternal Father had given to Him.

But Our Lord did not will to accomplish this great work by Himself. In addition to doing all things in union with the heavenly Father and the Holy Ghost, Christ also willed to associate His most holy Mother with Him in the great work of His mercy. "It is not good for man to be alone,"[5] said God when He willed to give the first woman to the first man; "let us make him a helpmate like unto himself." So also does the new Man, who is Jesus Christ, choose to have a helpmate in Mary, and the eternal Father gives the Blessed Mother to the beloved Son to assist Him and cooperate with Him in the great work of the salvation of the world, which is the work of His great mercy.

When Saint Catherine of Siena was in Rome, she pronounced several magnificent eulogies in honor of the Mother of God on the feast of the Annunciation in 1379—eulogies motivated and inspired by the Holy Spirit—of which these four invocations are most worthy,

5 Gen. 2, 18.

"O Mary, Bearer of Fire! O Mary, Peaceful Ocean! O Mary, Fiery Chariot! O Mary, Administrator of Mercy!"

Mary is called "Bearer of Fire" because she carried in her virginal body Him who is all-enkindled with love and charity toward mankind, who said that He came to bring fire to the earth, and proclaimed that His greatest desire was to inflame all hearts with love.[6]

Mary is called a "Peaceful Ocean" because she is an immense sea of grace, virtue and perfection, an ocean that is always calm and peaceful, that sustains and transports everyone to the port of eternal salvation without trouble or difficulty.

Mary is a "Fiery Chariot" completely inflamed with love, charity, goodness and meekness on behalf of true Israelites . . . "the Chariot of Israel,"[7] that is, of the true children (of God); but she is equally as terrifying to all the demons as she is meek and kind to men. Whoever honors, loves, serves and invokes Mary with humility and confidence will ascend to Paradise in a fiery chariot.

She is the "Administrator of Mercy" because God has endowed her with extraordinary goodness, meekness, generosity and kindness, with unparalleled power, that she may desire and be capable of helping, protecting, sustaining and comforting all the afflicted, the miserable, and those who have recourse to her in their needs and necessities.

Mary does this continually with regard to individuals, kingdoms, provinces, cities, houses and even the whole world, according to these words of one of the holiest and most learned Fathers of the Church, Saint Fulgentius, who lived almost twelve centuries ago. "Heaven and earth," he says, "would long since have been reduced to the nothingness out of which they were created, had not the prayers of Mary sustained them." These words must be understood to include not only the firmament but also the other skies which contain the sun, the stars and the moon.[8]

Let us, then, acknowledge and honor the Mother of the Saviour as the Mother of Mercy, with whom her beloved son willed to share His great mercy to associate her in the works of His clemency and benignity. Infinite and eternal thanks be rendered to Thee for this partnership! O my Saviour! O Mother of Mercy, may all the angels, saints and creatures forever sing the mercy of Thy son Jesus and His divine Mother! "The mercies of the Lord I will sing forever."[9] "Let the mercies of the Lord give glory to him: and his wonderful works to the children of men."[10]

---

6 Luke 12, 49.
7 4 Kings 2, 12.
8 *Caelum et terra jamdudum ruissent, se Maria precibus non sustentasset. Mythologia*, lib. 4.
9 Ps. 88, 2.
10 Ps. 106, 8.

Chapter Nine

"HE HATH SHOWED MIGHT IN HIS ARM"

Of the preceding verse the Blessed Virgin Mary praised and glorified the effects of divine mercy originating in the Incarnation of the Saviour and extending from one generation to another to all who fear God. In this verse she magnifies and exalts the prodigies of divine might which shine forth so admirably in this same mystery.

The great God, she says, hath put down the mighty with His arm. What arm is this? Saint Augustine, Saint Fulgentius and Saint Bonaventure all maintain that it is the Word Incarnate, according to the prophet Isaias, "And to whom is the arm of the Lord revealed?"[1] which text Saint John applies to the Son of God.[2] Since it is with his arms that man performs his actions, it is similarly through His divine Son that God accomplishes all things. "Just as man's arms," says Saint Albert the Great, "extend from his body, and his hands from both the arms and body, so also does the Son of God extend from the almighty Father, while the Holy Spirit proceeds from both the Father and the Son."

But what is the meaning of the words "He hath showed might"? They mean that God has acted powerfully, and that His power has produced admirable effects in His arm, through His only begotten Son and Incarnate Word, who is His arm. It is through Christ that the eternal Father created all things; it is through Christ that He redeemed the world; through Christ He vanquished the devil and triumphed over Hell; it is through Christ that God opened Heaven to us; it is through Him that He performed an infinite number of other miracles. "The words that I speak to you," says the Son of God, "I speak not of myself. But the Father who abideth in me, he doth the works."[3] Oh, what wonders are wrought by divine might in this ineffable mystery of the Incarnation! What a miracle to behold two natures, infinitely removed

1 Isa. 53, 1.
2 John 12, 38.
3 John 14, 10.

from each other, so closely united that they form but a single person! What a miracle to behold the Word Incarnate come forth from the consecrated womb of a virgin without destroying that virginity! What a wealth of miracles in the institution of the Blessed Sacrament of the altar! What a miracle, last of all, for divine might to have elevated a daughter of Adam to the dignity of Mother of God, and to have enthroned her as Queen of the angels and of the whole universe!

Among the works of God, some are attributed to His hands and fingers, like the Heavens, "The Heavens are the works of thy hands"[4] "I will behold the Heavens, the works of thy fingers."[5] Others are attributed to one of His fingers, "This is the finger of God,"[6] like the wonders that He performed through Moses in Egypt. But the incomparable work of the Incarnation is attributed neither to the hands or fingers of God; it belongs to the arm of His divine might because it incomparably surpasses all the other works of His adorable majesty.

"It is an admirable thing," says Saint John Damascene, "that He who is perfect God becomes perfect man. This God-Man is the newest of all things; indeed, He is the only new being that has ever appeared or ever can appear under the sun, in whom the infinite power of God is made manifest far more than in all that the universe encompasses. For what is there greater and more admirable than to behold God made man?"[7]

Let us listen now to Richard of Saint Victor who, in explaining these words of the royal prophet, *Descendet sicut pluvia in vellus*,[8] exclaims, "O the glory of the Blessed Virgin! O marvelous grace! Admirable dignity of the Mother of this divine Child! Oh, what goodness on the part of this adorable Child who, being the Son of God, wills to become the son of Mary! Oh, what dignity of the Mother of Jesus to possess the fruit of fertility together with the flower of virginity! What a marvel to behold a virgin who bears a son, not just an ordinary son but a son who is God! Truly the glory of Mary is a glory altogether unique. *Descendet sicut pluvia in vellus,* 'He will descend like rain upon fleece.' Who will descend? The only begotten Son of God. Whence and to what place will He descend? From the adorable bosom of the divine Father into the virginal bosom of His Mother."[9] So speaks Richard of Saint Victor.

4 Ps. 101, 26.
5 Ps. 8, 4.
6 Exod. 8, 19.
7 Saint John Eudes does not give the reference for this quotation.
8 Ps. 71, 6.
9 *Adnot. In Psal. 71.*

Will you listen, after that, to the holy Cardinal Hugues as he explains these words of the Psalmist, "Sing ye to the Lord a new canticle: because he hath done wonderful things."[10] What are these marvelous things? "They are," says this saintly cardinal, "that He has caused God to be made man, a virgin to become a Mother, and the hearts of the faithful to believe these two mysteries. It is a wonderful thing that God delivered up His own Son to the spite of slaves, His beloved Son to the hatred of His enemies, the sovereign Judge to the ignominy of criminals and condemned creatures, the First to the last (for a man is the least of all creatures), and the innocent to the impious.[11]

Here are two additional factors of the highest importance. The first is that nowhere is divine might more apparent than in the remission and destruction of sin, according to these words of holy Church, "O God, Who dost manifest Thine omnipotence more in forgiving us our sins and showing us mercy than in anything else." The wrong done to God through sin is so great that only the infinite might of an immense bounty can pardon it, and sin is such a frightful monster that only the arm of the Almighty can crush it.

The second wonderful manifestation of this adorable might is the virtue and strength that it imparts to holy martyrs and to all persons who suffer extraordinary afflictions, that they may bear them generously and in a true Christian manner for the love of Him Who suffered the torments and death of the Cross for their sake.

This is a brief summary of the countless miracles performed by the all-powerful arm of the Word Incarnate, miracles which He continues to perform daily for the glory of His divine Father, the honor of His most admirable Mother and the salvation and sanctification of mankind, to incite men to love and serve Him with all their hearts, as He loves them with all His heart.

10 Ps. 97, 1.
11 In Ps. 97.

Chapter Ten

"HE HATH SCATTERED THE
PROUD IN THE CONCEIT OF THEIR HEART"

Aside from the effects of divine might as indicated in the preceding pages, here is yet another of the greatest importance, proclaimed in the words of the Blessed Virgin Mary, "He hath scattered the proud in the conceit of their heart." What does that mean, and who are the proud? The holy Fathers explain this text in various ways. Some of them say that they are the rebellious angels whom God drove out of Heaven and cast into Hell for their pride. Others understand them to mean Pharao, Sennacherib, Nabuchodonosor, Antiochus and other enemies of the people of Israel. Saint Cyril and Saint Augustine explain them with reference to the demons that our Lord drove out of the bodies and souls of men when He came into the world. Saint Augustine writes further that we may also infer these proud to mean the Jews who scorned the humble coming of our Saviour, for which they were rebuked.

Hugh of Saint Victor and Dionysius the Carthusian say that these words designate all men dominated by pride, while Cardinal Hugues declared that these proud are the heretics whose minds are divided and at variance because of the diversity of their thoughts and errors. There are still others who assure us that these proud are sinners in general who rebel against the divine will.

Finally, certain holy Doctors write that we must apply these words to the emperors, kings, princes, philosophers and all the tyrants who have opposed the proclamation of the holy Gospel; personages whom God has exterminated and cast into hellfire. These also include all men who will persecute the Church until the coming of the antichrist, for the majority of the words of the *Magnificat* are prophecies expressed in the past tense, *dispersit superbos*, as if those things were already fulfilled, in order to show that they will just as certainly take place as if they had already happened.

Let us now examine the meaning of the words, "In the conceit of their heart." Saint Augustine explains them in this way, "He hath destroyed the proud by a secret and profound resolution of His divine will. For it was by a profound determination that God was made man and the innocent suffered in order to redeem the guilty; a most secret resolution of which the devil could not have had knowledge."[1]

But because the Greek reads thus, "In conceit of their heart," other doctors are led to offer this explanation; "He has destroyed and exterminated those whose hearts were filled with high esteem for themselves;" or else, "He has scattered the thoughts and resolutions that the proud were meditating in their hearts," in conformity with these words of the prophet Isaias; "Take counsel together, and it shall be defeated."[2]

Here is another most important secret which the Blessed Virgin reveals to us in the words "He hath scattered the proud in the conceit of their heart." They mean, according to the opinion of prominent writers, that not only does God disperse and annihilate the evil thoughts and pernicious designs contrived against Him and His friends by the wicked, but also that He converts all their pretentions into their own confusion, the glory of His divine majesty and the increased holiness and eternal happiness of those who serve Him. Furthermore, He opposes them with their own weapons, *Mente cordis sui*, striking back at them with the very same arrows launched by their malice against Him and His children, "The arrows of children are their wounds."[3] He makes use of their designs to fulfill His own. He causes the evil intentions of their impious minds to be turned to their own perdition and the advantage of His servants. God converts the obstacles which the wicked place in the path of the works of His glory into very powerful means employed to give them more firmness, perfection and brilliance.

Did not Satan's malice toward the first man lead to his own confusion while proving advantageous not only to man but to all posterity? God brought forth such immense good from the evil into which the temptation of the devil caused Adam to fall that Holy Mother Church sings, "O happy fault, that merited such and so great a Redeemer."

Did not the accursed envy and bad will of the brothers of Joseph serve divine providence as a means of exalting him even to the extent of sharing the royal throne of Egypt, and of earning for him the extraordinary title of the God of Pharao? Of what advantage to Pharao's successor was his hardness and cruelty against the chosen people except to drown him with his whole army in the depths of the Red Sea and to manifest still more strikingly God's protection of His own children?

1 *In Magnif.*
2 Isa. 8, 10.
3 Ps. 63.8.

What was the intention of the perfidious enemies of Christ and the evil spirits in treating the Son of God so ignominiously and cruelly as they did, if not to make His name infamous and hateful throughout the world? As we read, "Let his name be remembered no more."⁴ Thus they strove to thwart all His designs and nullify the great work that He had undertaken for the redemption of the world. Yet God employed their abominable hatred to fulfill the determination of His infinite bounty with regard to the human race.

What was the intention of the tyrants in slaughtering so many thousands of holy martyrs, if not to ruin and completely exterminate the Christian religion? And yet, did not divine might use this means to render its establishment more solid, holy, extensive and glorious?

Finally, we may truthfully apply to all who persecute and oppose the servants of God what Saint Augustine said of the godless Herod who slaughtered so many innocents in the attempt to destroy Him Who came to save the world, "Behold a wonderful thing, that the hatred and cruelty of this impious enemy of God and men was much more profitable to these blessed infants than all the friendship that he could ever have shown them and all the favors he could ever have bestowed on them."⁵

Thus does the all-powerful arm of the Incarnate Word overthrow the undertakings of the proud in the devising of their hearts, "He hath scattered the proud in the conceit of their heart."

It is through the humility of thy virginal heart, O Queen of Heaven, that all these great things are accomplished, since thy marvelous humility drew the divine Word from the bosom of His Father and clothed Him with flesh in thine own virginal bosom. We also look to thee to crush the head of the serpent, that is, to stamp out pride and arrogance. We may indeed say to thee, therefore, "Thou art the glory of Jerusalem, thou art the joy of Israel, thou art the honour of our people, for thou hast done manfully."⁶

This first phrase, "Thou art the glory of Jerusalem," is the voice of the angels, whose downfall has been atoned through thy intercession. The second, "Thou art the joy of Israel," is the voice of men, whose sadness has been changed into joy through thy mediation. The third, "Thou art the honor of our people," is the voice of women whose shame has been blotted out by the blessed Fruit of thy womb. The fourth, "Thou hast done manfully," is the voice of the holy souls who were imprisoned in Limbo and set free from captivity by thy beloved son, the Redeemer of the world.

4 Jer. 11, 19.
5 *Serm. 10. De Sanctis.*
6 Judith 15, 10–11.

O most holy and desirable humility of Mary, thou art the source of all blessings. O hateful pride, thou art the cause of all the evils of earth and Hell. "Every proud man is an abomination to the Lord,"[7] says the Holy Spirit; not only is the proud and arrogant man abominable in the sight of God, but "he is abomination itself."

O Queen of the humble, efface from our hearts whatever is contrary to humility, and make this holy virtue reign within us for the glory of thy beloved son.

7 Prov. 16, 5.

Chapter Eleven

"He Hath Put Down the Mighty from Their Seat, and Hath Exalted the Humble"

The time being ripe when the Father of mercy was pleased to fulfill His intention from all eternity to save mankind, His divine wisdom, whose resolutions are impenetrable, willed to employ means to that end which apparently had no capacity for or conformity with the greatness of this mighty work. What are these means? Here they are. God sent His only begotten Son into the world in a perishable and mortal state, in such abjection and lowliness that He Himself says, "I am a worm and no man"[1]: bearing as a title of honor in Scripture, *Novissimus virorum*,[2] "the most abject of men."

This adorable Father wills His only begotten Son, generated in His bosom from all eternity, and equal to Him in all things, to be born of a Mother who is in truth most holy, but so lowly and humble in her own eyes and in the eyes of the world that she esteems herself the least of all creatures.

Furthermore, this divine Father, wishing to provide helpers and co-workers to work with His divine Son in this supreme work of redemption of the world, chose twelve poor fishermen without learning, eloquence or any other qualities that might have distinguished them among men. He sent these twelve fishermen throughout the land to destroy a religion based on conformity with human inclinations, a religion rooted for several thousand years in the hearts of men and to establish instead a completely new religion which is opposed to the first and contrary to all the inclinations of human nature.

These twelve poor fishermen went everywhere to preach and establish this new faith while destroying the first religion. But how were they received? Everyone rose up against them—the great and the lowly, the rich and the poor, men and women, the learned and the ignorant, philosophers and priests of false gods, kings and princes. All men in general expended every effort to oppose the preaching of the Gospel which twelve fishermen strove to proclaim. They were seized and cast into prison with chains on their hands and feet; they were treated like rogues and magi-

1 Ps. 21, 7.
2 Isa. 53, 3.

cians; they were beaten, burned, stoned, crucified; in short, they were made to suffer all the most atrocious torments.

But what happened? They emerged victorious, they triumphed gloriously over the great, the powerful, the wise and all the monarchs of the world. They annihilated the religion, or rather the irreligion and abominable idolatry which hell had established throughout the world, and they established the Christian faith and religion in its stead. Finally, they became the masters of the world and God bestowed on them the principality of the earth, "Thou shalt make them princes over all the earth."[3]

God upset the thrones of kings and the pulpits of philosophers. He conferred the first empire of the world to a poor fisherman, whom He elevated to such eminent power and glory that rulers and magnates considered it a great honor to kiss the dust of his sepulchre and the feet of his successors. What is all that, if not the fulfillment of this prophecy of the Blessed Virgin, *Deposuit potentes de sede, et exaltavit humiles*. "He hath put down the mighty from their seat and hath exalted the lowly and humble"?

Notice that these words, as well as the other phrase of this inspired canticle, although expressed in the past tense, *deposuit*, nevertheless implies the past, present and future because they are uttered in a prophetic spirit. Indeed, the fulfillment of this prophecy has appeared manifestly in past centuries and will continue to appear more and more in the ages to come, until the end of the world.

In past centuries, did not divine might put down the proud Saul and replace him with the humble David? Did God not confound and destroy the arrogant Aman and the proud Vasthi to replace them by the humble Mardochai and the pious Esther? Did not Josue destroy more than thirty Chanaanite kings, turning their kingdoms over to the people of Israel?

Did not our divine Saviour deliver mankind from the bondage of the demons who before His Incarnation had subjected the world to their cruel tyranny? Did He not banish the rebellious angels from Heaven and the fallen man from paradise? And did He not restore mankind, after he had humbled himself through penance to the grace of His Creator? Did He not banish the godless Diocletian from his imperial throne to replace him with the pious Constantine? Did He not drive out the arrogant Eugene and give the throne of his empire to the humble Theodosius? Did He not exterminate the high priests, the Scribes and the Pharisees, to transfer their authority to poor fishermen

3 Ps. 44, 17.

chosen to share with Him the throne of His divine justice and the power which His Father had given Him to judge men and angels?

Thus it is that Christ humbles and destroys the great and powerful of this earth who misuse their power, and exalts the lowly and humble who practice the words of the Apostle, "Be you humbled therefore under the mighty hand of God, that he may exalt you in the time of visitation."[4] This Christ has always done from the beginning of the world; and He will continue until the end of time, even to the coming of the antichrist, who through his abominable pride will attempt to exalt himself even above God Himself, "Who opposeth, and is lifted up above all that is called God."[5] But He who annihilated Himself in order to confound the arrogant and exalt the humble will kill him with a single breath, "The Lord Jesus shall kill with the spirit of his mouth,"[6] casting him into the lower depths of Hell; and having resuscitated His two prophets Elias and Enoch, He will bring them publicly and gloriously into Heaven to shame their enemies who behold them.

O Queen of humble hearts, extinguish the accursed arrogance which reigns within us and replace it in our hearts with the humility of thy son and thyself, so that we thy children may resemble our most adorable Father and most amiable Mother.

4 1 Pet. 5, 6.
5 2 Thess. 2, 4.
6 *Ibid.* 8.

Chapter Twelve

"He Hath Filled the Hungry with Good Things; and the Rich He Hath Sent Empty Away"

Some Doctors of the Church explain these prophetic words with reference to the good and the bad angels, the humble and the proud angels, the angels obedient to God and the angels in revolt against God. The good angels, acknowledging that God brought them out of nothingness and drew all their perfections from His divine bounty, return all things to God and use their angelic qualities to pay Him homage, keeping for themselves only their nothingness. For that reason God allows them to pass from the state of grace in which they are into the state of glory, showering upon them the inestimable blessings that constitute the blessed eternity.

The bad angels, on the contrary, contemplating the excellence with which God has endowed their creation, find self satisfaction in them, appropriating their perfections and glorifying themselves as if they possessed these excellences in themselves. By insupportable pride and arrogance they oblige divine justice to strip away their brilliance and perfections, to reduce them to an extreme wretchedness and barrenness and to cast them into the depths of Hell.

Other Doctors explain these words with reference to the Gentiles converted to God by the Christian faith, and to the Jews remaining in their blindness. The Gentiles before the coming of the Son of God on earth existed in extreme poverty (which is indicated by the word *esurientes*), because they had no knowledge of their Creator and adored no other god but the devil. And when they embraced the Christian religion, God enriched them with its inconceivable treasures. The Chosen People, on the contrary, having uncompromisingly rejected the Saviour of the world and remaining obdurate, were stripped of all the gifts, graces and favors with which God had honored them, "The rich he hath sent empty away."

Still other Fathers of the Church understand these words to mean the holy patriarchs, prophets and all the just of the Old Law who felt an insatiable hunger, a burning thirst and a most vehement desire for the coming of the Redeemer and were thereby filled with grace and holiness, "He hath filled the hungry with good things." On the other hand, the arrogant priests of the Jews and the proud Pharisees, convinced as they were of their own wealth of virtue and holiness, and scorning the graces that the Son of God offered them, miserably lost the Law, the faith and the eternal salvation which God had placed in their hands.

The Blessed Virgin possessed such perfect faith and such an ardent love for the Saviour Who was to come on earth that her hunger, her thirst and her desires were much greater and livelier than the desires of all the patriarchs, prophets and saints who had preceded her or who were living in her time. Thus is it true that our adorable Saviour, so long anticipated, so fervently desired, so ardently begged of God, the only begotten and beloved son of her virgin womb, overwhelmed Mary with an infinity of inconceivable and inexplicable blessings during the nine months that she carried Him within her in the world, when, later, she received him so many times into her immaculate breast and motherly heart in the Blessed Eucharist after his Ascension, and above all since she possesses Him perfectly in Heaven.

Saint Augustine applies the word *esurientes* to the humble, and *divites* to the proud. "The humble," he says, "realize that of themselves they are nothing, and that they stand in extreme need of the help and grace of Heaven; but the proud are convinced that they are full of grace and virtue. That is why God takes pleasure in showering His gifts on the former and in depriving the latter of His bounty."[1]

These same words are also understood to mean all the poor whose hearts are detached from the things of earth, who love and embrace poverty for the love of Him who, possessing all the treasure of divinity, willed to become poor for love of us so that we might possess eternal riches. But we must understand the text to refer particularly to those who have voluntarily stripped themselves of all things through the holy vow of poverty, in order to imitate our divine Saviour and His most holy Mother more perfectly in their state of poverty, which was so extreme that the Son of God uttered these words, "The foxes have holes, and the birds of the air nests: but the son of man hath not where to lay his head."[2] Oh, what great treasures are encompassed by this voluntary poverty, since our Lord Himself said, "Blessed are ye poor, for yours is the Kingdom of God."[3] Oh, how dangerous is the possession of

---

1 *In Magnif.*
2 Matt. 8, 20.
3 Luke 6, 20.

worldly wealth, since He Who is eternal Truth also said, "Woe to you that are rich, for you have your consolation!"[4] And speaking through Saint Paul, He utters these terrible words, "They that will become rich, fall into temptation, and into the snare of the devil, and into many unprofitable and hurtful desires, which drown men into destruction and perdition."[5] That is why, if you love riches, do not love the false riches of this world but the true wealth of Heaven, which is the fear and love of God, charity toward your neighbor, humility, obedience, patience, purity, and the other Christian virtues which will lead you to the possession of an eternal empire.

This explanation of the aforementioned word, *esurientes*, is highly comforting. It is also a prophecy of the most holy Mother of God, referring to the enormous task yet to be accomplished of converting infidels, Jews, heretics and false Christians throughout the world. It was foretold and proclaimed long ago by the oracle of holy Scripture, by the mouth of the Church, and by the voices of the Fathers, Doctors and saints through whom the Spirit of God has spoken.

Open the sacred books and there you will hear the divine Spirit speaking of our Lord through the mouth of the royal prophet, assuring us that Christ will rule and reign throughout the world;[6] that all the kings of the earth will adore Him and all peoples will serve Him;[7] that all tribes will be blessed in Him and all nations will magnify Him;[8] that the whole universe will be filled with His glory;[9] that all generations without exception will adore Him and glorify His holy name;[10] that the whole world will be converted to Him; and that all the tribes of the world will fall prostrate before His face to adore Him.[11]

Do you not hear the eternal Father, speaking to His divine Son in the second Psalm, promise Him, as His inheritance, all the nations of the world and possession of the entire earth?[12]

Do you not hear the Church so often praying thus to God, "Let all the earth adore thee and sing to thee: let it sing a psalm to thy name"?[13] Are you not familiar with the solemn prayers offered by Holy Church each year on Good Friday for the sanctification of all her children and the conversion of all heretics, Jews and pagans? Do you not know that

4 Luke 6, 24.
5 1 Tim. 6, 9.
6 Ps. 71, 8.
7 *Ibid*. 11.
8 *Ibid*. 17.
9 *Ibid*. 19.
10 Ps. 85, 9.
11 Ps. 21, 28,29.
12 Ps. 2, 8.
13 Ps. 65, 4.

every day she obliges her priests to offer the Holy Sacrifice of the Mass to God for all men and to implore the salvation of the world in these words, "We offer unto thee, O Lord, the chalice of salvation, beseeching thy clemency, that it may rise up in the sight of thy divine majesty, as a savour of sweetness, for our salvation, and for that of the whole world"? Tell me then, I beg of you, would the Holy Spirit Who animates and guides the Church in all things permit her to offer prayers that were futile and unheard?

This great general conversion has been revealed by the Spirit of God not only to the prophets of the Old Law but also to the holiest men and women of the New Law. Does not the great Apostle Saint Paul assure us that all the Jews will be converted and that their conversion will be followed by that of the whole world? There is every reason to believe that God will not refuse His Grace to all other men.

Our Lord said one day to Saint Brigid, whose revelations have been approved by three Popes and two General Councils, "The time will come when there will be but one fold, one shepherd and one faith, and when God will be known to all."[14]

"You must realize," Christ revealed to her on another occasion, "that pagans will have such great devotion that Christians will be only their servants in spiritual life, and then shall we see the fulfillment of the Scriptures, which say that the people who know Me not will glorify Me, and that the deserts will be edified. At that time all will sing: Glory be to the Father, to the Son and to the Holy Spirit, and honor to all the saints!"[15]

All the holy Fathers[16] agree that after the death of antichrist the whole world will be converted, and although some of them assert that the world will last but a few days after his death, while others say a few months, some authorities insist that it will continue to exist many years after. Saint Catherine of Siena, Saint Vincent Ferrer, Saint Francis of Paula and a number of other saints have predicted this ultimate universal conversion.

Then shall we witness the fulfillment of this great prophecy of the Queen of prophets, *Esurientes implevit bonis*, although not perhaps so perfectly as we might wish; that is, with no one left on earth who did not know and love God. But if this conversion is not completely general it will prove, nonetheless, a delicious and magnificent feast for all those who possess a great hunger and burning thirst for the glory of God

14 *Revel.* Lib. 6 Cap. 77.
15 *Revel.* Lib 6. Cap. 83.
16 Dionysius the Carthusian in cap. 3, Epist 1 *ad Thess.*; Cornelius a Lapidé in cap. 2, *Epist. ad Rom.* vers 15.

and the salvation of souls. They will be overwhelmed with inconceivable happiness and joy upon seeing their Creator and Saviour known, served and honored throughout the world, together with His most worthy Mother, and beholding the demons who now possess so many rich treasures on earth—that is, so many souls of infidels, heretics and bad Catholics—dispossessed of all, according to these divine words, "And the rich he hath sent away empty."

Even if this prophecy is not completely fulfilled on earth, it will find its entire and perfect fulfillment in Heaven, where the insatiable hunger and burning thirst possessed by all the saints during their earthly lives for the glory of God and the salvation of souls will be perfectly satiated and slaked, and these words will be fulfilled in each one of them, "I shall be satisfied when thy glory shall appear."[17] There is no mind capable of understanding, nor tongue of expressing, the least particle of the inestimable and inexpressible blessing which God will shower upon them for their great zeal in promoting His honor on earth and for the salvation of the souls whom they have delivered from the possession of the devil.

O Mother of Mercy, who by thy prayers and merits didst hasten the time of the Incarnation of the Saviour of the world, hasten too, we pray thee, the desirable time of this great conversion which is so necessary for the salvation of so many souls who perish daily. Alas, take pity on them, O Mother of grace, and pray to thy son to have pity on all the works of His hands, to have compassion on them because of the many sufferings which His holy humanity endured and the Precious Blood that He shed in order to save these souls from falling into Hell.

17 Ps. 16, 15.

Chapter Thirteen

"He Hath Received Israel His Servant"

Almighty God fashioned two orders of creatures at the beginning of the world; angels and men; the angels in Heaven, men on earth. Both of them were so ungrateful that they revolted against their Creator; the angel through pride and man through disobedience to the commandment of God. The sin of the angel, being a sin of pride, was found to be so enormous in the eyes of God that divine justice obliged Him to drive the angelic sinner out of paradise and cast him into Hell; but His mercy, seeing that man had fallen into sin through the temptation and seduction of Satan, took pity on him and resolved to withdraw him from the miserable state to which he had been reduced, even making a pledge to that effect, and even the countless and enormous sins committed by the Jews, the Gentiles and all men since that promise were not capable of preventing its fulfillment, but they did delay it for many centuries, during which time the whole race of Adam, condemned and cast out by God, was plunged into an abyss of darkness and a whirlpool of inexplicable evils from which it was impossible for it to emerge unaided. The more humanity went forward, the more deeply mired it became in this gulf, the more it wallowed in the mud and filth for its sins.[1]

God was known only in Judea[2] and even there He was known very imperfectly and by very few persons. All the others were enshrouded in the darkness of hell. The whole earth was covered with idols and idolators, and the tyranny of Satan oppressed the whole world. The law of Moses revealed sin but it did not cure it. Thus it seemed that God, by an eminently just judgement, had entirely forgotten mankind abandoned in this deplorable state as a punishment for its crimes. His mercy did not manifest itself; there was evidence only of the terrible signs of His wrath which had cast one third of the angels into Hell, had engulfed

---

1 *Jacebat in malis, vel etiam volutabatur, et de malis in mala precipitabatur totius humani generis massa damnata.* Saint Augustine, *Lib. Enchiridii,* cap. 26 et 27.

2 Ps. 75, 2 "In Judaea God is known."

the whole army to be swallowed up in the waters of the Red Sea, had rained torrents of fire and flames from Heaven to reduce great cities to ashes, had delivered His people on several occasions to the fury of their enemies and had allowed men to suffer many other fearful punishments.

But finally the Son of God, mindful of His mercy which He seemed to have forgotten for more than four thousand years, *Recordatus misericordiae suae*, and of the promise He had made to Adam, Abraham, David and a number of other prophets, to draw the human race from the pit of evils, Himself descended from Heaven into the virgin bosom of the handmaid, Mary, where to His divine person He united the wretched human nature which He had abandoned, becoming man in order to save all men who long to be numbered among the true Israelites; that is, who seek to believe in Him and love Him.

That is what the Blessed Virgin announces to us through these words, "He hath received Israel his servant, being mindful of his mercy," for several holy Doctors explain them as the mystery of the Incarnation. This verse forms the conclusion of her inspired canticle; it is a recapitulation of its ineffable mysteries; it is the end of the Law and the prophets, the dispersal of the shadows, the consummation of the symbols. It is as if Our Lady were saying, "Here is the fulfillment of the predictions of the prophets; this is the fruition of the truth of the promises of God; this is what impels me to sing from the depths of my heart, "My soul doth magnify the Lord." This is the great cause of my joy and delight, "And my spirit hath rejoiced in God my Saviour." This is what will make me proclaimed blessed by all nations. These are the great things that the Almighty has done to me. This is the origin and inexhaustible source of the unfathomable graces and mercies that God will shed on generation after generation of all who fear Him. These are the greatest miracles of His infinite might and immense bounty. This is what will exalt the humble and bring ruin to the proud, "He hath received Israel his servant."

But what is this Israel? Several saints affirm that these words must be applied first of all to the people of Israel, the Son of God having willed to be made man and take birth from the Israelites notwithstanding their past ingratitude and the outrages that He was to receive at their hands. I say "first of all," for the divine Word also united Himself with all human nature and not only with the people of Israel.

But why does the Blessed Virgin say, "He hath received Israel his servant?" It is the Holy Spirit speaking through her and imparting two meanings by the word *puerum*. In the first place, He gives us to understand that the Son of God became not only man in order to make us God-like, but He also became an infant to make us children of God: *Puer natus est nobis*.

Secondly, the Incarnate Word is placed before us not only as man and child, but also as servant. It is the same thing that the Holy Spirit declares to us through the mouth of Saint Paul in these terms, "He emptied Himself, taking the form of a servant."[3] And do we not hear the voice of Our Saviour telling us Himself that He came not to be served, but to serve?[4] O superabundance of incomparable love! The sovereign Monarch of the universe takes the form of a servant in order to deliver us from the bondage of Satan and make us children of God! O my Saviour, we are unworthy to be Thy slaves; yet Thou, not content to call us friends and brethren, hast made us children of the same adorable Father whose beloved Son Thou art, and consequently His heirs and Thy co-heirs.

But Thou dost go even further, for, by another excess of unequalled goodness, Thou dost will to bear the title and to be in reality the spouse of our souls, our souls to be Thy true spouses as well, and consequently to be but one with Thee and to share all things with Thee.

That is still not sufficient to satisfy the ardor of Thy love for us. Thou dost will to be our head, and us to be thy members, and therefore to be but one with Thee, as members are but one with their head. Thou dost will us to be animated by the same spirit, to live the same life, to have but one heart and soul, and finally to be consummated in unity with Thee and the heavenly Father, just as Thou art one with Him. Is not this, my dearest Jesus, what Thou didst ask of Him for us on the eve of Thy death in pronouncing this prayer, "That they all may be one, as Thou, Father, in Me, and I in Thee; that they also may be one in Us."[5] "I in them and Thou in Me; that they may be made perfect in one, and that the world may know that Thou hast sent Me, and that Thou hast loved them even as Me."[6] O miracle of love! O prodigy of charity! O abyss of goodness!

O my Saviour, I am not amazed by the assurance that Thou wilt grant us possession of the same kingdom that the almighty Father hast given Thee, that Thou wilt invite us to feast at the same table with Thee, and that Thou wilt seat us on Thy throne, *in throno meo*, even as Thou art seated upon the throne of Thy Royal Father. If we are but one with Thee, we should possess the same kingdom, eat at the same table, share the same throne, be animated by the same spirit, live the same life and have but one heart and soul with Thee. Can we conceive of more admirable bounty? Has there ever been, and is it possible to imagine comparable magnificence. O human heart, how hard, how unfeeling, how unnatural thou art, if such goodness is incapable of softening thee!

3 Phil. 2, 7.
4 Matt. 20, 28.
5 John 17, 21.
6 *Ibid.* 23.

O monster of ingratitude, what wilt thou love if not Him who holds such a love for thee; indeed, who is all tenderness and love toward thee!

Such are the wonders contained in these words of the Mother of Jesus, "He hath received Israel his servant," since they teach us the mystery of the Incarnation, the source of all these miracles of charity.

But what is the primary cause of this ineffable mystery? and consequently, of all the infinite blessings which proceed from it? Do you not hear the most pure Virgin affirming in these words, *Recordatus misericordiae suae*? Yes, Mother of Grace, it is indeed divine mercy that is the origin of the Incarnation of thy Son and of all the immense treasures proceeding therefrom; and for all these things, next to the incomparable mercy, we are indebted to thy maternal heart. For by what other means didst thou bring the eternal Word from the adorable bosom of His Father into thine own virginal bosom and sacred womb? Do we not hear the Holy Spirit who, speaking through thee, declares that while the eternal King was dwelling in the bosom and heart of His Father, the most profound humility of thy lovable heart gave forth such a pleasing and powerful odor that, rising up to Him, it pleased God to the extent of attracting Him to descend to thee, where He became incarnate for the redemption of the world? Is it not what is meant by these divine words, "While the king was at his repose, my spikenard sent forth the odor thereof"?[7] It is the explanation offered by the saints, who say that the spikenard is a tiny but extremely fragrant herb which represents thy sweet humility.

But aside from the merit and strength of this holy virtue, how many ardent sighs didst thou send heavenward! How many tears didst thou shed! How many fasts and mortifications didst thou practice! How many earnest and ardent prayers didst thou offer to obtain from the Father of mercy the fulfillment of His promises regarding the Incarnation of His Son, and to draw the attention to this same Son to the prayers and cries of all the holy patriarchs, prophets and just persons who preceded His coming on earth! *Veni Domine, veni et noli tardare, veni et libera nos,* "O Lord, come without further delay, come to deliver us from all the evils which cover the earth."

After divine mercy, then, O holy Virgin, it is to the humility, love, charity and zeal of thine Admirable Heart that we are indebted for His adorable Incarnation, as indicated in these holy words of thy divine canticle, "He hath received Israel his servant." Oh, may all the angels and saints for ever sing to thee a canticle of gratitude, praise, blessing and immortal thanksgiving, in the name of the whole human race, for the inexpressible debt it owes to thee for all eternity!

7 Cant. 1, 11.

Chapter Fourteen

"As He Spoke to Our Fathers, to Abraham and His Seed Forever"

The final verse of the *Magnificat* sets before us the truth of the word of God and His fidelity to His promises. In Sacred Scripture He is justly called "faithful and true,"[1] being not only true to His words, but very Truth itself—essential, eternal and impregnable truth. Not only is God faithful to His promises, but He is fidelity itself, infinitely powerful, wise and good: infinitely powerful in overcoming all obstacles to the fulfillment of His promises; infinitely wise in fulfilling them most appropriately at the most suitable time and place; infinitely good in fulfilling His word in the manner most useful and advantageous to those to whom the promises were made.

Men speak freely and are quick to promise many things, but their words and promises are frequently nothing more than lies and frauds. God speaks little: *Semel locutus est Deus*.[2] He has but one Word in His mouth: *Verbum erat apud Deum*,[3] but with this single Word He gave being to all things: *Dixit et facta sunt*.[4] With this single Word He supports and preserves all things: *Portans omnia verbo virtutis suae*.[5] With this single Word he governs all things. With this single Word He makes and fulfills all His promises truthfully and faithfully and He always accomplishes even more than He promised. He promised Abraham, first of all, to give him a son who would be called Isaac and He gave him countless sons. He promised to multiply his children to equal the number of the stars in the Heavens and then gave him a son who is the Creator and sovereign Lord of Heaven and earth, man and God at one and the same time. God promised Adam and the other patriarchs and prophets to deliver men from the dark perdition of sin, and then He was not content simply to withdraw them from this wretched state and

---

1 Apoc. 19, 11.
2 Ps. 61, 12.
3 John 1, 1.
4 Ps. 148, 5.
5 Heb. 1, 3.

to free them from the bondage of Satan; He also became man in order to make them like God; He became the son of man so that men might become children of God; and He descended from Heaven to earth to transport them from earth to Heaven.

It is these promises made to Adam, Abraham and the other Fathers and patriarchs which the Blessed Virgin mentions in the final words of her divine canticle, "As He spoke to our Fathers, to Abraham and to his seed for ever," a promise that He fulfilled when He took flesh in her blessed womb. He declared this truth to the Jews when He said to them, "Abraham your father rejoiced that he might see my day,"[6] that is, the day of my Incarnation and birth, of my dwelling on earth, whence he hoped for his salvation and that of the whole world. "He saw it," that is, he knew Christ by faith, or else he knew Him through the revelations that the heavenly Father made to him, "and was glad."

We see, therefore, how God is true to His words and promises, a fact which should afford us wonderful comfort, because this most faithful fulfillment of the pledges of God provides us with infallible assurance that all His other promises to mankind will likewise be perfectly realized.

What are these promises? There are two kinds: those which belong to this life and those which concern the life to come.

What does God promise us in this life? He promises that He will preserve us from evil if we live in fear of Him, "No evil shall happen to him that feareth the Lord."[7] Yes, for all things work together for the good of those who love God, "To them that love God all things work together unto good."[8]

He promises to keep track of every step that we take in His service, "Thou indeed hast numbered my steps;"[9] to feel the wrongs that are done to us as if He Himself were wounded in the pupil of His eye, "He that toucheth you toucheth the apple of my eye;"[10] to cherish our good works like the apple of His eye, "The alms of a man is as a signet with him: and shall preserve the grace of a man as the apple of the eye."[11]

These are the promises made to us by our Saviour concerning our present life, but there are many others referring to the life in Heaven. Our most benign Saviour promises us that on the day of the general resurrection, not only will He cause our bodies to rise again, but He will also clothe them with the brilliance, incorruptibility, immortality and glory of His own most holy Body, "Who will reform the body of our

6 John 8, 56.
7 Ecclus. 33, 1.
8 Rom. 8, 28.
9 Job 14, 16.
10 Zach. 2, 8.
11 Ecclus. 17, 18.

lowness, made like to the body of his glory";[12] He will have us dwell with Him not only in Heaven but also in the bosom and heart of His Father, "Father, I will that where I am, they also whom Thou hast given Me, may be with Me";[13] He will make us kings of the very kingdom that the almighty Father conferred upon Him, "And I dispose to you, as my Father hath disposed to me, a kingdom;"[14] He will make us His Father's heirs and His own co-heirs;[15] He will share all His possessions with us;[16] He will give us the same glory that His Father has given to Him;[17] He will associate us with His angels, seat us on their thrones, have us live their lives and enjoy their felicity;[18] He will permit us to dine at His table;[19] He will seat us on His own throne;[20] we shall be through grace and participation what He is by nature and essence;[21] and, finally, we shall be but one with Christ and His eternal Father who are also but one, as we have already said.[22]

Those are the marvelous promises of our most bountiful Redeemer. But is it possible for such great wonders to be fulfilled? Yes, that is as certain as it is that God is God. It is what the Blessed Virgin tells us, "As he spoke to our Fathers: to Abraham and to his seed for ever."

O Christian, how admirable is thy religion! How holy and exalted is thy profession! How blessed and advantageous is thy state! Why dost thou not die of joy at the revelation of these rapturous truths! How is it possible for thy heart to remain cold and icy in the midst of these ardent flames of the love of thy God for thee? Oh, how fearful will be the furnaces of Hell for thee if, instead of loving the God who so loves thee, thou dost despise Him, outrage Him and trample upon His divine commandments! O my God, with all my heart do I wish to love Thee, not all for fear of meriting Hell, but purely for love of Thee. O my Saviour, I implore Thee to take full, complete and eternal possession of my heart.

Our adorable Saviour is not the only Being to be called the faithful and true, for Holy Mother Church ascribed this same quality to His beloved Mother Mary, "Virgin Most Faithful." This Virgin Mother has declared to her devotees, that among all the titles of honor in the lita-

12 Phil. 3, 21.
13 John 17, 24.
14 Luke 22, 29.
15 Rom. 8, 17.
16 Matt. 24, 47.
17 John 17, 22.
18 Luke 20, 36.
19 Luke 22, 30.
20 Apoc. 3, 21.
21 2 Peter 1, 4.
22 John 17, 22.

nies sung daily in her praise those most pleasing to her are, "Mother Most Amiable," "Mother Most Admirable" and "Virgin Most Faithful." And indeed with good reason she bears that title, being most admirably faithful to her words and promises.

Let us listen to her speaking, "Come over to me, all ye that desire me."[23] (i.e. the Holy Spirit, who causes her to speak thus.) *Omnes.* Not only some, but all—men and women, great and lowly, rich and poor, young and old, children and adolescents, the healthy and the sick, just men and sinners, faithful and unfaithful, learned and ignorant; for I desire to help all of you in your necessities and obtain the salvation of each and every one. Come to me, for I am the Mother of your Creator and Redeemer; to me, your Queen and Sovereign; to me, your Mother, your all-loving Mother, "The Mother of Fair Love."[24]

Come to me with great confidence, for God has given me all power in Heaven and on earth, and my love and tenderness for you are greater than all mothers have ever had, now have, or ever will have in their hearts. Come to me, for even as I have given life to your adorable head, who is my son Jesus, I can also give it to His members, "He that shall find me shall find life."[25] Come to me, for I have given you your Saviour, I can cooperate with Him in your eternal salvation, and I long to do so, "He that shall find me . . . shall have salvation from the Lord."[26] Come to me, for I will help you in all your needs. I will remain always with you to guide you everywhere and in all things. I will comfort your heart in afflictions. I will protect you amid the dangers of this life and defend you from the host of your enemies, visible and invisible. I will light your way in the dark and strengthen you in your weakness. I will sustain you in temptations and assist you specially at the hour of death. I will receive your souls when they leave your bodies and present them to my beloved son. Finally, I will lodge you in my bosom and my motherly heart. I will keep you always before my eyes and prove the fullness of my truly maternal love.

But listen to me, my children, "Now therefore, ye children, hear me."[27] "And blessed is the man that heareth me."[28] What have I to say to you? Cast your eyes upon my life on earth and consider the virtues that God granted me the graces to practice there. They are as so many voices saying to you, "Blessed are they that keep my ways,"[29] that is, who travel the road of faith, hope, charity, humility, obedience, purity,

23 Ecclus. 24, 26.
24 Ecclus. 24, 24.
25 Prov. 8, 35.
26 *Ibid.* 8, 35.
27 *Ibid.* 8, 32.
28 *Ibid.* 8, 34.
29 *Ibid.* 8, 32.

patience and the other virtues that I practiced on earth. Then embrace all these virtues in your hearts, and above all, cultivate a great love for my son Jesus Christ. And if you love Him, keep all His commandments faithfully, "Whatsoever he shall say to you, do ye."[30]

Finally, we must realize that my divine son and I love all those who love us.[31] Love us, therefore, as your Father and your Mother, and we will love you tenderly and ardently as our dearest children. And if you truly love us, strive to implant a love for us in the hearts of other men, and these words will be fulfilled in your regard, "They that explain me shall have life everlasting."[32]

These are the words and promises of our most bountiful Mother, and she will infallibly fulfill them on behalf of her true children, for she frequently accomplishes even more than she has promised.

O Jesus, only begotten Son of God, who has willed to become the only son of Mary and to accept us as her children and thy brethren, make us partakers, we humbly beseech Thee, of thy wondrous filial love for her, as well as of her admirable love for Thee, that we may love Jesus with the heart of Mary, and Mary with the heart of Jesus, and that we may have but one heart and love with Jesus and Mary.

30 John 2, 5.
31 Prov. 8, 17.
32 Ecclus. 24, 31.

Appendix One

MASS OF THE
ADMIRABLE HEART OF MARY

Mass of the Admirable Heart of Mary

INTROITUS

Gaudeamus omnes in Domino, diem festum celebrantes sub honore sanctissimi Cordis Beatae Mariae Virginis: de cujus solemnitate gaudent Angeli, et collaudant Filium Dei. Ps. 44. Eructavit cor meum verbum bonum: dico ego opera mea Regi. V. Gloria. Gaudeamus.

INTROIT

Let us all rejoice in the Lord while celebrating this festival in honor of the most holy heart of the Blessed Virgin Mary, a festival which rejoices the angels and suggests to them new canticles of praise of the Son of God. *Ps. 44.* My heart uttered a good work: I address my works to the King. Glory . . .

ORATIO

Deus, qui Unigenitum tuum, tecum ab aeterno viventem, in Corde Virginis Matris vivere et regnare voluisti: da nobis, quaesumus, hanc sanctissimam Jesu et Mariae in corde uno vitam jugiter celebrare, cor unum inter nos et cum ipsis habere, tuamque in omnibus voluntatem corde magno et animo volenti adimplere; ut secundum Cor tuum a te inveniri mereamur. Per eumdem Dominum.

COLLECT

O God who didst will that Thine only begotten Son who dost dwell with Thee from all eternity should live and reign in the heart of the Virgin Mary; grant us, we beseech thee, the grace to celebrate continually with one only heart, this most holy life of Jesus and Mary, to have but one heart with them, and one among ourselves, to accomplish Thy will in all things with a generous heart and resolute will, that so we may merit to become like to Thy heart. Through the same Lord.

LECTIO CANTICI CANTICORUM. CANT 4.

Quam pulchra es, amica mea, quam pulchra es! Oculi tui columbarum, absque eo quod intrinsecus latet. Tota pulchra. es, amica mea, et macula non est in te. Veni de Libano, sponsa mea, veni de Libano, veni: coronaberis de capite Amana, de vertice Sanir et Hermon, de cubilibus leonum, de montibus pardorum.

LESSON FROM THE CANTICLE OF CANTICLES (C. 4)

How beautiful art thou, my love, how beautiful art thou! Thy eyes are doves' eyes, besides what is hid within. Thou art all fair, O my love, and there is no spot in thee. Come from Libanus, my spouse, come from Libanus, come: thou shalt be crowned from the top of Amana, from the top of Sanir and Hermon, from the dens

317

Vulnerasti cor meum, soror mea, sponsa, vulnerasti cor meum, in uno oculorum tuorum, et in uno crine colli tui. Ego dormio, et cor meum vigilat. Vox dilecti mei pulsantis: Aperi mihi, soror mea, amica mea, columba mea, immaculata mea: quia caput meum plenum est rore, et cincinni mei guttis noctium. Pone me ut signaculum super cor tuum, ut signaculum super brachium tuum; quia fortis est ut mors dilectio, dura sicut infernus aemulatio. Lampades ejus, lampades ignis atque flammarum. Aquae multae non potuerunt exstinguere caritatem, nec flumina obruent illam. Si dederit homo omnem substantiam domus suae pro dilectione, quasi nihil despiciet eam.

GRADUALE

Estote imitatores Jesu et Mariae, sicut filii carissimi: et ambulate in dilectione, sicut et ipsi dilexerunt vos. Hoc sentite in cordibus vestris, quod et in Corde ipsorum: et omnia vestra in humilitate et caritate fiant! V. Convertimini ad Deum in toto corde vestro: et sit vobis cor unum et anima una.

ALLELUIA, Alleluia V.(Ps. 56:2 Mach. 1)

Paratum cor meum, Deus cordis mei, paratum cor meum, ut faciam omnes voluntates tuas corde magno et animo volenti. *Post Septuagesimam, omissis* Alleluia, V. et Sequentia, *dicitur* Tractus.

TRACTUS

Vide, Domine, quoniam tribulor, conturbatus est venter meus, subversum est Cor meum in memetipsa, quoniam amaritudine plena sum. V. Factum est Cor Virginis speculum clarissimum passionis Christi, et imago perfecta mortis ejus, quia stigmata illius in Corde suo portavit. V. Mortificationem Jesu semper in Corde et corpore suo portavit, ut vita Jesu manifestaretur in illa.

of lions, from the mountains of the leopards. Thou hast wounded my heart, my sister, my spouse: thou hast wounded my heart with one of thy eyes, and with one hair of thy neck. I sleep, and my heart watcheth. Open to me, my sister, my love, my dove, my undefiled: for my hair is full of dew, and my locks of the drops of the night. Put me as a seal upon thy heart, as a seal upon thy arm: for love is strong as death, jealousy as hard as hell. The lamps thereof are fire and flames. Many waters cannot quench charity, neither can the floods drown it: if a man should give all the substance of his house for love, he shall despise it as nothing.

GRADUAL

Be ye imitators of Jesus and Mary as their cherished children, and walk in their love as they have loved you. Conceive in your hearts the sentiments of their hearts and may all your actions be performed in humility and charity. Turn to God with your whole heart and have but one heart and one soul among you.

ALLELUIA. Alleluia (Ps. 56:2 Mach. 1)

My heart is ready, O God of my heart, my heart is ready. To do all that Thou willest with a generous heart and resolute will. (After Septuagesima Sunday, the Alleluia and Sequence are omitted.)

TRACT

Behold, O Lord, the grief which oppresses me; my heart is troubled within me for I am filled with bitterness.
V. The heart of Mary has become a faithful mirror of the passion of Jesus Christ, for she bore the stigmata in her heart.
V. She constantly bore the mortification of Jesus in her heart, and in her body, that the life of Jesus might be manifested in her.

SEQUENTIA

Laetabunda canant pie
Cuncta corda Cor Mariae.

Cor amandum omni corde,
Cor laudandum omni mente.

Cor aeterni Numinis
En factum est Virginis
  Cor aeternum.

Haec est Virgo sapiens,
Haec est Virgo rapiens
  Cor divinum.

Censors Patris Dexterae,
Fit Matris Deiparae
  Cor et Natus.

Flos Cordis Altissimi,
Flos Cordis Virginei,
  Flos et fructus.

Cordis nostri gaudium,
Exsili solatium,
  Cor Mariae.

Amoris miraculum,
Caritatis speculum,
  Liber vitae.

Fons vivus charismatum,
Thesaurus fidelium,
  Thronus Christi.

Rubus ignem proferens,
Incombustus permanens,
  Fornax Coeli.

O Fornax mirifica,
In te manent socia,
  Ras et flamma!

Ros mire vivificans,
Flamma beatificans,
  Corda pura.

Infundatur omnibus
Ros ille pectoribus:
Accendatur cordibus
  Flamma sacra.

O Jesu, Cor Mariae,
Ros, ignis, forts gratiae,
Ure, purga, posside
  Corda cuncta.

SEQUENCE

Now let all hearts rejoice and sing the praises of the heart of Mary.

Every heart should love her heart, and every heart give highest praise.

The heart of God Most High hath made Himself the Virgin's heart eternal;

She is the Virgin most wise, who has ravished the heart divine;

The Son, righthand of God the Father, has made Himself the heart and son of her, the mother of Incarnate God.

The flower of the heart of the Almighty, the flower of the Virgin's heart, is now become both flower and fruit.

O heart of Mary pure, thou joy of all our hearts, thou solace of our exile,

Thou miracle of love, thou mirror of great charity and book of life,

Thou art the living fountain of heavenly gifts, the treasure of the faithful, the lofty throne of Christ,

The burning bush, that glows with fire yet never is consumed, the furnace of celestial love,

O admirable fire, in thee there is mingled the miracle of flame and dew.

O wondrous dew, imparting life, O fire giving happiness to those whose hearts are pure,

Pour forth into our souls this dew of life, and kindle in our hearts the flames of love.

O Jesus, heart of Mary, O dew, O fire, O fount of grace, burn, purify, possess the hearts of all mankind!

O amor, propera,
Ubique impera,
In terris, ut super sidera!

Nova praecordia,
Nova fac omnia,
Ut Jesum laudent cum Maria!
Amen. Alleluia.

O love make haste to spread thy kingdom every where, upon the earth even as Thou dost reign beyond the starry firmament!

Renew our hearts in praise, make all things new on earth, singing forever the glory of Jesus and Mary. Amen.

SEQUENTIA SANCTI EVANGELII SECUNDUM LUCAM. Cap. 2.

In illo tempore: Pastores loquebantur ad invicem: Transeamus usque Bethlehem, et videamus hoc verbum, quod factum est, quod Dominus ostendit nobis. Et venerunt festinantes: et invenerunt Mariam, et Joseph, et Infantem positum in praesepio. Videntes autem cognoverunt de verbo, quod dictum erat illis de puero hoc. Et omnes qui audierunt, mirati sunt: et de his, quae dicta erant a pastoribus ad ipsos. Maria autem conservabat omnia verba haec, conferens in Corde suo. (Credo)

CONTINUATION OF THE HOLY GOSPEL ACCORDING TO SAINT LUKE (c. 2)

At that time: The shepherds said one to another: Let us go over to Bethelehem and let us see this word that is come to pass, which the Lord hath showed to us. And they came with haste: and they found Mary and Joseph, and the infant lying in the manger. And seeing, they understood of the word that had been spoken to them concerning this child. And all that heard wondered: and at those things that were told them by the shepherds. But Mary kept all these words, pondering them in her heart. (Creed)

OFFERTORIUM

Gaudete mecum omnes, qui diligitis me, quia Cor meum elegit Altissimus, ut poneret in eo thronum suum, et regnum Filii dilectionis suae. (Alleluia)

OFFERTORY

Rejoice with me, all you who love me, for the Most High has chosen my heart to set up His throne and to establish therein the Kingdom of the Son of His love. (Alleluia)

SECRETA

Tua, Domine, propitiatione, et Cordis sanctissimi beatae Mariae semper Virginis intercessione, auferatur a cordibus nostris concupiscentia carnis et oculorum, atque ambitio saeculi: tibique, cum hac oblatione, in igne tui amoris atque in flamma aeternae caritatis jugiter immolentur. Per Dominum.

SECRET

O Lord, by Thy mercy and through the intercession of the most holy heart of the Blessed Mary, ever Virgin, drive out from our hearts the concupiscence of the flesh, the concupiscence of the eyes, and the pride of life, and grant that with this oblation, these hearts may be forever immolated in the fire of Thy love, and in the flames of eternal charity. Through the same, etc.

COMMUNIO

Beatum Cor tuum, 0 Maria Virgo, thesaurus sanctitatis, fornax divini amoris, thronus omnium virtutum, sanctuarium divinitatis! Dei Genitrix, intercede pro nobis. (Alleluia)

COMMUNION

Blessed is Thy heart, O Virgin Mary! It is the treasure of sanctity, the furnace of divine love, the throne of all virtues, sanctuary of the Divinity: Mother of God, intercede for us. (Alleluia)

POSTCOMMUNIO

Domine Jesu Christe, qui miranda sanctissimae vitae, passionis et resurrectionis tuae mysteria, in sacratissimo Corde Matris tuae admirabilis conservari et glorificari voluisti: praesta, quaesumus; ut, meritis et intercessione ejusdem Cordis amantissimi, sicut te panem vivum, ac Regem nostrum, ex altari tuo suscepimus; ita in corde et corpore nostro viventem et regnantem portare et glorificare, nosque in te et propter te solum vivere valeamus. Qui vivis et regnas cum Deo Patre, in unitate Spiritus sancti Deus, per omnia saecula saeculorum.

POSTCOMMUNION

Lord Jesus Christ, who hast willed that the marvelous mysteries of Thy Life, passion and Resurrection, should be preserved and glorified in the most holy heart of Thy admirable Mother, grant us, we beseech Thee, through the merits and intercession of this most loving heart, that as we have received Thee at Thy altar, who art our living bread and our king, so we may bear Thee and glorify Thee living and reigning in our hearts, and that we may live in Thee and for Thee alone, who, being God, dost live and reign with God the Father, etc.

Appendix Two

Prayers in Honor of the Admirable Heart of Mary

LITANY IN HONOR OF THE MOST HOLY HEART OF MARY
For Private Recitation Only

Kyrie eleison.
Christe eleison.
Kyrie eleison.
Jesu, Cor Mariae, audi nos.
Jesu, Cor Mariae, exaudi nos.
Pater de caelis, Deus, miserere nobis.

Fili, Redemptor mundi, Deus, miserere nobis.
Spiritus sancte, Deus, miserere nobis.
Sancta Trinitas, unus Deus, miserere nobis.
Cor Jesu sacratissimum, miserere nobis.

Cor Mariae sanctissimum, ora pro nobis.
Cor Mariae, speculum divini Cordis,
Cor Mariae, compendium perfectionum Divinitatis,
Cor Mariae, imago perfecta Cordis aeterni Patris,
Cor Mariae, deliciae Filii Dei,
Cor Mariae, signaculum Spiritus Sancti,
Cor Mariae, sanctuarium Divinitatis,
Cor Mariae, triclinium sanctae Trinitatis,
Cor Mariae, thronus divinae voluntatis,
Cor Mariae, secundum Cor Dei,

Cor Mariae, custos divini Verbi,
Cor Mariae, speculum Passionis Christi,

Ora pro nobis.

Lord have mercy on us,
Christ have mercy on us,
Lord have mercy on us,
Jesus, heart of Mary, hear us,
Jesus, heart of Mary, graciously hear us,
God the Father of Heaven, have mercy on us,
God the Son, Redeemer of the world, have mercy on us,
God the Holy Ghost, have mercy on us,
Holy Trinity, one God, have mercy on us,
Most Sacred Heart of Jesus, have mercy on us.
Most holy heart of Mary, pray for us,
Heart of Mary, Mirror of the heart of God,
" Epitome of divine perfections,

" Perfect image of the heart of the eternal Father,
" Delight of the Son of God,
" Seat of the Holy Spirit,

" Sanctuary of the Divinity,

" Repose of the most Holy Trinity,
" Throne of the divine will,

" Heart like unto the heart of God,
" Guardian of the divine Word,
" Mirror of the passion of Jesus,

Pray for us.

Cor Mariae, cor unum cum Corde Christi,	" Heart which is but one with the heart of Jesus,	
Cor Mariae, spes et laetitia cordis nostri,	" Hope and joy of our hearts,	
Cor Mariae, fons totius consolationis,	" Source of all consolation,	
Cor Mariae, fornax divini amoris,	" Furnace of divine love,	
Cor Mariae, miraculum charitatis,	" Marvel of charity,	
Cor Mariae, centrum mansuetudinis,	" Center of meekness,	
Cor Mariae, abyssus humilitatis,	" Abyss of humility,	
Cor Mariae, domus sapientiae,	" Dwelling place of wisdom,	
Cor Mariae, thronus misericordiae,	" Throne of mercy,	
Cor Mariae, zelator animarum,	" Zealous for souls,	
Cor Mariae, thronus omnium virtutum,	" Throne of all virtue,	
Cor Mariae, abyssus gratiarum,	" Abyss of grace,	
Cor Mariae, thesaurus innumerorum bonorum,	" Treasure of innumerable blessings,	
Cor Mariae, caelum caelorum,	" Heaven of Heavens,	
Cor Mariae, Sanctum sanctorum,	" Holy of holies,	
Cor Mariae, abyssus mysteriorum,	" Abyss of mysteries,	
Cor Mariae, abyssus miraculorum,	" Abyss of marvels,	
Cor Mariae, liber vitae,	" Book of life,	
Cor Mariae, gazophylacium Ecclesiae,	" Treasure of the Church,	
Cor Mariae, oraculum Christianorum,	" Oracle of Christians,	
Cor Mariae, sidus amantium,	" Star of loving hearts,	
Cor Mariae, divinae legis tabula,	" Table of divine law,	
Cor Mariae, cordis fidelis regula,	" Rule of the faithful heart,	
Cor Mariae, raptor cordium,	" Ravisher of hearts,	
Cor Mariae, cordis nostri refugium,	" Refuge of our hearts,	
Cor Mariae, cordis nostri praesidium,	" Shield of our hearts,	
Cor Mariae, cordis nostri domus aurea,	" Golden house of our hearts,	
Cor Mariae, turris nostra fortissima,	" Our impregnable fortress,	
Cor Mariae, cordis nostri paradisus,	" Paradise of our hearts,	
Cor Mariae, cordis nostri jubilus,	" Sweet joy of our hearts,	
Cor Mariae, solatium exilii nostri,	" Consolation of our exile,	
Cor Mariae, Rex cordis nostri,	" Queen of our hearts,	
Cor Mariae, amator cordis nostri.	" Filled with love for us.	

Ora pro nobis. — *Pray for us.*

Propitius esto, parce nobis, Jesu.
Propitius esto, exaudi nos, Jesu.

Be merciful, spare us, O Jesus,
Be merciful, graciously hear us, O Jesus.

Per divinissimum Cor tuum, exaudi
   nos Jesu.
Per Cor amantissimum sanctissimae
   Matris tuae,
Per maximum ejus contra peccatum
   odium,
Per insignem ejus mundi contemptum,
Per profundissimam ejus humili-
   tatem,
Per mellifluam ejus benignitatem,
Per specialem ejus erga sibi devotos
   charitatem,
Per summum ejus in Patrem aeter-
   num amorem,
Per ardentissimam ejus in te dilec-
   tionem,
Per piissima illius desideria,
Per amantissima illius suspiria,
Per acerbissimos dolores illius,
Per temporalia et aeterna ejus
   gaudia,
Per excellentissimam ejus cum
   Corde tuo unionem,

Ora pro nobis.

O pretiosissimum Cor Jesu et Mariae,
   thesaurus cordis nostri, posside cor
   nostrum in aeternum.
O amantissimum Cor Jesu et Mariae, vita
   cordis nostri, vive in corde nostro in
   aeternum,
O dilectissimum Cor Jesu et Mariae, rex
   cordis nostri, regna super cor nostrum
   in aeternum.
Jesu, Cor Mariae, audi nos.
Jesu, Cor Mariae, exaudi nos.

Oremus

Omnipotens Deus, qui beatissimae
Virginis Mariae Cor amantissimum,
sacrarium Divinitatis, thronus omnium
virtutum, totiusque sanctitatis thesaurum
esse voluisti: da nobis, quaesumus, ejusdem sanctissimi Cordis meritis et
precibus, ipsius imaginem in corde nostro
jugiter portare; ut ejus imitatione, quae
tibi sunt placita semper facientes, secundum Cor tuum in aeternum effici mereamur; Per Christum Dominum nostrum.
R. Amen.

Through Thy most divine heart,
Through the most loving heart of
   Thy most Holy Mother,
Through her extreme hatred for sin,
Through her supreme contempt of
   the world,
Through her most profound
   humility,
Through her admirable benignity,
Through her wonderful affection
   for her devoted servants,
Through her surpassing love for the
   eternal Father,
Through her incomparable tender-
   ness towards Thee,
Through her most merciful desires,
Through her burning sighs of love,
Through her overwhelming sorrows,
Through her temporal and eternal
   joys,
Through her sublime union with
   Thy heart,

Pray for us.

O most precious heart of Jesus and Mary,
   treasure of our heart, possess our heart
   forever,
O most loving heart of Jesus and Mary,
   life of our hearts, live forever in our
   heart,
O beloved heart of Jesus and Mary,
   Ruler of our heart, reign forever in
   our heart!
Jesus, heart of Mary, hear us,
Jesus, heart of Mary, graciously hear us.

Let us pray:

Omnipotent God, Who didst will the
heart of the Blessed Virgin Mary to be
the sanctuary of the Divinity, the throne
of every virtue and the treasure of all
sanctity grant; we beseech Thee, through
the merits and prayers of this most holy
heart, that we may unceasingly bear the
likeness of her in our heart; so that, in
imitation of her, by accomplishing all
that is most pleasing to Thee, we may
merit to become eternally conformed to
Thy heart. Through Our Lord Jesus
Christ, Amen.

SALUTATION TO THE SACRED HEARTS OF JESUS AND MARY[1]

Ave, Cor sanctissimum,	Hail, Heart most holy.
Ave, Cor mitissimum,	Hail, Heart most gentle.
Ave, Cor humillimum,	Hail, Heart most humble.
Ave, Cor purissimum,	Hail, Heart most pure.
Ave, Cor devotissimum,	Hail, Heart most devout.
Ave, Cor sapientissimum,	Hail, Heart most wise.
Ave, Cor patientissimum,	Hail, Heart most patient.
Ave, Cor obedientissimum,	Hail, Heart most obedient.
Ave, Cor vigilantissimum,	Hail, Heart most vigilant.
Ave, Cor fidelissimum,	Hail, Heart most faithful.
Ave, Cor beatissimum,	Hail, Heart most blessed.
Ave, Cor misericordissimum,	Hail, Heart most merciful.
Ave, Cor amantissimum Jesu et Mariae;	Hail, most loving Heart of Jesus and Mary.
Te adoramus, te laudamus, te glorificamus, tibi gratias agimus;	We revere Thee. We praise Thee. We glorify Thee. We give Thee thanks.
Te amamus ex toto corde nostro, ex tota anima nostra et ex totis viribus nostris;	We love Thee with all our heart, with all our soul, and with all our strength.
Tibi cor nostrum offerimus, donamus, consecramus, immolamus;	We offer Thee our heart. We give it to Thee. We consecrate it to Thee. We immolate it to Thee.
Accipe et posside illud totum, et purifica et illumina et sanctifica;	Receive it, and possess it wholly, purify it, enlighten it, sanctify it,
Ut in ipso vivas et regnes et nunc et semper et in saecula saeculorum. Amen.	That Thou mayst live and reign in it now, always, and forever and ever. Amen.

1 This salutation which is at once a magnificent consecration to the Hearts of Jesus and Mary and a real treatise in abridged form of the devotion to these Sacred Hearts, has been recited since 1643 in the various Institutes of Saint John Eudes. The Blessed Virgin promised the Servant of God "to give to all who should recite it with devotion, desires to purify themselves more and more from all sorts of sin, in order to be more capable of receiving divine gifts and blessings." And, in fact, numberless graces which seem almost miraculous, have, at all times, been obtained, testifying to the efficacy of this prayer.

Salutation to the Blessed Virgin Mary[1]

Ave, Maria, Filia Dei Patris.	Hail Mary, Daughter of God the Father.
Ave, Maria, Mater Dei Filii.	Hail Mary, Mother of God the Son.
Ave, Maria, Sponsa Spiritus sancti.	Hail Mary, Spouse of the Holy Ghost.
Ave, Maria, templum totius Divinitatis.	Hail Mary, Temple of the Divinity.
Ave, Maria, candidum lilium fulgidae, semperque tranquillae Trinitatis.	Hail Mary, Immaculate lily of the resplendent and ever peaceful Trinity.
Ave, Maria, rosa praefulgida coelicae amoenitatis.	Hail Mary, Radiant rose of heavenly fragrance.
Ave, Maria, Virgo virginum, Virgo fidelis de qua nasci, et de cujus lacte pasci Rex coelorum voluit.	Hail Mary, Virgin of virgins, virgin most faithful, of whom the King of Heaven did will to be born.
Ave, Maria, regina Martyrum, cujus animam doloris gladius pertransivit.	Hail Mary, Queen of martyrs, whose soul was pierced with a sword of sorrow.
Ave Maria, domina mundi, cui data est omnis potestas in coelo et in terra.	Hail Mary, Queen of the universe, to whom all power has been given in Heaven and on earth.
Ave, Maria, regina cordis mei, mater, vita, dulcedo, et spes mea charissima.	Hail Mary, Queen of my heart, my mother, my life, my consolation, and my dearest hope.
Ave, Maria, mater amabilis.	Hail Mary, Mother most amiable.
Ave, Maria, mater admirabilis.	Hail Mary, Mother most admirable.
Ave, Maria, mater misericordiae.	Hail Mary, Mother of mercy.
Ave, Maria, gratia plena Dominus tecum.	Hail Mary, full of grace, the Lord is with thee.
Benedicta tu in mulieribus,	Blessed art thou amongst women.
Et benedictus fructus ventris tui Jesus.	And blessed is the fruit of thy womb, Jesus.
Et benedictus sponsus tuus Joseph.	And blessed be thy spouse, Saint Joseph.
Et benedictus pater tuus Joachim.	And blessed be thy father, Saint Joachim.

1 Saint John Eudes recommended this prayer for the conversion of sinners and advised his children to say it at the bedside of the sick. The Blessed Virgin promised him that "all who say it with devotion, or at least good will if they are in the state of grace, receive an increase of divine love in their hearts at each of the twelve salutations or benedictions contained in it; if they are in mortal sin, she will knock at the door of their hearts with her own sweet virginal hand to urge them to open it to grace." And she added that when persons are found steeped in sin and difficult to convert, it would be well to encourage them to say this salutation, or at least to consent to having it said for them.

Et benedicta mater tua Anna.	And blessed be thy mother, Saint Anne.
Et benedictus filius tuns Joannes.	And blessed be thy adopted son, Saint John.
Et benedictus angelus tuus Gabriel.	And blessed be thy angel, Saint Gabriel.
Et benedictus Pater aeternus, qui te elegit.	And blessed be the eternal Father who chose thee.
Et benedictus Filius, qui te amavit.	And blessed be the divine son who loved thee.
Et benedictus Spiritus sanctus, qui te sponsavit.	And blessed be the Holy Ghost who espoused thee.
Et benedicti in aeternum omnes qui benedicunt tibi, et qui diligunt te.	And blessed be forever all those who bless and who love thee.
Amen.	Amen.

Rosary of the Admirable Heart of Mary[1]

On the cross the *Creed* is said to adore all the mysteries of the Christian religion in the Sacred Heart of the glorious Virgin, in union with the faith with which this same heart was always animated, and in union with all the adorations and praises which it has rendered and will eternally render to these same mysteries.

On the three first small beads the following words are said in union with the love of the three divine Persons with regard to this most amiable Heart: *Ave Cor Sanctissimum beatissimae Virginis Mariae*. "Hail holy heart of the Blessed Virgin Mary."

On each large bead the Gloria Patri is said to thank the most Holy Trinity for all the graces poured so abundantly into this abyss of graces; and for all the favors which, through her intercession have been granted to the whole human race, and to ourselves in particular.

On the two first decades the following is again said:

Ave Cor Sanctissimum beatissimae Virginis Mariae. "Hail holy heart of the Blessed Virgin Mary."

This is done to fulfill our duties of respect towards this most worthy heart, in union with the devotion and praise which have been, are, and will be rendered it by all the hearts of angels and saints; uniting ourselves at the first Ave to the devotion of the Seraphim; at the second to the Cherubim and thus through the whole angelic choir from which we proceed to the hearts of the patriarchs, of the prophets, of the martyrs, etc.

On the third and fourth decades is said: *Per Cor amantissimum sanctissimae Matris tuae, O bone Jesu, fiat cor nostrum secundum Cor tuum*. "Through the loving Heart of Thy most Holy Mother, O Good Jesus, make our hearts like unto thine."

And this to beseech Our Lord by the heart all inflamed with love of His most Holy Mother, that our hearts be according to His Heart by a perfect imitation of the love, charity, humility, submission, obedience, patience, innocence, purity, hatred of sin, contempt of the world, entire disengagement from all that is not God, and of all the other virtues of this Adorable Heart.

On the fifth and sixth decades are said: *Per Cor amantissimum sanctissimae Matris tuae, exaudi nos Jesu*. "Through the loving Heart of Thy most Holy Mother, Hear us, O Jesus."

This is to supplicate Our Lord, by the Heart of His most Holy Mother by which He is more loved than by all the hearts of men and angels together, to graciously hear the prayers which we offer and to grant us the particular favors we ask either for ourselves or for others. Because He can refuse nothing which we ask with humility and confidence by this most loving, most lovable and most loved Heart.

At the end is said the *Salutation Ave Cor Sanctissimum*, "Hail, Heart Most Holy," (P. 358).

Benedicum sit Cor amantissumum et dulcissimum Nomen Domini Nostri Jesu Christi, et gloriosissimae Virginis Mariae Matris ejus, in aeternum et ultra. Nos cum prole pia benedicat Virgo Maria. Amen

"Blessed forever be the most loving Heart and the most sweet name of our Lord Jesus Christ, may His Mother, the Virgin Mary and her most merciful son bless us. Amen."

---

1 This rosary of six decades by Saint John may be said in Latin or English.

CONSECRATION TO THE ADMIRABLE HEART OF MARY

O most holy heart of Mary, ever Immaculate, ever Virgin, holiest, purest, noblest, greatest, inexhaustible fountain of goodness, sweetness, mercy and love; model of every virtue, image of the Adorable Heart of Jesus Christ ever burning with the most ardent charity, who lovest God more than all the Seraphim together; Heart of the Mother of the Redeemer, seat of peace, wherein mercy and justice are allied, whence peace between Heaven and earth has begun to be treated, who didst feel our miseries so deeply, who didst suffer so much for our salvation, who still lovest us so ardently and who dost merit by all these rights, the respect, love and confidence of all men: deign to accept my poor tribute of love.

Prostrate before thee, I render thee the most profound homage of which I am capable; I thank thee for the feelings of love and mercy with which thou art so deeply moved at the sight of our misery; I offer thee my humble thanks for all the gifts I have received from thy goodness, and I unite with all the pure souls who delight in honoring, praising and loving thee. They have learned from the Holy Spirit Who directs them, that it is through thee they must go to Jesus Christ, and offer to this God-Man their need of adoration.

Therefore, O most loving Heart, thou shalt henceforth be the object of my veneration, of my love and most tender devotion; thou shalt be the way whereby I shall go to my Saviour, as it is through thee that His mercy shall come to me; thou shalt be my refuge in every need, my consolation in every affliction; from thee I shall learn the purity, humility, meekness and above all, the love of Jesus. I shall ask for these virtues through thy merits and so shall infallibly obtain them. I presume to offer thee my heart sullied with a thousand sins. All unworthy as it is, I trust that thou wilt not despise it. Grant by thy powerful mediation that it may be purified and detached from every creature; penetrate it with sorrow for my sins; fill it with the love of the divine Heart of Jesus, thy Son, that it may be eternally united with thee in Heaven, there to love God forever. Amen.

Index

of Mary, 314

Fountain, symbolic of the Heart of Mary, 46

Fulgentius, Saint, 208, 245, 290, 291

Furnace of love, 6, 90, 105, 175, 213, 274

Gardens, fountain of, 48;

Germanus of Constantinople, Saint, 25, 40, 85, 87, 128, 208, 234, 246, 280

Gerson, John, 69, 88, 113, 186, 238, 239, 280

Gertrude, Saint, 193, 225

Golden candlestick, symbolic picture of the Heart of Mary, 84

Goodness of the Heart of Mary, 119

Grace, first grace, 201;
fulness of grace, 55, 111, 151, 201, 234;
gratuitous graces, 228 (See also Mediatrix)

Gregory of Nyssa, Saint, 79, 87, 142, 238

Gregory Thaumaturgus, Saint, 245

Gregory the Great, Saint, 69, 88, 89, 175, 245

Head, Jesus our, 13

Heart. (See Divine heart,)

Heart of Jesus, one with the Heart of Mary, 24;
three hearts forming but one, 10 (See also Divine heart,)

Heart of Mary, our heart, 38;
principle of life, 38;
source of all graces, 208;
source of salvation, 44

Heaven, symbolic picture of the Heart of Mary, 33;
the heaven of heavens, 30, 34, 35, 157, 326

Hilary, Saint, 149

Holiness of the Heart of Mary, 111

Holocausts. See Altar of holocausts.

Hugues, Cardinal, 293-4

Humility of the Heart of Mary, 275

Idiot, the. See Jourdain

Ignatius, Martyr, Saint, 176, 245

Ignatius of Loyola, Saint, 26, 188

Ildefonsus, Saint, 245

Immaculate Conception, 6, 31, 39, 65, 184, 185, 202-205, 230, 257

Immensity of God mirrored in the Heart of Mary, 109

Immutability of God mirrored in the Heart of Mary, 110

Incarnation, advanced by the Heart of Mary, 309;
consent of Mary to, 206;
cooperation of Mary in the, 97;
masterpiece of the divine powers, 291

Incognitus, 54

Infinity of God mirrored in the Heart of Mary, 109

Innocent III, Pope, 121

Irenaeus, Saint, 157, 213, 245

Jerome, Saint, 30, 42, 49, 55, 96, 114, 118, 176, 287

Jesus, arm of God, 291;
divine heart of Mary, 23;
His love for Mary, 101;
mercy of God, 287;
model of devotion to Mary, 101

John Chrysostom, Saint, 38, 54, 87, 127, 138, 156, 176, 181, 273

John Damascene, Saint, 31, 40, 65, 84, 89, 111, 127, 142, 181, 183, 207, 292

Jourdain, Raymund, 120, 121, 128, 213, 246

Justice, divine mirrored in the Heart of Mary, 134

Lake of lions, vision of St. Mary Magdalen de Pazzi, 139

Lanspergius, 194, 272

Lawrence, Saint, 87, 96, 134, 181

Life of God. See Compendium of the.

Light of the world, 39

Loaves of proposition, symbol of Jesus, 84-85

Love of the Heart of Mary, for God, 210;
for men, 214

Martyrdom of the Heart of Mary, 160, 242

Mass of the Heart of Mary, 317

Mechtilde, Saint, 101, 102, 103, 193

Mediatrix, 120, 126, 203, 271

Mediatrix, of grace, 155, 207, 213, 233
of religion, 156

Meekness of the Heart of Mary, 129

Mercy, divine, attributed to the